Doing the Town

DOING
THE TOWN

The Rise of Urban Tourism
in the United States, 1850–1915

Catherine Cocks

UNIVERSITY OF CALIFORNIA PRESS
Berkeley · Los Angeles · London

University of California Press
Berkeley and Los Angeles, California
University of California Press, Ltd.
London, England

Library of Congress Cataloging-in-Publication Data

Cocks, Catherine, 1967–
    Doing the town : the rise of urban tourism in the
    United States, 1850–1915 / Catherine Cocks.
      p. cm.
    Includes bibliographical references and index.
    IBSN 0-520-22746-8 (alk. paper)
      1. Tourism—United States.   2. Cities and
    towns—United States.   I. Title.
    G155.U6 C56 2001
    338.4'7917304929—dc21   00-064771

Printed in the United States of America
09 08 07 06 05 04 03 02 01
10 9 8 7 6 5 4 3 2 1

In memory of
Roland Marchand
1933–1997

Contents

Illustrations

Acknowledgments

Grants from the Graduate Division and the Department of History at the University of California, Davis, the Newberry Library, the Smithsonian Institution, the Huntington Library, United University Professions at the State University of New York at Oswego, and the Winterthur Library enabled me to do the research on which this book is based.

Like all researchers, I owe a great debt to the archivists and librarians who organize and manage historical collections. Especially helpful to me were Vanessa Broussard Simmons of the Archives Center of the National Museum of American History, Smithsonian Institution, May N. Stone at the New-York Historical Society, and Peter Blodgett at the Huntington Library. The staff at the Chicago Historical Society, the Newberry Library, and the Winterthur Library made those institutions excellent places to work. Thanks also to the staffs of the Washingtoniana room at the Martin Luther King, Jr., Memorial Library in Washington, D.C.; the Historical Society of the District of Columbia; the Rare Books Room at the George Washington University library; the Adams Building Reading Room and the Prints and Photographs Division at the Library of Congress; the New York Public Library; the San Francisco Public Library Local History Room; and the Bancroft Library.

The intellectual support and congeniality of my dissertation committee members, Roland Marchand, Karen Halttunen, and Cathy Kudlick, were greater gifts than I realized at the time. They enabled me to write a better dissertation more quickly than I would otherwise have done.

Roland's fame as a mentor was well deserved, and his premature death in 1997 is a terrible loss.

Thanks to the people who read and commented on pieces of the manuscript even though they didn't have to: Fraser Cocks, Charles McGovern, Amy Richter, and Erika Bsumek. Seth Koven read an early version of chapter 1 and allowed me to read part of his own work in progress.

For hospitality during my research trips, I would like to thank, first and foremost, Greg, Lauree, Jessica, and Helen Hickok in Brooklyn, who took me in, taught me how to read a New York City transit map, and allowed me to crash their Christmas celebration. In Washington, D.C., I am grateful to James Brooks and Rebecca Allahyari, Angela Blake, and Carolyn Höfig and Shannon Brown; and in San Francisco, Alice Ruby, Caroline Boyden, and Elizabeth Harris. In Delaware, thanks to Pat Elliott, who always found a room for me, and to Jeanne Solensky and Gretchen Buggeln. Thanks also to Karen Halttunen for twice needing a housesitter when I needed a quiet, pleasant place to write.

I had many opportunities to present my research: in 1994, at the California American Studies Association; in 1996, at the Newberry Library lunchtime colloquium, the American Historical Association–Pacific Coast Branch annual meeting, and the University of California at Davis History Department Scholarly Process colloquium; in 1997, at conferences of the American Historical Association and the Organization of American Historians and the Weekly Colloquium of the National Museum of American History; in 1998, at the Western History Association meeting; and in 1999, at the Winterthur Library Colloquium series. Thanks to the organizers, commentators, and audience members, especially Robin Bachin, Karen Sawislak, Terry Toulouse, Meredith McGill, Carl Abbott, Paula Elder, Lucy Barber, Steve Deyle, Nick Marshall, Bill Bowsky, Amy Richter, Patricia Cline Cohen, David Nasaw, David Glassberg, Paige Roberts, Charlene Mires, Patricia Gossell, Charles McGovern, Monica Rico, Hal Rothman, Neville Thompson, Gretchen Buggeln, and Richard McKinstry.

Mary Ryan, John Sears, and Alan Lessoff provided detailed, constructive criticism with which to begin turning the dissertation into a manuscript and the manuscript into a book. Monica McCormick has been a cordial and patient editor. Thanks to Lucy Barber for finding the photograph on the cover.

Thanks to teachers and friends for their wisdom, kindness, and humor: Donna Alvah, Joan Ariel, Becky Bales, Terry Bales, Lucy Barber, Angie Blake, Caroline Boyden, Ellen Broidy, James Brooks, Brian

Cooper, Valerie DeBrava, Jean Dittmar, Samantha Yates François, Liz Harris, Dave Hochfelder, Jill Hough, Shirley Jackson, Michelle Jolly, Kathleen Kennedy, Debbie Lyon, Susan Mann, Charlie McGovern, Bob Moeller, Heather Allen Pang, Belinda Peters, Liz Regosin, Amy Richter, Lynn Sharp, and Sharon Ullman. I am deeply grateful for their forbearance with my frequent Chicken Little impersonations.

My parents, Catherine Herlihy and Fraser Cocks, are the proverbial without whom. My grandmother, Lillias Campbell Cocks, took a flattering interest in the project and also provided some timely financial aid. There are no words to thank my sister Hanley, who, when we weren't walking through cities together, always kept my e-mail inbox full.

Introduction

I began this book unwittingly while researching the emergence of San Francisco's Chinatown as a tourist attraction for turn-of-the-century white Americans. To place my study in a larger context, I needed to know when and why Americans started visiting their own cities for fun and whether whites went to the neighborhoods of other ethnic minorities. But I found that historians were only beginning to study tourism and as yet had paid little attention to American cities. Indeed, in the study marking the beginning of historians' current surge of interest in American tourism, John Sears argued that nineteenth-century American tourists sought out natural wonders because the nation's cities lacked the historical relics and cultural institutions that made European cities so attractive. Although scholars have often chided middle-class reformers for acting like urban tourists, Neil Harris was alone in considering visitors who did not even claim to have philanthropic motives, and he did so briefly and with reference only to New York City.[1]

My preliminary research confirmed that even during the turn-of-the-century period that Harris wrote about, country resorts and natural wonders were far more popular than big cities. Then why bother to study the development of urban tourism in the United States? Because the tourists who chose to visit the nation's large cities by 1915 embodied a new sense of selfhood and enacted a new understanding of the sources and character of legitimate social bonds. The practice of urban tourism was an important sign of and contributor to the erosion of a Victorian, "refined" understanding of class, gender, and ethnicity and the gradual emergence of a cosmopolitan, commercial conceptualization of these social relations in the early twentieth century.

Studying the rise of urban tourism at the turn of the century brings together three important elements in this well-known cultural transformation: urban space, leisure, and commercialization. The popularity of city touring by 1915 marked a significant shift in the way that well-to-do Americans perceived, organized, and moved around in urban built environments. This change in spatial practice reflected and reshaped prosperous Americans' understanding of proper social relations between rich and poor, black and white, native and immigrant, and men and women. Equally important, the popularity of city touring by 1915 highlights the growing importance of commercial leisure in organizing social relations and public spaces. The people in this study did not just act like tourists; they *were* tourists, without pretense of any motive but innocent enjoyment for their jaunts about the city. Urban tourism modeled a cosmopolitan social vision in which stylized forms of cultural difference and commercial transactions, not personal knowledge or moral privilege, organized many spaces and interactions among people.

The organization and uses of urban spaces are central to my argument about the significance of city touring. Although often voyeuristic, it had important social and spatial aspects. Far from simply looking, tourists moved around the city in particular patterns, buying services . and souvenirs from the locals. Throughout this study, I assume that social relations take place in particular spaces and those spaces and social relations are mutually influential. Theorist Henri Lefebvre asserts, "(Social) space is a (social) product" and therefore "every society . . . produces a space, its own space." Space is neither empty nor innocent of ideology but rather a product of social forces and a force in itself. The concept of social space insists on the political underpinnings and the power of sedimented social relations and cultural assumptions, especially as they exist in the built environment and its uses. Further, it directs attention to nonverbal, nonrational interactions marked and shaped by the pathways and edifices of a particular landscape. As a result, it is a powerful tool for historians in trying to analyze cultural change.[2]

I use the term "spatial practices" to refer to both the shaping ideals and the patterns of movement characteristic of prosperous Americans in public, urban places between 1850 and 1915. While ideas about space and social relations helped to choreograph interactions among people of different social groups, the resulting dance also responded to changes in social composition and the built environment that exceeded the social vision implicit in existing spatial practices. Conventional ideas about space have a powerful effect on the shape and structure of a built environment but are not an objective description of them. One important reason for this disjuncture is that different groups in a society have unequal abilities to shape the built environment, as well as having different visions and making different uses of shared spaces. Because space is socially produced by interactions among these unequal groups, there can be no objective standard by which to judge representations of space such as maps or guidebooks. Any standard is a mode of representation with its own assumptions, intentions, and agents. Analyzing nineteenth-century urban description requires the historian to pay attention to the expectations and desires of writers and readers, for it was these that generated narratives, organized tours, and influenced the arrangement and uses of urban space.

The spatial practice of urban tourism was simultaneously a response to sociospatial change, a means of managing that change, and an agent of it. To understand its importance, one must examine the sociospatial practices characteristic of the mid-nineteenth century. Products of and actors in the spread of the market and rapid urbanization, the antebellum middle class asserted the legitimacy of its growing economic and social power by adopting the "refined" manners and dress previously characteristic of the gentry. This behavioral ideal demanded perfect self-possession of its practitioners in public and the enforcement of an elaborate code of etiquette, sharpening distinctions between the emerging middle and working classes.

Yet, despite their exclusive tendencies, refined practices also partook of the republican egalitarianism of which many mid-nineteenth-century Americans were so proud. For one thing, gentility appropriated courtly manners for an entrepreneurial middle class. For another, refined self-possession was supposedly available to all Americans if they worked hard enough, just like the ownership of real property that underwrote full political participation. Good character, not wealth or birth, was the only prerequisite. Indeed, for many middling Americans, the promise of true equality lay in uplifting all to middle-class standards of behavior. The ideology of refinement legitimated the middle class's claim to social authority and justified the new class hierarchy taking shape in the early nineteenth century without abrogating Americans' endorsement of formal equality.[3]

Tightly linked with refinement was the ideal of separate spheres, which divided the world into two opposing realms, public and private. The first was the realm of ambition and competition, politics and business, city streets and saloons, or men's affairs; the second was the realm of selflessness and nurturance, family and domesticity, home and church, or women's affairs. By separating these two, middling Americans sought to limit the socially transformative effects of the market economy without hindering its growth. Separate spheres sharpened both class and gender differences by attributing to well-to-do women a greater degree of natural refinement. This quality necessitated both their exclusion from the amoral competitiveness of the public world and the exclusion of unrefined working-class men from some semipublic spaces that ladies might occupy. The distinction masked the "aristocratic" character of gentility and separate spheres by attributing their divisive consequences to gender, a "natural" distinction, not class, an "artificial" one.

Both refinement and separate spheres responded to, increased, and sought to remediate a widely perceived rupture between appearance and essence. The transformation of the economy and the rapid growth of cities made it difficult to know who deserved the wealth and social rank he or she claimed and who did not. Early-nineteenth-century efforts to forge a republican political and social order similarly upset existing assumptions about status and authority. Mastering and enforcing an elaborate code of etiquette helped middle-class Americans to form a mutually known and accountable community amid the uncertainties of their time and place. The ideal of separate spheres was a geographic counterpart to refinement, offering a haven from disorder without eliminating the opportunities it offered.[4]

Well-to-do Americans had the means and the desire to realize these ideals to a degree that profoundly reshaped urban landscapes and the interiors of homes, hotels, and railroad cars, among other places. Many worked hard to enforce their ideal on others by reforming the urban built environment and instituting new conventions and regulations for its use. Yet their ability to realize these sociospatial ideals was far from complete, because of their sometimes conflicting aims, a limited ability to predict and manage social change, and resistance by many Americans. The conflicts that shaped the antebellum class system often concerned the uses of public spaces and the proper demeanor and social relations there.[5]

Having defined the world in opposing spheres, middle-class Americans, especially women, had to exercise great care in moving between the two. Moving in public, urban places was particularly dangerous, because cities brought together large numbers of anonymous strangers in public spaces and types of recreation apart from either the discipline of work or the bonds of affection in the private home. In American cities, many people were out of place in two senses: geographically dislocated and socially indeterminate. The growing number of wage earners, including a rising proportion of European immigrants, contested or simply ignored the dictates of refinement, often in the name of republican equality. As a result, walking in an American city in the mid-nineteenth century was an act fraught with moral and political peril, a danger the urban sketches of the period painted in the most lurid colors.

Such cities were not amenable to nineteenth-century tourism. Two traditions shaped pleasure travel in the antebellum period: the fading glory of the "Grand Tour," whose purpose was the education and social integration of the sons of the elite; and the burgeoning tradition of romantic tourism, whose purpose was the contemplation of and literary reflection on natural wonders by the middle class. Journeying to and effusing over the stunning beauty of Niagara Falls or the White Mountains was a most refined practice. Raw, young American cities were barren of classical history and art and unlikely to inspire romantic epiphanies. Although cities fascinated many Americans and foreign visitors because of the information they offered about the workings of the world's first modern republic, tourism in its nineteenth-century guises was not thinkable there.[6]

By 1915 urban tourism was not only thinkable, it was profitable. A growing number of tour agencies, railroad passenger departments, guidebook publishers, genteel travel writers, and city business organizations served and promoted pleasure travel in American cities. Urban tourism presupposed and encouraged the domestication of public, urban spaces for the well-to-do. It undermined the ideal of separate spheres and made refined self-possession less necessary for the expression and protection of status. In its place, urban tourism offered a model of urban space divided not into public and private but between places and peoples that were culturally resonant and commercially available and those that were not. Urban tourism offered a model of selfhood deriving from the appreciation and vicarious possession of urban landscapes and a wide array of cultural products and experiences, rather than self-possession and property ownership.

The promoters of urban tourism participated in a widespread campaign to rehabilitate public leisure and to make it the basis of a renewed, harmonious community in American cities. The popularity of city touring was one sign of the tendency to oppose leisure, not home, to work. Growing numbers of turn-of-the-century Americans saw in rationalized recreation the possibility of stable, amicable social relationships requiring no personal knowledge and thus better suited to an industrial, urban, and heterogeneous republic. The best way to address persistent class and ethnic divisions, many argued, was not moral uplift leading to the creation of a single community with homogeneous values but the cosmopolitan appreciation of cultural differences—in their proper place. Tourist itineraries defined and shaped the place of these differences in the turn-of-the-century city and deliberately commercialized them in order to make them safely, consistently available to a prosperous clientele. The result was to give the leisured transient a privileged social position.

The cosmopolitanism and leisured mobility of urban tourists seemed to many to be an ideal means of creating more harmonious social relations. Unlike residents, tourists moved through selected streets and sites in pursuit of innocent pleasure. Unlike residents, they did not allow local, partial concerns—the patterns of work, family, and community life—to limit their understanding or to define their sociospatial place. Because they were at leisure and because they were transient, they could see and appreciate the city as a whole. In short, at the turn of the century tourists offered to resolve urban social antagonisms by transcending the local and reconstructing it as a nationally available commodity.

As I hope the qualifiers "prosperous" and "well-to-do" have made clear, only a small minority of Americans could afford the money and time required by most pleasure tours between 1850 and 1915. Less well-off Americans often traveled to find work, contributing to the instability of urban life, but almost never for enjoyment. By 1915, as national and urban transportation networks improved, the length of the average workday declined, and real income rose, a growing number of Americans could afford to take short excursions. The ability of the comfortable but not wealthy to travel for pleasure was an important part of the social shift that made urban tourism possible. Still, mass tourism by any commonsense definition was not possible until after World War II.[7]

The relatively small number of Americans who were able to travel for pleasure before 1915 had a disproportionate influence on ideas about cities and leisure precisely because of their cultural and economic wealth. An entire guidebook industry developed to promote and supply the trade and in the process contributed to the rewriting of urban imagery that reached a broad and growing reading audience. Railroads and hotels competed for tourists' patronage, transforming and advertising the experience of travel and transience as the basis of a new kind of community. By 1915 those who could participate in commercial leisure seemed to many business leaders to be ideal citizens. The rise of urban tourism is one of the signs of the increasing centrality of consumption and leisure in defining meaningful participation in the social order.

Although the widening distance between tourists and the everyday lives of the communities they passed through was a prerequisite for city touring, tourists did not travel in a vacuum or go unnoticed by residents. Many people who never or rarely got the chance to travel for pleasure made money catering to tourists, complained about how annoying they were, or longed to join them. The presence of tourists, afoot or clustered on trolleys and special "seeing the city" cars, altered the composition and behavior of city crowds. The cultivation of sights attractive to tourists altered the physical landscape to a small extent, and to a greater extent transformed the meaning of walking in the city in a way that affected many city residents.

Studying the spatial practice of urban tourism for the most part means examining the ideal: the itineraries laid out in guidebooks and the destinations lovingly described in travel articles. Actual tourists, even the zealous ones who kept the detailed travel journals I was so grateful to find, often did not live up to these prescriptions. However, the prescribed itineraries represent the most conventional and thorough exposition of tourist possibilities. Extant travel diaries generally cover some of the ground that the guidebooks detail and rarely describe terrain not found in published works. Moreover, tourists were increasingly dependent on travel sketches, guidebooks, organized tours, and the conventional wisdom in organizing their travels, as they often lacked local connections by the turn of the century.

In designing this project, I decided to research four cities in depth: New York, Chicago, Washington, D.C., and San Francisco. Regionally diverse, they were all prominent in the popular imagination and drew large numbers of tourists by the 1890s. It is harder to justify my decision not to study closely the many other cities that were also tourist attractions during this era, especially New Orleans, Boston, Philadelphia, and Los Angeles. Frequent references in the primary sources and a brief investigation of secondary works indicate that the pattern I describe here was typical of most large American cities. Historical attractions were important in Philadelphia and Boston earlier and to a greater extent than in the four focus cities. Los Angeles's allure in the early twentieth century was not its urbanity but the many resorts in its hinterland and the warm, sunny climate. Thanks in part to the railroads, New Orleans's Mardi Gras became increasingly commercialized and nationally popular in the 1880s and 1890s, the same decades in which urban tourism was on the rise elsewhere. Probably not all cities experienced a growth in urban tourism or sought to promote it at the turn of the century, but the many cities that did contributed to a new and powerful set of ideas about urban space, commercial leisure, and social relations.

ONE

Strangers and Visitors

Or, The Impossibility of Tourism in
American Cities, 1830s–1870s

"Dear Oliver," Junius Mulvey wrote to his brother in 1854, ". . . I had been thinking for some time past of writing to you with a view of telling you something about the place where I have at length settled myself in preference to Cin[cinna]ti and every other place. . . . With Chicago I am very well pleased." Mulvey was one of thousands of Americans, along with immigrants from Ireland, Germany, and a slew of other countries, who contributed to the unprecedented rate of urban growth in the United States in the mid-nineteenth century. New York, home to more than 300,000 people in 1840, boasted a population in excess of half a million by 1850 and 800,000 ten years later. Chicago, claiming somewhere around 4,000 inhabitants in 1840, had boomed to more than 300,000 by 1870. San Francisco, long a provincial village, mushroomed with gold seekers and those catering to them in the 1850s, reaching nearly 50,000 by 1860 and 150,000 in 1870. Lacking large-scale commerce and industry, Washington, D.C., grew much more slowly. Still, its population almost doubled between 1840 and 1850 and rose enormously during the Civil War to reach 109,000 by 1870.[1]

In the same years, writing about cities also proliferated. Everything from mundane city directories to extravagant booster literature, urban sketches, melodramas, dime novels, and minstrelsy helped the many Americans new to cities or adjusting to their altered scale to understand the changing circumstances. All of these works addressed aspects of cities' sociospatial landscapes. But none, not even the many aimed at "strangers and visitors," cast American cities primarily as attractions for tourists. They made no clear distinction between strangers who had come to settle in a city and visitors passing a few days or weeks there. However long their stay, newcomers needed to gain a resident's familiarity with the city and its people as quickly as possible.[2]

The failure to distinguish clearly between pleasure seekers, visiting country cousins, business travelers, and migrants did not occur for lack of a word for or knowledge of pleasure travel. When Americans used the term "tourist," first noted in dictionaries in about 1800, they usually referred to people who were either going to Europe or making the round of natural wonders in upstate New York and New England.[3] Another common term, "excursionist," named people making short pleasure trips, those taking advantage of railroad rebates, and, by the 1870s, those participating in organized tours. Tourism and tourist businesses did exist in the antebellum United States, but cities were usually the starting and ending points of pleasure journeys, not their goal.

Pleasure travelers' preference for rural and pastoral scenes stemmed from the conventional meanings of tourism in the early nineteenth century. In the older tradition of the Grand Tour, young, elite men traveled through Europe to become familiar with great art, architecture, and history, while making contacts among the social elites of other nations. This mode of travel encompassed the serious social investigation that some elite travelers undertook. By the nineteenth century, a growing number of wealthy but not elite tourists, both men and women, sought a series of romantic encounters with nature whereby they could demonstrate their refined sensibilities through their emotional and literary responses. In both cases, the prescribed itineraries assumed and constructed a specific arrangement of space while mobilizing a corresponding set of social relations.[4]

Given these models of pleasure travel, the absence of urban tourism in the United States in the mid-nineteenth century was no oversight on the part of the fledgling tourist industry. American cities lacked the hallowed history and great art and architecture that attracted thousands to Europe. The chief contributor to the massive anthology *Picturesque America* (1872) lamented, "Our American cities are not usually picturesque." Why did they not possess the artful disarray that romantic tourists so desired? "Time has not yet mellowed their tints, nor age given quaintness to their structures." Even the successes of American cities made them unappealing to pleasure travelers: "Long rows of handsome business façades, and avenues of embowered cottages, however gratifying to the citizen, do not supply the stuff which the soul of the artist hungers for." [5]

Moreover, American cities tended to offend the sensitive with their ugliness and vulgar commercialism rather than inspire awe or aesthetic pleasure. Basil March, the groom in William Dean Howells's *Their Wedding Journey* (1871), insisted that his morning wanderings in New York with his new bride did not amount to touring; "it was the last place in the world where he should think of amusing himself or any one else." The newlyweds conceded that the city "was immense, it was grand in some ways, parts of it were exceedingly handsome; but it was too vast, too coarse, too restless" to inspire the affections of "any poet or scholar, or any woman of wisdom and refinement." Having met and courted amid the splendors of Europe, the Marches were only in the city to board a Hudson River steamer and consummate their union by touring the scenic splendors of the Northeast, where the finer emotions might flourish. [6]

The way that the well-to-do thought about urban social relations and arranged and moved through urban built environments precluded either elite or romantic tourism there. In the eyes of many observers, the ragged disorder of American cities was the material expression of the unsettled and often contentious social relations of the young republic. The growth of a market economy and rapid urbanization intensified the challenge that Americans faced in trying to forge a republican society in their newly established nation. The early nineteenth century witnessed the destabilization of older hierarchies and the formation of new working and middle classes. To establish their claims to elevated status and to create a limited, knowable community amid the urban crowds, middling people endorsed the ideology of refinement. It entailed the division of space into distinct public and private spheres. The refined individual maintained a careful self-possession in public and sought to avoid unregulated contact with less genteel, unknown people through elaborate rituals of recognition. [7]

The demands of refinement and its corresponding spatial ideal meant that strolling the city was a serious enterprise. Moving between the private and public realms and in public spaces tested both individual character and the ability of gentility to resolve the tensions between class differences and republican egalitarianism. In an effort to mold the competitive, anonymous crowds of the city into a legible and stable social order, those who wrote about cities in the mid-nineteenth century often portrayed the built environment and its uses as an allegory for relations

of class, ethnicity, and gender. The many Americans moving to and doing business in the nation's rapidly growing young cities had to learn to
perceive the deeper meaning of the scale, materials, location, and functions of buildings, as well as the dress and comportment of individuals
in the urban crowd, in order to move safely in public places. This knowledge served to construct and enforce the ideal of separate spheres and
the related social claims of the early-nineteenth-century middle class.

The many nonfiction works published between the 1830s and the
1870s describing American cities reveal these aims in their choice of subjects and imagery as well as in the spatial practices they prescribe. These
works fall roughly into two types: urban sketches and urban handbooks.[8] The sketches took the form of narratives about specific places,
people, and practices in a chosen city. Emphasizing the deceptiveness
and disorder of both the built environment and urban social relations,
sketch writers revealed the intimate relations among the uses of public,
urban spaces, an individual's character, and the state of the republic. Urban handbooks, in contrast, offered meticulous descriptions of government, religious, benevolent, and private enterprises. They directed the
reader-visitor along broad boulevards through progressive cities whose
elites were quickly redressing any social problems to be found there.

Both types of urban description urged on the reader-visitor the knowledge and spatial practices of the longtime resident in order to avoid or
ameliorate the dangers lurking in public places and unregulated social
interactions. "Enough is told in this volume . . . to convince the reader
that the only path of safety in New York is to avoid all places of doubt-
ful repute," James D. McCabe wrote in the preface to a work intended
for strangers to the city. "No matter how 'wise in his own conceit' a
stranger may be, he is but a child in the hands of the disreputable classes
of the great city."[9] Because of this emphasis on learning local practices,
neither the sketches nor the handbooks considered in any sustained way
the possibility of elite or romantic tourism, although both surely guided
the steps of many urban visitors. As the editor of *Picturesque America*
suggested, American cities might give joy (or sorrow) to the citizen, but
they had little to offer to the mid-nineteenth-century tourist.

"LEISURE IS THE PARENT OF MISCHIEF"

Between the late 1830s and the 1870s, sensational urban sketches frequently appeared in newspapers, magazines, and books. One type
among the many written and performed works addressing the character

of cities suddenly growing beyond experience, the nonfictional urban sketch provided the most specific detail about real places and people. Authors of such sketches, promising to reveal the city "by sunlight and gaslight," described in detail everything from public works to prostitution. Their politics varying from vaguely communitarian to strongly evangelical, the men who wrote the midcentury urban sketches shared the widespread belief that cities posed serious problems for the young nation. According to republican orthodoxy, the disparity between rich and poor and the anonymity that characterized urban life threatened the sturdy independence and mutual oversight necessary for the republic to succeed. Yet the untrammeled commerce of which cities were the physical manifestation resulted from the very freedom and social mobility that the republic fostered.[10]

The growth of a market, waged-labor economy and rapid urbanization exacerbated these long-standing fears in the mid-nineteenth century. The growing division of labor, the middle-class effort to divorce leisure practices from work, and the developing ideological and physical separation of work from home all contributed to conflicts between the working and middle classes over the uses of public, urban spaces. The very meaning of "public" space changed as the older moral economy and smaller scale of urban life gave way to competitive market relations and rapid city growth. City residents had long used the streets to buy, sell, socialize, and work, but more and more often commercial elites wanted the streets cleared for the rapid and unobstructed flow of traffic. Urban expansion and the development of new means of rapid transit, beginning with the horse-drawn omnibus in the late 1830s, reinforced the trend. Municipalities gradually ceded their common-law rights to oversee the uses of public, shared spaces, instead promoting a system in which abutting property owners controlled the streets, squares, and utilities.[11] The city's built environment shaped and reflected its political economy.

City spaces not only changed functions; they also took on new meanings for many Americans. For members of the emerging middle classes, home and workplace came to be physically separated from and ideologically opposed to each other. The private sphere of home and family represented a haven from and a moral anchor for the amoral, competitive market. In their efforts to uplift the lower classes, urban reformers sought to enforce this separation on working people as well. The men and women who preached genteel standards inveighed against practices in which work, leisure, and domestic life were closely connected spatially and ideologically. They sought to create separate places and times for activities they perceived to be quite distinct from each other. Expansion, a competitive real estate market, and this preference for specialized land use promoted the segmentation of urban areas according to class, function, and gender.[12]

The physical order that city reformers and developers wanted to impose on the chaotic urban landscape expressed a certain social vision. Motivating many urban reformers was a desire to extend the refinement that defined the middle class to all Americans. The ideology of refinement promulgated a strict code of individual self-control in public. Relying on the division of public from private behaviors and spaces, it nevertheless emphasized the importance of a correspondence between the two realms: sincerity was its highest virtue. Nowhere was such a code more needed than in the nation's large cities, where anonymity and the possibility of social mobility allowed for all kinds of deception. By dividing public from private and governing the presentation of self in public spaces, the sincere practice of gentility could lend order to urban social relations just as segmentation ordered its spatial organization.[13]

Because gentility was a matter of character rather than birth or wealth, it preserved a hierarchy of merit even as the new economic order disrupted older hierarchies and destabilized emerging ones. Far from undermining Americans' stated commitment to equality, refinement signified the belief that any real leveling depended on the individual achievement of a certain level of self-possession. For middling Americans, the ability of all to behave with propriety legitimized the existence of social differences in the republic, just as the supposedly universal possibility of becoming a property owner justified the existence of economic hierarchy. The proper use of public spaces served as an index of the possibility of achieving a truly republican society.[14]

But at midcentury, urbanites shared no consensus on the proper way to organize and occupy collectively owned streets, squares, and public buildings. All too often, these spaces were noisy, dirty, ill kempt, and inadequate to their purposes. Rather than bring citizens together in orderly colloquy, they provided the setting for often rowdy and sometimes violent contests over the meaning of republicanism and the role of ordinary people in shaping the political and social order. Although individuals built refined enclaves within cities, the urban landscape as a whole did not lend itself to refined conduct. American cities provided travelers and residents alike with evidence of the successes, failures, and peculiarities of the American experiment, but rarely with romantic epiphanies.[15]

In some ways, the journalists who wrote many of the urban sketches were typical of many of the people coming to American cities in the 1840s and 1850s. Socially and geographically, they occupied an uncertain place. Claiming to be literary men, they were employees of the popular, new cheap newspapers and closely associated with the dance hall owners, spunky, homeless newsboys, rowdy firemen, and nameless madams and prostitutes about whom they often wrote. Critical of the vices and inequities of city life, they also rejoiced in its freedom, heterogeneous crowds, and rapid pace. Sketch-writing ministers and doctors, in contrast, were often involved in the temperance and missionary work that characterized middle-class efforts to ameliorate the social and physical ills of urban life.[16]

Although usually sensationalized and often prurient, these works claimed a serious moral intent. They presented the city as a microcosm of the social problems plaguing the young republic. Their authors insisted that the reader-visitor had a personal stake in the contest over urban public spaces. Rather than the individual, uplifting encounter with the beautiful and the sublime that characterized rural and European tourism, visiting an American city in prose or in person was an exercise in confronting deception and disorder. The goal, as the journalist George Foster wrote, was to reveal evil "so that Philanthropy and Justice may plant their blows aright."[17] The urban sketches could easily serve as guides to the very haunts of vice and crime they virtuously warned against. Yet, whatever their actual uses, their authors all urged the reader-visitor to be morally vigilant, at least to protect himself or herself from temptation, if not to do battle against it. However hypocritical, such works did not depict a city suitable for aesthetic and spiritual communion.

Moreover, the literary approach typical of the urban sketch did not furnish the reader with a clear sense of urban geography. The authors offered little or no information on the layout of a city's streets or the precise location of its prominent buildings. Instead, they presented the city as a patchwork of neighborhoods characterized by the morals, ethnicity, and economic status of their residents. In Foster's New York, the well-to-do occupied Broadway and Wall Street, the native-born working class the Bowery and Chatham Street, while the immigrant lower classes dwelled in the notorious Five Points slum. San Francisco's Chinese population lived "in the heart of the city," just around the corner from American homes and shops. Knowing that Broadway was the "aristocratic" and the Bowery the "democratic" avenue of New York and that the two were not far separated gave the reader exact information about the sociospatial order but not directions for finding the two thoroughfares from the train station or pier. Presumably, a visitor's local host could provide that information. Writing in terms of light and dark, surface and depths, and kindred contrasts, authors described a city landscape whose character was determined by its social relations.[18]

Reinforcing the emphasis on social location was the brevity and serial format of the urban sketch, which framed the city as a discontinuous collection of places and peoples. The topical "slices" or "glimpses" of city life often appeared in newspapers before being collected and published as books. They provided no maps or continuous narration of the built environment, leaving the reader-visitor to find his—rarely her—way among the moral districts. Initially slim volumes, some compendiums contained up to eight hundred pages by the 1860s and 1870s. Lacking any explicit organizing principle, they mirrored the chaotic heterogeneity that many perceived in the cities themselves and probably encouraged people to read selectively.[19]

Notably, these works claimed to give their readers an accurate portrayal of urban life, not simply the city's built environment or notable attractions. Their titles often indicate their catholic scope and their interest in social practices as well as the built environment. Asa Greene titled his 1837 work *A Glance at New York: Embracing the City Government, Theatres, Hotels, Churches, Mobs, Monopolies, Learned Professions, Newspapers, Rogues, Dandies, Fires and Firemen, Water and Other Liquids, &c., &c.* Later writers fleshed out Greene's et ceteras, attempting to name in the title every topic covered in their hundreds of pages, from aqueducts to the stock exchange, noting department stores, express companies, prostitution, Sabbath customs, and the sewage system along the way.[20] Such entries assumed that readers wanted to understand a city's social and physical infrastructure in all its complexity, not simply its chief landmarks.

The urban sketch artists' emphasis on explaining the city's social structure was an attempt to impose representational transparency on urban social relations. The presence of great numbers of diverse people lent credit to each city's claim to be a metropolis, but it also troubled most writers. The social mobility that Americans celebrated in these years undermined the establishment of a legitimate social hierarchy in the city. If a person could not place others socially and geographically, how could the social order function? In an effort to reveal the true relationship between private essence and public appearance, the sketch writers spent a great deal of time unmasking urban deceptions, especially those perpetrated by fair-faced but black-hearted city dwellers on naive newcomers.[21]

Public spaces constituted the particular locus of such deceptions, especially the activities performed there apart from the discipline of work or the moral influence of home. "Leisure," as Junius Henri Browne declared in 1869, "is the parent of mischief." The members of the large transient population in Washington "have a vast amount of leisure time on their hands," John Ellis warned. "As they are thrown together with a comparative freedom from restraint, . . . the usual consequences of such promiscuous intercourse follow." [22] Leisured transients endangered both themselves and the local residents, so they had to be integrated into the social order as quickly as possible.

The growth of cities and the market economy made the moral economy and social relations of the city very different from those of the small town. Before the great wave of urbanization in the nineteenth century, most Americans lived in communities small enough for all or a good portion of the inhabitants to be known to one another. The city stood in direct contrast: "Its solitude is distressing. In the midst of a crowd the stranger is alone. He might live or die without any one's knowing or caring." The rapid pace of urbanization and the rise of wage labor meant the troublesome presence of thousands of unsupervised, single male "strangers" and a smaller but even more troublesome number of single female strangers. Because they were "unfamiliar" with the city—that is, not integrated into its social order through work and family—they could not tell true from false and respectable from vicious. Worse, they might not remember to try. Moreover, they came to the city with grand dreams of making their fortunes, putting themselves directly in the path of temptation.[23] As a result, they were easily taken in by those offering parodies of respectable social bonds: confidence men and prostitutes.

Confidence men usually offered the stranger both instant friendliness and a quick tour of the city, confirming the intimate connection between social and spatial orientation. Whatever they offered, their goal was to make money at the victim's expense. A common scam exploited the city's violation of the limits of a knowable community. "To a stranger there is no place so lonely and utterly desolate as a great city," declared one author. Bereft of the dense web of kin and acquaintance typical of small communities, the newcomer was all too ready to believe the false familiarity of the sharper, who had learned his name from the hotel register. "The visitor, thankful that he has found somebody to speak to in this great wilderness, becomes communicative. . . . He is only too happy to accept an invitation to call at a private club-house of a friend." [24]

Inevitably, the newcomer who placed such foolish trust in a kind stranger awoke the next morning hung over, penniless, and perhaps jailed on charges of public drunkenness. Ashamed of their behavior or unable to establish their good character, these hapless fools contributed to the coffers of blackmailers and suffered from official censure. Their disreputable activities, appearance, and location, all the results of an innocent trust in an amiable acquaintance, made it impossible for them to demonstrate their respectability to the strangers standing in judgment. At an extreme, such naïfs ended their lives as unidentified corpses buried ignominiously in the potter's field. The career of women so duped began with infatuation and seduction, then took a detour through prostitution and drink before ending in the same place. If the visitor was to avoid the toils of urban vice, he or she needed to learn an urban wariness of his or her fellows: "Honest men are not apt to take up sudden fancies for strangers." [25]

Trusting a city's built environment might be equally dangerous to the newcomer. One "respectable citizen of Buffalo," trying to avoid climbing a set of stairs in midcentury Chicago's uneven sidewalks, got lost and eventually fell into one of the young city's many mud holes. When the police finally responded to his cries of distress, they jailed him for being drunk and disorderly. Compounding his geographic ignorance was his lack of social ties: "Not being able to produce any witnesses who could prove the contrary, and the appearance of his dress being sorely against him," he was convicted and fined. His travails were a thinly veiled allegory for the uncertainty of urban life. The ups and downs of Chicago's treacherous sidewalks and streets symbolized everything from the volatility of the stock market and the rapidity of upward and downward social mobility to the evanescence of romance. [26]

Worsening the problems of scale that cities presented was the fast-advancing invasion of human relationships by market concerns. "The first impression one gets of cities," Browne noted, "is that everything in them is for sale." Fears that the cash nexus was making honest social relations impossible emerged most strongly in discussions of gambling and stock speculation. Both represented the institutionalization of the confidence man's business, for they entailed gaining wealth without productive work and relied on a modicum of trust motivated only by avarice. The first-class gambling houses resembled the finest private homes, and the players were all gentlemanly; yet they were sure sources of moral and financial devastation. And the legal speculation on the stock exchange was no better: "Every operator endeavors to outstrip his fellow. Device and deception, rumor and innuendo, ingenious invention and base fabrication, are resorted to. The greatest gambling in the Republic is going on, and the deepest dishonesty is concealed by the garb of commercial honor."[27]

The danger of both illicit gambling and its legal form in stock speculation lay in the illusion of instant wealth gained without hard work and the deceptive social mobility that resulted. The pervasiveness of such dishonesty made it difficult to place oneself in relation to other people. "Revelations of fraud are daily and startling. Men of high standing are thrown down, and desolation carried to their homes. Dishonesty, rash speculation, stock gambling, expensive horses, with women, wine, fast and high living, tell the story." The "work" of the speculator was indistinguishable from vicious leisure, and both entailed the greed-motivated pretense of amiability and trustworthiness that was the confidence man's stock-in-trade. To compound the problem, stock speculators and confidence men were not alone in their perfidy; on every street, tradesmen and beggars schemed to fleece the unwary as well.[28]

In short, the city and the market together abetted the perversion of natural social ties. The combination of social mobility and urban anonymity constantly endangered the ability of the refined individual to forge a respectable, mutually known, and stable community. Lacking local expertise, tourists were personally at risk in the city, but more important, they exemplified the commercial transience that the ideology of refinement sought to regulate. In the republic's intensely commercial cities, the price of moral integrity—or refinement—was constant vigilance, making pleasure travel unthinkable.

Efforts to separate private from public were among the chief responses of middling Americans to the distressing combination of urban anonymity and untrammeled market forces. They meant the division to create a protected realm of trust and intimacy beyond the reach of the market. Yet this private sphere was continually endangered by the market relations that made it both possible and necessary, nowhere more so than in cities. One of the most disturbing signs of the market's invasion of intimate relations was prostitution. Even more than confidence men, prostitutes offered a commercial parody of a key means of integration into the social order, courtship and marriage:

> Here are two ladies approaching us, magnificently attired, with their large arms and voluptuous bosoms half naked, and their bright eyes looking invitation at every passer by. . . . [T]hey look hard at you, and exclaim familiarly, "How do you do, my dear? Come, won't you go home with me?"[29]

The man who accepted the ladies' kind offer received not the moral and social benefits of marriage and family but, at best, an hour's or a night's physical pleasure and the temptation to sin again. At worst, he would lose his wallet, his will to do honest work, and perhaps even his life.

Symbolically undermining the moral order embodied in the idea of separate spheres, prostitutes also highlighted the troublesome nature of the relationship between self and commerce at a time when the market economy was transforming it. The members of the emerging middle class located virtue in private practices and realms, divorcing their tender scruples from a market increasingly conceived of as operating autonomously according to "natural" laws. The women assigned to this newly defined private sphere became the guardians of virtue, bolstering and absolving their men for combat in the marketplace. In public, self-possession was the chief armor against the social chaos caused by the market. Yet the developing capitalist market compelled many people to sell their labor power rather than products of it to survive. Wage laborers, especially prostitutes, could not separate themselves as easily as the middle classes from the imperative to buy and sell.[30]

The commerce in sex also demonstrated the hypocrisy of the middle-class separation of Christian morals from economic practices. If the market were unfettered, everything was for sale; if some things were not to be sold, the market had to be controlled by moral and not simply "natural" forces. Because the ideology of separate spheres idealized the desexualized, maternal woman in the private home as the linchpin of the social order, the increasing presence of prostitutes in the streets of American cities epitomized the violation of moral norms possible there.[31] Prostitutes enacted in public the evasion of gender and work imperatives through their immoral "leisure," yet they sold their bodies precisely because of those imperatives. They were powerful symbols of the potential of the market to corrode existing gender norms and thus to destroy the moral foundations of the republic.

The figure of the prostitute also marked the limits of respectable women's public presence. Urban anonymity made it impossible to know whether a given woman was respectable or not by her face or her dress. The fair faces and genteel good taste of high-class prostitutes were a commonplace in urban sketches. Therefore, women with reputations to protect had to be careful when and where they walked. On New York's Broadway, "[a] lady of respectability and standing does not lose caste by strolling out, *unattended,* during the hours of daylight, and no *gentleman* would presume to insult her, or even rudely address her"; but in the evening, "very few females, except those of dubious character, will be met in Broadway *alone!*" [32]

The specter of female sexual commerce meant that women who traveled in urban public spaces were always aware of their visibility. Unlike men, women could not easily adopt the "calm, yea, philosophic eye" that Browne recommended in order to see the city's "open and hidden mysteries at every angle; observe the places we enter, and analyze the people we encounter." Instead, they were the objects of that eye: "On almost any pleasant afternoon a crowd of ardent admirers of female loveliness may be seen upon some convenient street-corner discussing nonsense and insultingly ogling ladies as they pass." [33] Although some women did write about city life, their public presence was always much more problematic than that of middle-class and elite men.

Women's presence on city streets also represented the ability of women in large cities to abandon their domestic duties. The wealthy women who frequented the shops and ice-cream saloons were exploiting their husbands' wealth for their own pleasure instead of fulfilling their role behind the scenes as wives, mothers, and domestic guarantors of the social order. Many writers feared that their public leisure concealed a travesty of home life: adulterous spouses, neglected children, even abortions to enable them to participate in a lively social life.[34] Women's evasion of their proper role and space threatened to undermine the whole edifice of gentility on which the republic balanced so precariously.

Yet the presence of respectable women at leisure in the city's public spaces also signaled the social and economic openness that Americans celebrated as the consequence of their republican institutions. Women's display of wealth publicly enacted their male relatives' dedication to the market economy; their refined leisure justified men's amoral competitiveness as an agent of civilization. The ability of respectable women to occupy public spaces was a crucial indicator of the social power of their class. The extension of genteel regulations to public spaces such as theaters, parks, and major retail streets indicated the populace's growing refinement, and thus Americans' gradual attainment of the self-possession that would perfectly reconcile capitalism with republican egalitarianism.

Because women were supposed to represent private virtue, their public display of wealth and assertion of social superiority illustrated the deceptiveness of urban appearances and the related illegitimacy of social claims far more than did men's. "One would hardly believe he was in a republican country to see the escutcheoned panels of the carriages, the liveried coachmen, and the supercilious air of the occupants," Browne sniffed. Making things worse, the coach's female passengers "are fleshy, gross, and very showily dressed. They imagine they resemble duchesses." The seemingly refined ladies in another carriage were really high-class prostitutes.[35]

The spectacle of beauty and wealth in American cities, in short, directed the onlooker's attention to thorny social problems, not an uplifting awareness of historical or natural wonders. Encountering a city presented a challenge to the individual's moral principles and the nation's republican ones. No doubt thousands of men visiting the city used the sketches to find a place to drink, gamble, or purchase sex without much worrying about the moral and political implications of a night on the town. Plenty of women went shopping and riding or became prostitutes without considering themselves the cause of cultural demoralization. But even though neither cities nor urbanites quite lived up to the shocking, titillating urban sketches, their very preoccupation with vice and crime indicated a strong current of anxiety about the place of the city in a moral republic. The quest for beauty and uplift took one out of the American city, never into it.

Yet even the gloomiest of urban sketch authors did not lose all faith in Americans, their cities, or their principles. In addition to unmasking urban deceptions, these authors proposed to resolve some of the uncertainty characterizing urban life by categorizing residents in terms of their streets, buildings, dress, and leisure activities. One author admitted, "City life everywhere presents protean aspects," yet "[t]here are . . . certain localities that exhibit distinct characteristics." The particulars of place enabled him to define the "mixed multitudes" thronging the streets and to provide a trustworthy alternative to the confidence man's scam.[36] The urban sketch artists taught newcomers how to identify urban moral regions and characters accurately and thus how to negotiate city streets as safely and knowingly as residents.

Walking or riding along a city's chief streets was not only an introduction to the main business thoroughfares but also a lesson in social distinctions and how to negotiate them. In observing the "daily tide" of urban residents traveling between residence and business, the stranger learned to distinguish urban types amid the crowd and to connect them to the social hierarchy and the rhythms of work and leisure. George Foster claimed that "[e]ach division of the day has its distinctive class of omnibus riders." Earliest in the morning came the junior clerks and laborers, occupying the car with an "air of absolute independence and equality." Next to board were "the sleek and rotund burghers of Above Bleecker," using the egalitarian omnibus despite their pretensions to grandeur. Finally the wealthy women of the city emerged, "all muffled inscrutably from sight, and as careful of being seen as the inmates of the harem. It would be so vulgar to be caught in Broadway in the morning!" [37]

In one brief paragraph, Foster instructed his readers on the relationship among social standing, urban institutions, place, and gender. When and where people boarded the omnibus revealed the city's social and spatial organization. Clerks carried iron keys, laborers tin lunch pails, well-to-do men their portliness and fine dress, wealthy women thick green veils. Yet all patronized the omnibus; all were members of a single city, however complex and socially divided. Such descriptions illuminated the social order, but they had neither the depth of history nor the romance of foreignness. This was information meant to incorporate the visitor into the local sociospatial order, not to entertain or awe the beauty-seeking tourist.

In addition to lending order to city crowds, the authors of urban sketches described the social customs that regulated the interactions of middle-class and elite city dwellers. San Franciscans, Benjamin Lloyd reported, preferred to live in fine hotels and take their meals at the city's excellent restaurants. On Sundays, "small excursion steamers puff and pant" on the Bay, streetcars were crowded and carriages many, all containing well-dressed people on their way to church or to "the various picnic and pleasure grounds." Fashionable New York, Matthew Hale Smith remarked, "is distinguished by yellow kids. . . . [E]very man you meet, young or old, who makes a pretension to society, wears yellow gloves." [38] So informed, the visitor or newcomer could quickly adopt the local custom.

Often writers couched such investigations of a city's social arrangements in the language of natural history. Adopting the stance of the naturalist distanced the authors from the implications of their ambiguous social position and close acquaintance with vice and crime. In one instance, Foster undertook a lighthearted discussion of "the different genera of this interesting species," the Dandy. Others would detail the habitat, origins, and behavior of Rowdies, Hoodlums, Parvenus, Gamblers, Impostors, Thieves, Gamins, Beggars, Prostitutes, and other types. As in natural history, typing imposed order on a vast, heterogeneous mass of creatures, identifying both their unique characteristics and their relationships to others. Whether ogling the elite or inspecting the lowly, authors of urban sketches oriented their readers to the existing social and geographic order and hinted that they were as natural as those found among animals and plants.[39] The reader would presumably know where he or she fit and how to interact with other city dwellers.

The expansive later works also included short biographical pieces on the life and character of a city's prominent men—and a few women. Leading businessmen, clergymen, and politicians were representative subjects; the notorious abortionist Madame Restell received the most attention among notable women. These sketches tended to be didactic evaluations of the person's moral worth and financial acumen. Aside from predictable lessons about hard work and fair dealing, the biographical sketches also gave faces and personalities to a city's social leaders. Dry goods merchant Alexander Stewart's "manner is hard and repulsive. He is of the average height, slim, with a decided Hibernian face; sandy hair, nearly red; sharp, cold avaricious features." Renowned minister Henry Ward Beecher "is young-looking and vigorous. He has the face of a great orator. . . . He dresses plainly, with something of the farmer in his air, and lives simply."[40] Such widely available "inside" knowledge might approximate the personal oversight that neighbors exercised in small towns and mitigate the anonymity that threatened the city's social order.

In sum, unlike rural scenery and the historical ruins of Europe, American cities confronted their visitors with difficult moral and political issues. The spaces and activities typical of great cities were radically unlike those to be found in small towns or rural areas. They revealed that in many ways urban life had burst the bonds of community, although urbanites were struggling valiantly and with some success to create new kinds of social solder. Public, urban leisure in particular embodied all the perils of the great changes under way in the first half of the nineteenth century. The pervasive stink of commerce and less abstract wastes in cities' public spaces made them unsuitable for the kind of refined contemplation that characterized nineteenth-century tourism.

Yet people did go sight-seeing in cities, usually in conjunction with business or family visits. And alongside the sensational and encyclopedic revelations of cities "by sunlight and by gaslight" appeared books and articles emphasizing business, philanthropic, and cultural opportunities. These works offered visitors a rosy vision that emphasized the vigor and promise of American urban life. In praising the major buildings and streets, they insisted that the city did not pose a danger to individual morals or to the republic. Instead, they celebrated the rise of institutional and architectural anchors for the urban social order and built environment. Still, their authors shared with the urban sketch artists the beliefs that the built environment was an expression of the city's social relationships and that visitors needed a city dweller's familiarity with both. They too addressed not tourists but potential residents.

"LOCALITIES AND OBJECTS OF INTEREST"

The strangers and visitors who arrived in an American city at the middle of the nineteenth century often made a point of seeing the sights: "its miles of streets, its splendid public and private buildings, its extensive charities, and the enterprise and public spirit of its inhabitants." A party waiting for the next train west out of Albany, New York, "walked through the city and saw all the sights that could be seen by gas light, visited the state house," and then returned to the hotel to smoke "segars." C. N. Brainerd spent the hours between trains similarly, visiting Cleveland's "principal streets, public buildings, squares, &c.," during one stop and the same features of Chicago during the next. When the Utica, New York, businessman John Munn met with business associates in Chicago in 1853, they "spent two hours most pleasantly in a ride over the city at every step noting evidence of its great & rapid growth."[41]

Americans were interested in their young cities at midcentury and not simply fearful of them. Locally produced booster literature trumpeted each city's unparalleled opportunities for commerce and manufacturing. The rapid growth of Chicago and other midwestern towns attracted the attention of journalists as well as letter writers and diarists. Like the travelers above, journalists inspected public buildings and principal streets. The articles they wrote, detailing each city's trade, industry, and culture, appeared regularly in middle-class magazines. Often the implicit question was whether such overgrown towns yet qualified for the title of metropolis. The growth and maturity of these cities were a commentary on the nation's own progress as it expanded westward and industrialized.[42]

This kind of sight-seeing, although it might well be a pleasant activity, had a serious purpose distinct from the tourist's quest for romantic uplift. As did better-known foreign visitors to the republic, Americans sought evidence of how their society and government worked, especially in the troubling milieu of an expanding commercial-industrial city. Many Americans shared the faith that their republican nation exemplified social progress, and the institutions of government and social reform embodied this national virtue.[43] A city's broad avenues and government, commercial, and philanthropic buildings anchored the disorderly landscape and supplied evidence of a stable social structure. That such organizations existed in urban centers demonstrated that urbanism and republicanism were not necessarily at odds.

Like distinguished foreign visitors, American travelers did not encounter cities through enterprises catering solely to pleasure travelers. Until the 1860s, people journeying for pleasure enjoyed no special travel arrangements; they shared trains and itineraries with business travelers and migrants. City hotels were famous for being local community and business centers and serving as many, if not more, long-term residents as they did transients. Travel was usually an extension of people's business, familial, and social contacts. John Munn met neighbors and business associates on the train, stayed with them in the Sherman and Tremont hotels, and visited with the families of his partners in Chicago. His sight-seeing tour included a survey of the plots of land he had bought. Like Munn, most visitors to cities interacted with local people of their own class, not exclusively with other transients. This was not tourism in the same sense that it would become later in the century, when people visited places with little interest in their local significance and through the mediation of commercial tourist agencies.[44]

Just as urban visitors were not yet full-fledged tourists, the kind of information about cities readily available to them was not primarily designed for pleasure travelers. Encyclopedic versions of the urban sketch published in the 1860s and 1870s offered the information needed for Munn's kind of sight-seeing in generous amounts. In addition, other types of city description, especially urban handbooks and city entries in national tourist guides, focused almost exclusively on fine buildings and broad streets. Publishers produced the handbooks on a regular basis beginning as early as the 1830s, updating and expanding them over time and rarely acknowledging the author. Sometimes sponsored by a single business, they were close kin to city directories and booster literature. The reader of such works learned how to see the institutional and business structure of a city.[45] Despite the great difference in their subject matter and tone, both sketches and handbooks assumed that visitors wanted a resident's familiarity.

National travel guides, another important source of information for the visitor, seem to have been scarcer than the locally produced handbooks. In any case, they focused almost exclusively on resorts and rural scenery. Appleton's, a New York publisher, produced the first national tourist guide to the United States in the late 1840s, modeling it after the new Baedeker guides to European nations. The company intended its *New and Complete United States Guide Book for Travellers* specifically for pleasure journeyers. Unlike most such works, it incorporated major cities into the text and provided several city maps as well. Like Baedeker, Appleton's *Guide* emphasized places and services catering to transients. To a greater extent than contemporaneous descriptions of cities, it listed hotels, eating houses, theaters, railroads, and steamboats. By the late 1870s it had adopted Baedeker's format of listing this information at the head of the entry and leaving the description of sights for later. Mirroring the tourist's own priorities, this format also underscored the separation of the stranger's path from those that residents used.[46]

But the content and the approach of Appleton's *Guide* were otherwise very similar to those of the city handbook. After specifying the city's site by latitude and longitude and its advantages for commerce, both the handbooks and the city entries in national guides described the chief streets and buildings in an orderly, highly selective fashion. Some conducted the reader on a walk along major thoroughfares; others grouped like institutions together and left it to the reader to determine their geographic location. In either case, the city's success in harnessing market forces and remedying poverty, crime, and disease was on display. Broad streets, beautiful buildings, fine churches, and benevolent institutions all testified to the "well-directed spirit of enterprise, which is now so characteristic of New York, [and which] seems determined to make that city the most beautiful among the cities of either hemisphere."[47]

The precise location of a city's major streets was less important than the evidence they gave of metropolitan scale and grandeur as well as republican rationality. In these mid-nineteenth-century works, the gridiron system later so reviled was praised for its rationality and beauty, in contrast to the tangled, narrow, and inelegant streets of older cities. *The*

Great Metropolis (1849) informed its readers that New York's "streets were originally laid out according to the make of the ground, and some of them were crooked; and in imitation of European cities, many of them were narrow." But Americans were not content with this old-fashioned, imitative approach: "In later times care has been taken to lay out the streets straight, and of an ample width," with the result that "[n]o city can exhibit a more beautiful plan than this [northern] portion of New York." According to the authors of urban handbooks, the gridiron expressed the American dedication to social egalitarianism as well as modern rationality. At the same time, it served the purposes of the real estate market by dividing land into formally equal and fungible portions. It was an excellent symbol of American success in combining republican principles with commercial prosperity.[48]

Having explained a city's layout, the handbooks and guide entries then turned to its major avenues. First among thoroughfares, "Broadway is a noble street, 80 feet wide and straight as an arrow." Width, straightness, length, and the magnificence of its edifices were crucial features of a city's chief street, distinguishing it from less elevated byways and expressing the scale of urban population, building, and traffic. "All along Broadway, and its intersecting streets, the eye is greeted everywhere by long lines of marble and stone buildings, many of them of great architectural elegance."[49] Chicago's efforts in the 1850s and 1860s to raise itself out of the mud and construct just such broad streets and fine buildings marked its ambitious bid for metropolitan status. Without these features, no town could sustain a claim to cityhood.

The walk along a city's central street also introduced the visitor to the startling noise, pace, and volume of urban traffic: "The great characteristic of New York is din and excitement." Asa Greene was already warning newcomers in 1837 that crossing Broadway was a perilous enterprise: "[Y]ou must button your coat tight about you, settle your hat firmly on your head, look up street and down street, at the self-same moment, to see what carts and carriages are upon you, and then run for your life."[50] The width of major streets and the number of vehicles and their chaotic rush were unique to the burgeoning cities. The pedestrian had to take his or her chances when venturing to cross them.

Although the urban handbooks frequently called them "thoroughfares," major city streets were only beginning to be primarily channels for traffic in the mid-nineteenth century. The speed and volume of traffic permitted by such long, straight streets represented the abandonment of the community strictures accompanying and symbolized by the tangled

streets and distinct neighborhoods of the older city. Many urbanites
continued to trade and socialize in the streets, and the mixture of uses
resulted in many accidents and conflicts over the proper usage of public
roads. In systematizing the street layout and facilitating the development
of mass transit by the sale of franchises, municipalities initiated the
redefinition of streets as throughways, imperiling or literally marginal-
izing other uses of them.[51]

Noting the danger and disorder of city traffic undermined the handbooks' emphasis on order and progress somewhat. Yet from the 1830s
onward, the noise and rate of both vehicular and pedestrian traffic
marked metropolitan status and was an important element in the rivalry
between New York and Chicago. In conceding that Chicago might even
rival the eastern metropolis some day, Charles Dudley Warner declared
that the city's "throng of passengers and traffic, the intersecting street
and cable railways, the loads of freight and the crush of carriages, the
life and hurry and excitement are sufficient to satisfy the most eager
lover of metropolitan pandemonium."[52] Urban hustle would later come
to mark Americans' troubling inability to enjoy civilized leisure. But at
midcentury the rush of the streets was an index of the city's commercial
success and aimless loitering of the kind tourists indulged in an activity
to be discouraged.

Even more than broad and busy streets, Americans admired the edifices of progressive, republican institutions of government and philanthropy as evidence of the triumph of civilization over disorder. Although
American cities lacked the historical and artistic masterpieces of their
European elders, they nevertheless boasted humane asylums for the
blind and the insane, model workhouses and jails, evangelical missions,
and philanthropic hospitals. In addition to all the signs of a prosperous
city, New York "can boast something far more attractive to the eye of
humanity—far more suggestive of the true greatness of a people. We al-
lude to its institutions, founded by the benevolent and humane, for the
promotion of the temporal comfort of the unfortunate." Such institutions constituted "green oases, in the midst of a desert of selfishness."[53]
Without denying the evidence of dislocation and anomie that the urban
sketch artists deplored so graphically, the authors of urban handbooks
celebrated the emergence of institutions of order and humanity suited to
the scale of urban problems and wealth.

Yet, although the visit to such institutions had become conventional
by the mid-nineteenth century, they were not yet accustomed to accommodating masses of interested strangers. Certainly "localities and ob-

jects of interest," asylums were not yet tourist attractions. Some city entries in guidebooks did inform readers about the hours and conditions for visiting the city jail, asylums, workhouses, and hospitals, but in the 1850s and 1860s they often simply advised readers to apply to the pertinent official. Personal rather than commercial or institutional arrangements were necessary. On the other hand, the authors of handbooks assumed that visiting citizens would have ready access to government buildings and officials. One might not only visit city hall but also pay a social call on the mayor. As late as 1876, at least some ordinary visitors expected to be able to drop in on the president when they came to the White House.[54]

The way that handbook authors described such institutions highlighted their understanding of the interpenetration of the social order and the built environment. Even though the reason for visiting these buildings was their government or benevolent function, handbook authors described with pleasure the architectural grandeur of the exteriors far more often than they noted the good works practiced within. The New York Lunatic Asylum "is a large and fine building, attached to which are 40 acres of ground, tastefully laid out in gardens, pleasure grounds, and gravelled walks," with a fine view of the Hudson River. "The principal edifice is of stone, 210 feet long, and 60 feet wide. It cost, with its grounds, over $200,000, and contains about 150 patients."[55] That such a fine site and edifice were devoted to the care of the insane made the asylum a physical representation of urban order and progress.

Handbooks also directed the reader-visitor's attention to the buildings housing the municipal and federal government. In addition to their monumental character, they tended to contain what few historical relics Americans chose to preserve and display in the mid-nineteenth century. The *Great Metropolis* informed the reader that New York's fine City Hall, 216 feet long and 105 feet wide, "has more ornament than either the [Merchants'] Exchange or the Custom House, but less simple grandeur. . . . The front and ends are constructed of white marble, and the rear of brown freestone." Details of the building's architecture and interior followed, conducting the reader from an appreciation of the exterior to an exploration of the rooms within, especially those containing material traces of George Washington's short tenure there as president.[56] The attention to the materials and style of the building, accompanied by a reverential visit to historical relics, marked the beginning of the kind of tourism Americans practiced in European cities. But such objects and sites were as yet rare in the United States and would not be systematically cultivated until after the Civil War.

In addition to demonstrating that the city was a magnet for philanthropists as well as rogues, both the handbooks and many of the urban sketches offered loving descriptions of the possibility of social order through mechanization and labor discipline. The capacious urban sketches of the 1860s and 1870s delighted in detailing the organizational and technological improvements in fire fighting, crime detecting, parcel delivery, dry-goods retailing, and other large municipal and private enterprises. The detective force in New York "not only systematized, but classified," crime and, aided by the telegraph, maintained a constant knowledge of the whereabouts of all of the city's "adroit rogues." New York's police also had great "efficiency, discipline, and character," and within its headquarters, "[s]ystem, order, quiet prevail. . . . Every man has his place, and must be found in it." The Adams Express Company "is a model for convenience, elegance, and utility. . . . Order, system, and despatch reign throughout the house. . . . Every man knows his duty, has his place, and must do his work." [57] Juxtaposed to exposés of prostitution, gambling, and cheating, such pieces suggested that the preservation of the republic was not impossible even in the largest of cities. The anonymous crowds of strangers might be put in their rightful places, given determination, the latest technology, and the best business methods.

Having taken in the city's best public buildings and private enterprises, the stranger and visitor might also tour the city's churches, especially on Sunday when many other attractions were closed. Most handbooks assumed that visitors, like residents, would attend religious services that day, and travelers like David Clapp, John Kinsey, and Mrs. James Finley made a point of doing so. But by the mid-nineteenth century, a city's churches also functioned as important emblems of urban culture and history. Among the earliest urban edifices to have a distinctive architecture, they also had longer institutional, if not physical, histories in cities whose brief pasts had been mostly erased by commerce. Even though New York's Trinity Church had been rebuilt as late as the 1840s, its institutional existence and its cemetery rooted it in an earlier time, as did its Gothic architecture. Increasingly used for churches and university buildings in the nineteenth century, the Gothic style symbolized the stable moral and aesthetic virtues of a mythic medieval period. [58]

The Gothic style also heightened the contrast between churches and commercial buildings, as did the adoption of the classical style for government buildings. In most cities during the nineteenth century, churches followed the residences of the well-to-do away from the central areas, now devoted almost solely to commerce. Architectural style as well as location marked the process of city segmentation and visually expressed the ideological alignment of religion with private, domestic life. Although government buildings remained in business districts, their monumental, horizontal style and surrounding landscaping increasingly differentiated them from the profit-seeking enterprises around them.[59] This success in reorganizing the city according to the ideal of separate spheres raised the possibility of urban tourism in the late nineteenth century.

The tour of churches often included a tour of a city's finest residential neighborhoods, and it shared some characteristics with it. Unlike the urban sketch artists, the authors of handbooks did not criticize the fortunes or claims to social authority of the wealthy. Similarly, no mention of doctrine or sectarian disagreements marred their admiration for church exteriors. Many simply listed the city's best-known churches by denomination, race, and ethnicity, while others surveyed those with the most impressive architecture. The *Great Metropolis* headed its section on New York's religious buildings baldly: "Churches—Description of Several. Among the churches, some deserve to be particularly noticed, on account of their architecture." Having praised the banks, shops, and hotels of San Francisco, a Central Pacific railroad guide (1870) asserted, "The churches, however, are the finest edifices in the city. Here the Jews have erected a synagogue which, if not the most splendid, is, at least, one of the most splendid in the United States."[60] New York's fine synagogues also appeared in some handbooks, but generally Episcopalian churches and Roman Catholic cathedrals dominated the ranks of religious edifices worth seeing.

Imparting a kind of diffuse aesthetic awe, the authors of urban handbooks and city entries relegated doctrine to the individual's conscience. By the 1880s J. J. Burns and Edwin Smart could assure their readers that "all tastes and fancies in religion can be suited to a nicety."[61] As with the description of municipal and federal buildings, writers seemed little concerned with what actually went on within the doors of these institutions and more interested in their architectural and monumental presence in the urban landscape. Many works pointed to the number of churches and missions and the presence of excellent ministers as proof that the city was a haven of virtue as well as a den of vice. The particularities of faith were less important than the evidence of religiosity in general.

Fine business buildings marked a city's progress as well, despite the anxiety about commerce that pervaded the urban sketches. Chicago's claim to national eminence in the 1850s and 1860s would rest to a great degree on the fine new buildings and broad streets being raised out of the muck. Visiting the city in 1858, the journalist Caroline Kirkland wrote that "our Occidental Sultana dresses her fair head with towers and spires, and hangs about her neck long rows of gems in the shape of stately and elegant dwellings,—yet, descending to her feet, we sink in mud and mire." Twelve years later, the Englishman W. F. Rae reported, "A city of palaces has taken the place of a few miserable hovels." The great fire of 1871 would soon raze the palaces Rae praised, but solidity and magnificence of the edifices built from the ashes testified to the determined metropolitanism of the city's elites.[62]

Indeed, the fact that a growing number of commercial buildings had "architecture" was an important sign of the maturity of American cities. "Within these past twenty years, architecture has been making rapid advances among us," the cultural critic Clarence Cook wrote in 1855. Until then, only the Capitol in Washington, D.C., New York's City Hall, and a few other civic and religious edifices had "sufficient architectural importance to deserve a passing criticism." Cook's venture into art criticism heralded a change in the understanding of the relationship between the social order and the built environment. In claiming that architecture had arrived in the United States by 1855, Cook took the opportunity to counter the aesthetic philosopher John Ruskin's insistence on the correspondence between morality and aesthetics. "It is absurd to think," he wrote, that the Good, the True, and the Beautiful "can not exist independently of one another. . . . When, therefore, Ruskin connects architectural deformity with moral depravity . . . , he assumes for an essential what is only an accidental."[63]

Using the rarefied terms of moral and aesthetic philosophy, Cook claimed that public spaces might be the site of beauty without also being the site of a moral, republican community. Social relations might not have a direct, shaping influence on the built environment. To assert that there was no necessary correlation between inner and outer character undermined the basis of the ideology of refinement. It meant the acceptance of the anonymity and abstract market forces that characterized the city as against the face-to-face relations and moral economy of the idealized small town. The outer appearance need not represent the inner condition; metropolitan conditions made no necessary comment on the society sustaining them.[64]

If this were true, then moving between public and private and negotiating in public spaces need not be as socially and personally dangerous as most urban sketch artists assumed. The absence of sincerity in the landscape or in persons need not signal the collapse of the social order, but merely required a new approach to both landscape and social relations in which surface beauties could be taken for granted in public interactions and private evils left concealed. Such an attitude would make it easier for Americans to visit their cities without having to confront the social problems present there.

This growing distinction between society and built environment was not accidental, although it was hardly intentional. It derived in part from the apparent success that middling and well-to-do Americans had in creating refined spaces within cities in the second half of the nineteenth century. The most obvious triumph of refined ideas about the urban landscape was the construction of the great new city parks, begun in the 1850s with the movement to create what eventually became New York's Central Park. Up to that date, wealthy individuals had cultivated gardens as an expression of their own urbane gentility. The gardens provided a haven from the rough outside world but did not seek to alter it. A city's publicly maintained squares and commons, in contrast, hosted military displays, partisan and electoral activities, national holidays, and other occasions requiring large gatherings of citizens. The enactment of community in these spaces centered on the performance of the duties of a republican citizen—and all too often involved drunken rowdiness as well.[65]

But by the mid-nineteenth century, many Americans began to call for the creation of public gardens to serve the same purpose for the multitudes that private ones long had for the select few. The chief ideologue of the nineteenth-century parks movement, Frederick Law Olmsted, envisioned city parks as oases from the hustle and din of the city, its rationalized, inartistic design, and the uncertain social relations in the streets. Great public gardens would proselytize refinement to the masses, who would be able to enjoy the same romantic encounter with nature as did those wealthy enough to travel in the Hudson River valley and the mountains of New Hampshire and Vermont. Improving the environment would uplift people.[66] As Cook had suggested in reference to architecture, moral social relations were not a necessary precondition for beauty. The park advocates did not abandon the faith that a relationship existed between the environment and social relations, but they reversed the emphasis. Now beautiful places would produce a harmonious social order.

Although Olmsted designed his parks to encourage an individual's encounter with a romantic landscape, other urbanites (and Olmsted, too, at times) believed that the large urban parks could also serve to unite the urban community more effectively and genteelly than had militia exercises and drunken electioneering. Ideally, a city's broad, well-built avenues and squares were the site of the metropolitan promenade, where all citizens gathered peacefully and brushed elbows without regard to rank, enacting in their refined leisure the community's cohesiveness and legitimate social hierarchy. Both an activity and a space, the "promenade" represented the genteel vision of how to meld the city's disparate and contentious citizens through the practice of refined public behavior into a harmonious republican community.[67]

But as the urban sketch artists constantly warned, city streets and squares were dangerous and disorderly places. The jostling presence of uncouth workingmen, deceptive beggars, and fair-faced prostitutes made the streets socially uncomfortable for the respectable middle class. The rapid traffic, as well as the dust, mud, horse manure, and other wastes that gathered there, made many streets physically unpleasant as well. If streets were to be devoted to traffic in all senses of the word, then the promenade must move elsewhere. Adapting the principles of the genteel garden to metropolitan scale, the great urban parks offered an excellent site for the public, refined performance of community harmony. Contemporary accounts celebrated the success of this unifying function: "On Saturday afternoon it is a sight to behold"; "Tens of thousands, composed of the various nationalities of the city, assemble . . . ," including "the millionaire and the hod carrier; ragged newsboys and the Fifth Avenue Exquisite; ladies in the latest style, and female emigrants just arrived; madame flashing with jewels, and the scrubbing-woman."[68]

Following the lead of New York, Philadelphia, and other eastern cities, midwestern and western cities soon began to build parks of their own that in design, flora, and fauna resembled those of the East as closely as possible. The picturesque ideal mandated hills, woods, and quaintly bridged ponds and streams, however foreign they might be to

Chicago's marshy prairie or San Francisco's oceanfront sand dunes. In their pretense to naturalness, parks embodied a pastoral, genteel ideal that developed out of the social demands of urban life, not a longing for the rural. At the same time, parks brought to urban areas those scenic features that supported claims to refinement among rural tourists. Not surprisingly, then, a city's parks served as evidence of metropolitan status and attracted large numbers of well-to-do visitors.[69]

By the late nineteenth century, urban parks had become the chief public urban space for the practice of genteel leisure. Junius Browne claimed that New York's Central Park was "the only well governed part of the entire island." Parks were safe for the ladies; they permitted the exercise of aesthetic sensibility in the appreciation of natural, sculptural, and musical beauty; and they allowed the wealthy to see and be seen in their fine carriages. But despite protestations that they served the entire community, the parks identified as "promenades" usually hosted only the well-to-do, who endorsed the genteel social code and contemplative aesthetic required there. The new parks were generally located far from the city center, so that working people could afford neither the time nor the car fare to travel there.[70] A part of the broader campaign to improve cities, the parks movement contributed to the segmentation of the city by function and class.

The beginnings of suburbanization occurred during the same period that many cities planned and initiated their park systems. Like parks, many of the new, outlying communities were designed with curving streets and plentiful greenery; they were refined, carefully landscaped enclaves that might attract tourists as well as residents. The expansion of suburbs encouraged a growing number of the well-to-do to view cities as a place to visit rather than as the context of daily life.[71] Forwarding the segmentation of urban landscapes, both parks and suburbs embodied Clarence Cook's claim that beauty might be separated from morality. They constituted a solution to the deceptiveness and heterogeneity of the city that evaded rather than resolved the anxieties of the urban sketch artists.

Given the emphasis on republican institutions and monumental architecture in handbooks and in the city entries in national guides, it is not surprising to find that Washington, D.C., was the only American city to figure in written description as a tourist attraction in the mid-nineteenth century. Visitors had made a point of seeing it ever since its official opening in 1800. A planned city with no function except to serve as the site of the federal government and the location of some of the nation's largest and finest public buildings, it boasted just what sight-seers preferred and lacked the alienating urban scale and commercial hustle that marred other, wealthier cities.[72]

The existing descriptions of the national capital reflect its unique status among American cities of the period. Until the late 1860s, there were few or no urban sketches of the city. The handbook predominated, treating the architecture and ornamentation of the Capitol and other public buildings to the exclusion of all else. Indeed, many works did not even claim to be describing the city. The focus is made clear by one such work's title: *Public Buildings and Architectural Ornaments of the Capitol of the United States at the City of Washington.* Frequently reprinted works, such as *Morrison's Stranger's Guide for Washington City* (1840s–1860s), despite their titles, also described little aside from federal architecture.[73]

For instance, having noted the geographic features and selection of the site and the city's laggard commercial and industrial development, the 1868 edition of *Morrison's* proceeded to the meat of the matter: "The Capitol has a noble and commanding situation upon the brow of a hill." The building's substance and style suited its position: "The material of the old edifice is yellow sandstone, which has been painted white, to beautify and preserve it. The wings are of white marble. The architecture is Corinthian, and the style of finish, exterior and interior, is elaborate." In the ensuing pages, the guide detailed the major chambers of the Capitol and provided a plan of the building: "Every Room, Picture, piece of Statuary and object of interest in the Capitol will be found under its proper Alphabetical head, numbered to correspond with the number on the plan." Other guides emulated this pattern, explaining who was who in historical paintings and sculpture, demystifying the allegorical works, and often describing the heating, ventilation, and lighting systems of the enormous buildings.[74]

Like the handbook descriptions of official buildings elsewhere, Washington guides very rarely mentioned the political and official function of the buildings they described. Noting that the visit to the Senate and House of Representatives was most interesting when the Congress was in session, most authors went on simply to describe the construction and appearance of the chambers.[75] They avoided discussing politics as they avoided discussing religion, in order to appeal to a broad audience and to emphasize the success of the republic, not its persistent conflicts. In short, the significance of the capital's landscape lay in its evidence of refined republicanism. It was successful to the extent that it excluded the contentious, greedy, and deceptive everyday conditions of urban life.

In passing over the local, Washington handbooks largely neglected the social customs of middling and elite urbanites that typified the sketches of other cities. Instead, the self-styled guides to Washington often included an explanation of official etiquette. This codification of official usage was very different from the quasi-ethnographic description of social customs such as New Year's Day visits and the use of class markers to criticize urban social relations. Its purpose was not to reveal the composition of and relations between classes but to prescribe specific behaviors for people assumed to be middle or upper class.[76]

The etiquette detailed in Washington guides rested on the assumption that most of the people who came to the city were part of, or sought to be part of, the official social structure. According to *Bohn's Hand-Book of Washington,* "Few strangers ever visit Washington during the sessions of Congress without being invited by a friend to a reception." Therefore, it was appropriate to detail the days on which various high-ranking officials held receptions, who was expected to attend, and who would or would not return calls (the First Lady never did). Visits to Washington were expected to follow the older pattern of elite leisure travel or to be part of the network of national political patronage.[77]

Despite its admittedly grand public buildings, Washington came in for a considerable amount of criticism precisely because its local conditions did not live up to the promise of republican splendor. The journalist "Viator" claimed that the soldiers who came to defend Washington during the Civil War "experienced a sensation of intense disappointment as they marched up the dusty Avenue, and saw so little that was in keeping with their ideas of a city, as formed by the contrast with Baltimore, Philadelphia, and New York." John Ellis, writing in 1869, agreed: "As a general rule, . . . there is little to see after one has explored the public buildings and grounds. The city does not offer many attractions to the stranger, and few care to remain after seeing the National property." Until the 1870s most of the city's streets were unpaved and ungraded, its private and municipal buildings small and undistinguished. If it seemed undefiled by the vices of the great commercial entrepôts, it also lacked their fine business buildings, city halls, shops, theaters, hotels, churches, and mansions.[78]

Only in the late 1860s and the 1870s did a few authors apply to the national capital the conventions of the urban sketch, at the same time that the city was being "improved" and the sketches were swelling to hundreds of pages. Such works made it clear that Washington had its share of gambling dens and prostitutes. Even within the august Capitol building the mighty were engaged in political and sexual misbehavior, particularly with their extravagantly dressed female constituents—another sign of the danger of women's entry into public places.[79] But such accounts of Washington remained exceptional. Long before any other American city, Washington offered itself as primarily an aesthetic and historical object for visitors.

Because it was so unlike other cities, Washington was the only one to enjoy a prominent place on the tourist circuit in the mid-nineteenth century. The handbooks' emphasis on federal architecture and neglect of local society privileged the interests of American visitors as the true owners of these grand buildings, notwithstanding their residence elsewhere. Guides to the city of Washington portrayed it as a national park in which Americans might enact a national promenade. In contrast, the descriptions of most American cities emphasized learning local ways of seeing and moving. By the late nineteenth century, the approach typical of Washington sketches became increasingly possible in other cities. It did so because of changes in urban built environments, new understandings of the relationship between place and community, and an altered view of the role of leisure in shaping social relations.

Among the heralds of change were the appearance in 1876 of *Appleton's Illustrated Hand-Book of American Cities* and the opening of the Philadelphia Centennial Exposition. In many ways a spin-off from the company's successful national tourist guide, the *Illustrated Hand-Book of American Cities* broke with the tradition of urban description in addressing itself exclusively to pleasure travelers. Like that of the national guide, its preface trumpeted its focus on the tourist's needs: "[T]he present work contains a larger amount and greater variety of that kind of information which is really useful to the tourist and sight-seer than many more voluminous and pretentious works." In addition, "No mention is made of anything which is not thought worth the traveler's attention."[80] The content of the new guide did not actually differ much from the standard entries in the national guide or those of city handbooks. Nevertheless, the existence of a guidebook devoted to tourists and to American cities at the same time suggested that the urban anxieties of midcentury were quieting and the interest of pleasure travelers growing.

The rise of regional, national, and international expositions played a key part in stimulating pleasure travel and redirecting some of it to-

ward cities. All of the major fairs in the United States between 1876 and
1915 were urban events. City elites in government and business campaigned for them, financed them, and controlled them. They intended
these events to enhance their city's reputation as well as to celebrate the
nation's history and industrial prowess. To encourage millions of strangers to visit the exposition and its host city, they bargained with railroads, hotels, and newly formed tour companies to provide excursions
and accommodations at special rates, stimulating the burgeoning tourist
industry. At the same time, publishers like Appleton seized the opportunity to provide new forms of urban description.[81] Finally, the grounds of
the expositions provided a model for a refined and republican urban
landscape, and the way that visitors perceived and moved around the
fair grounds offered an alternative to existing urban spatial practices.

The emergence of new ideas about leisure, pleasure travel, and urban
life signaled the reconceptualization of urban space and social relations
in ways that made urban tourism possible. The institutions of travel,
particularly trains and hotels, had an important part to play in the rehabilitation of leisure and urbanity. In trying to reconcile the contradic-
tions among profit, refinement, republican egalitarianism, and the ideal
of separate spheres, trains and hotels both legitimized public leisure and
shifted the boundary between public and private spaces and behaviors.

TWO

Refining Travel

Railroads and Extra-Fare Cars,
1850–1915

"Dear Clarinda," W. M. Steele wrote to his wife from Chicago in March
1857, "I have had quite a romantick journey I assure you." Embarking
from Boston on the 8:30 A.M. express train, he had traveled westward
in the company of a party of friends bound for Kansas. More than nine
hours later they arrived in Albany, New York, "too late by ten minutes
to connect with the express train going west and so had to wait five
hours for the next train which was at 11 o'clock at night." The party
passed the time pleasantly in sight-seeing, supper, and a dance. Steele's
letter continued: "Well at last we started in a night train to ride 2 hundred miles—now that is a horrible thing to think of aint it." Steele arrived in Rochester, New York, as the sun was rising. There he parted
from his friends and boarded another train heading for Niagara Falls
and into Canada on his way to Chicago.[1]

By the turn of the century, one could make the trip between New
York City and Chicago in just twenty-four hours, and, according to the
Railway Review, "[n]o other day's travel is so delightful and so fleet-
ing." Between 1850 and 1915, railroads, luxury car manufacturers, and
tour companies worked hard to transform "a horrible thing to think of"
into a genteel fantasy. They made the cars more comfortable physically
and socially for their passengers by manipulating the design, decoration,
fare structure, and staffing to reflect refined ideas about the proper relations between rich and poor, black and white, men and women. The
elegance, fine service, and speed of the finest "express" and "limited"

passenger cars made them the embodiment of metropolitan wealth and sophistication.[2]

The transformation in rail service addressed difficult social questions. Railroads, as well as hotels and tour companies, often referred to their customers as the "traveling public" and cast themselves as servants of that public, yet they were thoroughly commercial enterprises.[3] As public carriers, they confronted many of the same problems with the character and uses of public space that occurred in cities. As privately owned businesses, they had to negotiate in every ticket sale the difficult relationship among gentility, commerce, and republican principles. To a considerable extent they succeeded in associating commercial exclusiveness with republican egalitarianism. Like middle-class urbanites, they did so in large part by extending the reign of refinement outside the middle-class home. In the process, they helped to make semipublic leisure more respectable.

But the commercial extension of refinement tended to blur the boundary between private and public, commercial and familial, eroding the power of the ideal of separate spheres. The experience of George Pullman and his exclusive passenger-car service exemplified the difficulties. Nationally celebrated for its good taste and refined service in the 1870s, the Pullman Palace Car Company was vilified in the 1890s for everything from monopolistic practices and excessively high fares to unsanitary furnishings and bad taste.[4] By the early twentieth century, a growing number of middling Americans found the luxuries of the Pullman cars a barrier to their participation in the "traveling public" rather than a guarantee of propriety there. Increasingly, they demanded cheaper, more efficient, more "modern" accommodations. The extension of refinement had made the ideal both more desirable and less necessary as a safeguard for public interactions among strangers.

The waning importance of refinement signaled an important shift in the spatial ideals of well-to-do Americans, one that opened up the possibility of urban tourism. The luxurious Pullmans and other extra-fare cars embodied a kind of metropolitan gentility based on transience and distinct from any local social order. By making refined public accommodations available to almost anyone with enough money, the Pullman company represented the sharpening of class divisions as proof of the nation's egalitarianism. Any white person might earn the money to pay for a seat in the extra-fare car, and those who had not could be excluded without a twinge of anyone's republican conscience. Disentangling refinement from a known community and providing it for a fee encouraged well-to-do Americans to regard commercial transactions as guarantees of their status and security rather than threats to them. This change diminished the importance of the refined distinction between public and private. The growing comfort of well-to-do Americans with social transience was an essential precondition for the rise of urban tourism in the 1890s.

"VEXATIONS AND ANNOYANCES"

From the railroads' small beginnings in the 1830s, Americans believed that they would transform the nation. The slender paths of wood and iron would transport raw materials, people, and information more quickly and profitably than ever before. Independent of the limits of animal strength and water transport, the railroads offered an exhilarating rate of speed compared to stagecoaches and barges. Promoters claimed the steam trains would erode sectional differences, bind the nation together, promote its manifest destiny in the West, and even abolish space altogether. In addition to encouraging the growth of a far-flung urban network, the railroads brought urban amenities to rural areas, rural people and resources into the cities, and disseminated a metropolitan ideal and experience across the nation. And as early as the 1840s, railway companies were serving and promoting pleasure travel in the northeastern states.[5] In short, railroad cars were a particularly modern, mobile kind of space in which Americans vested much social hope as well as capital and labor.

But in the middle decades of the nineteenth century, the railroads suffered from woeful limitations, especially for their human freight. The rapid proliferation of railroad companies in the mid-nineteenth century did not mean the development of a coordinated national network. The railroads developed at a time when governments were relinquishing their traditional prerogatives over such semipublic enterprises. Although state subsidies and federal land grants were critical to the capitalization of many roads, especially the long, risky western ones, neither level of government exerted much regulatory power until the late nineteenth and early twentieth century. The absence of any governmental effort to coordinate the roads, combined with the relatively small budgets and local interests of many early railroad promoters, meant that the early tracks often connected regional centers to the towns in their hinterlands without concern for wider networks.[6]

The existence of many separate, short lines made traveling any distance rather difficult. Mrs. James Finley noted, "We got to Farley at one pm—left at 8 ½—the trains up this way dont connect the roads belong to different companies." Separate lines had separate stations, not always convenient or easy to find for the traveler. In the late 1870s the Boston railroad investor George Bethune sent his servant ahead with his baggage for a hunting trip on Long Island. But when he arrived at the station, "neither man nor baggage was to be found." Bethune wrote, "I at once suspected that he had misunderstood me and gone to the wrong railroad." And so it was; on his return some days later, Bethune's servant met him "at the Albany station. He had gone to the Lowell road by mistake." [7]

Further, the many short lines usually advertised and distributed their timetables locally. Often travelers and even ticket agents could not determine the best route to take. Departure and arrival times might reflect either local time, determined by the height of the sun, or the time in the city where the particular railroad had its headquarters. The resulting profusion of times could defeat the most dedicated student of travel. In any case, mechanical failures and weather made schedules more often prescriptive rather than descriptive. [8]

Even the perfectly informed traveler faced wearying difficulties. Railroad companies did not begin to coordinate their ticketing to facilitate long trips until the late 1850s and the 1860s, when "coupon tickets" containing passes for all the necessary roads became available. Even with tickets in hand, transferring passengers had to detrain, collect their baggage, and find the railroad they needed, which might be at a different station somewhere else in the city, before continuing their journey. The different track widths used by the various railroads often required travelers to move from one car to another even when they did not have to change stations. The lack of bridges meant ferry rides where the railroad met rivers or lakes. [9]

But the chief limit of the railway network in the middle of the nineteenth century was that it was not yet very extensive. In 1850 the United States boasted just over nine thousand miles of track, 60 percent of it in New England and the mid-Atlantic states. By the start of the Civil War, that total had more than tripled to exceed thirty thousand miles and the tracks stretched west toward the frontier from Wisconsin to Texas. The war both hindered and promoted railroad growth. It diverted raw materials and trains to the war effort, but the centrality of the railroads to waging war underscored their national importance. In the short term,

the absence of Southern lawmakers from Congress enabled that body
to agree at last on a northern route for the first transcontinental road.
In the long term, the political upheaval that accompanied the war de-
cisively turned national economic policy toward domestic industrial
growth and away from transatlantic commerce.[10]

With increased federal and state assistance, the railroads expanded
rapidly after the war. By 1900 the United States had five transcontinental roads and some two hundred thousand miles of track, more than all
the nations of Europe combined. More significant was the acceleration
of a trend toward consolidation and coordination that had begun in the
1850s. The New York Central and Pennsylvania Railroad systems had
started to engulf their local competitors before the war. By 1906 the latter encompassed lines originally owned by two hundred companies. In
that year a mere seven corporations controlled more than 60 percent
of the nation's total trackage. Even before achieving this degree of cen-
tralized control, railroad managers had instituted standard time zones
(1883) and a standard gauge or rail width (1886). Both agreements
eased the burdens of travel: passengers did not have to change cars as often, and they did not have to figure out myriad local times in determin-
ing train schedules.[11] Wherever they were, rail travelers remained within
an urban-industrial time and space increasingly distinct from the local
places they passed through.

Mid-nineteenth-century rail travel was also remarkably uncomfortable. In the 1840s and 1850s the typical American coach car was a long
box crossed with several rows of benches divided up the middle to provide an aisle. Cars ranged from thirty to forty feet long, six to seven feet
high, and about eight and a half feet wide. The two-person seats were
closely spaced, narrow slabs of wood with low backs, thinly upholstered
with leather or broadcloth cushions. The small windows allowed in little
light or air but plenty of dust, ash, and cinders, especially in the summer
when passengers had to open the windows to ventilate the car. Poorly
lighted by oil lamps, heated by a coal or wood stove, and equipped with
doors on both ends, the cars could be stultifyingly hot or bone-chillingly
cold, depending on the season, where one sat, and how often people
went in and out. The railroad might provide a tank of ice water and a
communal cup; otherwise, passengers had to carry their own refresh-
ments. When toilet facilities existed, they often amounted to little more
than a hole in the train floor. Finally, the light, cheap tracks and cars of
many early railroads made for a jarring, deafening, and unsafe ride.[12]

Figure 1. "Discomforts of Travel," *Frank Leslie's Illustrated Weekly* 45 (1876): 389. Photo courtesy of the Newberry Library, Chicago.

The coach car was bad enough for the short journeys that most travelers made in the 1850s and 1860s. But for overnight passengers, it was agony. (See fig. 1.) No matter how they slumped in the seats, propped up their feet, and cushioned their heads and necks, it was impossible to find a restful position. If the car were crowded, one could not even stretch one's legs or curl up on a seat. Travelers had to bring their own food, wait for the boys who constantly walked through the train selling apples and similar items, or rush out at the twenty-minute station stops in search of a meal. In the morning, the weary pilgrims had little or no water with which to wash their dusty faces and no privacy in which to change clothes. "[W]e were as dirty as the dust and swet could make us," John Kinsey wrote ruefully of the first leg of his trip to Chicago. "[Y]ou could write your name in most any man's coat." An all-night train ride was indeed "a horrible thing to think of," as Steele wrote to his wife in 1857.[13]

But the physical "vexations and annoyances" were only the beginning of the traveler's woes.[14] The mid-nineteenth-century railroad car was also a socially uncertain space in which travelers entered into an often unwanted intimacy with a group of heterogeneous strangers. Like city streets, the railroad passenger car was an indisputably public space offering neither the discipline of work nor the affectionate bonds of domesticity.[15] Yet unlike the streets, the cars were privately owned commercial services. The railroad companies sought broad patronage at the same time that they tried to diminish the social and physical discomforts of travel. The cars exemplified the efforts of mid-nineteenth-century Americans to put commerce at the service of the republic by providing refinement for a fee.

Like crowded urban thoroughfares, the American coach car was a celebrated symbol of the nation's vaunted egalitarianism. Many Americans scorned the class system typical of European train travel, which carefully distinguished and separated railroad passengers into three and even four classes. The physical embodiment of this clearly articulated and fixed hierarchy was the compartment car commonly found on English and Continental railroads. It featured a row of individual rooms accommodating four to eight people in facing seats. The quality of the car and the compartment depended on one's class. At midcentury, these cars had no aisle. The conductor walked along the depot platform to collect tickets before locking the passengers in for the duration of the journey.[16]

In contrast to this "aristocratic" railway carriage, the single-cabin coach was democratically open, an emphatically public space. Labeling the English traveler "a peculiar man" who preferred to be locked into his compartment and to keep his fellow passengers at arm's length, one pundit insisted that "[t]he sine qua non of the comfortable American car" was that "the traveller must be at liberty to move, to change his seat, to leave the car. . . , to find out what is going on outside, to communicate his feelings to strangers."[17] For Americans, aisleless cars with sealed compartments mirrored the rigid European class system; the lack of physical mobility symbolized the absence of social mobility. The open coach car, with its central aisle and two doors, offered precisely that freedom of social interaction essential to a republican society.

Of course, American railroad companies had pragmatic reasons for favoring the open coach car. Without interior walls, it was lighter than the compartment car and could seat more fare-paying passengers at one time—about fifty to the compartment's twenty-four. The low capitalization and rapid construction of many midcentury American railroads

led their builders to use light tracks that could not support heavy locomotives and cars. But these exigencies did not invalidate the symbolism
of the coach car. A well-defined class system began to emerge in the late
1860s at the same time that tracks became sturdier, locomotives more
powerful, and cars heavier. This system embodied the American preference for at least the appearance of egalitarianism: the majority of passengers in the United States traveled "first class" in the day coach, while
their European counterparts traveled third class in similar cars.[18]

The emergence of different kinds of railroad accommodations
stemmed from the fact that many well-to-do Americans found the democratic atmosphere of the coach car as dismaying as its physical discomforts. Urban portraitists coupled their exuberant pleasure in the
colorful, jostling, heterogeneous crowds in city streets with grave
reservations about the social order that regulated—or failed to regulate—them. Those who wrote about the railway cars were similarly am-
bivalent about the consequences of anonymous egalitarianism for republican social relations. An aggregation of strangers, the "traveling
public" gathered on the cars did not necessarily exercise its social pow-
ers effectively or in the proper direction. This urban uncertainty was the
theme of a lighthearted song titled "The Charming Young Widow I Met
in the Train." It featured a cynical confidence woman and a naive country boy, with entirely predictable results.

On receiving a letter notifying him that he had inherited "a large sum
of money" from a recently deceased uncle in Boston, our protagonist at
once left Vermont for the city. In keeping with his new status as a man
of means, "to book myself by the 'first class' I was fain." Soon after he
entered the car, a young and lovely woman entered: " 'Twas a female a
young one and dress'd in deep mourning/An infant in long clothes she
gracefully bore." The young man promptly "fell deep in love," but they
traveled in proper silence until the Young Widow "enquired the time by
the watch that I wore." The proprieties satisfied by this polite query,
"conversation/Was freely indulged in by both, 'till my brain/Fairly
reeled with excitement." Their growing intimacy permitted her to indulge in a burst of grief over her lost husband, and she "leaned her head
on my waistcoat." Alas, despite all the signs of gentility and sincerity in
the Young Widow's appearance and manner, she decamped at the first
station stop. The young man from Vermont was left with the baby but
without his watch, his purse, his train ticket, or his innocence.[19]

The song's banal message was that appearances were deceiving and strangers not to be trusted. Like city streets, the cars were full of strangers who were not what they seemed and who were most to be suspected when they greeted a newcomer cordially. But, significantly, the Young Widow was not the only one to don a disguise. The narrator also attempted to present himself as what he was not: an urban man of means. The Young Widow owed her success to her ability to perform gentility without sincerity. The Young Man's sincere and sensitive gentility betrayed the sophistication he claimed, leaving him vulnerable to her canny deception. The song's lighthearted tone and predictable outcome invited listeners to laugh at the Young Man's naïveté. Like the authors of mid-nineteenth-century city description, the song proposed an urban wariness as the solution to social deceptions.

The possibilty of deception was always accompanied by the possibility—indeed, the necessity—of discriminating observation. Railroad cars, like city streets and omnibuses, offered an excellent opportunity to study humankind in its artificial habitat. The veteran train conductor Charles B. George noted, "Human nature displays itself in a thousand different and often unexpected ways on a railroad train." The concentration of dissimilar, unacquainted people in public spaces promised to reveal the truth not just about individuals but about the social relations they constructed, for such spaces did not provide the ideal division of public from private that enabled genteel self-possession. On the cars, structural aids to defining social boundaries, such as class distinctions in service, gender segregation, compartments, or even reserved seating, were scarce until the introduction of extra-fare cars in the late 1860s. And surely the sheer discomfort of train travel rubbed tempers raw. The result, as George noted, was that "[t]he mask that is worn so successfully in church and society is dropped."[20]

Take, for example, Benjamin Taylor's description of a woman awakening from an uncomfortable night on the train. In the dim morning, "[t]he seats are heaped with shapeless piles of clothes. Folks are shut up like jack-knives or bagged like game." One particular heap drew his attention because of the "dainty hat" and a "muff like a well-to-do cat" nearby:

> It is shaped like an egg, and it is an egg. . . . A snug gaiter with a foot in it emerges at one end, and a disheveled head at the other. Forth comes a hand, and at last the chrysalis is rent, and the occupant is hatched out before your eyes. But it is anything but a butterfly. It is a crumpled, drowsy piece of womanhood, who slept in her head but not in her hair.

The writer watched as the woman attached her "back hair" and care-fully arranged her curls over the proper phrenological bumps until she had provided visible evidence of all the right characteristics of respect-able femininity. Next she washed her face, straightened her collar and skirts, and donned her "dainty hat"; only then did she present the gen-teel appearance appropriate to public places.[21]

Like the Young Widow, this female passenger achieved ladyhood by manufacturing the correct appearance, something that usually hap-pened in private. By revealing the artificiality of genteel gender roles, both the song and participant observation on the cars implied that refinement itself was a social deception. Neither George nor Taylor proceeded to ask whether such manufactured personae deserved to be the basis for legitimate social privilege, perhaps because ladies were the chief offenders. Women's mendacity could be attributed to their gender rather than their class and therefore was not a danger to the American experiment. Nevertheless, the troublesome gap between reality and ap-pearance implicit in the genteel ideal underlay the many, strenuous ef-forts of mid-nineteenth-century Americans to conceal the underpinnings of refinement from public spaces such as railroad cars.

In addition to the lack of privacy, the cars compromised the efforts of genteel individuals to behave properly in public. For one thing, the coach car was often disgustingly dirty, its "seats foul with the scrapings of dirty boots, [its] floors flowing with saliva." The copious spittle of the many tobacco chewers made the floor brown, slippery, and smelly. The refined American might concede with republican charity that these "unkempt, unwashed, tobacco-chewing, heavy-shod and loosely expec-torating mortals" were "well enough in themselves," but only if one did not have to associate with them.[22] This sentiment was not simply snob-bery; it was part of the larger debate about the social meanings of republicanism.

Insults to the sensibilities of genteel travelers were always also in-fringements on their republican rights in the use of public space. All the passengers in the coach car had bought the same ticket, entitling them to a seat of their own in a shared space. But the most commonly noted of inconsiderate travelers, the "railway hog," failed to respect this basic equality. The railway hog used every stratagem imaginable to occupy two, three, as many as four seats, even when other travelers had to stand. Close kin to the railway hog was the man who propped his dirty-booted feet "upon the back of your seat, and wants you to beg pardon for being so near them," spat tobacco juice on the floor or the shoes and skirts of his unwilling companions, opened windows regardless of others' wishes, and generally treated a shared, public space as an opportunity to exercise his individual preferences.[23] Such behavior was liberty degraded to license.

The absence of structural distinctions in the car undermined the ability of refined passengers to maintain the proper self-possession and social distance from other riders. Conductor Charles George found it amusing "to notice the way some people try to draw a line between themselves and their neighbors." The combination of proximity and heterogeneous crowds of strangers made making acquaintances impossible to avoid yet dangerous to undertake, as the tale of the "charming Young Widow" demonstrated. Taylor warned his readers of the "Might I?" man, "an animated cork-screw, forever trying to pull the cork from the bottle of your personal identity. 'Might I?' begins his acquaintance by stealing—stealing a look at you out of the corner of his eye, the meanest kind of pilfering."[24]

Both the Might I? man and the railway hog illustrated the close connection between property and propriety. For genteel, middling Americans, only the self-possession of the refined individual could reconcile social order with the personal freedom guaranteed by the republic, just as the ownership of real property ensured both white male political equality and a well-regulated society. Both placed a limit on liberty and indicated the origins of proper social distinctions amid the ideological and economic fluidity of the republic. At midcentury neither was completely successful in imposing order and transparency in social relations but remained powerful ideals motivating Americans of a variety of political perspectives.

Of course, the published songs, complaints, and colorful sketches highlighted only the more annoying, amusing, and unfamiliar aspects of rail travel. Daily experience was rarely as vivid as songs and anecdotes. Diaries and letters from the 1850s suggest that many people traveled in groups or with companions, as W. M. Steele did between Boston and Rochester. John Munn, the Utica, New York, businessman with interests in Chicago, made the arduous journey to that muddy town regularly in the 1850s. A business partner or subordinate often accompanied him, and he frequently encountered business and family friends on the cars and in the city's hotels. He and other "gentlemen" also often supervised and escorted ladies traveling alone. One such lady, Mrs. James

Finley, passed smoothly from one set of friends to another on a trip from
Iowa to Delaware. With their aid and company, she investigated several
towns and factories along the way.[25] Like visitors to large cities, many
travelers found the anonymity and social heterogeneity of the new public spaces mitigated by the presence of kin, relatives, and business
associates.

Far from mirrors of reality, published accounts nevertheless underscored the kind of cultural work necessary to make sense of new possibilities and dangers that opened up in the cars. Like city streets, the passenger cars concentrated and highlighted the ongoing renegotiation of
class, gender, and republican principles in public spaces. As privately
owned public carriers, railroads necessarily directly confronted the relationship between commerce and republicanism that bedeviled Americans on the sidewalks and in the stock exchanges of the nation's cities.
The railroads' chief response was to make some of their cars conform to
genteel sensibilities.[26] In doing so, they expressed a characteristic mid-
nineteenth-century faith that the commercial provision of refinement
could uplift all Americans and thus construct a genteel yet egalitarian
social order. Simultaneously, they eroded the boundary between private
and public and made well-to-do Americans feel more at ease in the latter realm.

DEMOCRATIC LUXURY

Railroad company officials were well aware of the social and physical
discomforts of their passenger cars. Even before steam cars ran regularly
in the United States, inventors patented designs for reclining chairs and
sleeping berths. In the 1850s several railroad companies ran sleeping
cars featuring two- and three-tiered rows of bunks without mattresses or
bedclothes. Some lines experimented with class distinctions as well. But
it was not until the 1860s, with the spread of luxuriously furnished
sleeping and day cars, that gradations in accommodations became standard. The usual explanation for the railroads' growing attention to riders' comfort has been the expansion of the railroad network: as longer,
overnight journeys became more common, passengers demanded and
railroads began to provide cars with comfortable seating and retractable
berths.[27]

Certainly the increase in the number of travelers and the distances
traveled spurred competitive railway lines to offer improved services.

The consolidation of lines also must have made the provision of specially constructed sleeping cars more profitable for the railroads. But the improvement of railroad accommodations and the imposition of a standard class system occurred in the 1860s, about the same time that middle-class and well-to-do Americans were also beginning to create or refurbish urban, public spaces for refined activities. They expected such spaces to provide a haven from the excesses of democracy in the streets, yet also to uplift the dangerous masses. Genteel public places, they hoped, would foster just the kind of self-possessed individuals essential to the smooth functioning of a republican, capitalist society.[28]

The man who would come to dominate the luxury passenger car industry, George Pullman, understood his endeavor in just these terms. If the cars were beautiful, men would cease to spit on the floor and to put their boots on the seats. They would learn to exercise their freedom without annoying others. Like the great urban park systems planned and constructed in the 1860s and 1870s, the new passenger cars were socially exclusive spaces with egalitarian intentions. Higher fares, seat reservations, increased space for passengers, lavish, expensive decoration, sleeping and dining accommodations, and good servants constituted the material context of refined, commercial republicanism.[29]

The formula for the layout and use of the most common of the extra-fare cars, the sleeping car, emerged in the 1860s and dominated the industry well into the 1920s. Its design followed the existing cultural and financial preference for an open coach. Like the first-class car, it had a center aisle with rows of two-person seats in facing pairs along each side. But aside from their arrangement, these seats had little in common with their cousins in the ordinary day car. They were "easy chairs" thickly cushioned and upholstered in velvet or plush. The car itself was no mere box but "a luxurious and richly furnished parlor."[30] Its woodwork was richly carved and inlaid; gilt mirrors, soft carpets, and great swathes of cloth at the doors and windows embodied the ideal midcentury refined interior.

At night, the facing seats slid down to form berths, "not simply shelves where persons are crowded into to pass sleepless nights, but elegant staterooms, luxuriously furnished with soft hair mattresses, and amply large enough for two persons." From a cabinet above the seats another berth was lowered, and curtains enclosed the whole, so that "every berth [was] separate and distinct from the other," providing the physical distance and separation of public from private that gentility re-

quired. The upper and lower berths together formed a "section." In contrast to earlier sleepers, the railroad lines now furnished sheets, blankets, and pillows and promised that they would be cleaned between each
use. Men were politely requested to remove their boots when they got
into bed. Many cars also included a drawing room or compartment,
walled off from the body of the car and often containing its own toilet
and washbasin.[31]

The lavish decor and the increase in creature comforts were not the
only innovations of the 1860s. The new cars were more expensive to
build, heavier to haul, and accommodated fewer passengers than the ordinary coach car, so railroads had to charge more for their use to make
a profit. But instead of designating the palace cars first class and the
coach cars second class, American railroad companies imposed a surcharge for the use of the luxury cars. After paying the cost of a first-class
ticket, the traveler paid two dollars more to secure a seat or berth in an
extra-fare car. Passengers with second-class tickets were not permitted
to buy space in the extra-fare car.[32]

Although the surcharge established a clear difference in quality of accommodations and discriminated among passengers, it did so in a peculiarly American fashion. The general faith in the possibility of upward
social mobility distinguished economic condition from imputed class
distinctions. The unfortunate who had to sit up all night in the first-class
coach now might soon rise in the world and become a patron of the
extra-fare car. A writer for the Baltimore & Ohio Railroad claimed, "It
is simply a question of cash, not of caste." Contemporaries often portrayed the extra-fare cars as a democratic, and thus typically American,
luxury: "The wealth of a railway bondholder cannot give greater luxury or privacy in traveling than the poorest man can command for two
dollars."[33]

William Dean Howells made this point with his usual gentle irony in
Their Wedding Journey. Having spent some few hours in the first-class
coach because they thought it more "in the spirit of ordinary American
travel," the newlyweds Basil and Isabel March got bored with observing
"the varied prospect of humanity" and bought seats in the extra-fare
car. But the return to their usual social level entailed no rejection of
democratic principle: "this seemed a touch of Americanism beyond the
old-fashioned car." Comparing the luxury surrounding them to that enjoyed by "enchanted princes in the Arabian Nights," they nevertheless
insisted that "the general appearance of the passengers hardly suggested

greater wealth than elsewhere; and they were plainly in that car because they were of the American race, which finds nothing too good for it that its money can buy."[34] The only insurmountable obstacle to partaking in the commercial amenities of a republican society was being black. African Americans struggled with little success to obtain access to the extra-fare cars from the 1870s onward.

The imposition of a surcharge rather than a system based on explicit class distinctions also stemmed in part from the decision of George Pullman, one among several sleeping-car manufacturers in the 1860s and 1870s, to lease rather than sell his cars to the railroads. This arrangement allowed him to retain control over their management. The "extra fare" went to his company, while the regular first-class fare remained with the railroad. This decision had significant consequences. "'The essential element of the Pullman system,'" the company's lawyer told *Railway Age* in 1879, "'was its entire and absolute uniformity.'" Passengers knew exactly what to expect when they paid for a Pullman berth and stepped into the beautifully finished cars. "The sight and feeling" of the Pullman car, one writer sighed gratefully, "make the traveler at home no matter where he may go, or in what distant and lonely locality he may be placed." And that home was an urban one: "the traveller has no privations of primitive beds and coarse fare to endure," for "every day the city rushes through the wilds."[35] The extra-fare cars constituted a space at once genteel and transient, distinct from a particular community yet fostering a national community of the refined. By making the well-to-do feel "at home" amid metropolitan splendor and surrounded by strangers, the extra-fare cars eased mid-nineteenth-century fears about public spaces and social interactions.

Pullman's leasing system also contributed to uniformity in another sense; it helped to make through travel more common. His cars—and those of his competitors—were broader, higher, and heavier than ordinary ones, requiring infrastructure to suit. They could be attached to the locomotive of any railroad and even lifted from one wheel truck to another to accommodate changes in gauge. Competitive pressures moved railroads to be sure that their tracks and depots could accommodate the Pullman or other extra-fare cars where the demand existed. The leasing system enabled the railroads to avoid the costs of building and maintaining the extra-fare cars. They could arrange to run the heavy cars when the traffic on their road merited the costs of hauling them.[36]

An excellent promoter, Pullman did everything possible to publicize his cars. As early as the 1870s he dominated the business. By 1899 the Pullman Palace Car Company held a virtual monopoly on the manufacture and operation of extra-fare cars. Only a few railroads continued to run their own palace cars. But whatever the manufacturer or the railroad, the extra-fare cars offered their passengers a degree of exclusiveness and luxury entirely impossible in the day coach. Although the Pullman Palace Car Company manufactured and sold ever more luxury cars and served a steadily rising number of passengers in the late nineteenth and early twentieth century, most American travelers could not afford the extra-fare cars and continued to ride the day coaches. Without overtly imposing class distinctions, the surcharge functioned to exclude the "coarse faces and coarse conversation" that plagued the genteel passenger.[37]

Complementing the greater creature comforts and social exclusiveness, the design and operation of the extra-fare cars largely precluded the crowding so common in the day coaches. The luxury cars were wider and longer than their predecessors. The seats were bigger and softer, and often there were fewer of them. Most important, "[i]n the ordinary car the passenger [took] his chances of a seat when he enter[ed]. In the sleeping car he [was] the absolute owner, for the journey, of a certain selected portion, the purchase of but one berth entitling him to a whole seat, or twice the space belonging to him in the day car."[38] Having title to a seat meant that each passenger knew his place, eliminating much of the uncertainty and discomfort of the coach car.

Acquiring property in a seat enabled travelers to draw social boundaries much more easily than they could in the first-come, first-serve day coach. "There is a certain sense of ease and comfort upon taking a seat in one of the palace cars," an unnamed journalist declared in 1870, "especially if you have secured a section and are not annoyed by the presence of a stranger on the seat in front of you." Having purchased an entire section, the traveler could choose whether to make contact with others: "If continued silence becomes irksome, it will be no difficult matter to scrape an acquaintance." On the four-day journey between Chicago and San Francisco, "[t]he track is your home . . . , and the passengers form a family."[39]

Another writer inadvertently acknowledged that this casual familiarity characterized men's interactions on the cars to a greater degree than women's. The palace car, he claimed, "has its peculiar school of manners, and not a bad one, whose principal feature is the duty of being always ready to chat with your male fellow-travellers." Yet, although women passengers had to be more cautious about making acquaintances on the cars, most people believed that the ladies were much safer on the extra-fare cars than in the day coach. One teenaged girl confided to her travel journal in 1872, "It is astonishing with what facility one 'picks' up acquaintances on the cars, and it is worse than foolish to hold aloof from the free and easy manners which generally prevail in travelling." In charge of her two sisters during a trip from Boston to Florida, Anna Douglas sniffed that "a gentlemen who scraped acquaintance with us. . . . was too familiar with me" but expressed no anxiety about his presence and easily made friends with the "very refined pleasant lady" also on the cars.[40] As in cities, the creation of refined public spaces entailed a measure of class segregation that eased the rigid propriety that respectable women had to observe in public.

In addition to providing properly genteel interiors, Pullman and his rivals also tried to ameliorate other discomforts. "The chief horror" of railway travel in the United States, one journalist pronounced in 1869, was the absence of proper arrangements for meals. "[T]he 'fifteen' or 'twenty minutes for dinner,' shouted at the hungry and exhausted traveler" at selected station stops ". . . is simply a summons to frenzied battle with tough meats, cold vegetables, soggy hot bread, boiled tea and swill rye coffee. . . . With one eye upon the clock, the traveler bolts the unsavory repast." The inevitable result was a "deranged digestion," that most typical ailment of the mid-nineteenth-century middle class.[41]

The physiological discomfort corresponded to a breach of propriety. Dining was an important ritual for well-to-do Americans, not simply a nutritional opportunity. But twenty-minute station stops did not leave much time for elegance or polite conversation; "more than half of the time [was] taken up washing yourself and quarreling with the waiters." Bret Harte recalled one hungry passenger who, having received his breakfast buckwheat cakes as the call to board sounded, "frantically enwrapped his portion of this national pastry in his red bandana handkerchief, took it into the smoking-car and quietly devoured it en route." Such a necessity prevented him from exercising the "certain degree of artistic preparation and deliberation" that Harte felt the pancakes required.[42]

The introduction in the late 1860s first of the hotel car and then the dining car made such breaches of propriety unnecessary and doubtless calmed the digestive tracts of many passengers. The hotel car was an

Figure 2. "Dining Saloon of the Hotel Express Train," *Frank Leslie's Illustrated Newspaper* (January 15, 1870), after Albert Berghaus. Library of Congress, Prints and Photographs Division, LC USZ 62-14133.

otherwise ordinary sleeping car with a compact kitchen and pantry at one end. (See fig. 2.) Passengers could eat their meals at appropriate hours on tables placed between their seats, so they did not have to "wait and eat with the other animals at the general feeding place." Introduced a year later, the dining car was entirely devoted to food service, containing a kitchen and several tables for two or four passengers each. On both, and in the later buffet car, the menu, service, and prices matched those of first-class restaurants. Both cars served only passengers who had paid the surcharge.[43]

After the advent of the hotel and dining cars, many more types of extra-fare cars appeared. These included parlor cars with two single

Figure 3. "The Observation Car," *Summer Excursion Book: Season of 1891* (Pennsylvania Railroad Company, 1891), 269. Courtesy of the Winterthur Library, Printed Book and Periodical Collection.

rows of swiveling easy chairs, glass-enclosed observation cars for particularly scenic routes (see fig. 3), club cars with fully stocked bars, and composite cars combining several functions. By the early twentieth century, the finest luxury trains boasted cars with barbers, bathtubs, libraries, stenographers, and baby nurseries. The idea behind the extra-fare

cars remained largely the same amid these elaborate permutations: to assure passengers of a refined environment and refined fellow travelers.
The all-Pullman Chicago and New York Limited, the *Railway Review*
observed, "attracts the exclusive type of travelers and tourists. . . . The
most exacting patron . . . at once feels that satisfaction that comes of
finding himself among his kind of people for the day's journey."[44]
Buffering travelers from local conditions and the heterogeneous "traveling public," such accommodations made rail journeys much more appealing and fostered a transient community of the refined among those
who could afford the surcharge.

Crucial to providing this atmosphere was the presence of well-trained
servants whose deference confirmed the gentility of the space and the
passengers. It also promoted the illusion that the company and the passengers had a face-to-face, individual relationship rather than an impersonal, industrial one. As the Pullman company's instruction manual,
Car Service Rules, stated in 1888, "[T]he good effect of [liberal expen-
ditures and the latest improved and most elegant cars] upon the traveling public will be largely neutralized by inattention or indifferent service." The chief providers of this personalized service were conductors
and porters. The conductors had higher rank and took charge of all tickets and cash transactions on the cars. But the porters came into most direct and frequent contact with the passengers and were chiefly responsible for upholding or degrading a railroad's reputation.[45]

Although other companies also provided porters to serve their extra-
fare cars, it was the Pullman porter who became a popular icon. He was
an essential element in that "uniformity of service" that was the company's goal. At his best, the porter represented the ideal servant. Perfectly suited to the genteel fantasy that the luxurious palace cars embodied, "[h]e had that happy faculty of just knowing what was the right
thing to do at the right moment, and if he was not wanted you would
think the earth had swallowed him up, and in the moment he was
wanted he appeared to descend from the clouds."[46] Pullman porters
came to play this imaginative role in large part because from the late
1860s they were almost always black men.

Evidence of George Pullman's decision to hire recently emancipated
black men to serve as porters appeared in press accounts of his cars as
early as 1868. Why he did so is not known. Probably the same capitalist paternalism that prompted him to construct a model town for his
workers and led him to see the extra-fare cars as an instrument of human improvement informed the choice. As did many white Northerners,

he likely believed that centuries of enslavement had diminished blacks' willingness to work hard and get ahead. In hiring former slaves, Pullman may well have seen himself contributing to racial uplift by giving them the opportunity to learn the self-discipline necessary for survival and social mobility in a free labor economy.[47]

Whatever his philanthropic motives, Pullman was also taking advantage of the fact that in the 1860s black men had few alternatives to the same backbreaking, dead-end agricultural labor they had performed as slaves. His commitment to racial uplift did not extend to hiring or promoting black men to be conductors or passenger agents. On call twenty-four hours a day during journeys sometimes as long as a week, porters caught what sleep they could on the sofa in the men's washroom. For their long hours, they earned pitifully low wages: about $27.50 a month or $330 a year in 1915 if they worked full time, far less than necessary to support a family. But they did earn more than farmworkers, and they could expect a small degree of upward mobility from temporary to full time and from ordinary sleeper to exclusive limited train. The job took them all over the country and could be combined with other employment or education. Many of the men who worked as porters were leaders in their own communities.[48]

The porter's duties made him the janitor and the waiter of his car. He was responsible for constantly dusting all of a car's elaborately carved wooden surfaces, wiping down sinks and toilets, cleaning out spittoons, and sweeping carpets and floors. In the evening, at the request of passengers, he had to "make down" the car, lowering the upper berths and putting sheets, blankets, and pillows on the lower ones. He might well have to help passengers climb into the upper berth by providing a ladder or his shoulder. In the morning, he was responsible for making all signs of the bedding vanish again without discommoding the passengers. The personal services he was expected to provide included waking passengers for their stops, polishing their boots and shoes, bringing passengers water, fans, and other small items, answering their questions, opening and closing windows, and generally catering to travelers' wishes. In a car with a buffet, he took dining orders and served the food as well.[49]

The porter's ability to perform according to a white, middle-class ideal of racial servility was a critical element of the Pullman car experience. An editorial in *The Nation* counted "[t]he attentive colored servant" among the features making the Pullman sleeping car "a characteristic product of our national life." The common belief among whites that African Americans were particularly well suited to menial service made passengers look upon porters with special favor. "He is thoroughly adapted to his work," one journalist claimed. "It is difficult to imagine how [the porter's job] could be better performed by any other class of people. Certainly white men would not fill this difficult role as well as our colored brethren." A passenger noted with approval that, while another company's black porters were too proud for his comfort, on the Pullmans the situation was much better, "the colored porters knowing their places." As one porter told an interviewer, "You had to con a lot of them, get inside them and make them feel like they were the boss. They *were* the boss. *Everyone* was your boss; that's how we were trained."[50]

But travelers were not always pleased with porters. Their complaints illuminated the difficult balance of power and servility that porters negotiated on the job. No issue agitated passengers so much as tipping. Many travelers resented the expectation that they should pay the porter for services that were part of his job: "Why, when you pay two dollars for the privilege of sleeping . . . on one of G.P.'s palaces on wheels, do you have to pay his servant, who is taking good care of his property, a quarter of a dollar when you bid him good-bye in the morning?" The gratuity destroyed the myth that a natural, personal, and congenial relationship of mastery and servitude governed interactions between passenger and porter. Only the tip motivated the porter's "profound salaam," and a traveler's refusal to give one earned him (women were notoriously poor tippers) "the porter's look of contempt and surprise." In order to get tips, porters foisted on passengers services they did not want, from polishing their shoes to whisk-brooming their clothes. The more enterprising might emulate the apocryphal man who installed a "snorograph" in an empty berth. His ability to silence the stentorian rumbles earned him the cash gratitude of his passengers.[51]

The constant fuss about tipping on the cars and in other institutions highlighted the continuing problem that commerce posed for the ideology of refinement, despite Pullman's efforts to reconcile the two. The gratuity revealed that, rather than a gentleman, the passenger might be a cheat, and, rather than an ideal servant, the porter might be a small-time, unavoidable confidence man. When the passenger's gentility and the porter's faithful servitude were the result of a commercial rather than a personal interaction, the contradiction between refinement and republican egalitarianism became painfully clear. Once denaturalized, the

Pullman porter's servility became an effect of market relations shaped by racism rather than the natural result of a hierarchy rooted in character.

The complaints about tipping also revealed the Pullman company's benevolent gesture in hiring black men to be a sham and its service to passengers to be strictly a matter of profit, not philanthropy. Many newspaper exposés of the tipping question and the efforts of porters to unionize at the turn of the century noted that the company did not pay porters a living wage. Without tips, porters argued, they could not support themselves and their families. During the recessions of the 1870s and 1890s, the "traveling public" grew resentful of the Pullman company's unchanging fares, continued profits, and domination of the extra-fare car business. The porters' inadequate wages exacerbated travelers' sense that the company's claim to be providing a service to humanity was merely a mask for greed.[52] Capitalism, like the porter, might not be the willing servant of gentility that Pullman claimed.

Passengers were also often offended by the small power that porters exercised over the car as company representatives. Frequently, newspaper articles portrayed porters as tyrants who ruled their unfortunate charges with an iron fist: "The moment it is dark, he puts his passengers to bed. . . . What to him is the wail of the wretched traveler who is thrust into a stifling berth [at eight in the evening]?" He then took away the passengers' shoes, not to polish them but "as a guarantee that they will not get out of bed without permission."[53] Critics lamented that their very refinement led them to accept this tyrannical treatment without a complaint. A necessary adjunct to gentility, porters could sabotage the extra-fare car passenger's sense of rightful mastery by refusing to subordinate their own wishes to the traveler's.

The porters' race compounded their always potentially difficult relationship with the passengers. An essential element of their role, it also exacerbated the fears of some whites about racial intimacy. Promoting its own dining cars against Pullman's hotel cars, the Chicago, Burlington & Quincy Railroad (CB&Q) warned readers that on the hotel cars "your highly-flavored sable attendant . . . sleeps in the buttery. Oh, faugh! Can your sensitiveness stomach it?" Its dining cars, in contrast, were used for no other purpose but food service. The unattributed rebuttal to this claim merely reversed it, claiming that the Pullman hotel car staff slept in a room "isolated from the grand saloon, from the drawing-room, from the berths, and from the kitchen." On the CB&Q, in contrast, the dining saloon at night hosted "nigger-nests": "From five

to seven 'buck niggers,' to say nothing of the 'wenches' they not unfre-
quently [*sic*] entice into these cars at night."[54]

The salacious racism of these claims was uncommon in the press, but
the concerns about racial intimacy were not. The Pullman company's
manuals specified that porters had special blankets reserved for their
use. Under no circumstances were they to use the same blankets that
passengers did. Nor were they to occupy a passenger berth at any time
or use the communal brush and comb provided in the men's washroom. Porters, like other servants, were expected to know their masters'
desires so intimately as to anticipate them. But when equality accompanied proximity, the presence of blacks threatened whites' claims to racial
superiority.[55]

The tensions that made the porter's life so difficult and the Pullman
company's goal of perfect service impossible to obtain also shaped many
of the other complaints that Americans lodged against the extra-fare
cars. Initially enthusiastically received, the palace cars soon ran afoul of
the very requirements of refinement their designers had hoped to meet.
First among the criticisms of the open-section sleeper was the lack of privacy. True, the berths offered far more of this precious commodity than
did the day coach. Each section had a wooden partition at head and foot
and dark green curtains that could be tied or buttoned closed (although
a few gaps might remain, as the travel writer and novelist Helen Hunt
Jackson found to her dismay). The porters were to provide the ladies
with an additional, inner curtain as well.[56]

But there remained the problem of getting undressed for bed and then
dressed again behind the curtains. A double berth was only about three
and a half feet wide and about that high. There was no place to stand
behind the closed curtains and very little headroom. The contortions required to dress in a Pullman berth quickly became the butt of jokes. One
man new to the cars asked to borrow a pair of suspenders from his son:
"Busted mine tryin' to put my pantaloons on layin' down. Done it,
though. Got all dressed layin' flat—boots, pantaloons, coat, collar,
necktie—hull business." Asked why he had not left the berth to put on
his collar and coat, the old man explained, "Wimmin in the car." Many
women felt the same compunction, strengthened by the fear of sexual
improprieties: "What self-respecting women [*sic*] cares to travel when
she must robe and disrobe almost in public, and sleep without protection from the intrusion of strangers?"[57]

Then there was the problem of making one's toilet. At first undiffer-
entiated, as they were on coach cars until the 1880s, the washrooms on

extra-fare cars soon became gender-specific. To use them, the traveler had to put on enough clothing to be respectable and then make his or her way down the aisle amid similarly half-dressed, frowzy fellow passengers. This was a particularly difficult trial for refined women: "the spectacle of half-dressed men passing before you on the way to the washroom is not pleasant, nor quite decent." Even more disturbing was women's fear of the spectacle they presented to male onlookers while performing such unladylike acts as climbing into an upper berth. Once again, the essence of the problem was the inadequate separation of public from private spaces and behaviors. Without such divisions, genteel self-possession was impossible.

> Who could accept with smiles the company of six adults at the combing and washing stages of one's toilet? Who could rise in the society, and under the close personal scrutiny, of twenty-nine fellow-beings, jostle them in their seats all day, eat in their presence, take naps under their very eyes, lie down among them, and sleep—or try to sleep—within acute and agonized hearing of their faintest snores. . . ?[58]

Moreover, there was the problem of sharing accommodations. The Pullman company sold individual berths, the nocturnal counterpart to a seat. Two seats constituted a half-section, four a section. Although the company insisted in the 1860s that the three-and-a-half-foot-wide double berth provided plenty of room for two people, anecdotal evidence suggests that only newlyweds, mothers and children, and earnest YMCA men chose to share it. But strangers did routinely have to share a section, and this situation caused some anxiety among passengers, especially women.[59]

Tales of inadvertent, improper contact between men and women on the sleeping car at night were common. They played on both the troubling possibilities of intimacy among strangers and how easy it was to forget which of the identical green-curtained berths one had rights to. Despite women's constant anxiety about their vulnerability on the cars, most tales cast them as the chief violators of privacy. A typical tale featured a virtuous gentleman, "enjoying the sweet repose which is known only to single blessedness," awakening to find "a fair and buxom lady" in his berth under the fond impression that he was her husband. Failing in his attempt to apprise her quietly of her mistake, he finally shouted, "'Madam, you have got into the wrong berth.'" Exclaiming, "'Oh, my God, I have got into the wrong berth,'" she departed rapidly. In the morning she refused to acknowledge him.[60]

Newlyweds were another frequent target of jokes. The young bride who audibly instructed her loving new husband to stick his foot out of the berth to guide her on her return exited the washroom to find a foot protruding from every pair of curtains. While women walked in their sleep or lost their bearings, men—especially the chief habitués of the sleeping cars, the drummers or traveling salesmen—amused themselves by playing jokes on other passengers. One mischievous fellow seized the wayward hand of a sleeping traveler and shook it vigorously, only to be belted across the corridor. In the morning, none other than Susan B. Anthony emerged from the berth.[61]

The attempt to reconstruct the nation's race relations after the Civil War complicated matters further. In the 1870s Pullman gradually extended service into the South as the region's rail network improved and Northerners' interest in southern investments and resorts grew. Reinforcing the Fourteenth Amendment's promise of equality, the Civil Rights Act of 1875 prohibited racial discrimination in access to all public institutions—including, many whites feared, the sleeping cars. As usual, they portrayed the dangers of racial equality in sexual terms. At Jacksonville, Florida, "a large, black negro entered the Pullman sleeping car and presented to the conductor his check for the upper berth of No. 15." Who occupied the lower berth but "a Baltimore lady," whose race need not be specified. She fled to the coach car to save herself from a fate worse than death, the sharing of a section with a black man.[62]

White southern newspapers published violent polemics against Pullman's supposed commitment to forcing whites and blacks to sit and sleep together as equals. But the company seems to have taken a much less principled stand. While instructing its conductors to abide by the law requiring equal access regardless of race, the Pullman company also advised them to seat passengers with consideration for whites' racial prejudices. Pullman managers surely knew, as one Chicago editorialist pointed out, that most blacks were too poor to travel, much less purchase a first-class ticket and an extra-fare berth. In any case, state Jim Crow laws and the Supreme Court's endorsement of "separate but equal" in 1896 soon absolved the Pullman company of the responsibility. By 1915 the company distributed to its crews a booklet listing all the state laws they had to obey, including several mandating racial segregation. Although African Americans continued to challenge the practice, they would have little success until the 1950s.[63]

The solution to the concerns about the absence of proper gender and racial segregation on the cars was, of course, the compartment car. Many of the ladies who found themselves embarrassed and offended in the open-section sleeper implored the railroads to provide what Americans called "drawing-room" cars. State racial segregation laws required the erection of "substantial" wooden partitions between black and white areas where completely separate cars were not available.[64] But the one sustained effort to introduce the compartment car to the United States failed, illuminating the continuing conflict between profits and gentility that Pullman claimed to have resolved.

In the 1880s "Colonel" D'Alton Mann marketed luxurious "boudoir" cars of a type that had brought him considerable success in Europe. But the nickel-plated handrails and gold doorknobs and hinges that accompanied the greater privacy failed to overcome traveling Americans' reluctance to pay the higher fare railroads charged for the heavy, low-capacity cars. The Pullman company absorbed Mann's company along with another competitor in 1889. To a great degree Mann failed because Pullman, who favored the open-section plan, already dominated the industry. Until the twentieth century, Pullman's preference rested on a sound economic basis. When railroads did provide the expensive drawing-room cars, they often went unsold or ended up accommodating unacquainted passengers. Female passengers on the boudoir cars found that the only thing worse than sleeping with an entire car full of strangers was to be shut up in a small compartment with them. Finally, the name "boudoir" and the use of the cars by well-known actresses seem to have given the Mann cars a whiff of immorality.[65]

The exclusion of lower-class people, the luxurious furnishings and attentive service, the provisions for privacy and genteel rituals such as dining—all made the extra-fare cars the first resort of well-to-do Americans when they traveled. They embodied the material wealth and social exclusivity of the best urban homes and institutions. When complaints about the shortcomings of the cars multiplied at the turn of the century, it was not because the cars had deteriorated but because the terms of the negotiation of republicanism and class differences in public spaces were changing. The common denominator of the complaints about the extra-fare cars was a rejection of the refined standards of the 1860s and 1870s in favor of a new ideal of "comfort" and "efficiency." By the 1890s growing numbers of well-to-do Americans subscribed to the view that the elaborately carved wooden paneling, the richly patterned and textured fabrics of the walls and seats, and the ubiquitous gilt-framed mirrors of the usual extra-fare car were the height of bad taste, not good. Many of them also became convinced that the lavish decor trapped health-threatening dust and germs.[66]

Worst of all, the gaudy glory of the average Pullman car raised the cost of traveling higher than many thoroughly respectable Americans could afford. A lively debate raged in the press from the 1890s about whether the standard two-dollar fare kept out undesirables or excluded the deserving middle classes. In response to calls for decent, second-class sleeping cars to serve refined but not wealthy would-be travelers, the California railroads promoted the "tourist car," a streamlined version of the standard sleeper initially intended for the "better class" of emigrants. The tourist car lacked the rich upholstery and paneling of the standard sleeper but retained many of its other features. The other major reform of the era was a federally mandated lower surcharge for the upper berth, which passengers, especially women, testified was hard to get into and even less comfortable and less well ventilated than the lower.[67] Both developments reflected the gradual decay of the refined ideal as the means of reconciling economic disparities with republican values.

In a sense, Pullman's very success stimulated the vilification of the cars he had designed to be uplifting as well as profitable. In their heyday, the extra-fare cars put metropolitan commerce in service to republicanism and refinement simultaneously, at least in the eyes of the well-to-do. Thanks to the two-dollar surcharge and the spatial and social segregation it paid for, the traveler no longer had to to suffer the vagaries of local conditions or the rudeness of unrefined fellow passengers. But that two dollars expressed no permanent class difference, only the market's reward for self-possession and hard work, qualities any person of character would demonstrate. It facilitated the creation of a community of the refined whose roots lay in commercial patronage and transience rather than mutual knowledge.

But improved traveling accommodations and the vigorous publicizing of them helped to stimulate a desire to travel among a broadening range of middling Americans. Many came to see the extra-fare car's exclusive luxury as a barrier to their participation in the "traveling public" rather than a precondition for it. Refinement had promised transparent, trustworthy relations among self-possessed strangers. The new ideal of efficiency promised an urban, cosmopolitan anonymity that would open public spaces to a wider range of Americans. Both claimed to be the best vehicle for republican egalitarianism; both were socially exclusive in practice. But the latter frankly made urban, commercial re-lations the guarantor, rather than the destroyer, of republicanism.

Urban hotels underwent a similar shift from refinement to commer-cialism in their spatial organization, services, and furnishings between 1850 and 1915. Even more than the railroads and extra-fare cars, big-city hotels played a key role in structuring the relationship that their pa-trons enjoyed with the public spaces of the city. The "traveling public" they housed represented in miniature the larger ideal public of the na-tion. Its relationship to the city similarly mirrored a larger shift in atti-tudes toward cities, urban life, and the material conditions for a repub-lican society.

THREE

At Home in the City

First-Class Urban Hotels, 1850–1915

"Emerging from the ferry-house to the street, it seems as if Bedlam were broken loose, such is the horde of shouting and scuffling hackmen trying to capture the people and their baggage," the journalist Joel Cook reported of his arrival in New York in 1889. "[T]hose not trying to get possession seem anxious to drive their hacks over you." Joining the baggage and elbow-grabbing crowd were the hotel runners, "dilating with terrible fluency on the virtues of their respective houses." The baggage transfer wagons crowded about and the horse-drawn cars of the street railway clanged by in the muddy streets, while a lone policeman tried uselessly to impose order.[1]

Similar descriptions of urban arrival scenes were common in travel writing and city description throughout the nineteenth century. Even as the extra-fare cars furnished their riders with an ever more refined and luxurious means of travel, and even as train stations grew larger and grander, they remained enclaves of genteel order in a stubbornly vulgar environment. Just outside their walls lay all the money-grubbing hustle, clamor, and stench of urban life, its "whirling, grinding, smashing, shrieking, seething, writhing, glittering, hellish splendor."[2] The new arrival's most pressing task was to find a haven from the city's chaos, a substitute for the private home.

In order to find this sanctuary, the traveler had first to plunge into the melee, arranging to have his or her baggage transferred, driving a hard bargain with one of the proverbially grasping hack drivers, and ordering

him to drive to a hotel. The experienced traveler would have already selected a hostelry appropriate to his or her status and finances by con-
sulting a hotel register or gazette, or the train porter or conductor. Old
hands might even have written or telegraphed ahead to make reservations, but the practice was not common until the 1890s, and even then
only at the best hotels. The inexperienced traveler had to rely on the in-
variably deceptive promises of a hotel runner or the hack driver's knowledge of city hostelries. In any case, he or she had to make the rounds of
the hotels in search of something both respectable and affordable, mean-
while wearing out his or her feet or wallet.[3]

Most Americans wealthy enough to be traveling for pleasure in the
mid-nineteenth century stayed only at the best city hotels, for lodging
at a "first-class" hostelry was "a strong presumption of social availability." Where the traveler "stopped" while in the city signaled his or her
social status to the local elite, many of whom resided semipermanently
at such fine hotels in the mid-nineteenth century. Other travelers, such
as middle-class young men traveling rough and exposition visitors,
might select cheaper, second-class rooms. People sojourning for several
weeks or months had the option of living in a boardinghouse or making
long-term arrangements with their hotel's manager. But most travel
guides assumed the elevated cultural and financial status of their readers
and listed only a city's leading hotels.[4]

The finest city hotels sought to attract equally fine patrons in a variety of ways between 1800 and 1915. The term "first class" always signaled the finest architectural facades, the most up-to-date plumbing,
heating, and lighting technology, the most lavish interior decoration,
and the best service.[5] These features announced the hotel's claim to urbane luxury and prominence and by extension the guests' social status.
But even more important to the promotion of its good reputation and
the comfort of its guests, closely related matters, was the arrangement of
the house's interior structure and social relations.

Like the extra-fare cars, the best city hotels both served and undermined the separation of private from public, character from commerce,
by providing refined, semipublic spaces for a fee. At midcentury the best
hotels promised to protect their guests from the dangers of urban life by
offering patrons a substitute for home and family. Their spatial organization and services fostered among guests the mutual acquaintance
needed to sustain genteel interactions. A commercial proxy for the private sphere, a first-class hotel also represented the possibility of achieving a refined republic. By 1915 hotels instead offered to patrons the best

of urban life, guaranteeing luxurious accommodations accompanied by the personal freedom of anonymity and commercial privilege. Their public rooms merged with the attractions of the surrounding city, while their guests felt no necessary fellowship.

The best city hotels were institutions critical to the development of urban tourism. For one thing, magnificent establishments like San Francisco's Palace Hotel, Chicago's Palmer House, and New York's Waldorf-Astoria were important tourist attractions by the turn of the century.[6] But even the hotels whose names did not become widely known forwarded the erosion of the ideal of separate spheres that made city sightseeing possible in the United States. Like the extra-fare cars, by the late nineteenth century the first-class hotels created a distinct set of transient spaces in which well-to-do visitors could move comfortably without entering into the social relations of the community around them. In selling refinement for a fee, hotels helped to expand the realm of gentility and yet attenuated its connection to good character. Together, the greater social distance between visitors and locals and the waning of the ideal of separate spheres tended to lessen the moral significance that walking through the city had possessed at midcentury. This change opened up the possibility of urban tourism.

"THE TANGIBLE REPUBLIC"

In the United States, the hotel had its beginnings in the early decades of the nineteenth century, when purpose-built hotels replaced the overgrown houses that had long sheltered transients and furnished space for formal dinners and meetings. Financed by groups of merchants, the new, unusually large, pillared buildings constructed of stone instead of the usual wood often rivaled government edifices in their dominance of the city's built environment. First-class hotels were important centers of business and social life in antebellum cities. City boosters commonly agitated for the erection of a fine hotel in order to convince potential investors of their town's sure rise to metropolitan standing.[7]

In addition to building impressive facades and vast, vaulted public rooms, hotel financiers added every new mechanical improvement in heating, plumbing, and lighting that came along. They decorated the interiors to the height of fashion, providing many Americans with their first encounter with the material expression of gentility. One guest at Chicago's Sherman House in the 1860s launched her authorial career in the newspaper of her hometown Literary Society with a description of the ladies' parlor: "The room is carpeted in rich Brussels. The massive chairs and sofas are cusioned [*sic*] with rich Damask. On the center tables are always found beautiful and interesting books." She confessed, "All these things are novelties to one like myself accustomed all my life to rural scenery." [8]

Like that of the extra-fare car, the hotel's refinement was not a denial of republican egalitarianism but its supreme achievement. Both domestic and foreign travelers noted that hotels in the United States played a larger role in the public life of cities than did similar institutions in Europe. They were far bigger and fancier than most European guest houses, for example, offering semipublic rooms as well as beds for the night. Moreover, they usually contained a large proportion of long-term residents, forming a somewhat exclusive community that included some of the town's leading citizens. The line between commercial guest houses and private homes was not as distinct at midcentury as it would later become. Large numbers of well-to-do urbanites chose to live in a hotel or boardinghouse to avoid the costs of running a household. [9]

For contemporaries, a more compelling explanation than expense was the peculiar gregariousness of Americans—the men, at least. Unlike refined Europeans, Americans of all levels liked to be in company and eschewed privacy. Even if an American valued his solitude, to indulge in it would brand him "aristocratic" in the eyes of his fellows, an unbearable social stigma and an impediment to ambition. In short, contemporary observers believed that the hotel hosted community gatherings not simply because so many American cities had no other halls but also because the republican experiment had broken down class barriers and fostered a love of the public life, whether in railroad cars or in hotels. As early as the 1820s, Americans fondly called the first-class hotels "palaces of the people." They were royally magnificent spaces in which the refined republic took visible form. [10]

The special locus of the everyday staging of republican social relations was the hotel's dining hall, because of both the room's arrangement and the "American plan" of hotel keeping, which required guests to pay a single, daily tariff that included both room and board. The fee covered three to five meals per day and did not change if a guest missed a meal. The hotel staff served meals on a strict, limited schedule, causing great irritation to those who arrived late, left early, or preferred not to rise with the dawn. Summoned by a gong, the patrons entered the

long dining hall in a company. At the nicer hotels, they might do so cere-
monially for the midafternoon dinner, making the meal a formal occasion for the display of wealth, social position, and marriageable daughters. Often, they sat at long, communal tables, elbow to elbow with
other lodgers.[11]

Like the first-class coach car, the hotel's communal dining room, with
its long tables and simple service, was a handy symbol of the egalitarianism of American institutions. Travelers from England and Europe frequently objected to the promiscuous mixing of classes there. But when
one New York hotel announced the institution of private dining rooms
and specially prepared meals, the writer Nathaniel Willis declared that
the shared dining hall was "the tangible republic." Were some guests
permitted to avoid it, "the cords will be cut which will let some people
UP, out of reach, and drop some people DOWN, out of all satisfactory
supportable contact with society."[12] This division of the republic into
mutually unknown extremes was precisely what the authors of the midcentury urban sketches found most disturbing about urban life. Could a
republican society exist if the cords of recognition and daily social interaction were cut by private exclusivity, on the one hand, and public
anonymity, on the other?

Of course, relatively few antebellum Americans could afford to pay
the three- to four-dollar price of meals and a bed at the nicer hotels. But,
as with the surcharge for access to a sleeping car, the absence of overt
class barriers lent the appearance of democratic access, and the preva-
lent faith in social mobility compensated for the remaining disparity.
The point was not that the "society" contained in microcosm in the hotel dining room included everyone but that everyone had a chance to
meet its criteria for membership. Those people who dressed, behaved,
and ate genteelly were welcome at the table of any first-class hotel. Self-
possession, not material wealth or birth, was the key.

Aiming to encourage the mutual knowledge necessary to a refined order amid urban uncertainty, hotel keepers elaborated on the familial
ideal that underpinned the American plan in the social and architectural
arrangements of the hotel. Managers endeavored to make guests into
members of a community by organizing them according to gender and
status under the landlord's benevolent, patriarchal care. This model had
its origins in the less commercial, status-oriented hospitality of prominent families of an earlier era. It also reflected the values of the mid-
nineteenth-century middle class, for whom refinement marked the suc-

Figure 4. "Dining Room Scene in a Hotel," *Chicago Illustrated, Comprising a Full Description of the City* . . . (Chicago, 1884), 31. Courtesy of the Winterthur Library, Printed Book and Periodical Collection.

cessful combination of the market with republican principles. Hotels provided the material and spatial arrangements that corresponded to these values. In turn, these arrangements enabled the hotel to create simultaneously a haven from the city and an exemplary, highly visible enactment of refinement.[13]

The landlord's paternalism began with the patron's entrance. Having greeted and perhaps shared a glass of whiskey with new guests, the landlord himself often presided over meals. Following the "English" style of serving popular in the antebellum United States, waiters placed all of the food on the table at once. The landlord then carved the roasts and solicited guests for their preferences. Sometimes his clerks took this task, joining the community of guests as if they were the sons as well as the employees of the landlord. Since guests paid a fixed rate, they were free to eat as much as they liked. Normally, hotel keepers provided their guests with a wide range of dishes, coffee, tea, and ice water, although they often charged an extra fee for alcohol. Even when the best hotels introduced "French" cooking, involving more elaborate preparation and embellishment of the basic meats, vegetables, and sweets, eating at a hotel did not differ in style from a meal in a well-to-do household (see fig. 4).[14]

The spatial organization of the mid-nineteenth-century hotel reinforced the social aims implicit in the American plan. Guest houses of
all classes provided their patrons with much less privacy than would
their counterparts at the end of the century. Hotel keepers routinely expected guests to share a room and perhaps a bed with strangers of the
same sex if the house was crowded. The price the guest paid ensured
only accommodation, not a room of one's own. During Chicago's midcentury boom, hotels were often so crowded that travelers found no
rooms available. "I applied immediately for a room and was told that
they could accommodate no more that all the rooms & beds were full
and that not even a cot was to spare," wrote a miserable Junius Mulvey
to his brother in 1854. Cold, wet, and weary, he trudged through fierce
winds to another hotel, where he eventually "got a cot in one of the parlors where a large piano & four cots & other luggage filled the room." [15]

In addition to rooms and beds, throughout much of the nineteenth
century guests shared communal bathing and toilet facilities. The lavish
suites designed for the many long-term guests often included private water closets, but most short-term hotel patrons had to leave their rooms
to use the toilet or to bathe. Boston's monumental Tremont House, built
between 1827 and 1830, offered eight privies and eight basement bathrooms, but New York's Astor House trumped this stunning achievement
in plumbing within ten years, offering seventeen basement baths and
privies on every floor when it opened. By the 1850s all the best hotels
had large, lavish bath establishments in their basements where hotel patrons paid a fee to bathe. Men could purchase a shave at the barbershops
near the lobby. [16]

Technological limitations in plumbing and other mechanical arts par-
tially determined the organization of the hotel's space and amenities. But
equally important was the imperative to preserve "the home feature" in
a commercial establishment with a significant public role in the city. The
hotel was an anomaly: a commercial household in a society that increasingly posed domesticity and business as antagonists. "Hotel life is
of necessity one of restlessness, bustle and hurry," the editor of *Hotel
World* wrote regretfully in 1876. "[T]he hotel-keeper is fortunate, who
possesses the tact necessary to dispel as much as possible of this excitement, by making his house more of a home." [17]

Aside from tact, the chief means of making the hotel homelike at
midcentury was to incorporate the same separation of work from home
that characterized middle-class urbanites' efforts to mitigate the city's

industrial-commercial disorder and to display their own uplifting refinement. This separation entailed a growing degree of gender segregation, beginning at the hotel's entrance. The main doorway into the building usually fronted on a chief thoroughfare and was noticeably different from an ordinary portal. It led directly into the hotel's rotunda or lobby, a large hall that often boasted walls and floors of marble dotted with comfortable chairs and couches. At the back of this pillared expanse was the clerk's desk, where guests requested rooms and signed their names in the register. By the 1850s "ladies" were expected to enter by a separate, less ornate, entrance on a side street that led not to the lobby but upstairs to the parlor. In doing so, respectable women avoided one of the least exclusive semipublic spaces in the hotel and moved immediately into one designated domestic, although it too was semipublic, open to all of the hotel's guests. The separate entrances enforced a division of labor as well as space: men made the party's presence official and paid for all accommodations.[18]

Once in residence, men and women continued to occupy distinct spaces outside of their bedrooms. Female guests used the delicately furnished and decorated parlors to receive calls, read, write, sew, play the piano, and enjoy other acceptably feminine leisure pursuits. Many parlors fronted or overlooked the street. Safe behind the large windows, women could observe the urban promenade without risking its democratic excesses. They also served as a display of wealth and refinement for passersby. Men, although they might pass time in the drawing rooms when accompanied by women, also had the option of going to the lobby, the bar, the reading room, and, in many cases, the billiard room. With the partial exception of the lobby, these were male-only spaces, usually located on the first floor close to the entrance hall and accessible from the street. They were furnished with heavy, thickly cushioned, and plainly upholstered pieces and ornamented in dark colors and designs.[19]

Because the parlors provided a safe, domestic haven for the ladies and for those gentlemen in temporary retreat from the world, the lobby could serve as a refined interior street. It connected the hotel to the city outside its doors but excluded most of the dangers and discomforts of wheeled traffic, promiscuous crowds, garbage, and weather. Retaining some of the character of city streets before the nineteenth-century rise in the volume and speed of traffic, the lobby added the material context of refinement with its marble walls and floors, vaulted ceiling, and pillars. Here respectable men could lounge in the comfortable chairs, talk business and politics, chew and smoke tobacco, get their boots polished, and buy newspapers and tickets for the theater, railroads, and steamboats. Open to properly dressed and well-behaved city residents ("rotunda chair boarders") and hotel guests alike, the lobby came much closer than the less accessible second-floor parlors to exemplifying the republican promise of the first-class hotel. The exclusion of respectable women and lower-class males not employed by the hotel allowed it to do so.[20]

As elsewhere in the city, gender segregation inscribed and obscured the enforcement of class, racial, and ethnic differences by invoking female refinement, rather than economic disparities, for the exclusion of "common" people and middle-class women from certain public and semipublic spaces. That gender segregation was far from rigorous underlines the importance of its function in enforcing other kinds of discrimination. Men were welcome in feminine spaces like the parlor if they accompanied a female guest and observed the proprieties. Similarly, respectable women could and did enter hotel lobbies (though never bars), but as in any public space they had to observe careful decorum in order to maintain a good reputation. Ideally, they entered such public spaces only when escorted by a gentleman, whose physical protection was less important than the symbolic assurance that this woman was properly part of a male-headed family.[21] In performing their social ideal in semipublic spaces, middling and well-to-do Americans made such proprieties a prerequisite for public participation. They excluded those who were "unrefined," an attribute of character that shifted the blame for exclusion to the excluded.

Two engravings of the parlor and the lobby of first-class hotels illustrate the institution's ambition to provide both a haven and a visible, exemplary enactment of propriety. "Grand Parlor in a Hotel" showed small groupings of men and women in a large and magnificently furnished parlor (fig. 5). In these refined surroundings, they played the piano and sang, read newspapers, and engaged in genteel conversation. The upright posture and firmly planted feet of all the figures as well as the distances between them demonstrated the thoroughly respectable character of the guests and, implicitly, the contrast between the refined interior of the hotel and the mannerless masses in the streets. The small groupings and the sparse population of the room also suggested the possibility of privacy in public. In "Rotunda of the Palmer House, Chicago," properly suited and hatted men occupied the chairs and benches,

Figure 5.   "Grand Parlor in a Hotel," *Chicago Illustrated, Comprising a Full Description of the City* . . . (Chicago, 1884), 33. Courtesy of the Winterthur Library, Printed Book and Periodical Collection.

whose construction and upholstery were clearly less elaborate than those of the parlor (fig. 6). Others strolled about the marble floor or stood chatting. One man escorted his small son, but otherwise all those present were adult men. At the back appeared the clerk at his counter, registering more guests. To judge from these two images, the hotel's semipublic spaces mirrored the proper division of the domestic from the commercial, thus supporting the social claims of the middle class.[22]

But first-class hotels did not always achieve the tranquil ideal portrayed in the parlor and lobby engravings and claimed in many hotel advertisements. Contemporary descriptions of hotel lobbies often emphasized their atmosphere of urban hustle and male camaraderie. Crowds of resident and transient men, lounging, standing, smoking, talking, and spitting, filled many a rotunda with noise and confusion. "On entering the hotel," one ailing New Yorker wrote of his 1867 visit to Chicago, "I found the hall filled like a merchants' exchange, and made my way to the office, not without some difficulty. . . . Porters, waiters, guests, all are in quick motion; and one or the other is pretty sure to knock you over." New Yorkers used the lobbies of the first-class hotels as after-hours offices and stock exchanges, while some southern hotels hosted slave

Figure 6.   "Rotunda of the Palmer House, Chicago," *From the Lakes to the Gulf* (Chicago, 1884), 19. Courtesy of the Chicago Historical Society (Engraving 1CH1-30174; Library qF25H F9).

auctions.[23] And at least some of the affable gentlemen sheltering in the hotel's refined embrace were sure to be confidence men, lingering near the front desk to overhear or glimpse the names of potential marks.

Crowds of women and children might make the most genteelly furnished parlors equally noisy and fractious. Authors of etiquette books had to instruct their readers on the maneuvering necessary to maintain the illusion of domestic privacy in a semipublic space: "Should a visitor come in to see one of the boarders who may be sitting near you, change your place, and take a seat in the distant part of the room." Ladies who talked too loudly, played the piano constantly, or monopolized the writing desk earned the dislike of their fellow guests.[24] The tea party ambience promised in the Palmer House engraving was not at all assured, even when the hotel was not jamming cots around the piano and piling trunks in the corners.

The growing size and lavishness of first-class urban hotels from the 1850s into the twentieth century steadily distanced them from their original model, the well-to-do household. The proliferation of specialized spaces increased the hotels' ability to provide an ideal balance between domesticity and commerce, yet also began to undermine the familial ideal governing social relations in midcentury hotels. As a result, their ability to host a representative public diminished as well. For example, once one room had served as a bar, office, and lobby, but as early as the 1820s, first-class hotels had separated these spaces and given each a more lavish treatment, just as they had walled off the parlor from the lobby. This differentiation of functions indicated the growing separation of the substance of hospitality from the selling of it. Male patrons less often drank companionably with the innkeeper, his clerks, and fellow guests as a prelude to joining their company officially. By the turn of the century, hotel moralists were warning clerks and managers to avoid "good fellowship" at the bar.[25]

It was an innovation in the organization of service—the institution of the "European plan"—that most clearly revealed the growing difference between the hotel and the household. The new plan highlighted the centrality of commerce in the first-class city hotel's operation and threatened to tarnish its republican glamour. The plan's premise was the separation of the two essential elements of accommodation, room and board. Now, a patron could pay simply for a room and find his or her meals elsewhere. The dining room of the American plan hotel brought the guests together physically and symbolically as a community. The European plan frankly acknowledged that guests were strangers who did not necessarily want to become acquainted. The nostalgic Henry Bohn, editor of the *Hotel World,* complained, "The European plan scatters the social forces of a hotel, sends them straggling to the dining room, creates a little bunch here and little gathering there."[26]

The change from American to European plan was gradual and piecemeal, stemming from many smaller "improvements" in hotel service during the mid-nineteenth century. Many first-class hotels served guests privately in their parlors upon request from the 1830s or seated them at smaller tables accommodating only six to eight people. At the same time, the "French" style of service replaced the English: waiters served diners from the kitchen or a sideboard rather than place all the dishes on the table. The *Hotel World* credited the Leland family, managers of New York's Metropolitan Hotel (opened in 1852), with the honor of being the first house to abandon a fixed schedule for meals. The Lelands instituted practices that departed from the familial model and underscored the commercial nature of the hotel's hospitality: "They announced the novel but welcome idea . . . that the landlords should accommodate the public—not the public the landlords. They arranged the meals so that the table should be always accessable [*sic*]." Finally, they also "introduced the printed bill of fare."[27] These modifications of the American plan gave the guests more autonomy and privacy, but they eroded the republican, familial practices that had sustained the American plan hotel's ability to mediate between private and public.

Increasingly popular in the 1870s, by the 1890s the European plan predominated among large, urban first-class hotels. Other changes meant to rationalize hotel service and make it more profitable accompanied the switch. Lacking a monopoly on the house's guests, the dining room became a restaurant open to the public. The printed bills of fare more and more often listed a price for each item, initiating the à la carte style of dining. In adopting such innovations, hotel managers began to abandon the effort to make hotels small, knowable communities with an intelligible social order. Instead, they advertised the guest's freedom to choose where, what, when, and with whom to eat and keep company. These were particularly urban and commercial freedoms that enabled transients to inhabit the hotel without becoming part of a local social network.[28]

The European plan offered significant advantages to big-city hotel keepers. By making the meal service optional and extending the hours of service, hotel men did not have to employ an army of waiters to serve all of the house's guests simultaneously. Fewer waiters working longer hours could serve the same or a greater number of diners at less cost to the hotel. Under the American plan, guests commanded all the resources of the host's kitchens for a fixed fee, whereas under the European they paid for each item selected. The meal became a revenue producer rather than an extension of hospitality, and the burden of food costs shifted from the hotel to the guests. Finally, by opening its dining hall to the public, the hotel increased the number of potential customers but diminished its ability to function as a domestic haven.[29]

The rationalization of dining extended beyond simply the menu or the service; it encompassed an ambitious campaign to alter Americans' eating habits. Hotel keepers joined health and nutrition reformers in criticizing Americans for eating too much of the wrong kinds of food. At breakfast, for example, "fruit, then fish, eggs, steak, vegetables, and time and again several kinds of meat were ordered." And that was not all: "At the finish 'cakes and syrup' were thrown at you. The guest, believing he had paid for these articles . . . did his best to make 'way with the whole combination." But times had changed and enlightened hotel keepers adopted the European plan: "[T]oday men are guided in ordering meals by the cost as well as by the appetite. Today the proprietor is not so anxious to donate food stuffs for the demoralization of the guest's health." Allowing guests to choose and charging for each item "has done away with gormandizing [*sic*], stuffing, over-feeding." And what was good for the guest was good for the hotel: "it is businesslike and profitable." [30] Efficiency, rather than hospitality, justified the new plan; commerce would improve the lot of the inner man as well as the outer. In its small way, the à la carte menu signaled the rejection of the separation of spheres that once protected tender morals from the merciless market.

The introduction of à la carte service and printed menus made dining at a restaurant quite unlike family or even formal private dinners among the well-to-do. Eating out became an urbane practice requiring special expertise. Americans had to learn to read and order from the long, complex menus. The unfamiliarity of many of the items and hotel keepers' tendency to use French instead of English terms ("menu" instead of "bill of fare") compounded the difficulty. Oscar Tschirky, maître d'hôtel at the Waldorf-Astoria in the early twentieth century, offered a sample dinner menu involving eleven distinct courses. Each course offered several choices, including exotica such as frog legs and escargot that few Americans would have encountered on their dinner plates at home. The restaurant owner George Rector admitted that the menu "was based more on the vanity than on the palate of our diners." [31] Dining out had become an exercise in cosmopolitanism.

Sophisticated diners noted the perplexity of novices with amusement. In one anecdote, a group of excursionists arrived at "the Grand Hotel" for dinner, and "managed, after much perturbation of spirit, to get their dinner ordered from the 'printed programme.'" One young man then mistook his consommé for coffee and added cream and sugar before tossing it down. Advised by the waiter of his mistake, he said with aplomb, "That's all right, I know what it is, and that's the way I take it." One headwaiter advised his charges that sometimes "a guest does not know how to order from a menu card, but even so a waiter is more apt to give offense than to receive thanks should he attempt to enlighten him." [32] Visitors took part in an experience that symbolized refined urbanity when they sat down to eat at a first-class restaurant. Even well-intentioned advice undermined their social performance.

Despite its social perils, dining out was an important part of an excursion to the city by the early twentieth century. Organized tour groups were assured fine meals at their hotels. Many unorganized tourists planned at least one fancy dinner at a fine restaurant, or they patronized their hotel's dining room to the same effect. "It appearing to be the sentiment of the party" of four Civil War veterans visiting Grant's just-completed tomb in New York in 1897 "to have a first-class dinner in style, they took a carriage to the . . . Windsor Hotel. . . . Oh, but it was great!" But the pleasure of the experience no longer stemmed from the diner's participation in a republican ritual. In 1912 the journalist Julian Street pictured two hapless suburbanites, visiting New York for a night on the town, joining a "silk-stocking bread line" at the door of their hotel's Palm Room restaurant.[33] The grandeur of the occasion more than made up for the absence of egalitarian community and their humiliating dependence on the charity of the maître d'hôtel.

In adopting the European plan, the first-class hotel brought its patrons closer to the city. The commercial aspect of its hospitality became increasingly overt and pervasive, endangering the previously crucial "home feature." In "the 'American Plan hotel,'" one hotel journal editor wrote in 1910, "the guest roamed about unmolested as if he were in his own household."[34] Now, guests constantly had to make choices about which services to buy rather than have ready access to the house's amenities for a single fee. The opening of the hotel's dining room to nonresident customers pushed back the boundary of "private" spaces and increased the hotel's integration with the urban landscape and urban society. Now the all-male lobby and bar were not the only rooms where guests and locals mixed; they might share dining rooms, tearooms, and cafés as well. In such spaces the patrons did not form a community of fellows and could not represent "the tangible republic" in the same way as they had at midcentury. Only commercial patronage and physical proximity united them, creating a consummately urban relationship that earlier hotels had sought to moderate.

First-class hotels continued to increase in size and amenities at the turn of the century, achieving what contemporaries believed to be the absolute height of luxury during the great hotel building boom of the 1890s and 1900s. The symbol of the new era was New York's Waldorf-Astoria (1892–97), which broke the thousand-room barrier when it opened in 1897. Dozens of even larger and more lavish hotels sprang up in the years following the Waldorf's dazzling success. But the grand hotels of the early twentieth century did not have the same republican connotations of their predecessors of the 1850s or even the 1870s. Increasingly, they hosted previously "domestic" events for the fabulously wealthy nouveaux riches whose wealth derived from their domination of the emerging national, corporate economy. According to legend, the smashing success of the Bradley-Martin charity ball that celebrated the opening of the Waldorf-Astoria spurred urban elites to rent banquet halls and hotel ballrooms more and more often. Such celebrity events drew in the society columnists of the new mass-circulation metropolitan newspapers who, much to the delight of hotel managers, devoted long, detailed columns to the lavish events.[35]

The extravagance of the grand hotels and the presence of the very rich attracted local and out-of-town sight-seers. Onlookers crowded around great hotels when a society ball was going on, gawking at the richly clad, bejeweled millionaires. This "society" was not the same as that invoked by Nathaniel Willis at midcentury: its members flaunted rather than effaced their exclusivity. They were celebrities rather than public men, embodying individual charisma rather than social values. Long urban landmarks, the great hotels now became tourist attractions. Chicago's Palmer House had provided guides for those who wanted to explore its interior as early as 1879; the Waldorf-Astoria followed suit twenty years later.[36]

First-class hotels also served a new kind of patron at the turn of the century: conventioneers. More and more often, veterans, fraternal, professional, trade, and business associations held annual, national meetings. This new kind of stranger arrived in the city in order to affirm pre-existing social ties and had little interest in entering the day-to-day life of the city's residents. Rather than parlors, these visitors required more and larger meeting halls and sample rooms. Moreover, in soliciting the patronage of such organizations, city hotel managers found themselves competing in an ever more important national market.[37]

The changing organization, scale, and clientele of the first-class hotels transformed their role as a site for the constitution and representation of a republican society. At midcentury visitors had wanted to stop at a fashionable hotel in order to join its select company. As a boarder at New York's Astor House wrote in 1857, "We must place ourselves as we are among the best people."[38] The integration of guests symbolized both the importance of a knowable community and the possibility of social mobility. By the turn of the century, the great hotels had simultaneously become more public, blurring the boundaries between the hotel proper and the city streets and enterprises outside its doors, and more private, enclosing and renting the spaces once dedicated to creating a refined community. Like à la carte restaurant service, the renting of the hotel's "domestic" areas transformed the spaces in which midcentury Americans had enacted the tangible republic into sites for commercial, private, or professional events. Such events could not enact a refined community in the way that the more exclusive gatherings of the 1850s had.

This change and its broad social context did not go unnoticed in the
hotel trade journals. Some observers lamented the loss of the "homelike" atmosphere of a bygone generation of smaller, American plan
houses and explicitly identified the new with the urban-industrial economy. "[T]his hotel is too large to give satisfactory service," the editor of
one journal complained of the Waldorf-Astoria. "[T]he guest loses his
identity in such a large hotel; loses that personal recognition of clerks
and employees that makes a hotel homelike." Sadly, the hotel had
become "simply a great, big, elegant luxurious hotel accommodation
'factory.'" [39] Unlike this man, many city dwellers and visitors prized the
urbane splendor of these hostelries—especially the Waldorf-Astoria—
more than any homelike comforts. Indeed, for many, the point of staying at such a house or just visiting it was its magnificent distance from
the everyday.

But the palace hotels in many ways represented the final flourishing
of the nineteenth-century tradition of commercial hospitality. As early
as the 1870s in New York, they faced growing competition from family
and apartment hotels for long-term residents. They found their ability
to attract the increasing number of transients challenged by the new
"businessmen's" hotels. This new type of middle-class hotel was unlike
either palace hotels or second-class hostelries and boardinghouses. It offered a large number of single rooms designed for rapid turnover instead
of suites for long-term guests. The public rooms and bedrooms tended
to be small and less lavishly decorated. Standardized in construction, design, and furnishings, these hotels adopted every labor-saving device
available to cut labor costs. They did not pretend to be a home, much
less to foster community. [40]

Having rejected or modified the costliest features of the palace hotels,
the businessmen's hotels could then offer unheard-of amenities for relatively low prices. The chief developer and promoter of this type of hotel
in the early twentieth century, Ellsworth Statler, advertised his Buffalo
(1908) and Cleveland (1912) hotels as offering "A Room and a Bath for
a Dollar and a Half." No other hotel in the country, and only Cesar
Ritz's luxury hotels outside the United States, could claim to offer every
guest a private bathroom, and none for so low a price. Despite the in-
credulity of more experienced hotel managers, Statler's houses were
enormously successful. "The private bath is no longer a luxury; it is a
necessity," hotel journal editors acknowledged. Within a few short
years, Statler owned the world's first "chain" of hotels. Other hotel managers and investors soon followed his example. [41]

Notably, the businessmen's hotels catered almost wholly to transient visitors, especially the ubiquitous traveling salesmen to whom their name referred, but they also welcomed a new, expanding category of travelers: urban tourists. Less well-to-do than city visitors of the past, the tourists of the 1890s and 1900s also had plans that distinguished them from many of the patrons of first-class hotels. Once vacations had involved relatively long stays in one place. Now, just as urban hotels were gaining a greater share of vacationers, "the tendency [was] to make shorter stays and frequent more points—summer recreation [had] become a sight-seeing tour." Even the business trade, once a steady, year-round money-maker, had changed. The growing numbers of conventions, "now tending toward a combination of business and pleasure gatherings, create[d] a tremendous demand for a day or a few days at a time and [left] hotels half empty at other times."[42] Given these conditions, hotel keepers had no stable community into which to integrate travelers, even if they wished to try.

The businessmen's houses seemed to many to represent a particularly modern, efficient kind of republicanism. Hotel journal editorials argued that "[t]he need in the hotel world today is not more palaces where only the multimillionaire can afford to stop, but hotels so built and located that they can give comfort, homelike atmosphere and good food at the price the great middle class can pay." The aesthetic sins of the palace hotels, like those of the Pullman cars, were the material signs of an un-American snobbishness. "A majority of travelers," John Willy, editor of the *Hotel Monthly*, insisted in 1909, "would prefer to stop at a hotel of the plainer type, more consistent with their democratic ideas. . . . They have no use for hifalutin wall or ceiling embellishment nor for obsequious service. They want the modest, unassuming quarters where they can feel at home."[43] Luxury was no longer the only means of assuring gentility. Indeed, it seemed now to deny decent people the comforts they deserved. The palace hotels, like the palace cars, had lost the odor of democracy they had enjoyed in their early days.

The rejection of older, more ornate taste signaled the emergence of a "modern" aesthetic, one that valued smooth surfaces, clean lines, and ease of use. "I would not sacrifice one jot of beauty and elegance," wrote one self-declared prophet of the future hotel, but "money should be made to yield more comforts to mind and body, and a less surfeit to the sense."[44] Staying at a businessmen's hotel was not simply an economic choice but one representing a modern rejection of the overt exclusivity and material excess of a previous generation. The rationalized simplicity of the new hotels now represented egalitarian access to modern amenities.

In the extent of their rationalization of space and services, their catering to middle-income travelers, and their rejection of the lavish decor of the palatial houses, the businessmen's hotels exemplified the general trend toward commercialization. Making it easier for a wider range of people to stay in cities cheaply and respectably, they also provided only a bedroom. For the parlors, dining rooms, and lounges that had long mediated between hotel patrons and the city, the guest at a businessmen's hotel had to go elsewhere, probably to one of the growing number of commercial tearooms, bars, restaurants, and cafés. There, visitors to the city might feel themselves immersed in the exciting, brightly lit life of the city, but they would not be integrated into a community of fellows. Distanced from the day-to-day life of the city's residents, most would interact with the locals chiefly in making purchases and asking for directions.

The changes in the organization of the hotel's space and service are only part of the story. The hotel keepers' effort to provide the material context for an ideal public realm could not succeed without the cooperation of their workers and patrons. Between 1870 and 1915 the rationalization of the hotel's spatial structure and service also affected its labor relations and the treatment of guests. Discussions about hotel employees and customers in hotel trade journals revealed the extent to which rationalization eroded the influence of the ideal of separate spheres and cleared the way for urban tourists.

MASTERS AND SERVANTS

The keepers of first-class urban hotels always sought to provide an ideal social order as a necessary complement to their houses' material luxuries. In doing so, they confronted the tension at the heart of urban description at midcentury, the contradiction between a market economy and a republican political order. All men were created equal, but some were richer than others. According to the ideology of refinement, this disparity arose from differences in character, and thus the rich constituted a legitimate elite. Among the chief institutional evangelists of refinement, the best city hotels promised their patrons an environment in which the legitimacy of their privilege would be confirmed at every ring of the bell.

Not surprisingly, the editors of hotel journals continually returned to the importance of having capable yet submissive servants. They, no less than well-to-do housewives, battled constantly with the "servant problem." "The management and judicious selection of help . . . in our large hotels is no small item," editor William Smith reminded the readers of the *Hotel World* in 1877. "The hired help and actual workers in a hotel, as will be conceded by all, are the mainspring of the house and make or destroy its reputation." Unhappily, the poor quality of service in the United States was proverbial among both citizens and visitors to the republic throughout the nineteenth century. As the anonymous author of *Forty Days in a Western Hotel* (1867) put it, "[T]he sense of freedom is so strong at the West, it spoils all men for service." [45]

But fortunately for the hotel keepers, American egalitarianism had its limits. The formal equality of white men rested on the legal and customary subordination of African Americans and white women as well as the economic and social marginalization of working people. Many immigrants also faced considerable discrimination, although only Chinese and Japanese newcomers were explicitly barred from becoming citizens and taking certain types of work. Hotel managers manipulated the existing hierarchies of race, class, and gender in order to secure self-effacing servants without endangering the characteristic American dedication to egalitarianism.

The struggle to define the conditions for republican deference emerged most clearly in a debate conducted on the editorial pages of hotel journals over who would make the best dining room waiter. As soon as the hotel trade journals began to be published regularly in the 1870s, their pages were peppered with arguments about the merits of native-born white men, European immigrant men, black men, and white women as dining room servitors. In the years just after the Civil War, black men seem to have dominated high-class personal service jobs. Even before emancipation, black servants in the North may have signaled a family's—and presumably a hotel's—claim to high social status by analogy to the "aristocratic" planter families of the South. As William Smith put it, "[E]verything goes to prove that the colored men are the best" waiters, because "[t]hey are naturally subordinates, and where white men only take the position as a matter of convenience and aspire to higher positions . . . the height of the negro's ambition is a rush of good-feeing patrons and the position of 'head.' " The natural subordination of black servants conveyed the natural privilege of white patrons. "What a complete gentleman," Isabel March rhapsodized in Howells's *Their Wedding Journey.* "There ought never to be a white waiter. None but negroes are able to render their service a pleasure and distinction to you." [46]

Yet, despite the racial stereotype that underwrote the hiring of black men to be Pullman porters and dining room waiters, some employers expressed doubts about their suitability. If they were naturally subordinate, they were correspondingly less capable than the less deferential white men. The "weak spot of the colored waiter," one trade journal editor declared, was that the headwaiter "has to watch him like a cat watches a mouse lest he forgets [sic] this and that." Compounding this inbred simple-mindedness was their cupidity: "they are taught from their youth up to hold out their hand for 'a stamp'; it is second nature, and nine times out of ten if they are not fee'd your dinner will be a very uncomfortable one." [47]

Like the much-maligned Pullman porters, black waiters labored under the stereotype of being especially insistent about receiving gratuities. But they were hardly alone in more or less openly soliciting tips. Uncommon before the Civil War, the practice of tipping spread with the introduction of the European plan and the commercialization of other services. It seems to have been endemic among a wide range of service workers by the late nineteenth century. Having tipped the Pullman porter, Julian Street's suburbanites set off for their hotel, feeing all the way: "So the station porter takes your little bags to the taxi and gets *his,* and the taxi driver drives you . . . to the hotel and gets *his,* and the carriage starter. . . , and the bellboy." In the course of their stay, this couple would also tip the hat- and coat check boys, the barber, the washroom attendant, the headwaiter, the waiter, and more taxi drivers. Paying for unwanted services, Street wrote, was "the metropolitan custom." [48]

For hotelmen as for the Pullman company, this urbane practice marred the attempt to provide perfect service: "Instead of the unobtrusive service of the ideal hotel there is developed an obtrusive service, seeking the gratuity." Servants who too obviously demanded remuneration made the guests uncomfortably aware that the hotel keeper was only selling them hospitality, not extending it to his refined equals. Tipping also brought the class tensions of the street into the first-class dining room. "The waiter takes your tip . . . in the spirit in which it is offered. That is to say, there is complete ill-will on your side and on his. You give him the dollar because you are one of custom's cowards; he takes it as though it belonged to him; as though he was collecting an old debt." [49]

The hotel journal editors also had other reasons for deploring the practice of tipping. Although one argued that the combination of à la carte service and the desire for a tip made waiters more mindful of the patron's wishes, others replied that only those guests who could afford to pay well received attention. Failing to tip condemned the guest to poor or no service, and even small disparities made a difference: "The man who gives 10 cents or 15 cents does not receive the same attention that is bestowed upon those who are more liberal." Another editor agreed, adding that tips disgusted guests as "unearned." [50] The marketplace law of supply and demand was not supposed to apply to the refined hotel meal. An unwanted consequence of rationalization, the tip seriously jeopardized the practice of refinement by revealing the commercial, rather than natural, character of the relationship between master and servant.

By the turn of the century, white, often European-born men and white women gained favor over black men in the eyes of hotel journal editors. According to them, white waiters of both sexes became more common and black men less so in first-class dining rooms. Most likely the race of the workforce reflected the location of the hotel and the growing availability of low-skilled, white male labor in major industrial cities. But in the trade journals, editors pronounced that black men were losing their natural place as waiters because they had abandoned their deferential, selfless ways of yore: "If the colored man, who is a natural born servant, wishes to regain his prestige he must demonstrate his willingness and ability to give good, clean, quick service." Hotelmen's hiring preferences were one small part of a nationwide abandonment of the commitment to black Americans' civil rights at the turn of the century. By 1908 one editor suggested that training black men to wait table in second-class establishments "might aid in the solution to the negro question" but that "[o]ur high-priced, profitable hotels, will, of course, always employ trained, white, male waiters." [51]

The ideal white, male waiter combined intelligence and self-direction with the deference thought natural to black men. Raised in societies Americans believed to be more hierarchical and mannerly than their own, European-born men still possessed an intelligence native to their race. Of course, not all European immigrants were good material for dining room service; the Irish certainly did not qualify. The model immigrant waiter hailed from some civilized northern European nation and managed to combine subservience with a whiff of aristocracy. "All our waiters were educated in their profession on the other side [i.e., in Europe] and spoke six or seven languages," George Rector claimed, and many had attended the College of Waiters in Geneva, Switzerland. Probably few hotelmen and restaurateurs could match Rector's boast truthfully, but George Boldt of the Waldorf-Astoria also sought out waiters who spoke several languages.[52]

A few employers experimented with hiring white women to wait table by the late nineteenth century. Like black men, white women were thought to have a natural aptitude for the work. But, again like black men, white women could not quite meet the standard set by white men: "While all admit that the work is of a class for which the female is better adapted, still the tendency to shiftlessness, neglect and even evil deportment, is so common in the class that apply for and fill such places" that the best hotels hired them only as dishwashers, laundresses, and chambermaids. In such positions, they remained safely hidden from the patrons. The precedent for hiring women to serve in restaurants was poor. The "waiter girls" who worked in some saloons at midcentury danced and sometimes had sex with patrons who bought drinks. Female workers tempted guests into private vice rather than affirm their elevated public status.[53]

By the end of the nineteenth century, however, hiring white women was starting to look like a good prospect. After 1883 Fred Harvey's successful importation of legions of white, female servants for his network of first-class, railroad depot restaurants in the West proved that waiting table could attract respectable, competent women workers and simultaneously provide diners with a refined experience. Other employers cogently pointed out that women would do the same work for half or less the already low wages of male waiters. Moreover, they were less prone to solicit tips and to strike.[54] The natural subordination of women workers could lessen the incursion of the commercial into hotel service without hindering rationalization. But the managers of first-class eating houses seem to have preferred the more costly, less docile white men, perhaps because their service signaled the class superiority of the patrons more powerfully than the work of "naturally subordinate" groups did.

But selecting waiters of the ideal race, origin, and gender did not guarantee excellence in service. The waiter's behavior and cleanliness were essential to the quality of the diner's experience, and hotel managers tried to enforce rigid standards. Beginning in 1901, the *Hotel Monthly* editor, John Willy, published a series of columns titled "The American Colored Waiter." The author was John B. Goins, "a well-known colored headwaiter." Goins devoted much of his column to the waiter's wardrobe and daily dress code, advised his readers on how often to bathe and launder their clothing, and reminded them often that they were not to talk, lean against walls, or otherwise indicate that they were not constantly vigilant of diners' comfort and yet respectful of their privacy. Above all, "every accessory must be in perfect keeping with the character of the service—rich and immaculate—and the waiter should spare no pains to make himself harmonious with his surroundings." [55]

Just what constituted "harmony" for this particular accessory to the dining experience caused some friction between hotel managers and waiters. George Boldt, the first manager of the Waldorf-Astoria, insisted that all the waiters shave their faces and then extended that requirement to the porters, hack drivers, and other men standing in wait to serve hotel patrons outside. Despite objections from the employees and other New Yorkers about this piece of tyranny, Boldt remained adamant, and either the man or the facial hair was removed.[56] The order indicated a thoroughly modern concern with cleanliness and its visual corollary, clean lines, in keeping with the contemporaneous changes in the decor of some extra-fare cars and hotels. It also suggested the extent to which hotel keepers would go to assure their patrons' comfort.

The only other area of hotel service to gain the amount of attention that the dining room did was the front desk. Here stood the hotel clerk, whose "chief duty is to 'face the audience'. . . ; doing his part to make the hotel what it should be, a home with the kindly atmosphere; delivering service to patrons of widely different tastes and dispositions." But clerks seemed rarely to achieve this ideal in the eyes of the customers. From the 1870s, they suffered from a bad reputation. "[T]he conventional American hotel clerk," Howells wrote, was a well-kept young man who sported diamonds on his shirt and fingers. "A gentle disdain for the travelling public breathed from his person." When the honeymooning Basil March inscribed his name in the register, the clerk "did not lift his haughty head to look at the wayfarer. . . ; he did not answer him when he begged for a cool room" but merely provided a key, called the bellboy, and resumed his conversation about a "mighty pooty gul" with a friend lounging nearby.[57]

The sympathetic editors of the hotel journals acknowledged that the clerk had to perform as a diplomat on what even hotel managers sometimes admitted was a low salary. Drawing on forty years as a clerk and supervisor, Henry Mower insisted: "As a class, they are hard-worked, attending closely to business, with seldom a holiday, many of them with families to support, and rarely a dollar they feel they can spend on themselves." The hotel clerk stood in much the same position as the department store saleswoman. Like her, the hotel clerk had to dress and behave with refinement equal to that of the hotel's patrons, an affluent group of men and women, yet also had to be appropriately deferential. The proverbial diamond pin on the clerk's shirtfront, which guests saw as an offensive claim to a status and wealth his position belied, might signal his own defensive insistence on social equality. His notorious indifference to waiting patrons confirmed his own, limited control over the hotel's resources.[58]

Further, the clerk bore the burden of trying to reconcile impossible demands with the hospitality of the house. In spite of his subordinate position, he was required to act as the human gatekeeper to the upper, private regions of the hotel: "[H]e must be able to read character as well as counterfeit money at a glance. He judges every guest as he registers his name. . . . He knows whom to assign the best rooms, and to what persons to say that the house is full." He had to make guests feel welcome and yet prevent them from damaging the house's furniture or, more important, its reputation. If patrons wanted to cash checks, the clerk had to choose between insulting their respectability and financial status by denying them the privilege or risking the ire of his employer for landing the hotel with bad paper.[59]

Moreover, as the century ended, clerks faced a greatly decreased chance of rising into the ranks of managers and hotel owners. As in other occupations, the trend toward salaried, midlevel managerial jobs and decreasing entrepreneurial opportunities was evident. The growing specialization and commercialization of hotel work meant that clerks no longer mingled socially with the guests. At midcentury, in contrast, they had often helped to carve the roasts at dinner and had the opportunity to become acquainted with long-term or frequent guests. By 1900 most hotel clerks seem to have come from the lower-middle classes and less often from the same ranks of society as the patrons they dealt with. Then, too, the vigorous protests of hotel journal editors and hotel keepers that the hardworking, honest, courteous clerk would inevitably end his life the prosperous owner of his own hostelry have a suspicious fervency:

> Did you ever see a turtle
> That w's crawlin' 'long the ground,
> . . . Making little headway, but
> Just tryin' all th' more
> . . . Well, that's the way with fellows

If they struggle and they try;
They're bound to find the current
That will help them, bye and bye.

That John Willy had to wish at the New Year in 1911 for the clerk to be regarded as "a gentleman as a matter of course" revealed the depths to which the front-desk man had fallen.[60]

The formation and membership of hotel workers' organizations solidified horizontal divisions that reflected the ongoing specialization of hotel work. The first was the Hotel Men's Mutual Benefit Association (HMMBA), established in 1879 to provide funeral benefits for all its members and their families. It was similar to many such groups founded by workingmen in the nineteenth century. At its founding the organization comprised mainly clerks but also included managers and proprietors. Suggesting the extent of its benevolence, longtime clerk and supervisor Henry Mower dedicated his 1912 memoir to the association that had helped to sustain him in his old age.[61]

But at the turn of the century, the organization's activities indicated strongly that its members were mostly managers and owners. The annual meetings had become three- and four-day extravaganzas during which the members gathered in the several first-class hotels of a particular city to be fêted by the local hotelmen. In 1910 the meeting took place in San Francisco, requiring the participating members from outside the Pacific Slope to travel for two to five days just to reach the city. They traveled in two large excursions of the New York–Boston and Midwest delegations and took time to do the sights along the way. The northeasterners traveled via New Orleans and stopped to see the San Antonio, El Paso, and Los Angeles hotels before coming north. The midwesterners took the more direct route from Chicago, but tarried to crowd thirty-five members into the hollowed-out trunk of a redwood tree before arriving in the city.

Once in San Francisco, the HMMBA members and their wives lodged and attended several lavish meals and meetings at the St. Francis and Fairmont Hotels, the city's finest. They visited Mount Tamalpais, Golden Gate Park, and the Cliff House, as well as taking a steamship tour around San Francisco Bay with a stop to visit a wine cellar. The homeward journeys were more varied, with some members choosing to visit the Pacific Northwest and Canada, others returning via Salt Lake City, Omaha, and Chicago. This was not a vacation most Americans could afford. It was also more extravagant than many other conventions

of the period. Even when the HMMBA meetings were held in cities in
the East and Midwest, closer to the homes of most members, the costs
in time and money were considerable. No one but hotel owners and
managers could afford to host or attend such affairs.[62]

By the twentieth century, the HMMBA's inability to represent all hotel workers was manifest. Associations of stewards and clerks had
formed at the city and state level as early as the 1890s, as had hotel managers' groups. In the twentieth century, the stewards formed the International Stewards Association, while the clerks united several smaller
organizations into the national Hotel Greeters of America in 1910. Less
noted by the editors of hotel journals and decried when they did receive
mention were waiters' persistent efforts to unionize in order to protest
their long hours, low pay, and poor working conditions.[63]

In the meantime, hotel journal editors exhorted managers and owners to organize an association to meet the challenge of increasing government regulation. Ben Branham, the editor of the *Hotel Bulletin,*
pointed out, "The H.M.M.B.A. is not the body to assume the functions
of such an association. Its objects are benevolent and social." One alternative was the American Hotel Protective Association (AHPA),
founded in 1911 to protect hotel managers from deadbeats by creating
an information network. Like the HMMBA, the AHPA's limited functions hindered its ability to serve as a viable national lobby. Just two
years after its creation, participants at an AHPA meeting formed a new
organization, the National American Hotel Congress (NAHC). Its purpose was to "improve and elevate the hotel business by securing the
needed uniform laws, fixing the status of the name 'hotel,' eliminating
many evils and accomplishing other good deeds." It was not until 1917
that the NAHC transformed itself from a midwestern regional organization into a national one with a new name, the American Hotel
Association.[64]

In short, by the turn of the century, professional and trade organizations had clearly defined and reinforced the horizontal lines dividing hotel workers. Hotel journal editors still printed exhortations emphasizing
unity: "A motto for hotel employees: Be loyal to your house." But the
lower-level employees, from waiters to clerks and stewards, developed
strong loyalties to each other and to their profession. The erosion of the
paternalistic, relatively unspecialized organization of the mid-nineteenth
century undermined the naturalization of social hierarchy so crucial to
providing a refined yet republican experience. By 1915 deference was
more clearly than ever a commodity that the patron bought. The same

blurring of hotel boundaries that turned the hotel into "a little world" rather than a home away from home made the relationship between the patron and the house's employees a businesslike one, with all the advantages and disadvantages of the cash nexus.[65]

The one element of the hotel business that could unite hotel workers from the manager to the lowliest chambermaid and bellboy was, of course, the customers. Like department store managers and saleswomen, hotel keepers and their employees were continually frustrated by their patrons. The perfection in furnishings, spatial organization, and service that hotelmen promised was difficult to deliver; the most harmonious accessory to the dining experience could not satisfy all customers. To offer their guests the best of everything, landlords had to charge prices their demanding guests complained about. To ensure the respectability and profitability of the hotel, they had to question the respectability and financial soundness of their patrons.

At the center of the moral questions plaguing hotels in the mid- to late nineteenth century was the ambiguity of its domestic yet commercial service. The segregation of space and the harmoniousness of the house's accessories could only do so much to disguise the fact that a hotel was a profit-making enterprise. An unusual piece published anonymously in 1883, "The Horrors of Hotel Life," highlighted the paradox of selling domesticity. Its author warned that, for all the guest knew, the soap beside the pitcher and washbasin "was used by the last guest to wash his body, his feet, or the syphilitic sore that marks him for death, and by him was laid back in the soap dish. . . . That same guest used the towel" and then dropped it on the floor. Next the chambermaid haphazardly cleaned the chamber pot, water pitcher, and basin with the contaminated cloth. Compounding this series of filthy acts, the hotel's penny-pinching laundry washed it with careless haste and the maid placed it, deceptively clean, once again by the equally misleading washbasin. Such horrors did not confine themselves to the bedroom: waiters blew their noses on the dining room napkins and maids used them for menstrual cloths.[66]

The horrors the author described were especially potent symbols of the dangers of a transient life among strangers. Syphilis at once brought to mind not simply a horrible disease but the illicit sexual activity presumed to be its cause. Hinting at illness and female sexuality, mucus and menstrual blood were two of the less publicly mentionable of body fluids. Although unique in its hysterical tone and explicit examples, the article all too accurately identified the central difficulty of the hotel business. On the one hand was the home, where mutual care and perfect knowledge ensured cleanliness of mind and body, and on the other the hotel, a large commercial operation in which the patronage of strangers, the desire for profit, and the carelessness of servants made the most ordinary and necessary actions perilous. To insist that syphilis, mucus, and menstrual blood invisibly stained the hotel's snowy linen violently upset the efforts of first-class hotel managers to balance the domestic and the commercial.

In invoking the purity and order of the home against the avaricious disorder of a commercial enterprise, this critic shared common themes with others who wrote not of physical filth but of the moral dangers of hotel life. From the early years of the nineteenth century, middle-class and elite Americans had a much-lamented tendency to reside in boardinghouses and hotels instead of private homes. "[T]he promiscuous herding together of families and individuals in the urban boardinghouses," one self-appointed critic argued in 1878, results in the "gradual loosening of family integrity and coherence, in lowering the standard of personal refinement and self-respect." [67]

Although the American plan hotel, designed to have more suites for long-term, family residence than single rooms, and the boardinghouse, a family home opened to paying guests, offered a close approximation of familial arrangements, both institutions suffered from a fatal flaw. The residents were unrelated strangers. Given the guests' mutual anonymity and the commercial motives of the landlady, they could all too easily be those fair-faced but deceptive characters, confidence men and prostitutes. No matter how fine, the boardinghouse and the hotel were ultimately commercial institutions, not households of intimately known people united by sentiment and law. They were not havens from the city but tiny microcosms of it. [68]

But the dangers did not end there. Hotel living abrogated the all-important isolation of the family as a haven from outside influences that only the freestanding residence could provide. Hotel families did not have to share the ritual family dinner together; instead, the meal became a social, not a domestic, occasion. As Benjamin Lloyd wrote in his 1876 account of San Francisco, "[R]estaurant living is entirely opposed to domesticity. It interrupts the private social intercourse and family meetings of members of the same household, and eventually weans them from home; thus tending to destroy the very traits and principles that our republic would have engendered." [69]

The member of the family most freed of familial obligations by hotel living was, of course, the wife and mother. Residing in rooms without

the necessity of keeping house and without the proper, complete authority over her children, a woman could fall into idleness and vice. Instead
of acting as a moral counterweight to the deceptions and competitiveness of the public realm, she would have the leisure to join it, shopping,
meeting friends, perhaps even having an affair. Meals did not serve as a
showcase of her housekeeping, cooking, and affective skills but rather
encouraged her vanity and preference for society instead of her family.[70]
Most common in the 1860s and 1870s, these complaints embody the
same fear found in the urban sketches, that commerce would enable
women to escape the bonds of their sex and that the republic could not
survive without its anchor in a moral private realm overseen by a dili-
gent and self-sacrificing mother.

Not surprisingly, women often favored hotel residence precisely because it relieved them of the burdens of maintaining a house and serving a family. Hotel managers sometimes advertised their houses' ability
to relieve patrons of such daily cares. But despite the frequent criticisms of hotel living, hotel keepers shared the mainstream ideas about
gender roles and family life of their contemporaries. They insisted on
the respectability of their accommodations, even as some acknowledged that they were not, perhaps, the best place for families. The physical structure and the services of the hotel were designed to reproduce
and encourage the prevailing ideals in gender segregation and refined
behavior.[71]

Unfortunately, gender segregation only worked properly in housing
men alone or men and women clearly and respectably linked by marriage or family ties. The woman traveling alone presented a serious problem for the hotel keeper. First came the practical problem of her registration at the hotel. Properly, she should enter by the segregated ladies'
entrance and bypass the bustling lobby, avoiding the gaze and remarks
of the men gathered there. Some hotels offered separate registration facilities in the second-floor ladies' parlor.[72] But the problem of registration only symbolized far more troublesome issues raised by the lone
woman's presence.

In the hotel keeper's catalog of problem guests, she was among the
most dangerous, for any immorality on her part undermined the hotel's
respectability in a way far more serious than passing bad checks or leaving without paying the bill, typical male crimes. To maintain its first-
class business in domestic accommodations, hotel keepers had to assure
their potential patrons that all their female guests were entirely respectable. If they were not, the establishment degenerated into an assignation

house; the city invaded the private sphere. Junius Browne devoted an entire chapter of his 1869 collection of New York sketches to the "adventuresses" who frequented boardinghouses and first-class hotels, wreaking havoc on male egos and good marriages. George Rector claimed that his turn-of-the-century New York hotel was ruined by the rumor that it harbored fast women.[73]

Hotel managers tried very hard to prevent such women from taking up residence. In practice, this effort to police the morals of female guests led hotels, and restaurants as well, to refuse to serve women traveling alone. Ernest Ingersoll advised the readers of Rand McNally's *A Week In New York* (1891), "It is well, therefore, for '[lone] women,' especially if young, to write or telegraph in advance of their intention to arrive at a certain time; or better yet to take a letter of introduction." He hastened to add that the "great probability is that she will meet with no more obstacle than if father or husband were with her; but if she does, she has only to insist upon her legal right, so long as her behavior is justifiable."[74] The next step was to take a cab to police headquarters. By that time the beleaguered woman would surely have given up hope of getting a good night's rest.

In general, the "solution" to the woman problem from the 1850s through 1915 was the provision of segregated facilities, but the nature of that segregation changed over time. Common in many institutions, the separation of unmarried women from men made it easier for guests, onlookers, and hotel managers to have faith in the respectable behavior of patrons. In addition to the ladies' entrances, parlors, and tearooms, by the early twentieth century some of the largest and fanciest hotels offered a women's floor, complete with a female clerk. Here, women traveling alone to shop or do business could register and reside without endangering their own or the hotel's reputation. At Chicago's La Salle Hotel, the management even hired a few "belle hops" to save female guests the distress of dealing with the boys who usually ran errands in hotels.[75]

Another solution was the all-women's hotel, a more definitive form of segregation. In the 1870s the dry goods magnate Alexander Stewart had attempted to establish a working-women's residential hotel in New York. The venture quickly failed because no working woman could afford to live there and very few respectable, middle-class single women could live outside of a family household. The hotel was renovated shortly after its opening in 1878 to become the first-class Park Avenue Hotel.[76]

But by the end of the nineteenth century, the idea of a women's hotel resurfaced, this time among female entrepreneurs.

In 1901, after three years' work to finance it, the Woman's Hotel Company launched the construction of the Martha Washington Hotel in New York. Like Stewart's effort, the hotel was intended to provide decent accommodations for respectable young women, but its founders had a more upscale clientele in mind. The Martha Washington catered mainly to the growing numbers of white, middle-class women engaged in professions or pursuing higher education and living outside of a male-headed household. For the most part a residential hotel serving few transients, it was one of many turn-of-the-century attempts to house working women in institutions that provided some of the security and oversight of the private home and yet acknowledged their growing independence.[77]

Women alone were not the only ones presumed immoral; even married women accompanying their husbands might face embarrassing difficulties. When a man was traveling with his wife, he signed the register with his name followed by "and wife." ("And lady" was dangerously ambiguous.) This phrase notified the hotel staff that the woman present in his room was respectable, but, unfortunately, the honor system was not entirely reliable. For example, a man might claim a woman as his wife who was not; or he might forget to indicate that his wife accompanied him; or he might invite women to his room without notifying the hotel.[78] These were urban dangers: the hotel keeper could not personally vouch for the paying guest, and the guest felt no necessary compunction in abusing the host's hospitality, for they were unknown to each other. The propriety of the relationship between the guest "and wife" rested on the guest's word alone, not community knowledge.

In each case, the hotel's reputation suffered. Managers were eager to minimize the damage by evicting the wrongdoers. But neither the clerk nor the hotel manager always had perfect insight into the legal standing and moral character of the guests. The result was that mistakes were made. One hapless night clerk confused Martins and Mortons, concluding that whoever they were, they were not properly married to their roommates. He compelled the Martins to leave the hotel at night, both Mrs. Martin and Mrs. Morton became ill, and "[b]oth husbands and both wives . . . filed separate suits."[79] News of similar lawsuits regularly appeared in the pages of hotel journals at the turn of the century.

But by that time, hotel managers more and more often denied any responsibility for the private transgressions of their patrons. They insisted that the problem lay with the guests who abused the house's hospitality and called for criminal penalties to be levied against hotel guests who committed immoral acts: "Let the burden rest upon the parties who use the hotel and not the parties who run the hotel."[80] Holding patrons, rather than the landlord, to blame once again underscored the abandonment of the effort to create a moral community within the hotel. As frankly commercial enterprises, hotels did not need to police their patrons' morals but simply to provide services as long as their behavior did not offend. Not refinement and mutual knowledge but public decorum and a bill paid in full would assure a harmonious social order.

The decline of refined standards went hand in hand with increases in single women's income and a growing range of respectable reasons for their presence in public. As a result, women alone and in groups began to receive a more hospitable welcome at many restaurants and hotels. The *Hotel World* noted, "It begins to look very much as if the attitude of hotel keepers in the metropolis [New York] were experiencing sudden and radical change. Woman patronage, without male escorts, is invited." A number of small but symbolic events signaled the growing acceptability of women's presence in semipublic, commercial institutions. In some first-class hotel restaurants, men were now permitted to smoke in the presence of women. One New York hotel decided to allow women to smoke in public wherever men were allowed to do so, to the dismay of some hotel journal editors.[81]

By the early twentieth century, the new policies in hotels and restaurants suggested that gender segregation was no longer a necessary element of refinement. The hotel architect Henry Hardenbergh wrote in 1901, "[T]he setting apart of rooms for . . . women is being abandoned." The Martha Washington eased its women-only policies in 1908, when the management opened a restaurant that both sexes could patronize. Yet gender segregation persisted and even flourished in the early twentieth century; what changed was its character. City hotels increasingly offered women amenities previously restricted to men—a bar and a billiard room, for example. The Martha Washington permitted cocktails to be served in celebration of its new restaurant, accepting that women as well as men might enjoy alcohol. The great internal corridors of the palace hotels, especially the Waldorf-Astoria's Peacock Alley, replaced or supplemented the ladies' parlors, allowing women to lounge, gossip, and promenade in semipublic splendor as men did in the hotel's central rotunda. In 1911 a speaker at the Chicago Hotel Association even de-

clared proudly that there should be no hotel "to which a father could
not enter with his daughters and walk about its first floor." [82] One imag-
ines an updated image of the Palmer House's lobby, now showing a father escorting his young daughter instead of his son.

If their anxieties about fornication and female smoking were easing
somewhat by the 1900s, hotel managers now faced another looming
threat, and it too derived from the lessening influence of the ideology
of refinement. The editors of hotel journals wrote with increasing frequency in the 1890s and 1900s in defense of the hotel bar, for the startling success of the Prohibition movement threatened their claims to provide genteel sites for male leisure. Hotel keepers wanted a statutory
definition of "hotel" that would clearly distinguish between hotels and
saloons. The difference, they argued, was that the hotel bar and dining
room served alcohol in a domestic space, and, as commercial homes, hotels had to serve patrons what they wanted. But by the turn of the century, the tasteful furnishings and artwork adorning the hotel bar no
longer sustained such claims, for hotels were ceasing to be homes away
from home. Betraying the weakness of their argument, hotelmen argued
defensively that fewer men were drinking anyway and hotel bar profits
were smaller than ever. [83]

The hotelmen's turn to the government for legal aid in establishing
their good repute exemplified their new understanding of their public
role. Instead of policing their patrons and fostering community among
them, they sought to protect their houses' reputations by legislating distinctions in accommodations. The editors of hotel journals in the early
years of the twentieth century continually harped on the need for a legal
definition of the word *hotel*, distinguishing respectable hostelries not
just from saloons but also from cheap lodging houses and brothels. "It
is a well known fact that there are many places conducted under the
name of 'hotel,' . . . which are not in fact hotels," Harry Hess, attorney
for the Ohio State Hotel Association, declared in 1911. "These alleged
hotels . . . are in truth and in fact 'dives.'" [84] Not only were saloons,
lodging houses, and brothels sometimes criminal, they were low-class. A
statutory definition of these differences in clientele and services would
aid hotel keepers' efforts to construct a thoroughly modern public realm,
bolstered by the power of the state rather than by means of the patrons'
collective and visible respectability.

The difficult questions of Jewish and African American patronage
also occasionally challenged the efforts to maintain an exclusive, refined
social climate in first-class hotels. There seems to have been some sym-

pathy for Jews who were refused rooms, at least in the 1870s. Noting the exclusion of a "Mr. Oppenheimer" from a leading hotel in the resort town of Saratoga, one editor commented, "The Jews are going to open an opposition hotel. No Gentiles need apply. . . . [but] Christians will be admitted." [85] But at least among some Christian hotel keepers, either personal or commercial anti-Semitism led to the refusal to accommodate Jewish travelers.

African Americans did not even gain a sympathetic line in the hotel journals. They appeared there only as waiters or troublesome legal problems. "A number of negroes have created something of a sensation by visiting several of the leading hotels and demanding drinks," the *Hotel World*'s New York correspondent reported in 1903. In all but one bar, the men received their drinks; in the exception, the other patrons forced them to leave. The consensus among hotelmen was that "the best way out of the trouble is to obey the law but discourage the patronage as much as possible." In restaurants, a later piece advised, "by using a little ingenuity some portion of the room may always be reserved for emergencies . . . without offending race or caste." [86] The civil rights laws of the 1860s and 1870s caused hotel keepers as much—and as little— worry as they did the Pullman company.

In 1915 as in 1850, the managers of first-class hotels promised their patrons the finest in everything. Their scale, interior splendor, good service, and technological wonders made them exemplars of the best that cities had to offer to the well-to-do. But in 1850 hotels had also labored to protect their guests from the dangers of urban life through the organization of their interiors and services. By 1915 first-class hostelries had largely abandoned their efforts to resemble the well-to-do household and to host the tangible republic. Guests had an increasing range of commercial choices and a decreasing obligation to integrate themselves into a community. The city outside came into the hotel and hotel guests ventured out of it to eat and amuse themselves.

Like the extra-fare cars, first-class city hotels undermined the sociospatial ideal that joined refinement and republicanism by providing the former for a fee. As their urbanity and commercialism became more apparent, their claim to contain a microcosm of the republic dissolved. Hosting fewer locals and long-term guests, hotels adapted their spaces and services to a rising number of transients with little or no expectation of joining local, respectable social circles. As a result, hotels created physical and social spaces not just open to transients but dedicated to them and increasingly distinct from the spaces that locals used. The travelers who occupied these spaces engaged in spatial practices separate from the everyday movements of city residents. In short, by the 1890s first-class urban hotels helped to create the cultural and material context in which urban tourism was plausible.

But extra-fare cars and splendid hotels in and of themselves were not enough to make American cities part of the tourist's itinerary. To attract pleasure travelers, the nation's cities had to offer respectable amusements, splendid public places, and a new understanding of the consequences of public leisure. Urban geography had to be transformed both imaginatively and physically for city touring to become attractive. The nation's tour companies and city businessmen's organizations took that task upon themselves.

FOUR

"Why Not Visit Chicago"

Tour Companies and City Business Organizations, 1870–1915

"There is a fascination about the great metropolitan cities of the world that cannot be entirely explained," Richard Henry Little mused in about 1905. "[T]hese great metropolitan cities . . . act as wonderful magnets upon humanity." Little provided several explanations for this strange urban magnetism: the great wealth that enabled cities to build magnificent buildings and improve urban landscapes; "the combined mental radiation from such enormous numbers of people"; cities' appeal to a natural human gregariousness; or perhaps "the [individual's] opportunity of seeing all kinds of his fellows of high and low degree, of observing how they live and what they do." Ritually invoking the beauties of Paris and London, Little then turned to the subject of his essay: "The Charm of Chicago." [1]

This startling juxtaposition of an American city, less than one hundred years old and notorious for its vulgar commercialism, to two of the great capitals of Europe marked an important change. In the mid-nineteenth century, Americans had flocked to urban centers to find work, to do business, and to explore and alleviate the dangerous social conditions existing there. Many had disported themselves in the streets, ice-cream parlors, saloons, and concert halls. But urban social relations and spatial organization did not lend themselves to the refined pursuit of the beautiful and the historic that was the essence of nineteenth-century tourism. When they entered the nation's cities, well-to-do Americans necessarily confronted the tensions among their republican principles, their refined ideals, and the vigorous expansion of a market economy. Whether delighted or despairing, they were not tourists.

By the 1890s, however, the United States's largest cities attracted growing numbers of visitors whose only aim was to "do" the town, "seeing all kinds of [their] fellows of high and low degree." Several factors contributed to this development. Travel was easier and more comfortable, and a widening range of people had time and income to devote to touring. The first-class city hotels and the extra-fare cars provided spaces that fostered refinement while accommodating social and physical transience. By charging prices that excluded the unrefined, these institutions mitigated the reluctance of genteel people to take their leisure in public. At the same time, the splendid urbanity and commercialism of hotels and extra-fare cars eroded the opposition between culture and commerce, public and private. As Little suggested, urban crowds might exercise a magnetic attraction on the gregarious visitor rather than endanger the refined individual. Together, these changes made urban tourism possible.

But the possibility of urban tourism did not add up to its actuality. The expansion of refined public spaces and the partial reconciliation of refinement with commerce did not automatically lead well-to-do Americans to write or read about "the charm of Chicago" without laughing, much less to plan a visit. Behind the emergence of domestic urban tourism lay vigorous efforts by tour companies and city businessmen's organizations to promote pleasure travel as the means to individual and civic regeneration. Little's essay, suitably enough, appeared in a membership booklet of the Chicago Association of Commerce, an organization founded in the early twentieth century to promote the city's business interests. Like other city business associations, it played a key role in encouraging urban pleasure travel and shaping tourists' itineraries once they arrived.

By the 1890s tour companies regularly boasted about the reinvigorating power of travel, encouraging Americans to conceive of leisure, not home, as the opposite of work. Their expanding services tended to separate pleasure travelers from other passengers and from the residents of the places they passed through. Even more than extra-fare cars and fine hotels, organized tours offered their members a refined community based on transience and commercial patronage, not mutual recognition. Having eased the social concerns that the well-to-do had felt about public, urban leisure, tour companies also created short city excursions to appeal to a new class of tourist, comfortable but not wealthy. These conceptual and practical changes underlay the growing popularity of urban tourism.

The efforts of tour agencies and city business organizations to promote pleasure travel and to popularize urban destinations were part of a widespread reevaluation of the uses of leisure and public space in the United States at the turn of the century. Liberal clergy more and more often conceded the possibility of wholesome theatricals and dancing. Progressive reformers agitated for small parks to provide poor city residents with healthy opportunities for play outside their cramped apartments. The leading reformer Jane Addams argued that simply watching a baseball game could unify sadly divided communities. Advocates of the City Beautiful movement campaigned for the construction of neo-classical city centers intended to rehabilitate public life.[2]

Organized businessmen shared with these diverse movements the assumption that the provision of fine public spaces devoted to rationalized leisure was the best hope for forging legitimate social bonds in an irredeemably urban, industrial society. Public leisure was now to be the parent of virtue, not vice. Yet, while most reformers saw public, regulated leisure as the last haven of culture against the expansion of commercialism, many businessmen believed that it reconciled the pursuit of profit with strengthened community relations.[3] Consequently, they placed commercial leisure at the center of their vision of a renewed civic social order.

From one perspective, viewing public recreation as the means of reviving urban community was the culmination of long-standing efforts to refine the city and city dwellers by extending the reign of the middle-class home outward. But doing so breached the boundary between the private and public spheres. As a result, the vision of cities as harmonious landscapes combining beauty and commerce required a new set of spatial practices. For their promoters, tourist itineraries embodied a way of seeing and moving through a city that enabled the journeyer to perceive it as an integrated whole, not a patchwork of antagonistic regions. Ideal urban citizens, tourists modeled a kind of vicarious, collective ownership that promised to obviate conflicts rooted in work and the division of wealth. Now visitors would teach city dwellers how to live in the city rather than learn local customs.

"THE RAW AND THE COOK'D"

Travel businesses were among the chief agents of the changing meaning
of pleasure travel in particular and leisure more broadly. In promoting
travel as a good in and of itself, they altered the rationale for tourism and
contributed to the rehabilitation of leisure. By means of organized tours,
they helped to separate tourists from the societies they traveled through,
diminishing the sense of moral obligation that animated the ideology
of republican refinement. Both the growing social distance between travelers and locals and the commercial rehabilitation of refined leisure
made it possible to conceive of the nation's cities as appropriate for refined leisure. Tour companies began to exploit that new possibility by
the 1890s.

As the twentieth century began, tour companies and railroad passenger departments urged Americans to travel, not in search of aesthetic uplift or social progress, but because "[o]ne who works with mind or body
or both . . . requires relaxation. . . . The mind is strengthened and in-
vigorated, and the spirits quickened by new and interesting experiences
and adventure." And this quickening was not to be had in the dull environs of everyday life: "One should travel a good distance from home
to realize these advantages." [4] This approach had an obvious appeal for
the enterprises promoting travel, but it had not been common before the
turn of the century.

Indeed, campaigns to encourage pleasure travel had not always been
common, even though the railroads had served and augmented the
tourist trade as early as the 1840s, particularly in New England. The
railroads increased access to the White Mountains region of New
Hampshire and Vermont and relatively quickly extended the circuit up
into Canada, including Montreal and Quebec, and descending through
Maine. Travelers soon could reach the major northeastern resorts, especially those near Niagara Falls, by rail. The change in the means of transportation did not necessarily transform the reasons for or the experience
of travel. Although excitingly fast for passengers accustomed to stage-
coach travel, the relatively slow speeds of many trains, between twenty
and forty miles per hour, complemented and encouraged the leisurely
contemplation of beautiful landscapes. The New York Central boasted
of the beauties of its route through the Hudson River and Mohawk valleys; the Southern Pacific called its line between Portland and Los Angeles "The Road of a Thousand Wonders." [5] From the 1870s, express

trains and extra-fare car consists often included an open back platform or a large-windowed observation car. Even in such a contested, public space as the railroad car, the traveler had ample opportunity for the aesthetic quest proper to the good nineteenth-century tourist.

But although the tourist trade was potentially lucrative, some railway men were reluctant to encourage it. In 1850–51 the men who controlled the "Northern Lines of Railway" held a convention in Boston to discuss this aspect of their business. By their own admission, some of their number had indulged recklessly in the excursion trade in the summer of 1850. They had offered fares at less than half price on the routes to popular regional resorts in the hope of encouraging traffic. But the result seemed to be a diversion of regular riders to days when the excursion fare was available. A greater number of riders had not materialized to offset the lower ticket prices. By the end of their meeting, the railroad managers resolved to place some nonbinding limits on the excursion trade. One resolution gained unanimous support without any debate: "That Excursion Trains shall never be advertised by Railroad companies."[6]

Given the intense rivalries of mid-nineteenth-century railroading, the resolution probably did nothing to curb fare wars, including excursion rates. But its unanimous endorsement by the conferees indicates that, although railroads served pleasure travel at midcentury, their managers thought it was a potential threat to the more important regular traffic. Writing half a century later, the economist Walter Weyl attributed their reluctance to promote tourism to moral qualms: "In the beginning it was assumed, although tacitly, that traveling for the mere sake of traveling was not to be encouraged." Whatever their scruples, the railroad managers' opposition to pleasure travel steadily declined as the roads consolidated their mileage and developed the administrative infrastructure to make excursion rates reliably profitable. In 1906 one chronicler of the expansion of American railroads declared confidently that "the desire for travel is universal."[7]

If this claim were true, the credit belonged in part to the tourist agencies, a growing number of which had encouraged touring since the 1870s with an abandon that would have unnerved the cautious New England railroad men of 1850. By the 1890s the tour companies were competing with more and more railroad passenger departments and travel information bureaus. These businesses were conveniently located in train stations, downtown business centers, and even department

stores in many large and midsized American cities. They appealed to an
increasing number of potential travelers whose real income and leisure
time were on the rise. Producing a growing stream of promotional publications to advertise an ever-increasing list of resorts and routes, including the nation's major cities, they transformed the rationale for touring
and the experience of pleasure travel.[8] One result of this change was the
emergence of big cities as tourist destinations.

The earliest tour companies served English travelers to the Lake
Country and to Europe. The most successful grew out of the unpaid efforts of Thomas Cook, an English cabinetmaker, printer, and evangelical reformer. In 1841 Cook negotiated with the Midland Railroad to organize a short excursion for the temperance organization to which he
belonged. Pleased to have full cars, within a few years the railroad began to pay him a commission for arranging similar outings, and Cook
went into the business full time. By the 1850s he had similar contacts
with railroads throughout the British Isles and Europe. The scope of his
services expanded from obtaining railroad tickets to reserving seats, hotels, carriages, and other necessities for his clients.[9]

Cook's goals in launching his business were admirable: he sought to
uplift ordinary English men and women by offering them the same privilege of travel that the wealthy enjoyed. The opportunity to go abroad
not only diminished the differences between the middling and the well-
to-do at home but also promoted international tolerance and diverted
men and women from immoral recreations, especially alcohol. Although
his business steadily upgraded its image and attracted a wealthier (and
less straitlaced) clientele, Cook continued to speak of the philanthropic
ends of his business and occasionally ran excursions at a loss for workingmen. Like George Pullman, Cook understood his profitable enterprise also to be an important public service through which "the broad
distinctions of classes are removed without violence or any objection-
able means."[10]

Cook first brought his system to the United States in 1865, after the
"disorganisation of the Great Republic" had ceased. But, despite Cook's
Christian and republican aims, American railroads did not welcome him
or his business. A few years later, Cook wrote that "jealousies of Agents
and rivalries of competing lines . . . frustrated my plans" so thoroughly
that he conceded defeat in 1867. Nevertheless, he saw great opportunities for the tour business in the United States. Apparently no such enterprises yet existed and railroad excursion and through-ticket programs

were not extensive or well organized. In 1871 the firm returned to the United States, now in partnership with an American, E. M. Jenkins, whose European journey with a group of Knights Templars Cook had arranged.[11]

What Cook had to overcome was the same fear that the New England railway men had expressed in 1850—that cheap excursion travel would diminish regular traffic without increasing the total number of passengers to compensate. To succeed, Cook & Son had to acquire the right to act as ticket agent for as many railroads as possible, and American railway managers apparently feared his system might benefit other roads to their detriment. They were reluctant to promise a uniform low rate per mile for travelers with Cook's tickets when they did not know what other roads might do. The tour company worked hard to assure them: "it was never our intention or expectation to interfere with local or ordinary traffic; . . . our wish was to create a new traffic, by inducing people to travel."[12]

Following Cook's example, tour agencies made it their business to encourage pleasure travel as distinct from other forms. The result was the creation of a set of institutions and spatial practices that tended to separate tourism from everyday life and tourists from other travelers and from nontravelers. Like the extra-fare cars and hotels, tour agencies furnished refined spaces whose occupants were transient and defined by wealth, yet identified with egalitarianism and uplift. Such institutions and spatial practices solidified the social distance between the refined and the unrefined and furthered the rehabilitation of public leisure. Pioneering refined communities shaped by commercial patronage rather than mutual recognition, tourists modeled social relations designed for an urban, industrial, and class-divided society.

Again, Cook's firm led the way. Despite continuing "objections arising from rivalry and competition," Thomas Cook & Son finally inaugurated a series of American tours like those it offered in England and Europe in May 1874. These "tours" were model itineraries for which the agency had tickets available. As an agent for multiple roads, the company could provide prospective travelers with much more extensive information about routes and fares than a railroad's own ticket agent. Cook and his employees were also admirably inventive in creating dozens of similar but not quite identical itineraries from a limited range of routes. Although a severe economic depression afflicted the United States in the 1870s, the nation's first tourist agency survived and even claimed that business was booming: "Our American tourist business in this sec-

ond year of its infancy has been very large"—larger than that done by
all the railroad companies in New York.[13]

Although Thomas Cook & Son was the biggest and best known of
nineteenth-century tour agencies, other companies soon joined the field.
E. M. Jenkins, the Cooks' partner, split with them in the 1870s when
they accused him of being profligate with their money; by the early 1880s
he had launched his own tour company. The premier American firm was
Raymond & Whitcomb, founded in Boston in 1879 to serve the high
end of the trade. The firm erected a luxury resort hotel in Pasadena in
the 1880s, helping to launch southern California's career as a tourist
mecca, and sponsored elegant tours throughout the United States and
around the world. Advertisements in travel magazines and the few brochures preserved in archives suggest that many other Americans also decided to go into the tourist business. By 1893 the competition was fierce
enough to prompt *Cook's Excursionist* to warn its readers "[t]hat numbers of incompetent and irresponsible persons, whose only qualifica-
tions are the possession of considerable assurance and an office sign, do
pose as tourist agents." [14]

The railroads' general passenger departments also began courting
pleasure travelers more actively toward the end of the nineteenth century. Changes in the way railroads and tour companies publicized their
expanding services marked the campaign. The simple timetables and
travelers' guides of midcentury became brightly written and often illustrated folders promoting the scenery and comforts of the road. They
talked about travel instead of simply providing information. More and
more often, the railroads offered general incitements to travel in addition to advertisements for their lines. They targeted journeyers who had
more in mind than reaching a destination and hoped to encourage this
frame of mind in all passengers. In doing so, they contributed to the rise
of the tourist as a distinct social type defined by transience and nonpar-
ticipation in the local social order.[15]

The New York Central Railroad, for example, began publishing a
line of folders called *The Four-Track Series*, selling them to patrons perhaps as early as the 1870s. In the 1890s it produced a monthly bulletin
containing timetables, lists of railroad officials, notes on train routes,
tips for travelers, advertising, and random jokes. In 1901 a monthly titled *The Four-Track News*, "designed as an auxiliary" to the folders,
first appeared. Using a double-column, short-item format, it combined
travel trivia and middlebrow humor with more or less undisguised pro-
motions for the New York Central and the resorts and cities along its

lines. This information might be useful and entertaining to any traveler, whatever his or her reason for journeying.

Apparently a success, the journal rapidly grew in size and included longer, topical features and fewer jokes. In 1902 it gained a new subtitle, "A Monthly Magazine of Travel and Education," and boasted that in "form and size" it now "corresponds to the popular style of current monthlies." As a result, it could now "publish handsome, full-page half-tone illustrations" and feature articles by some of the best writers of the day. In 1906 the periodical became a large-format, glossy magazine titled simply *Travel*. The editorial duties shifted from the road's general passenger agent to a professional editor. Rather than an auxiliary to the railroad's promotional brochures, the magazine now presented itself as "a periodical for those active-minded men and women who are interested in the recreation, opportunities and cultural advantages which travel affords."[16] In short, it was aimed at tourists and intended to encourage pleasure travel.

The *Four-Track News* and *Travel* had plenty of competition. Beginning in 1897, the Baltimore & Ohio Railroad published *The Book of the Royal Blue*. The Southern Pacific's *Sunset* entered the lists in 1898 with the aim of illustrating "in pictures and text, the beauties and opportunities of the territory served by the railroad." In 1914 the staff and stockholders bought the magazine from the railroad and turned it into an independent promoter of the Pacific West; tourism continued to be an important topic. Thomas Cook & Son had begun publishing an American edition of its *Cook's Excursionist* in 1873. It remained chiefly a vehicle for publicizing the company's many itineraries and organized tours until 1903, when it, too, gained a glossy new format. Other tour companies also put out journals that both advertised the company's wares and promoted travel in general.[17] The existence of such periodicals indicated the commercial incentive to generate interest in leisure journeys. This kind of literature also embellished the distinctiveness and attractiveness of tourism as a social activity.

During the same years, travel information bureaus proliferated, usually as adjuncts to newspapers, magazines, guidebook publishers, and organizations of resort owners. New England, New York, and the San Francisco Bay Area supported associations dedicated to promoting tourism in the early twentieth century. By 1912 the tourist business had become big enough to support its own trade show, the Travel and Vacation Exhibition, in New York. The institutional infrastructure of pleasure travel lacking in 1850 now existed.[18] These proliferating institutions of travel constructed a new kind of transient space that enabled well-to-do Americans to travel apart from the kin and class networks in which travelers at midcentury had been embedded. When they joined a tour, travelers stepped out of the context of their everyday lives and existed apart from local social relations. That new distance eased anxieties about public interactions and raised the possibility of urban tourism.

In enabling tourists to travel outside of local spaces and social relations, tour agencies both embodied and ameliorated the consequences of industrialization and urbanization. Often, the most important service that the agencies offered was good information about services, access, and destinations. "Those who contemplate making a journey are prone to spend a great deal of time . . . going from one railroad office to another making inquiries," an advertisement for Lansing's General Ticket Office lamented. "Often, alas! all this labor and expenditure results only in confusion and doubt." In a world made strange by anonymity and distance, tour companies promised that the "[i]nformation is authentic because someone connected with the Ask Mr. Foster bureau has been there." [19] Professional, systematic knowledge promised to replace the traveler's personal knowledge or reliance on local contacts.

With the expert help of an agency employee, one could plan an itinerary or choose one already set up and purchase all of the tickets necessary, often at a slight discount. Doing so eliminated the uncertainty about routes, times, and fares that plagued midcentury travelers. Since credit networks were limited and travelers had to carry easy-to-steal cash or difficult-to-use letters of credit, making one payment at the start for all railroad tickets, baggage transfers, and sometimes hotel rooms and meals likely relieved travelers of much anxiety. This method, or simply buying tickets from the railroad, was known as "independent" travel.[20] It departed least from the way travelers made arrangements without the aid of a tour company.

Independent travel still left plenty of chance for physical and social discomfort on the cars or at one's destination. The alternative was the "personally conducted" tour, which went much further to separate tourists from their everyday lives as well as from locals. In extending his business to Europe in the 1850s, Thomas Cook had accompanied his parties in order to manage all interactions with the locals—thus "personally conducted." His firm soon became famous for this innovation, and as it expanded he hired other men to act as conductors.[21]

Significantly, this modern, efficient, mass-produced version of the Grand Tour involved more egalitarian social relations than its aristocratic model. Calling his conductors "business managers," Cook insisted on their superiority to the low-class couriers hired by the wealthy: "they are gentlemen of education, who mingle with their parties on terms of perfect equality." The conductors performed the same duties as couriers, but they were respectable professional men, not servants; they represented a company, not a class. The organized tour not only expanded access to travel but also replaced uncertain, individual service relationships with institutional, professional ones. The conductor, unlike many couriers, was not a local; his loyalties lay with the company and his duties focused on the travelers. The innovation in management opened a new physical and social distance between travelers and the societies they traveled through.[22]

This altered service relationship accompanied and encouraged a growing conceptual distance between leisure and work. The gentleman conductor's presence and the prearranged itinerary assured tourists that they could devote themselves entirely to refined sight-seeing. They did not need to worry about logistics, the character of their guide, or the worthiness of what they saw or did not see: "Our conductors know precisely what to do in every place they go. . . ; if one day is sufficient to see a city or town, only one day is given." The contrast with "independent" travel was striking:

> Only those who have traveled in one of these 'Personally Conducted' parties can properly appreciate the relief and benefit obtained by the tourist through having nothing to do with the cares and details of the journey. . . . [A]ll that the members of our parties have to do is to enjoy themselves.

Stephen Merritt, a vacationing minister, heartily agreed: "We write and sight; we eat and sleep; we talk and walk; and go to heaven on wheels."[23]

In advertising their services in this way, the tour companies participated in the rehabilitation of leisure. As early as the 1860s, cultural leaders such as the Reverend Henry Ward Beecher were assuring their prosperous listeners and readers that time spent away from work and domestic obligations was not necessarily wasted or a step on the path to perdition. By the turn of the century, most liberal Protestant clergy agreed that an occasional, wholesome respite from labor renewed a person's vigor and commitment to the work ethic. Railroad passenger departments and tour companies adopted and energetically promoted this idea. "All sensible people recognize the fact," *Cook's Excursionist* lectured in 1892, "that by taking a rational amount of rest and recreation, a man not only obtains more pleasure and satisfaction in life, but is enabled to accomplish more and better work." [24] An alternative to drink in the 1840s, tourism had become by the 1890s the rational complement to a life of disciplined labor.

Tempering the social discomforts of the railroad cars in the United States was an important part of removing the tourist from the everyday and lessening the dangers of public leisure. Like the extra-fare car, the organized tour promised both to extend opportunities once available only to the rich to the middle classes and to exclude those who were not refined. The exclusionary tendency in refinement and the rehabilitation of leisure went hand in hand: public recreation became acceptable and even virtuous to the extent that the troubling presence of unrefined people and activities were removed from public spaces. In turn, the redrawn spatial and social boundaries eroded the mid-nineteenth-century sense of a shared moral community, making urban tourism thinkable.

In assuring their clients that they would have "first-class" accommodations throughout the tour, tour companies promised the greatest comfort and the greatest exclusivity available. "In the belief that our patrons demand everything possible in the way of first-class and elaborate service," one Raymond & Whitcomb brochure declared, the company provided vestibuled Pullman sleeping, parlor, and dining cars for all of its California tours. Many tour companies also chartered extra-fare cars for their tours, but Raymond & Whitcomb went a step further and leased a locomotive as well, enabling the company to set the schedule and speed of the train "expressly for the purpose of affording superior facilities for sight-seeing." [25]

Whether in chartered cars or on chartered trains, a personally conducted tour ensured even more than the extra-fare car that the traveler would not encounter socially heterogeneous crowds and, in turn, that tourists increasingly occupied social spaces distinct from local ones. "In the cars [our travelers] form a select company, and are relieved of the annoyance of being placed in proximity to strangers, and, as it often happens in the common way of traveling, undesirable people." Tour companies did not have to work very hard to exclude such undesirables. The cost of many excursions in money and time put them out of the reach of the vast majority of Americans. At a time when a respectable middle-class income ranged between $900 and $1,500 annually and credit cards were rare, typical excursions cost a few hundred dollars and took a month or more. On the short side was a two-week, $150 trip from Chicago to Yellowstone in 1908. To go all the way to California on this tour required forty days and $350. Such tours offered their members some

savings, for the first Baedeker written for the United States (1893) esti-
mated the cost of train travel at $10 per day or $20 for a full twenty-four
hours.[26]

But the party itself, no matter how "select" and carefully separated
from the outside world, still posed the problem of unacquainted strangers brought together by commercial patronage. Tour companies made
two rather contradictory claims to assuage this anxiety. First, they
claimed that members of the party would form a "small and congenial
company of fellow-travelers" much like a private touring party. The
amiable Reverend Merritt praised Raymond & Whitcomb for fulfilling
this promise: "The people comprising the company without exception
are very nice; no airs, no foolishness, Catholic and Protestant and Jew
we are one. . . . [A]ll seem to be very unselfish, except the smokers and
that band."[27]

Second, the tour agents pointed out that families or friends in the
party would be seated together, guaranteeing them more privacy than
they would find traveling outside the tour. The Buffalo businessman Augustus Franklin Tripp, offical recorder of an 1893 trip to California that
he and his wife took with nine acquaintances, meticulously detailed the
collective side trips and Kodak adventures of "the Buffalo eleven" without remarking on the other forty-odd excursionists in the party.[28] The
tour companies promised, and often delivered, urbanity at its best: not
only were the members of the party refined people, but one did not have
to associate with them in any case. The personally conducted tour, like
the first-class urban hotel, created a public space and activity that diminished the importance of mutual knowledge in regulating public social
interactions.

In addition to excluding the unrefined, tour companies addressed the
problem of social interaction with strangers by making sure that their
travelers had a generous amount of space. Each adult passenger enjoyed
a double berth to himself or herself, and married couples usually had
an entire section. In the daytime, this meant that every two people had
rights to four seats and a window. Moreover, on most tours members of
the party had the same seat and berth throughout the journey. Reserving a particular seat and berth strengthened the passenger's temporary
ownership of it, ensuring both a physical and a social space of one's own
on the cars. The tour company's provision of such social and structural
boundaries enabled their already "select" parties to enact gentility more
easily than they might in the ordinary extra-fare car.[29]

But in spite of the manifest benefits of organized tours in relieving the

traveler of work, worry, and the presence of "undesirables," they earned
bitter scorn from their earliest days. Organized tourists were treated like
sheep, the critics claimed, given "little time to breathe, certainly . . .
scant opportunity to see anything, or to appreciate what they saw." According to their enemies, the mass-produced nature of the organized
tour defeated the real purpose of pleasure travel: aesthetic contemplation and personal enlightenment. Instead of empowering its participants, the tour undermined their autonomy, just as other forms of mass
production promised to emancipate but instead trapped people into ever
more rigid and numbing lives.[30]

Tour companies both defended the organized tour's purposes and denied that it had a mass-produced character at all. Packaged travel, tour
company owners insisted, enabled the many to enjoy the broadening influences of travel once restricted to the wealthy. While the "wealthy traveler is indeed a monarch," still, the member of an organized tour need
know "nothing of the delays and unpleasant experiences which Dame
Rumor reports as falling to the lot of strangers and unprotected tourists." Besides, tour companies did much to make their tourists feel like
monarchs. In addition to elegant accommodations, they offered their
members souvenir menus and membership lists, flowers for the ladies,
and other tokens of appreciation.[31]

In addition to splendid material conditions, organized touring served
philanthropic ends, according to its partisans. Although few companies
could claim the humble and virtuous beginnings of Cook & Son, all
shared its assumption that pleasure travel was broadening. An editorial
in the *Toronto Empire* asserted:

> There can hardly be a stronger means of advancing the work of civilization
> and promoting the true spirit of Christianity, in spreading peace and good-
> will amongst mankind, than by bringing the nations nearer to one another,
> and making each acquainted with the virtues of the other. This is best accom-
> plished through the encouragement of travel.[32]

Because it enabled those without great personal fortunes or cultural expertise to do their part in the civilizing mission, organized touring was
both Christian and democratic. Its increasingly industrial character was
cause for celebration rather than denigration, for modern technology
and business practices represented the possibility of social improvement.

Even as they defended themselves as agents of civilization, the tour
companies also constantly emphasized the complete independence of the
traveler within the structure of the "personally conducted" tours: "We

demonstrated by our system that a party of select people may journey together, and yet be independent, that they may be relieved of all personal care by deputizing details to a central power without in any way sacrificing their individuality." Given its republican organization, the tour company's expertise and efficiencies of scale heightened rather than diminished a traveler's freedom, all the while assuring comforts the lone traveler might not be able to obtain.[33] Commercially provided refinement promised social exclusiveness, upward mobility, and egalitarianism all at once—the American dream.

Class snobbery and offended privilege lay behind many of the criticisms of organized tourism, yet there was some truth to them, too.[34] It did tend to transform the character of pleasure travel. By separating tourists from networks of kin and class embedded in local communities and emphasizing the opposition between tourist leisure and everyday work, the organized tour offered an experience quite different from the elite Grand Tour and middle-class romantic tourism. Although tour members continued to believe that travel was educational and to seek the beautiful and the sublime in natural monuments, they did not regard the experience as an entry into adulthood or an occasion for spiritual uplift. Rather, they expected to be rejuvenated in order to return to their usual lives. As a haven from mundane pressures, the experience of leisure assumed some of the ameliorative duties of the middle-class home. This broadening of ideas about leisure and travel meant that tourism could now encompass gregarious as well as contemplative pleasures without implicating the tourist in the local social order. As a result, it became possible to conceive of American cities as tourist destinations.

Another complaint against the organized tour centered not on its implications for the members but on its impact on others. The personally conducted party formed a visible, single-purposed crowd that might well overwhelm the independent traveler, the locals, and the sights. The very separation of tourists and their spatial practices from the local threatened the usual uses of the landscape and social relations there. Tour companies routinely insisted that theirs were not such "large and promiscuous excursions." Raymond & Whitcomb protested that its patrons would not be subject to "any special or ostentatious display, which would naturally be obnoxious to persons of quiet tastes."[35] A creature of modern, industrial society, the organized tour would nevertheless avoid any negative consequences because its members were so refined.

But the tour company's disclaimers did not always describe reality. At least one Raymond & Whitcomb tour included forty sleeping cars and eight dining cars, accommodating about eight hundred people. Amy Bridges noted overlapping waves of tourists in groups of one hundred or more when she traveled with Raymond & Whitcomb in 1882 and 1886–87. Also, participants in the tours were not always averse to the public attention they attracted. One member of a tour that brought vestibuled trains to the southern states for the first time rejoiced not only in the personal attention from hotel keepers and Pullman officials but also in the fact that "at every stopping-place we are the observed of all observers." Bridges's fellow tourists too were far from shy and retiring. At a station in Arizona, "a good many of the excursionists promenaded and danced Shaker dance and Verginia Reel and played the [thumb] game having so much sport that the inhabitants looking on with interest said it was more [fun] than an Apache war dance."[36] Tourists, like hotel guests and city residents, enjoyed such gregarious public pleasures more than cultural critics thought seemly.

The growing importance of wholesome recreation to the occupation of public spaces made them more hospitable to respectable white women. Like the promoters of extra-fare cars, tour companies claimed that the luxury and exclusivity they provided made traveling alone easy and safe for the ladies. Gillespie and Kinports assured its potential customers, "Ladies without escort can make the trip without experiencing the slightest unpleasantness or being in any way oppressed by doubts and difficulties incident to travel in the ordinary way." The Pennsylvania Railroad even hired a female chaperone to accompany its personally conducted tours.[37]

Critics of the tours labeled them effeminizing and female dominated precisely because of the buffers they placed between tourists and the rest of the world. Such comments conveyed the extent to which the tours challenged the gender and class assumptions underlying the construction and uses of public spaces. Men's masculinity suffered to the extent that the tour mediated their participation in public interactions, while the women entering public spaces courtesy of the personally conducted tour revealed a brash lack of femininity. Although well-to-do women probably did feel more comfortable traveling when cushioned by the exclusivity and personal attention of a guided tour, the success of firms such as Cook & Son and Raymond & Whitcomb required a larger and wealthier clientele than single women. The few extant travel diaries suggest that older married couples predominated among excursionists.[38]

Through their services and advertisements, tourist businesses contributed to the increasingly acceptable idea that just those spaces and ac-

tivities affiliated with neither work nor home were the arena of freedom
and the reward for virtue. The rehabilitation of leisure was perfectly
compatible with a refined passion for scenery and a rejection of the commercial hustle of urban life: "Leave Babylon by the fastest express for
Arcadia," cried one minister to his congregation. For many middle-class
Americans, big cities were both the site and the symbol of white-collar
work. Increasingly nostalgic for a simpler past, they often envisioned
rural areas as pastoral havens from labor, notwithstanding the many
who labored there. According to a writer for the Southern Pacific Railroad's *Sunset* magazine, "Every earnest man frequently asks himself . . .
How can I increase my efficiency?" He advised not application to the
job at hand but a country vacation: "The man who is ambitious to do
the most and best work will, if he be wise, take a month out of his summer each year and invest it in pure air and sunshine." Seaside, mountain,
and lake resorts proliferated at the turn of the century as more people
were able to take summer vacations to "soak out all the grittiness of
the city."[39]

Still, highlighting people's need for rest and change in and of themselves, rather than as a means of uplift, opened the door to a wider range
of destinations, and some firms moved quickly to promote new possibilities. "Thoughts of Rest and Recreation now begin to call up mental
pictures of delightful and cool summer resorts of lakes, mountains and
seashore," sighed one Illinois Central Railroad folder; and, it added, "of
the attractions of the large and interesting cities. . . . Why not visit Chicago[?]. . . . It is a city everyone desires to see." The city could offer the
benefits of travel as well as any beautiful landscape, for, as the anonymous author of *Hints for Strangers, Shoppers, and Sightsee-ers* [sic]
noted, an "occasional change of air, water and general surroundings
is as essential for the recuperation of our physical system, as is rest or
recreation for our mental ones." Change of scene itself, rather than a
particular scene, was the important thing, at least according to New
York City's *Guide Magazine:* "[Men] want change and recreation, and
when they start out on the road to get it the road brings them right here
to New York."[40]

Drawing on and fostering such attitudes, from the 1890s on, tour
companies more and more often created and advertised tours with cities
as destinations, not just stops along the way. The initial occasion for city
tours, the slew of national and world's fairs and spectacular celebrations
of various centennials across the United States, furnished ample evidence that Americans were eager to entertain and enlighten themselves

in the nation's cities. Occurring in or near big cities, the fairs and festivals stimulated the founding of many tour companies, excursion offers, and hotel information bureaus. In addition to proving the attractiveness of urban areas to tourists, expositions and city festivals indicated that a rising number of middling Americans who could not afford the months'-long luxury tours that dominated tour offerings now earned enough to consider a short summer vacation trip.

To attract such people, the tour companies began to offer shorter, more affordable tours to both resorts and cities. Noting the addition of "a numerous array of low-priced tours" to its repertoire in 1890, Raymond & Whitcomb explained, "They have been arranged with a view to meeting the wishes of large number of our patrons who find it inconvenient to absent themselves from home or business ties for the time required in the longer excursions." By the 1890s, if not earlier, Cook's offered three-day tours from East Coast cities to Washington, D.C., for between $9 and $13.25. As with all its other tours, members of these parties enjoyed the best rail and hotel accommodations. If they chose to pay the higher price, they were entitled to a carriage drive around the city and a steamboat ride up the Potomac to Mount Vernon during their stay. The Baltimore & Ohio and the Pennsylvania Railroads offered similar tours, as did Raymond & Whitcomb and other eastern firms.[41]

In some ways the Washington city tour epitomized nineteenth-century tourism; in others, it presaged the twentieth-century mode of pleasure travel. Participants in these tours did much as their predecessors in visiting the capital had: they visited the Capitol and other major public buildings and usually made the pilgrimage to the now-restored Mount Vernon by steamer or the new electric rail connection. Several rounds of construction and reorganization since the 1870s made Washington more than ever exemplary of the kind of city worth touring in the nineteenth-century sense. It had magnificent public buildings and extensive parks, and it inspired strong historical and aesthetic associations. But it was unusual for a tour to focus only on a city and for it to be so short, providing only a day and a half for sight-seeing. This was a tour deliberately arranged as a respite for busy, middle-class Americans. The entrance of other, less traditionally attractive cities like Chicago in the lists underscores the direction of the change.[42]

Moreover, by the early twentieth century, urban and tourist promoters regularly claimed that cities made excellent "summer resorts," invoking the outdoor pleasures associated with the many mountain, lake, and seaside hotels. The idea that a large city could be a pleasant place in summer was novel indeed. American cities had long been unpleasant and unhealthy places in the summer, when hot weather exacerbated the stench of human and animal waste and factory pollution. Poor waste removal systems and inadequate water supplies combined with the effects of crowding and bad food to encourage epidemic disease. The gaslit theaters closed because of the heat and the elite social season ended. Those who could afford to left the city in summer.[43]

Better sanitation, more frequent and effective street cleaning, enlarged and cleaner water supplies, and less dusty, less absorbent pavements all mitigated the evils of the city summer for well-to-do urbanites by the turn of the century. The creation of parks and driving boulevards provided pastoral oases for those who had the leisure and money to take advantage of them. New cultural institutions and refined places of leisure abounded, including libraries, opera houses, roof gardens, department stores, and tearooms. Electricity provided nearly heatless and excitingly modern lighting inside major buildings and along main streets.[44]

Guidebooks and advertising flyers pointed out all of these things. They also increasingly noted the opportunities for outdoor activities in the city, another novelty. Nearby beaches and parks approximated the more usual oceanside and rural resorts, and by the twentieth century electric trolleys made them more accessible to a wider range of people. In many cities, parks began to boast tennis courts and baseball grounds; bicycles and well-paved roads to ride them on proliferated; the suburbs sprouted golf courses; and yachting, riding, and driving occupied the very rich to an even greater extent than before. Municipal festivals began to include formal, regulated athletic contests in swimming, sailing, track and field, and other sports.[45]

The growing vogue for athletics and the provision of urban spaces for them were central elements in the rehabilitation of public leisure. Even as recreation lessened the formal political aspects of the uses of public spaces, it enabled more people to enter such spaces and participate in community (usually small-group) activities. The emergence of cities as summer resorts also indicated a transformation in the meaning of leisure and of nature. Through much of the nineteenth century, scenic tourism and the parks movement rested on and were shaped by the understanding of nature as the privileged locus of a solitary and refining act of communion. The self-conscious, romantic quest for spiritual and aesthetic uplift stood opposed to the market-driven exploitation of natural resources typical of American expansion and industrialization, echoing the division of private and public in everyday life. By the end of the century, "nature" was increasingly the backdrop for group exercise and play, especially in cities where open spaces were limited and highly regulated. Leisure was increasingly seen as a break from and reward for numbing industrial labor, not an alternative to it. Given these attitudes, cities could exercise a powerful attraction.

Like the tourist cars and businessmen's hotels, the weekend city tour was efficient, relatively inexpensive, and thoroughly modern. This compressed break from the daily grind represented the industrialization of urban space and spatial practices. Casting leisure as an appropriate public activity precisely when it was most distinct from work or other obligations transformed the content and meaning of both leisure and public, urban spaces. The new spaces and social activities relied on the increasingly firm distinction between travelers and locals. This social distance vitiated the sense of a shared moral, political realm that had been at the core of both republicanism and refinement in the mid-nineteenth century. It made urban tourism both possible and, in a cultural sense, necessary. Responding to and seeking to shape the changes under way, city businessmen's organizations by the 1890s came to see tourism as a means of creating a renewed, cosmopolitan, and prosperous community. Their efforts to promote this ideal did much to popularize urban tourism.

SELLING THE CITY

American cities had always had their boosters. They were centers of the national passion for the land speculation that flourished along with westward expansion and urbanization throughout the nineteenth century. Merchants, industrialists, and real estate developers dominated the economic and political leadership of many emerging cities during the mid-nineteenth century and zealously promoted the economic development of their hometowns. The long-standing link between pride of place and plans for pecuniary gain remained strong at the turn of the century. But between 1850 and 1915, the character of the cities that such men sought to develop changed considerably.[46]

As they responded to and shaped these changes to suit their interests, city boosters took a growing interest in encouraging tourism, something they had not done before the turn of the century. They endorsed City Beautiful plans and less ambitious proposals for urban embellishment, sponsored world's fairs and commemorative festivals, and continually solicited the growing number of professional, fraternal, labor, and trade

associations holding conventions at the turn of the century. The men
who spearheaded this expansion of boosterism argued that a city attractive to tourists would not only improve a city's economic outlook but
also renew the civic loyalty and foster cordial class relations. Making
money and strengthening the community would go hand in hand.

The business associations' concern with civic loyalty and class relations was not new in the 1890s, but the political and social changes of
the time had made it more urgent. For all the dire warnings of the urban
sketch artists in the mid-nineteenth century, a fragile compromise then
existed among the white men who dominated the public realm. A slew
of challenges ripped apart this compromise by the turn of the century.
The accelerating pace of industrialization deepened the class divisions
and the inequitable distribution of wealth and political power, just as
George Foster and his ilk had feared. Emancipation led to bitter struggles over the place of black Americans in both public affairs and public
places. Immigration from a growing range of European and a few Asian
nations made ethnicity and nativity increasingly important political issues. Women's social activism, their growing presence in the waged
workforce, and the suffrage movement illuminated the erosion of the
boundary between public and private as well as the division's inequitable effects. The rising number of massive, national corporations and the
belated, piecemeal efforts of city, state, and federal governments to balance profits and the public welfare undermined the older ideal of the au-
tonomous republican citizen.[47]

These challenges to the mid-nineteenth-century political economy
politicized the assumptions on which the old order had rested and gal-
vanized new social groups. For many middle-class Americans, refinement and the ideal of separate spheres were no longer adequate means
of organizing a moral and republican community. In competition with
corporate leaders and agrarian and industrial radicals, they began to re-
imagine the sources of legitimate social bonds. Many different groups
strove to realize a new order at least in part by creating new kinds of urban spaces and by reorganizing the existing social relations, spaces, and
spatial practices.[48]

One sign of this reimagining on the part of urban businessmen was
their growing interest in promoting tourism. At the turn of the century,
businessmen in many cities established new or substantially reorganized
advocacy groups called the Merchants' Association or the Chamber of
Commerce. Through these groups, they claimed to represent the city's
best interests in opposition to the selfish, parochial interests of working-

class and ethnic groups.[49] "Improving" the urban landscape and attracting tourists to admire it took a prominent part in the efforts of organized businessmen to sell their vision of a reunified city greater than the sum of its parts.

In the mid-nineteenth century, neither municipal governments nor businessmen had made much of an attempt to plan for urban growth. Individual real estate developers used various means to stabilize property values, but most Americans agreed that long-term, communitywide planning was at odds with the rights of property owners and the market relations believed to underwrite equality of opportunity. Besides, putting that much power in the hands of elected officials invited corruption, as the municipal and state politics of the late nineteenth century amply demonstrated.[50]

Beginning with the parks movement of the 1860s, however, some Americans promoted a more managerial approach to urban growth. The creation of appointed commissions to control the development of parks and major utilities pointed the way toward a kind of urban planning that seemed to avoid the dangers of corruption yet also would ameliorate the ugly, unhealthy chaos of the mid-nineteenth-century city. Such planning offered both refined landscapes on an urban scale and the easing of social tensions, as all residents came to inhabit a lovely, well-serviced city. Not coincidentally, the new commissions also tended to limit the influence of partisan politics. Commissions promised to reform politics partly through uplift and partly through the exclusion of the unrefined, just as parks did for the city and its residents.[51]

The growing interest of businessmen in city planning and embellishment derived in part from their experience with national and international world's fairs. Beginning with the first American world's fair, held in New York in 1853 in emulation of London's Crystal Palace exposition two years before, American events were sponsored and largely funded by the host city's business elites. The large world's fairs and the written and pictorial images of them suggested the limits of existing cities and the possibilities of planned and policed ones. As they were intended to, the expositions also demonstrated the marvelous civilizing capacity of capitalism.[52]

The grandeur of the architecture and the careful landscaping of the exposition grounds offered not simply a revamped built environment but also a model of how people should occupy cities and how they should come together in an urban community. Walking amid the enormous, magnificent display halls on the exposition grounds, visitors performed a particularly refined version of the urban promenade. Although written accounts of expositions generally emphasized the cross section of Americans to be found there, the cost of transportation and entry largely excluded those who did not abide by the rules of gentility. Low attendance figures and constant battles over Sunday opening, the only day that working-class Americans could attend, underscore the expositions' exclusivity. And, although fairs were usually located in a great urban park, they celebrated commerce.[53] They represented the reconciliation of refinement and business values, easing the anxieties of the well-to-do and yet also challenging the division of public trade from private values.

The key to reuniting culture with moneymaking in public was the relationship of fairgoers to the exposition. Their chief activity was uplifting leisure, safely anchored by the refined art and architecture of the exposition landscape. Just as the fine buildings and the rhetoric of cultural progress and national pride obscured the commercial substance of the fair, so the visitors' leisure obscured their relationship to paid labor. Images of exposition grounds portrayed the ideal behavior: in them, small groups of well-dressed men, women, and children quietly and respectfully admired their surroundings. These figures were intended to show scale, but their dress, grouping, and relationship to each other also dignify them as emblems of genteel leisure. (See fig. 7.)

Contemporary commentators readily perceived the spatial, architectural, and social lessons of the expositions. Visiting the unfinished grounds of the World's Columbian Exposition in 1892, Julian Hawthorne rhapsodized to his sister: "[T]he Fair is a world. . . . in which ugliness and useless[ness] have been extirpated, and the beautiful and useful alone admitted." Such a world would be at its best "when the vast grounds and illimitable floors are thronged with the countless thousands of well-dressed people" instead of the "Micks and Dagos and the scattered and dazed sightseers who now mottle the barren spaces."[54] Hawthorne's socially and architecturally knowledgeable fairgoers were the essential counterpart to the ideal urban landscape. Neither workers nor "ethnics," their presence and their sensitivity to its high-cultural meanings represented the city's financial and social success.

Significantly, these citizens constituted themselves as members of a leisured public by looking. The receptive visitor identified himself or herself with the splendid commercial achievement of the fairs, conflating the republic with the market. As one humorous account of the Centennial Exposition put it, "[O]nce within the enclosure we began to feel our citizenship to a greater degree than ever before. . . . [A] calm ob-

Figure 7. "Horticultural Hall, Centennial International Exposition, 1876,"
in E. S. Marsh, *Memoir of the Centennial Exhibition of 1876* (Philadelphia,
1876), plate. Courtesy of the Winterthur Library, Joseph Downs Collection of
Manuscripts and Printed Ephemera.

server might have looked with some reason to see the genuine American
sprout feathers and spurs before he had been inside half an hour." But
this imagined proprietorship was the only kind ordinary Americans
had of the world's fairs. Although the Centennial and later expositions
did receive some government subsidies, they were largely funded and entirely controlled by private organizations of businessmen. A less wealthy
citizen might buy a subscription to the fair but gained no rights over its
construction or administration by doing so. Of course, ordinary Americans did build, maintain, and demolish the fair grounds, but, while
architects, sculptors, and other professional employees might be celebrated, the workmen and women were not.[55]

On the exposition grounds, the city of the urban handbook existed
without its shadow, the city of the urban sketch. The fair's buildings
and displays aestheticized and celebrated both industrial and mercantile
wealth and the possibilities of urban life. Just as the ideologues of republican gentility promised, the leisured contemplation of commercial
and cultural progress brought Americans together in harmony and national pride. No dangerous crowds infested with undetectable pick-
pockets, overly friendly strangers, and women of dubious virtue inhab-
ited this ideal city. Pedestrians had the uncontested right-of-way on the

broad paths; few carriages were permitted and trains and omnibuses were carefully restricted or excluded. The dangers of frightened horses, grade crossings, sparks, and cinders, as well as the noise and filth that railroads and horses produced, were scrupulously contained on the periphery of the main grounds. Here, no one need doubt the intrinsic beneficence of the market.[56]

The expositions, unfortunately, were only temporary solutions. Built for a few months' use, most of the magnificent buildings were destroyed after the fair's closing, although the landscaped grounds persisted as parks. Those convinced of the importance of properly constructed urban landscapes therefore began to campaign for the reconstruction of permanent cities to look more like expositions. They called their ideal "the City Beautiful." Originating in the mid-nineteenth-century parks movement and incorporating the village improvement societies founded as early as the 1850s, the City Beautiful movement grew increasingly coherent in response to Chicago's Columbian Exposition of 1893. It reached the height of its influence between 1900 and 1910.[57]

Like the many middle- and upper-class white men and women who supported other "progressive" causes in these years, City Beautiful advocates sought to reconstruct the social bonds strained or broken by urbanization and industrialization. What distinguished them from both earlier parks activists and their contemporary opponents was, first, the optimistic belief that cities could and should be made beautiful. They proceeded, as an anonymous author wrote in San Francisco's *Merchants' Association Review* in 1903, "on the principle that city life is a great and commendable thing. . . , and that there is no good reason why it should be squalid when it can just as well be splendid." The city constructed according to this principle would minister "alike to the material well-being of the public and the elevation of its ideals of citizenship."[58] Urban beauty, like its rural counterpart, would inspire and shape harmonious social relations.

Second, urban landscape reformers cast aside a long tradition of urban fiscal conservatism and urged municipalities to invest millions of tax dollars in improving the built environment. They justified their apostasy by claiming that the construction of public works and monuments would forward both the material and the civic welfare of a broadly conceived urban public. There was a larger good, they believed, than immediate profit or the particular interests of landowners. This characteristically Progressive belief in the state's responsibility for the collective welfare undermined possessive individualism and the ideal of separate spheres that sustained it.[59]

Favoring an austere neoclassical architecture bearing connotations of republican grandeur, City Beautiful advocates aimed to mold motley individuals into an urban community. They began with monumental civic centers built around large, public plazas. Such open spaces and surrounding landscaping would distinguish these government and public, cultural buildings from commercial edifices, whose imperative was to maximize rentable space. The great civic centers were to anchor a larger urban composition articulated by broad, tree-lined, radial avenues and encircled by boulevards joining the parks that ringed the city. Deliberately breaking the gridiron pattern that had been so popular in mid-nineteenth-century city design, the new model embodied the triumph of civic community over the forces of individualism and commercial utility. When combined with the harmonizing of architectural styles and cornice lines throughout the city, the carefully designed street plan would bring a unity to the urban built environment that would generate greater pride and cohesiveness among the citizens.[60]

Apart from improving large urban parks, two chief concerns governed City Beautiful plans: traffic and sight lines. In their designs, planners sought to redress the sprawl and segmentation of American cities, whose physical organization mirrored and encouraged the mutual ignorance and distrust of city dwellers. The great radial avenues and encircling boulevards were intended to make urban traffic flow more easily and swiftly and to link the city's people in a promenade of truly metropolitan scale. Properly closed off by large, imposing government buildings and embellished with monuments and statuary, the avenues would direct both motion through the city and the visual perception of it. The aim was to constitute an architectural and aesthetic mold for an ideal community.[61]

Of course, if the City Beautiful was to exercise its unifying, uplifting power, people had to exercise themselves. Urging New Yorkers to erect fine buildings and statuary in their city, the architect Henry Rutgers Marshall pointed out in 1895 that "in order that a person may gain a sense of beauty from these works, he must move from spot to spot."[62] The citizen of the City Beautiful was intended to experience its landscape primarily as an edifying display rather than the context for everyday life. The reorganization and better articulation of the city would encourage residents to transcend the parochial identities and politics rooted in the spaces of work, home, and neighborhood. The tourist, whose mobility and leisure enabled him or her to perceive the city as a single, designed, and meaningful whole, provided a model for the urban resident.

The link between plans for urban improvement, civic renewal, and tourism was more than metaphorical. Many businessmen agreed with the necessity of reforming urban life and landscape and found the City Beautiful model appealing. Even supporters, however, questioned the financial and political feasibility of the ambitious plans. So did the many working-class men who routinely voted against the higher taxes and bond measures necessary to fund them. Addressing these doubts, men and women who spoke on behalf of the City Beautiful plans argued that such reforms made economic as well as spiritual and aesthetic sense. Fine-looking cities would attract tourists, who would spend money, which would benefit the city's businesses and, in turn, the entire urban population.[63]

Speaking before San Francisco's Downtown Association in 1911, Joseph Redding proposed that city beautification advocates adopt the following line of reasoning to explain themselves to voters reluctant to foot the bill: "We are going to tax the stranger for all this; we are going to make our city so wonderfully attractive that thousands upon thousands of strangers will come within our gates all the year round, and we will fascinate them into spending and buying among us in every conceivable way." Redding's proposal was far from unusual; it followed the lines laid down by the dean of American City Beautiful planners, Daniel Burnham, who urged people to recognize "the commercial value of beauty."[64]

Endorsing the concept, business associations in New York, San Francisco, and Chicago sponsored and promoted ambitious City Beautiful plans. In Washington, congressional support was crucial. In the first three cities, the plans met with little immediate success, although some elements of them were eventually constructed. Washington represented the City Beautiful movement's most visible success in the early twentieth century, in part because of the inability of the city's residents to reject congressional plans for a monumental city core.[65] Despite the mixed results, the support of organized business for such plans, the deep interest of planners in mobility and visual effects, and the belief that tourism would provide the funds demonstrated the growing importance of urban visitors to the way that many Americans envisioned improved, socially harmonious cities.

The popularity of this urban vision also demonstrates the simultaneous extension and erosion of the refined spatial ideal. In some ways, the City Beautiful was the refined home writ very large, and its aim was the uplift of all who dwelled within. The realization of such an ideal would eliminate the need for the division of public from private, spatially and socially. Yet the City Beautiful abandoned the emphasis on mutual recognition in the regulation of social relations that lay at the heart of refinement and replaced it with an emphasis on architectural beauty. The Committee on Municipal Art of the Washington Board of Trade praised its citizens for realizing "that the more beautiful the city was, the more pleasure and pride its people would feel in it, the more they would work for its advancement, and the more it would attract strangers to it." [66] The walls would speak, so that citizens had no need to address—or to doubt—each other. The presence of admiring tourists would mark a city's success.

City elites across the nation learned the lessons that the expositions and the City Beautiful movemement taught, but the immediate catalysts for the growing interest in tourism differed in each city. San Francisco's leaders were concerned about the great strides in industry, trade, and tourism being made by rival Pacific Coast cities, especially Los Angeles. The multiplication of transcontinental railroads to five by 1900 had diminished San Francisco's dominance of domestic travel to the Far West at the same time that southern California was attracting growing numbers of tourists and home seekers. Portland and Seattle were also growing more quickly than the Bay city by the early twentieth century. To stimulate the slowing pace of growth in San Francisco, several businessmen's organizations worked vigorously to attract business investment, new residents, and tourists.[67]

For a time, plans to reorganize and beautify the city were prominent in the efforts to attract newcomers and to suture the divisions among San Franciscans. The Association for the Improvement and Adornment of San Francisco, formed in 1904, included in its statement of purpose not simply the projects implied in its name but also the hope "to stimulate the sentiment of civic pride." As soon as it had gotten launched, the Association invited Chicago's Daniel Burnham to devise a plan to improve San Francisco. Not surprisingly, the resulting plan incorporated the standard City Beautiful features: a monumental civic center to anchor the city, radial avenues, and an encircling boulevard to improve the traffic, the vistas, and the residents' interaction. It also suggested the cre-

ation of parks atop the city's tallest hills and the modification of the gridiron street plan to allow for comely—and sensible—winding roads up
the city's steep slopes.[68]

The San Francisco plan came to nothing, despite the 1906 earthquake
and fire that razed the center of the city. As in other places, entrenched
real estate and commercial interests, a strong commitment to the rights
of property owners, and the weakness of the municipal government
combined to prevent any large-scale urban reconstruction. But businessmen continued to assert that a beautiful city would promote tourism
and better San Francisco's reputation as well as its economic situation.
They launched campaigns to clean and pave city streets and sidewalks,
to erect ornamental lampposts in the high-class retail area around Union
Square and in Chinatown, and to improve the waterfront. Their most
ambitious effort was the Panama-Pacific International Exposition, held
in San Francisco in 1915. Organized business justified nearly all of these
projects with reference to the opinions and purses of visitors.[69]

Washington, D.C.'s elites had an even greater interest in tourism than
did San Francisco's. The capital's local leaders had struggled throughout
its first century of existence to establish and attract industry and commerce, to little avail. The lack of local control over fundamental issues
of municipal government, the burden of the untaxable federal presence,
and the absence of local capital undercut every project. Following the
Civil War, however, the city's fortunes seemed to be on the upswing.
Growing nationalism and the passion for commemoration benefited
Washington and the historical sites in its immediate hinterland, especially Mount Vernon. The expansion of the federal government brought
more people to the city and led to the extension, renovation, and construction of government buildings.[70]

The nongovernmental areas of the city also received increased attention. Changes in the district's and the city's governing systems enabled
a bold local real estate entrepreneur, Alexander Shepherd, to undertake
huge "improvements" in the early 1870s. He masterminded and supervised the massive, rapid construction of a sewage and water supply system and the grading and paving of streets throughout the city. Although
the ambitious project was poorly planned, poorly executed, and plunged
the city into debt and scandal, it began the process of providing Washington with the amenities common to its larger metropolitan cousins.[71]
No longer would visitors find it to be an undistinguished, medium-sized
town unsuited for its exalted function as the nation's capital.

The increasing prestige and power associated with holding federal elective office also benefited Washington's built environment. In the last third of the nineteenth century, members of Congress began to move out of boardinghouses and into hotels and rented homes. They more often brought their wives and families with them to the city and stayed for longer periods. The wealthier legislators built or bought fine, new residences, endowing Washington with a booming real estate market and the kind of exclusive residential areas of which other cities boasted. The influx of elected and appointed federal employees buoyed the local economy and underwrote the expansion and improvement of private concerns such as hotels and shops until they, too, more closely resembled their counterparts in larger cities.[72]

Leading efforts to attract tourists was the city's Board of Trade, composed of prominent local merchants. It occupied a position quite different from that of other business associations because of the city's unusual government. Washington residents lost the right to vote in 1874, following revelations of Shepherd's mismanagement and the massive debt his improvement scheme incurred. Congress then turned the city over to three appointed commissioners who effectively ran it. The Board of Trade took the place of both city council and businessmen's organization. It had no municipal government to hinder or aid it; nor did it have any responsibility to an electorate. But it was severely limited by the power of the three commissioners and the goodwill of Congress, which was fickle and limited at best.[73]

Like their predecessors among Washington's resident elite, the members of the Board of Trade hoped against hope to bring industry and commerce to the capital. But they also took a rising and more realistic interest in attracting pleasure travelers and convention visitors. In 1898 the organization's annual report acknowledged frankly that "[m]uch of Washington's strength, like that of a woman, is in its beauty; its face is its fortune. Among the Board's most important committees, therefore, are those which labor to increase the city's material prosperity by developing its external attractiveness."[74] At midcentury such a comparison would surely have evoked visions of the city as a painted whore and the city fathers as panderers. But by the 1890s, urban beauty was a resource to be exploited.

The Board of Trade deliberately turned Washington's historic liability, the lack of industry, to its advantage. In doing so, the Board contributed to the emergence of a new standard in evaluating urban attractiveness. By the 1890s the city had more to offer than simply a few impressive federal buildings scattered widely across the muddy landscape of a medium-sized town. Filled with fine homes, parks, and tree-lined streets, it was free of factory pollution and had relatively few of the industrial laborers whose poverty, strange tongues, and political protests made the public spaces of other cities so unfriendly to middle-class and elite Americans. Despite Congress's rejection of an ambitious plan to redesign the central city in the early twentieth century, downtown Washington steadily gained in open spaces, historical monuments, and public cultural institutions, while evidence of industry and local residences receded. The city was becoming a metropolitan suburb.[75]

In keeping with its built environment, Washington offered a leisurely, cultured pace of life, in contrast to the urban hustle of industrial and commercial entrepôts. Rufus Rockwell Wilson wrote in 1902 that Washington "is a city of authority and leisure," as the daily promenade along Pennsylvania Avenue revealed: "The people who make up this parade are different from those of other American cities. . . . There are no strained faces among them, such as one encounters in New York or Chicago, and all walk as if conscious of the fact that they have time at their command." In Washington: "You will find a welcome . . . as in no other great city of the Union, for business is subordinated there, and the tourist finds a Mecca where the gods welcome him and bid him see."[76] The nation's premier urban tourist destination epitomized the growing faith in beautiful urban surroundings and public leisure as the foundation for renewed and harmonious social relations.

Booming commercial centers and well established as the largest and second-largest cities of the nation, New York and Chicago had less financial need and prestige staked on the tourist trade than did San Francisco and Washington, D.C. Nor was the imperative to lure new residents and business investments quite as powerful. Nevertheless, as the Publicity Bureau of the Merchants' Association of New York pointed out in 1914, "no city is too large to profit by having its name constantly before the outside public."[77] Both this organization and the Chicago Association of Commerce had committees devoted to publicity and conventions, and their publications demonstrated a lively interest in attracting visitors with money to spend.

To a greater extent than the other cities, New York and Chicago associations linked tourism with business travel, seeking to encourage buyers for hinterland concerns to come to the city—and to bring their families. The Chicago Association of Commerce, for example, invited everyone west of the Atlantic seaboard states "to buy in Chicago and take a vacation in Chicago." The Merchants' Association of New York made arrangements for reduced railroad fares for commercial buyers and provided space for them in its rooms. The annual report offered no comparative figures but claimed that the program saw a 500 percent increase in 1906. Chicago undertook a similar program with the slogan "Chicago—the Great Central Market." [78]

Both associations found that visiting buyers wanted more than commercial information: "A great many of the out-of-town merchants registering at the offices of the [New York] Association request information as to hotels, theaters, restaurants, ferries, railroad offices, street car routes. . . , pleasure resorts, short excursions, etc." To meet this demand, as well as to publicize the city's attractions, both associations published guidebooks and circulars in various forms. One hopeful Chicago publicist wrote that such "reading matter is quickly digested by the recipient's entire family. Women and children begin to impatiently inquire when their trip to Chicago is to come off." [79] The San Francisco organizations and Washington's Board of Trade also sponsored the publication of guidebooks and folders but seem not to have undertaken regular programs to attract wholesale buyers.

Of course, Chicago and New York entered the competition for pleasure and business travelers on a different footing. By the turn of the century second only to the eastern metropolis in population and commerce, Chicago had long been infamous for its residents' excessive devotion to gain, its muddy streets and smoke-fouled air, and the general absence of refinement. It had the reputation of being the most remorselessly urban city in the nation. In the 1850s Caroline Kirkland had compared the city to a bejeweled but dirty-footed oriental sultana. In 1907 an anonymous writer for the Chicago Association's journal was still protesting: "Muck, murder, and murk: This is the message of the alien sensationalist." [80]

The Association responded by exhorting the local newspapers to counter such slander and insisting on the pleasures of Chicago's climate and its multiplicity of attractions, from soaring skyscrapers to vast parks, great theaters, and excursions on the lake. Although ardent insistence that Chicago had culture as well as wealth was as old as the city, the point became crucial if the city was to attract tourists, not just business investment. Defending the city's reputation now involved efforts to alter existing patterns of tourism in the city. One speaker before the Chicago Association of Commerce declared in 1910: "There was a time, and I am glad to see that time passing, when strangers came to this city. . . , the first thing we did was to take them out to the stockyards." Not to offend the powerful packinghouse owners, he hastened to add,

"That is a wonderful institution out there. . . ; but it isn't the most esthetic thing to show to visitors the first time they come to Chicago and
forget many other things in which this city is forging to the head." The
Chicago Art Institute also notified the Association, rather plaintively,
that it wanted a higher profile among business visitors and was prepared
to offer special deals to convention-goers.[81]

New York's organized businessmen seem to have felt somewhat less
pressure to redeem their city's reputation, but they did have to combat the persistent idea that cities lacked the spiritual quality and refined
significance of the countryside. George Englehardt, author of the lavishly illustrated, oversize "guide" that the Merchants' Association produced in 1902, wrote, "The world, it is true, knows New York fairly already. . . . as the greatest port, center of finance and center of trade," but
he insisted that New York was not only a commercial center: "it is something else and something more—something better, higher, grander." He
cited the city's fine architecture, its "charming scenic situation," and the
existence of great institutions of art, education, science, charity, and
religion.[82] The effort to lure tourists required that cities be imagined
as places of beauty, refinement, and high culture. Fine architecture, not
stock speculation, the Art Institute, not the stockyards, were what
counted now.

By the twentieth century, attracting the annual meetings of large, national organizations had taken a central place in the efforts of organized
business to promote urban tourism. In a sense, conventions represented
the institutionalization of expositions, and they literally and imaginatively furthered the integration of American cities into a larger national
whole. Representatives of national, often professional, ties, convention-
goers came to cities in pursuit of specialized interests, not to join the
local social order. As a result, they modeled new, cosmopolitan social
relations that were not embedded in a particular community or place.
Organized businessmen sought to construct publicly owned convention
centers that would bring together urbanites in a similar manner, overcoming the parochial, everyday occupancy of urban spaces.

The convention trade existed before the interest of business organizations in encouraging it. Its growing importance stemmed from several
developments. Following the Civil War, the improvement, expansion,
and consolidation of the railroad network made travel easier, faster,
safer, and more comfortable throughout the nation. The last third of the
century also witnessed a great surge in the formation of voluntary associations. Veterans' and commemorative groups seem to have led the

way, but professional, business, and trade organizations were not far behind. The existence of national travel and communications networks,
as well as national stimuli—memories of the Civil War, occupational
ties, and expanding markets—all motivated nationwide associations to
gather in frequent, if not annual, conventions.[83]

By the turn of the century, attracting conventions was one of the basic functions of businessmen's associations. The anonymous authors
of articles in the various journals of these groups never tired of estimat-
ing the number of conventions won, the number of visitors they would
bring, and the amount of money the guests would spend. Particularly attractive were the very largest groups, among which loomed the many
fraternal lodges and the Grand Army of the Republic, the Union veterans' group. One reunion in San Francisco, far from the center of the nation's population, drew some ten thousand former soldiers.[84]

National veterans' and lodge conventions were enormous public
events. In addition to meetings and speeches, they often included massive marches through the city's main streets complete with brass bands,
elaborate decorations, and electric illuminations. They created tourist
events as well as constituting them, drawing national attention to the
host city and, in the dreams of local businessmen, spreading its fame
throughout the nation. City business organizations counted the arrival
of such large groups as great coups and urged railroads and hotels to
provide special discounts and other services.[85]

By the early twentieth century, the business associations that had been
engaged in promoting the convention trade for a decade or more were
seeking greater municipal participation. For the most part, city governments left the job of encouraging tourism to private business. Some
mayors might agree to issue official invitations to sweeten the persuasive
efforts of the association's convention committee. In a few cases, city
councils contributed to the financial incentives offered to prospective
visiting organizations. But, despite the frequent pleas of businessmen's
organizations, municipal leaders did not feel themselves obliged to fund
such endeavors. The partial exception was Boston, where the mayor attempted to set up a partnership with the local businessmen's organizations for the purposes of promoting tourism in 1906.[86]

But some business organizations were convinced that encouraging
the convention trade was a vital public matter. Accommodating conventions promised to provide the facilities for strengthening the local
community as well as profiting the city's hotels and restaurants. The
chief means proposed for achieving these goals was the construction of

a large, publicly owned convention hall. The idea derived from the existing City Beautiful emphasis on public buildings as the locus and symbol of civic community. The monumental civic centers that anchored such plans often included not simply buildings housing the government but also a public auditorium. This great hall was intended to be a center for great community ceremonies, but, businessmen pointed out, it could also host large conventions at a profit to the city.[87]

In campaigns for building such a civic auditorium cum convention center, businessmen's organizations made two pragmatic arguments. First, the existing halls were too small to host the largest meetings. National political conventions and fraternal orders had more delegates than could be easily accommodated in any existing single room. And increasingly important trade groups, such as that of the automobile industry, required more extensive exhibit space. Hotels continued to expand their rentable, semipublic spaces, but these were not large enough either. In San Francisco there were literally no major halls left standing after the 1906 fire. Second, no single enterprise or entrepreneur could command the resources to build and maintain a convention center, and the business groups had demonstrated that they were not united enough to do so either.[88]

But their appeal to municipalities was not simply expedient. Promoters agreed with urban landscape reformers that cities needed new and uplifting public spaces, especially those to be used for leisure. Fine theater and opera performances, art galleries, civic centers, sculpture, and monuments "are the attractions great cities have for the multitudes of people to whom culture and aesthetic gratification are a main object in life—and of such people the most thriving and successful communities are formed," claimed the San Francisco *Merchants' Association Review*. With an auditorium to host such events, the city "can make for itself a high destiny," while reaping the profits of the conventions using the space.[89] A great and refined public space, the public convention hall would enable city dwellers to come together literally as the proper civic spirit would unite them emotionally. And once again, tourists would foot the bill.

The Chicago Association of Commerce's campaign for a publicly funded convention center underscores the distance between the older conception of the public as the body of citizens gathered to debate political matters and the emerging understanding of a public united through commercial leisure. The Association declared that such a municipally sponsored hall would be the "Town Hall of the Nation." Implied by the name was its opposite: city hall, symbol and site of bitter struggles over the division of municipal resources and power. Though city-owned, the town hall was not meant to be a forum for political battles. Rather, it was to be a "public home" for the citizens at the same time that it hosted large, profitable conventions.[90]

Chicago's "town hall" was to be located in Grant Park on the lakefront, conveniently near the downtown area and freight, passenger, and recreation piers. Drawing in hundreds of thousands of people to attend trade and professional meetings, it would offer them both ideal working spaces and an alluring proximity to the city's pleasures. An imagined summertime convention delegate "leans back in his chair. . . . Through the wide south windows he looks upon the picturesque life of the river. . . . Strains of music, perhaps, drift in from afar on the recreation pier." Eventually, the delegate "tires of convention discourse" and ventures out to the pier and beach. Similarly, in winter when conventions met less often, the hall "would take in the outdoor life of Grant Park," including the circus and athletic competitions.[91]

Like the city that organized businessmen and City Beautiful advocates promoted, this convention center was abstracted from social relations and made to serve as a symbol of community cohesion. This vision of unity through business and leisure banished political discontents and indicated that good citizens should stand in much the same relationship to the city as did convention-goers. The ideal of separate spheres had indeed fallen on hard times if a public hall could replace the private hearth as the source of social virtue and moral community. The municipally owned convention center, in short, represented the sea change in American thinking about the sources of urban social bonds and the growing importance of tourism in financing and imagining a renewed, yet thoroughly modern, urban community.

Organized businessmen believed that their campaigns for city beautification and tourism would inspire civic spirit and social unity. The Chicago Association of Commerce published its guidebook "for the dual purpose of properly guiding and assisting in the entertainment of visitors to Chicago, and to instruct Chicagoans themselves in subjects of civic interest." Business associations also urged local residents to acquire the knowledge and visual orientation characteristic of tourists. Having "endeavored to impress upon the citizens of San Francisco the value of an optimistic attitude both towards ourselves and strangers visiting the city," the Pacific city's Convention League also emphasized "the necessity of their being informed as to the many places of interest in and around San Francisco."[92] Such knowledge would encourage a proper appreciation of the city as well as enable the locals to help tourists find and interpret the sights.

This piece of advice suggested that the construction of appropriate spaces and organized business's campaigns to encourage tourism would mean little if Americans did not know what was worth looking at or how to move about their refurbished cities correctly. The creation of cosmopolitan urban tourists required a great deal of "education" in the form of promotional literature. In this realm, organized business had the help of railroad passenger departments, tour companies, and a variety of publishers that produced new kinds of urban description at the turn of the century.

FIVE

"An Individuality All Its Own"

Tourist City and Tourist Citizens, 1876–1915

"This little pocket folio is intended to aid the out-of-town visitor in locating the many places and objects of interest which have an undying and ever-increasing fascination for those whose opportunities are limited," declared the anonymous author of *The Tourist's Hand-Book of New York* in 1905. The slender, fifteen-cent paperback pamphlet had been written specifically for the modern tourist: "The subject matter . . . has been variously treated by other writers and historians in times past, but as far as we are aware, no attempt has heretofore been made to arrange or classify such material in a way that would insure not only acceptability, but *accessibility* as well." [1]

The author of this convenient little guidebook exaggerated its singularity. Far from unique, it exemplified a form of nonfictional urban representation new in the late nineteenth century: the city guidebook. Beginning in the 1870s, publishers associated with the railroads and tourist enterprises began to produce growing numbers of such works. In the same years, middle-class mass-circulation magazines frequently published self-consciously literary urban sketches whose authors wrote about American cities as they long had written about Old World metropolises. Melding the earlier traditions of travel writing and urban description, the new guidebooks and urban sketches focused on cities but were addressed chiefly or exclusively to pleasure travelers. They tended to distinguish the cultural significance of American urbanity from its social consequences and to celebrate the former. These works integrated

American cities into national and international tourist networks by portraying them as subjects appropriate for respectable leisure and literature.

These turn-of-the-century city guidebooks and urban sketches promoted new ways of approaching and moving about the cities that helped to create the tourist as a distinct social type and tourism as a distinct spatial practice. Like the extra-fare cars, businessmen's hotels, and organized tours, the guidebooks and urban sketches of the 1890s and 1900s sharpened the distinction between residents old or new and those visiting the city to see the sights. With the aid of cheap guidebooks, even those visitors "whose opportunities are limited" and who lacked local contacts or a hired guide knew where to go and how to get there. The detailed itineraries and new forms of transit, especially the tourist trolleys and "seeing the city" cars, enabled pleasure travelers to encounter the city as they might have a rural resort at midcentury: a site of leisure safely distant from the anxieties and obligations of everyday life.

Organized city tours also promised to restore the vital sense of community that the nation's sprawling cities had lost but on a new, modern basis that transcended older, parochial loyalties. The idea that each city had a "personality" or "an individuality all its own"[2] played a key role in both making cities appealing to tourists and conveying a sense of social unity. Complementing this perspective, the new guidebooks and urban sketches often portrayed urban landscapes as tidy artistic compositions. Treating cities as objects of literary and pictorial art rather than as social aggregations helped well-to-do Americans not just to make sense of but to take pleasure in the rapid changes in the scale and character of urban landscapes and their denizens at the turn of the century. The spatial practice of tourism promised to weave the many fragments of the city together precisely because it was a public, mobile form of leisure that provided an alternative to the strict division of public from private characteristic of mid-nineteenth-century sociospatial ideals.

Of course, urban tourism was in its infancy in the early twentieth century. It never surpassed the popularity of rural resorts, soon to be reinforced by the rise of autocamping in the 1920s. Further, the urban vision promoted in guidebooks was only one among many competing ideas about social relations and city landscapes. Even the most uninformed and wholehearted tourists had a broader frame of reference than their guidebooks. Muckraking journalists, Progressive reformers, and realist novelists published reams of pages detailing the persistence of urban degradation and spiraling class conflict. Despite their relentlessly cheerful banality, the guidebooks shared these concerns. As guides to public leisure, they expressed the same preoccupation with reconciling cultural and class differences through wholesome recreation as did more critical writings. What distinguished the guidebooks was their bland faith that industrialized leisure made the landscape of modernity livable; that, by "doing" the town, the ideal urban tourist transformed life into art and division into unity.

URBAN PERSONALITY AND THE TOURIST

The idea that places had personalities was a venerable convention in travel writing, yet it had not been much applied to American cities in the mid-nineteenth century. The cities of earlier sensationalist sketches competed for the title of wickedest city of them all, and each claimed peculiar regional characteristics, but none claimed to have personalities. By the end of the nineteenth century, the authors of the new guidebooks and urban sketches began to make just that claim on behalf of American metropolises. The journalist and railroad publicist Edward Hungerford titled his 1913 collection of sketches *The Personality of American Cities*. The chamber of commerce's 1915 guide to San Francisco asserted that the city "has evolved an individuality and a versatility beyond any other American city." Like people, cities had ceased to have character, the result of a disciplined struggle to be good, and began to have personality, a unique yet conventionally appealing collection of people-pleasing traits.[3]

Asserting that cities had personalities was a thoroughly modern, industrial means of making them readily available and intelligible to a national readership—and to tourists. The idea of an urban personality packaged a city as a salable commodity for a national clientele. Succinctly differentiating one city from all the others, it gave a simple, compelling reason why it was worth visiting, despite the fact that the markers of metropolitan status remained standard: fine commercial and governmental buildings, mansions, parks and boulevards, good shops and theaters, and so on. Ridiculing the pretension of the man who claimed to see Paris in New York, Hungerford argued that "New York does not aim to be a replica of any foreign metropolis. She has her own personality, her own aggressive individualism." Like the brand name of a mass-produced product, personality gave a city an imaginative profile that distinguished it from other, very similar sites. The similarity was not accidental; by the turn of the century both goods and cities were increasingly competing on a nationwide, rather than simply a regional, basis.[4]

The idea of the uniqueness of places smoothed the tourist's path into any city by casting it as a meaningful entity similar to Niagara Falls or other natural monuments. A city's personality derived in part from the character of the city's setting and built environment and in part from the character of its citizens taken in the aggregate. Bay windows, cosmopolitanism, and lighthearted hospitality, alternately attributed to the city's "Latin" heritage, its pioneer spirit, or its temperate climate, characterized San Francisco. Soaring skyscrapers, frenetic hustle, and up-to-dateness stood for New York and its residents. Contending for the title in urban hustle and claiming a more loquacious civic pride, Chicago also boasted that it was the most typically American of the nation's cities, notwithstanding its considerable proportion of foreign-born residents. Tinctured with a romantic southern aristocracy and host to Americans from all regions, Washington residents exhibited a greater degree of civilized leisure.[5] These were characteristics requiring no long acquaintance to perceive, for they were immanent in the same crowds and facades that had seemed rife with deceit, chicanery, and indifference to midcentury urban sketch artists.

The guidebooks and urban sketches that promoted the idea of city personality were themselves thoroughly modern products of the industrial economy. Because guidebook authors addressed a far more specific audience and were employees of the tour industry, they had a different relationship to their readers than had their predecessors in urban description. Mid-nineteenth-century writers had not been shy of addressing their readers directly, often inviting them to join the authors in entering a low dive or presenting a card at the finest New Year's Day soirées. The urban sketches and compendiums were works by singular authors reaching out directly to their social equals. They spoke man to man, with an occasional piece of advice for lady readers.

The circumstances of their production supported this direct address to some degree. Although often serialized in newspapers before publication or periodically updated and expanded for reissue, the earlier urban sketches remained individual pieces of writing by identifiable human beings who offered their own experience to augment the reader's. The journey these authors depicted also often included encounters with individual, named city dwellers, both actual and apocryphal. Biographical sketches of famous city dwellers served as an urban approximation of the personal knowledge that small-town residents were supposed to have about local elites. Fallen women, redeemed drunkards, Mose the Bowery B'hoy, and finicky dandies spoke out in these pages, populating the city with knowable, if also highly stylized, characters. Urban description between the 1850s and the 1870s embodied the personal expertise and wary, yet appreciative view of the city's residents and activities that the authors themselves possessed.

The early urban handbooks, in contrast, were far more likely to be compiled or edited by a publisher and credited either to him or to the firm. Yet the publisher was usually a local man, established in the city he wrote of and presumably familiar with it. Sometimes the handbooks were thinly disguised advertising pamphlets for the city's businesses or even a single enterprise. Offering less intimate expertise, the writers of these works were vitally connected to the economic and social interests of a particular city. Works national in scope, such as *Appleton's General Guide* or *The Hand-Book of American Cities,* often made extravagant claims for the breadth and depth of the research done in every locale named; they also solicited corrections and updates from readers.[6]

In some ways drawing on the example of urban sketches, the new city guidebooks followed the precedent of the urban handbooks and national guides. They were often sponsored, compiled, and edited by publishers or interested enterprises such as railroads, hotels, and businessmen's organizations. Yet they also differed from the handbooks in downplaying government and philanthropic institutions to focus more narrowly on the tourist, transient services, and the city's amusements and landmarks. Although many guidebooks incorporated the descriptive mode of the urban sketch, now the publisher or sponsor's name overshadowed the author's.[7]

The waning of the author's visibility corresponded to the rise of a national tourist industry. The consolidation of the many competing railroads of the 1850s into a small number of large ones meant that railroad passenger departments now advertised national routes of travel to a nationwide clientele. By the 1890s a few large publishing houses specializing in the production of guidebooks had also developed. The best known was Rand, McNally, a Chicago company that had been printing tickets and travel guides for the railroads since the 1860s. By the last decade of the nineteenth century, the company was publishing urban guides under its own name. Unlike Appleton's, which continued to print its *Gen-*

eral Guide through the 1890s, Rand, McNally specialized in travel and geography-related materials, but it was not owned or run by a railroad company. It joined other regional and national firms in producing single-city guides in addition to the more usual resort and route guides. The Standard Guide Company, for example, was associated with the Florida-based tour information company, Ask Mr. Foster, and a chain of information bureaus. A national market had emerged for travel to urban locations even apart from regional or national tours.[8]

Local publishers and hotels continued to print handbooks, guides, and souvenir folders, and individuals continued to write and publish urban guides throughout this period. Business and street directories remained common and now grew thicker than ever to incorporate more enterprises, telephone numbers, and the proliferating means of mass transportation. Still, the development of publishing companies and railroads trying to reach national markets with highly specialized works signaled a less intimate relationship between guidebook and tourist. No longer did a guidebook's author stand as a surrogate friend to his social equals; now, large companies extended a generic welcome to a broad range of users. Ernest Ingersoll wrote and updated guides to New York for the Rand, McNally company, while the passenger agent C. A. Higgins wrote a long-lasting route guide for the Southern Pacific Railroad Company, including a lengthy entry on San Francisco.[9] In both cases, the authors were employees of the company. They were more like hired guides than personal friends. Although both midcentury and turn-of-the-century authors hoped to make money from their writings, the later works were not simply literary commodities but also advertisements for specific companies.

The expertise of the new-style guidebooks did not pretend to be local or personal; rather, it was corporate and businesslike—and, according to the companies, more reliable as a result. Rand, McNally informed readers of its 1891 New York guide, for example, that "'guide-books,' unfortunately so called, are often prepared primarily in the interest of certain advertising [enterprises], and hence are both partial and untrustworthy." In contrast, the makers of Rand, McNally's guides were quite independent: "in no single case has any remuneration, [direct or] indirect, influenced them in anything herein written or omitted." This proud statement, however, did not indicate that business interests had vanished from the guide. Like turn-of-the-century newspapers and magazines, Rand, McNally sold advertising space in its guides, trusting this commercial transaction to provide the "independence" that the sponsorship of single enterprises or political parties denied.[10] Like Thomas Cook's conductors, the guidebook writer embodied a new, professional position at once distancing tourists from local, particular social relationships and gaining them broader access to public places and information.

Still a popular form, urban sketches also changed in substance and distribution at the end of the nineteenth century. Writing about natural scenery had long been an integral part of the experience of viewing it. American cities had been the site and subject of ambitious literary efforts at least from midcentury. The journalist and urban sketch artist George Foster, for example, had sought literary fame and fortune, goals he believed had been frustrated by the vulgar nouveaux riches whose wealth bought them cultural preeminence. But, however popular, the sensational subject and style of much city description did not qualify as literature.[11]

Turn-of-the-century urban sketches began to situate American cities within the literary conventions of pleasure travel, just as tour companies, railroad passenger departments, and businessmen's organizations were literally putting them on the tourist's map. The authors of the later city sketches largely abandoned the earlier, sensationalist and reform-minded approach to focus on the charming, eccentric, or picturesque aspects of metropolitan life. Adopting a breezy, lighthearted voice, the new generation often turned its eyes away from the slums and ceased to question what lay behind closed doors. Often visitors to the city of their musings rather than residents, the urban sketch artists of the turn of the century dallied among the city's cultural and recreational resources without much concern for any iniquities. Adopting the opposition between work and leisure forming in other arenas, they left the almshouses and asylums to reformers without literary pretensions or to novelists experimenting with a gritty new aesthetic and got on with the business of making popular art.[12]

The greater professionalization of writing and publishing was as important to the change in urban sketches as it was in city guides. The later writers had ready access to a broad, genteel audience through the pages of the middle-class, mass-circulation magazines that proliferated in these years. Upscale magazines such as *Harper's* commissioned journalist-litterateurs to roam the country, particularly the Midwest and the West, visiting all good-sized cities. This practice was not entirely new; mid-nineteenth-century journals had published many essays on the phenomenal growth of midwestern cities. The articles that resulted from the earlier writers' visits, however, tended to be serious discussions of each city's industrial and commercial importance, usually accompanied by a lament about its cultural impoverishment. Like the contemporaneous urban handbooks and sketches, their first concern was for the moral economy of the new city.[13]

Neither industry nor social structure dominated the new style of sketch, although both might be treated. Turn-of-the-century urban essayists tended to emphasize not a city's role in the development of an American, industrial republic but its cultural significance for the development of a distinctively American literature and art. To express a native culture, each city had to have a unique, easily recognizable identity. City personality and national literature went hand in hand. Hungerford declared that he intended the sketches in *The Personality of American Cities* to portray "something of the flavor and personality of a typical American town."[14] A sensual experience had become the key to understanding both cities and America, where once the discipline of natural history dominated the metaphors.

Notably, both Hungerford and the popular writer Julian Street, author of *Abroad at Home: American Ramblings, Observations, and Adventures* (1914), visited only sizable cities, ignoring the vast rural areas and small towns so long thought the repository of a genuine, if democratically plebeian, American culture. And they understood their mission to have a cultural significance unrelated to the mundane facts of industry and commerce. As he packed in his New York flat for his venture into the provinces, Street received a telegram from a "literary friend" advising him that "*you are going to discover the united states dont be afraid to say so.*" Why be afraid? The journalist confessed that the project seemed at once worthwhile and yet "ridiculous, and ponderous, and solemn with an asinine solemnity."[15] Perhaps American cities did not yet merit the serious literary treatment of European sites, but Street nevertheless boldly risked their integration into the canon of travel literature.

Street's account revealed the incorporation of American cities into a tourist circuit in another way as well, one less rarefied than a claim to literary significance. Although Street disavowed tourism, his approach exemplified the tourist's. He had long wanted to roam the United States, "not as a tourist with a short vacation and a round-trip ticket, but as a kind of privateer with a roving commission." The problem with tourism was its industrial regimentation and vicariousness of experience: "we Americans . . . rush about obsessed by 'sights,' seeing with the eyes of guides and thinking the 'canned' thoughts of guidebooks." And too often journalists "go in search of some specific thing," such as corruption or comedy. Street rejected both kinds of structure: "I claim the right to ignore, when I desire to, the most important things, or to dwell with loving pen upon the unimportant. . . . I shall mention things which people told me not to mention."[16]

In taking this tack, Street expressed the reigning ideal, if not the reality, of twentieth-century pleasure travel. His scorn for the industrialization of experience was one of the chief motives for pleasure travel in this era. Moreover, Street's insistence on the primacy of the artistic temperament expressed the growing separation of the cultural from the economic that helped to underwrite urban tourism in the United States. Street's wanderings would not produce an evaluation of social, commercial, and industrial factors shaping American urban life. Rather, he invoked the spiritual and aesthetic quest of earlier, romantic tourists to assert that the significance of his urban wanderings lay in the literary rendition of an entirely personal experience. Governed by whim, pleasure travel was emphatically not work; and yet, through its very lack of concentrated enterprise, it enabled the perspicacious traveler to discern a deeper truth about the places he or she visited. Leisure and self-indulgence might be the key to wisdom as well as personal pleasure. It was this kind of experience that tour providers promised to tourists and that city boosters believed would foster civic loyalty.[17]

The idea of city personality rested on the reconceptualization of the city as a living entity composed of the built environment and the citizens, both animated by civic spirit. This view was not unique to guidebooks. Its endorsement by advocates of the City Beautiful movement revealed both its political implications and how different it was from mid-nineteenth-century understandings of urbanity. Earlier reformers, notably the landscape architect Frederick Law Olmsted, had conceived of cities as artificial constructs whose alienating effects on human beings needed to be leavened by rustic oases. In contrast, the idea of the city-as-organism assumed urban vitality and insisted on the interconnectedness and functionality of its constituent parts:

> The city that was a short while ago a mere aggregation of human cells has become a highly developed organism, with specialized members, definite needs, and ordered functions. It is growing a nervous system. A certain measure of civic spirit pervades it, so that it is recognized that what harms any part of it harms the whole.[18]

To portray a city as an individual or an organism abstracted it from its social relations and recast it as a singular subject whose needs and purposes were already given in its physical structure. The realm of debate was radically limited, but the mobility and interconnection of parts ensured the participation of all—precisely the ideal of the tourist city.

The city-as-organism also lent itself to a forgiving attitude toward the urban evils that so appalled earlier writers: "Faults? Chicago has plenty of them, and knows it. So has the human race—and the universe, too, for that matter. But the faults of Chicago are those of youth," insisted one travel writer in 1907. A chamber of commerce–sponsored guide to San Francisco informed the visitor, "You have reached a city so rich in its varied types and personal elements, so versatile, so human in its strengths and weaknesses. . . , that it is fit to rank among the dominant communities of the world." [19] The evangelical and republican urgency of earlier authors faded in the face of a belief that urban areas were just going through a stage. Their adolescent awkwardness and emotional extremes would soon pass away with the normal onset of adulthood.

Set in the context of the turbulent urban politics of the turn of the century, the assertion of a unitary and unifying urban personality with an organic basis and life cycle was wishful thinking at best. At worst, it lent itself to cynical political maneuvering. It could easily be used to invoke a preexisting, apolitical unity to which all city dwellers owed allegiance. Any dissent became a betrayal rather than a legitimate exercise of democratic citizenship. Certainly this usage was implicit in the insistence of business organizations that any opposition to their plans indicated selfish, partisan "class interests." But to see the idea of urban personality simply as a fantasy or a Machiavellian stratagem caricatures the complex mix of class interests and social anxieties that shaped elite and middle-class Americans' responses to urban conditions at the turn of the century.[20]

Many Americans wanted to believe that no irreconcilable conflict existed between capital and labor, black and white, native-born and foreign-born. Some larger set of values, whether derived from Christianity, the Declaration of Independence, the new social sciences, or a carefully stylized urban built environment, could surely bring Americans in general and urbanites in particular together in harmony. Despite its limits, the imagined unity of the city's personality indicated a continuing concern about the conditions enabling a legitimate social hierarchy in the city and a yearning for a sense of community. Guidebook writers and sketch artists expressed the same preoccupation with healing the rents in the social fabric that characterized muckraking, early social science, and realist writings. In these genres, writers hoped that finding literary or statistical means of representing the deep divisions among city residents would reveal the way to overcome them.[21] Implicit in the assertion of an organic personality magically incorporating all of the human and physical elements of the city was the hope that it really could be so.

Investing hopes for social harmony in the idea of urban personality marked a significant change in the ways that Americans understood the constitution and enactment of proper, republican social relations. It marked the demise of an older vision of moral community based on the creation of a "tangible" or knowable republic by means of face-to-face relations and refined behavior. The idea of city "personality" signaled the abandonment of any attempt to integrate visitors into the social structure of the city; instead, it integrated the city into the nation. Knowing that San Franciscans were particularly warm and hospitable people, a key aspect of the city's personality, would replace for most tourists any real experience of the hospitality of city dwellers. What welcome they did encounter would come from workers in the tourist industry: hotel employees, paid guides, and souvenir sellers. Occupying a distinct "stranger's path," tourists perceived each city in terms of the personality traits that made it nationally distinctive rather than through local patterns of social interaction.[22]

As well as signaling and encouraging the integration of American cities into tourist itineraries, the idea of city personality smoothed the path of the broadening range of Americans who could afford to travel by the 1890s. The traces of this change appear in the guidebooks' recommendations for how best to see the city. Earlier urban descriptions rarely made mention of the money or time to be spent in sight-seeing, although they might steer visitors to relatively expensive practices, such as hiring carriages, or time-consuming ones, such as walking up Broadway and Fifth Avenue from the Battery to Central Park. These were itineraries meant to introduce the well-to-do, genteel visitor to the social structure as much as the built environment of the city. Guidebook writers, in contrast, often assumed that visitors had limited time, money, and social contacts—and wanted to maximize their use of all three. As the publicist Frank Morton Todd declared, "To enable the stranger to appreciate and enjoy these quite exceptional scenes, with the least inconvenience and expenditure of time and money, the San Francisco Chamber of Commerce has prepared these directions for little jaunts on the street cars."[23]

The replacement of the promenade by "little jaunts" hinted at the altered relationship the turn-of-the-century tourist would have to both the urban built environment and city dwellers. Responding to the fear that the rationalization of city visits would devalue the experience, guidebooks typically promised tourists that they could still achieve the personal enlightenment and serious analysis of the places and peoples that travel was supposed to offer. The guides routinely insisted that to know a city required weeks, if not months or years: "To become well acquainted with the National Capital, and to thoroughly enjoy its many distinctive features, an extended visit is necessary." Unfortunately, this kind of travel was no longer possible: "But as hundreds of visitors are pressed for time, and yet desire to see as much as possible, and the most interesting things, a few hints and suggestions may be of service." [24] No longer leisured gentlemen and ladies, modern tourists wanted the fastest and cheapest means of getting to the right places.

The guidebook presented itself as a substitute for the old-fashioned intensive investigation as well as an aid in the modern goal of the efficient use of leisure time. Not only was the *Tourist's Hand-Book of New York* "intended to aid the out-of-town visitor in locating the many places and objects of interest," but it would also help him or her in "avoiding those long and tedious side trips." The guidebooks' emphasis on efficiency highlighted the industrialization of leisure that eased lingering fears about the perils of enjoying oneself in public. Hutchins Hapgood lamented that Americans "hurry our business in order to get at our pleasure, and hurry our pleasure to get at our business." Indeed, the leisure that most city guides encouraged was far from the "gentle loafing" that Hapgood dreamed of and that tourists often indulged on the long verandas of resort hotels in Saratoga and Monterey.[25]

City guides commonly insisted that sight-seeing was hard work. If the tourist attempted anything like the thoroughness and tight scheduling most published itineraries demanded, it certainly was. Advising readers to begin their tour of New York at the Battery in the south and to work northward, the anonymous author of *New York City Illustrated* (1902) added: "Don't recoil at the term 'work,' for if you see anything like the better part of all that is to be seen in New York you will have accomplished a good deal more of work than of play." A brochure distributed by the tourist agency Ask Mr. Foster provided a detailed schedule for seeing the national capital. Under the heading "ECONOMIZE TIME," it specified to the half hour how much time a visitor should spend at each site.[26]

As well as affiliating tourists with the waning tradition of elite travel, the strenuousness of tourism distinguished its practitioners from other, socially dangerous representatives of urban leisure of the period: tramps and bohemians. According to a slew of state laws criminalizing begging and vagrancy in the 1870s, a tramp was any person wandering about without visible means of support. Guidebook authors and urban sketch artists used the term "bohemian" loosely to describe the "careless and disreputable" men (and a few women) who lounged about in a few shabby café-saloons, justifying their unusual dress and dissipated habits as the signs of artistic temperament.[27]

Tourists certainly might fit either description, since they roamed through the city's streets and institutions without any obvious source of income and often took tea or stronger beverages in city cafés. Visible industry, along with the brevity and commercial structure of the tourists' visit to less than genteel places and people, was an important antidote to misspent leisure. The obvious cost and propriety of their clothing and their use of carriages, hotel rooms, and, increasingly, guidebooks, cameras, and tourist trolleys also helped to distinguish tourists from tramps and bohemians. Although they might occupy a park bench or enjoy a fine, slow-paced dinner, they did not sit idle on stairs or in beer gardens; they did not have the time to waste. Tourists' modern efficiency in touring enabled them to partake in pleasures once available only to the rich. City touring thus embodied and expressed spatially the cultural position of a new middle class defined largely by its cultural capital and efficient use of resources.[28]

The Chicago teacher Helen Boyden, her mother, and a friend made up a particularly well-disciplined party. On their first day in New York in the summer of 1894, the three women rode the Fifth Avenue stage north, taking in the sights, and spent several hours touring Central Park and the nearby Metropolitan Museum of Art. Then the ladies boarded the elevated and rode down Broadway to the Battery on the waterfront, noting the parks, squares, churches, and other important buildings along the way. By then: "It is late so we board the 3rd Av. El. and ride across Wall Street over the famed Bowery," ever vigilant for sights. After having supper with their local host, they visited Madison Square Garden's rooftop summer theater before finally retiring. No one would mistake these sturdy voyagers for the leisured poor or dissipated artists; nor were they the philanthropic or business-minded sight-seers of the 1850s. Hapgood lamented that the American "always retains an ele-

ment of strenuousness," even while playing. Boyden, with a week remaining in her monthlong summer vacation, told herself sternly, "Ma is
quite ill & I am worn out but must not give up." [29]

At the same time that they portrayed American cities as unified
"personalities" deserving of literary and artistic treatment, the new city
guidebooks and urban sketches created a distinct and thoroughly modern social role for the tourist. Because of their mobility and efficient
use of leisure, tourists were the lifeblood of the urban organism. They
circulated a holistic vision of the city even as their movement articulated its parts and connections. To fulfill this social function, tourists
needed to know what to see and how to see it. Turn-of-the-century
guidebooks and city sketches gave them this information by recasting
urban landscapes as tidy artistic compositions and offering detailed itineraries. Both the composition and the itinerary shaped a distinctive
spatial practice that enabled tourists to perceive sprawling, divided, and
often squalid cities as a series of lovely sites available to the cultured
transient. Undermining the distinction between public and private, this
new geography replaced it with an opposition between work and leisure
that privileged the latter as the realm of freedom and potential social
reconciliation.

CREATING URBAN LANDSCAPES

An essential element of a city's personality was its built environment, or
at least select parts of it. Both the new style of urban sketch and the city
guidebook tended to portray cities primarily as visual, architectural artifacts rather than arenas of personal interaction. Like City Beautiful advocates, turn-of-the-century authors of urban description insisted that
cities could be objects of beauty and refinement just as natural scenery
was. But Americans had to be trained to see this beauty, as they were
learning to appreciate stark western landscapes through travel sketches
and photographs.[30] The authors of guidebooks and city sketches intended to impart this skill by encouraging people to move about cities
in a way that endowed the landscape with the spatial and social unity
that the city's personality presupposed. By overcoming the parochial
tendencies of local residents, the tourist's itineraries offered a means for
realizing the new, cosmopolitan, and leisured social bonds that reformers, city boosters, and travel entrepreneurs envisioned.

Teaching Americans to see urban beauty at the turn of the century

was an easier task than it would have been fifty years earlier. By the late
nineteenth century, the expansion of first-class retail, theater, and hotel
districts created refined enclaves at the heart of many cities. These areas
were concentrated celebrations of the power of industrial capitalism to
provide both material abundance and meaningful freedoms to the individual, especially middle-class white women. Magnificent skyscrapers
extended the reach of a modern kind of gentility into the business district as well. The rapid spread of electric trolley lines at the turn of the
century accelerated the development of residential suburbs. The number
of well-off city dwellers fleeing expanding areas of manufacturing, industry, and the neighborhoods of working-class and foreign-born residents rose quickly as well.[31] In other words, as they grew in area and
population, American cities became increasingly segregated by class,
ethnicity, function, and gender. By directing the visitor to a city's show-
places, urban sketches and guidebooks portrayed these sprawling, divided cities as visually coherent landscapes readily available to the
knowledgeable onlooker.

The guides and urban sketches often began by presenting the city as
a composition, usually seen from afar. Authors of urban description had
long urged visitors to climb church steeples (or the Capitol Dome) to
survey the city from above, and views from the water were equally important for San Francisco and New York. Lithographed and photo-
graphed panoramas of the nation's growing cities had been popular at
least since midcentury. But often the city's buildings were less important
in such views than was evidence of the city's commerce, in the shape of
ships or lumberyards. Mid-nineteenth-century images tended to depict
"cityness" by means of an indistinct, vast sprawl of uniform low buildings, long, straight streets, and isolated steeples and domes seen from a
then-impossible aerial vantage point (see fig. 8). As late as 1876 the veteran travel guide producer John Disturnell could write, "The panoramic
view of the approach to [New York] City from the sea is very fine." But,
he sniffed, "[t]he view of the City is less prepossessing," for "little of
it is visible from the water, and it has no very striking object to arrest
the eye."[32]

By the early twentieth century, such a statement would have been lu-
dicrous. More and more often, written and pictorial panoramas drew
the approving eye past the picturesque and prosperous forest of masts
and steamship smokestacks to distinctive urban landscapes. The newer
views directed the reader's attention to the city's profile as limned by its

Figure 8. Bird's-eye view of New York City. Engraving by Frank Leslie, 1853.
Library of Congress, Prints and Photographs Division, LC-USZ62-23779.

tallest edifices and seen from actual approaches to the city or from a
lofty rooftop. By 1891 New York made a nicely composed painting
when viewed from the harbor: "the massive commercial and office buildings at the lower end of the city group themselves into a magnificent
mountain of stately architecture. . . . The focal and foreground point of
the splendid scene is the Battery."[33]

Aided by guidebooks, stereoscope slides, and postcards, people came
to recognize city profiles, soon dubbed "skylines," and were eager to as-
cend to the observation decks that the owners of tall buildings so kindly
provided to test their ability to recognize both individual landmarks and
the overall pattern. Static images of important buildings, often shot at an
angle that portrayed the hotel or city hall or church looming up in a
landscape empty of other buildings, continued to dominate the multi-
plying numbers of stereographs and postcards produced at the turn of
the century. But a growing number of street scenes depicted both soaring walls and a long stretch of pedestrian and vehicular traffic. Such images attempted to portray the city in motion by incorporating large
crowds, streetcars, and other symbols of mobility in the frame.[34]

The cover of the guidebook "New York Illustrated" (1914) is a strik-

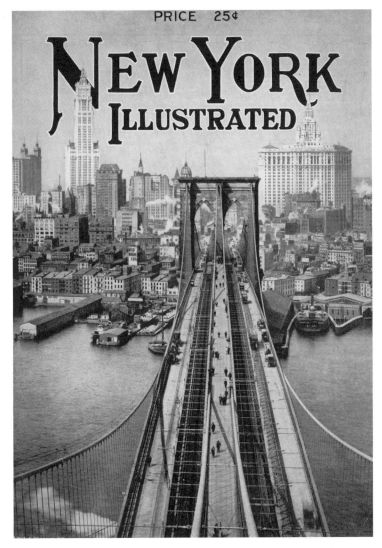

Figure 9. Brooklyn Bridge looking toward Manhattan, "New York Illustrated" (1914). Archives Center, National Museum of American History, Warshaw Collection.

ing example of the pictorial representation of the tourist city. Tall buildings spike the city's profile, while the sweep of the Brooklyn Bridge toward Manhattan invites the visitor's approach (fig. 9). At the center of the booklet, a drawing picked out the looming office buildings of the business district in impossible size and detail. At the tip of the island, the

Figure 10.   Lower Manhattan skyscrapers and Battery Park, "New York Illustrated" (1914). Archives Center, National Museum of American History, Warshaw Collection.

exaggerated Battery Park is perfectly designed to balance the skyscrapers (fig. 10). Aesthetically and literally, it provides the viewer with a place to rest and from which to view the city. Like guidebook narratives, this image shows a legible, orderly, and grand urban landscape.[35]

The new method of perceiving cities as distinctive, dynamic wholes resulted in part from the availability of new building technologies and new forms of mass transportation. Rising far beyond the structural capacity of masonry and quickly overtopping the tallest church steeples, steel-framed skyscrapers made striking landmarks amid a sea of five- and six-story buildings. New York and Chicago entrepreneurs continually vied to build the world's tallest building, and even San Francisco businessmen built upward in spite of the danger of earthquakes. Despite the criticism that such buildings barred sun from the streets and neighboring edifices, dehumanized the urban landscape, and increased traffic congestion, only Washington enjoyed an effective limit on building height before 1915, thanks to congressional fiat. But the perception of the new tall buildings, sometimes clumped and other times widely separated, as elements endowing the city with a visual, expressive unity was not simply a function of their presence. The growing tendency to perceive the city as a unified work of art rather than an agglomeration of buildings, streets, and people endowed the tall buildings with a cultural significance their builders fully exploited.[36]

The panoramic view from above or from the water was only the initial, orienting step into the city. Guidebooks also offered a new mode of moving about cities, one that allowed tourists to avoid the perils and pitfalls so common in midcentury urban description. Unlike earlier works, the guidebooks provided detailed information about what the sights were, how to get there, and what the tourist should make of them. More and more often, detailed itineraries and maps highlighted tourist attractions, ensuring that visitors would not overlook anything worth seeing or see anything not so worthy.[37] Like the conducted tours, guidebooks rationalized the landscape so it could best serve the casual visitor, and in the process separated pleasure travelers further from the everyday and local social relations. One of their aims, after all, was to eliminate the visitor's need to ask for directions.

The exposition handbooks published for the Centennial Fair and the World's Columbian Exposition in 1876 and 1893 had set a precedent for the new city guidebooks. Like the goods displayed on the fairgrounds, the host cities and others along the railways were exhibits of the nation's history and progress. The relatively few city guides produced for the 1876 fair were quite similar to the existing urban handbooks. However, they explicitly addressed temporary visitors to the city, and they demonstrated more interest in naming the "points of interest" than had been characteristic of such works previously. Thus one Philadelphia guide included a map that showed the location of the fairgrounds, the main lines of transportation, and the "location of important buildings" and "points of commercial interest," as well as the "built-up portion of Philadelphia as it was one hundred years ago." Whereas some handbooks and the national guides had included maps, urban sketches never had. Combining the two genres, guidebooks now began to offer specialized tourist maps instead of reprinting existing city plans. Although more topographically accurate than the moral geography of earlier works, tourist maps were equally selective, emphasizing architecturally or historically important buildings and sites rather than neighborhoods.[38]

The guides to the exposition grounds influenced the development of the city guidebook proper in other ways as well, by providing an ideal urban landscape and a characteristically modern way of moving through it. Expositions had begun under one roof in the innovative Crystal Palace in London in 1851. Americans had imitated that model in the not very successful New York fair of 1853. But by 1876 the volume of exhibits, the number of participants, and the scale of ambition had grown. Beginning with the 1873 Vienna exposition, large, landscaped parks containing several exhibition buildings replaced the single hall. Located in Philadelphia's extensive Fairmount Park, the Centennial grounds covered 236 acres and included five shared exhibit halls (Main, Machinery, Art, Horticulture, and Agriculture) as well as dozens of state and foreign buildings.[39] Later world's fairs would make the 1876 event look small.

Given the sheer size of the grounds of the Philadelphia fair, the construction of an intramural railway was a pragmatic concession to the limits of human physical strength. But the three-mile, narrow-gauge, double-track railroad circling the fairgrounds was much more than that. The tiny railroad was itself a display of American industrial strength, a miniature version of the nation's vast railway network, which included more than ninety-three thousand miles of track in 1880. Further, it had a crucial role to play in the tourist's experience of the fair: "On arrival on the grounds, take a seat in one of the narrow-gauge railroad cars. . . . The tour of the entire grounds is thus made, occupying twenty minutes, at the cost of five cents, and giving an excellent general idea of the grounds and relative location of buildings."[40] Riding on the intramural railway enabled visitors to encounter the exposition as a coherent, visual whole before they passed among its walls and crowds. In cities, a growing variety of mass transportation similarly offered a means of seeing the city at once distant, like the view from above, and mobile, encompassing areas too distant to be seen from a single perspective.

The grounds and buildings of the World's Columbian Exposition in Chicago in 1893 made forcefully apparent what was only suggested at the Centennial celebration: the fairgrounds constituted an ideal city. Planned as an architectural ensemble, uniform in style and color, the "White City" also boasted monumental buildings and statuary, plentiful and clean modes of travel, broad streets, elegant waterways, artistic lighting, and good policing. The notorious ugliness, dirt, and danger of the host city, Chicago, furnished an all-too-obvious contrast. In 1912 Charles Moore, the director of the Panama-Pacific International Exposition (1915), made a grand claim for host San Francisco: "Her whole house will be open, decorated, lighted, swept and made ready. The city is the site."[41]

Corollary to the exposition's ideal built environment was an ideal mode of inhabiting a city, one foreshadowed by the cultural uses of the intramural railroad at the Philadelphia fair. The grounds and buildings of the great expositions constituted an urban built environment specifically created to move through and to look at: a tourist's city. The magnificent, though temporary, edifices and the lavish displays of manufactured goods and produce presented the ideal urban landscape as an artifact of aesthetic significance and commercial abundance. The broad avenues reserved for foot and pushchair traffic eliminated the vehicular dangers of city streets, and the cost of admission—usually fifty cents—excluded the human ones.[42]

Ordinary, permanent cities would never achieve the unity of style, careful spatial organization, cleanliness, and personal security that exposition grounds provided, Moore's claim for San Francisco notwithstanding. Nor could real cities ensure the supremacy of leisurely contemplation that the world's fairs encouraged. The near-impossibility of implementing the plans promoted by the City Beautiful movement for the nation's largest cities proved that. But by the 1890s urban guidebooks nevertheless began to write about real cities as if they were expositions. Landmarks proliferated nearly as quickly as exposition buildings and statuary, the gifts of philanthropic millionaires, proud ethnic and veterans' organizations, and public subscription campaigns.[43] And the means of getting about the city quickly also increased, making possible the mobility that allowed exposition visitors to master the grounds before setting foot in them.

Mid-nineteenth-century urban description had rarely made mass transportation the basis for a tour of the city, merely advising visitors to be wary of the chicaneries of hack drivers. Most of the earlier works, in fact, did not bother to explain how the visitor was to get to the city hall, prison, almshouse, college, church, or hospital described as among the city's salient features. The spatial practice of the visitor was not so different from that of the resident as to require special directions, and most visitors would have had local hosts to guide them. In contrast, guidebook writers frequently offered detailed advice on how to "do" the city. Lacking local connections, tourists needed instructions about not just what to see but how to see it, if they were to grasp the city's personality quickly and efficiently.[44]

Urban railways were crucial to the new focus and practice of tourism. A growing number of turn-of-the-century tourists likely did not have the money to spend on frequent or extensive carriage rides, and in any case there were simply more "modes of conveyance" and many more miles of track in the nation's sprawling cities. By 1900 Chicago, San Francisco, New York, and Washington, D.C., all had both horse-drawn and electric rail systems plying their streets. San Francisco and Chicago also had cable cars, invented to make the former city's steep hills accessible for business and housing. In addition, Chicago and New York featured elevated steam and electric railways, and in 1904 the latter opened its subway system. These services often cost a mere five cents a ride. Steamboats also served commuters and excursionists in each city.[45]

In giving detailed instructions about how to reach the important landmarks and how to board and pay for trolley rides, guidebook writers assumed that visitors were unfamiliar with the city. They also assumed that the main-street promenade was no longer sufficient to introduce the tourist to a city's characteristic buildings and residents. That experience would remain important, particularly in New York, but it increasingly became associated with a visit to the first-class business, retail, and theater districts, not an experience of the city's social structure. Instead, echoing many exposition guides, one author advised the tourist that "the best way to familiarize himself with a city is to ride over the main lines of the street railway." Traveling from Boston to Daytona, Florida, in 1892–93, the sisters Anna and Bessie Douglas spent several hours riding from one end of the streetcar line to the other during their brief stay in Jacksonville.[46]

Tourists' reliance on mass transportation affected their experience of the city. Traveling relatively quickly through the landscape, the rider could perceive the buildings and people there as the elements in a panorama. A popular form of entertainment at the time, panoramas were great circular murals past which the viewer walked. They promised to make the surrounded viewer feel as if he or she was participating in a dramatic, usually terrifying event such as the Battle of Gettysburg, the Great Chicago Fire, or the eruption of Mount Vesuvius. However magnificent, of course, they remained painted representations, and the visitor was in little danger of death by fire.[47]

Rapid transit permitted passengers to treat the passing city in a similarly spectatorial, fascinated manner. In a much-quoted passage from the novel *A Hazard of New Fortunes,* William Dean Howells had New York newcomers Basil and Isabel March board the elevated:

> She now said that the fleeting intimacy you formed with people in second and third floor interiors . . . had a domestic intensity mixed with a perfect repose that was the last effect of good society with all its security and exclusiveness. He said it was better than the theatre.[48]

Such an encounter contrasted sharply with the promenade, which plunged the stranger and the visitor into the urban crowds. Walking on State or Market Street, Broadway or Pennsylvania Avenue, offered an intensity far from domestic and very little exclusivity. The stroller was necessarily a player as well as an onlooker. Riding the cars removed the tourist from participation in the everyday and simultaneously offered it to him or her as spectacle. As Isabel March's words suggest, this distance endowed the city with all the "security and exclusiveness" of elevated social circles, making city touring safer and more accessible for the refined.

Moreover, like the rail circuit of the exposition grounds, a ride over a city's streetcar lines gave the rider a primarily architectural sense of the city's differences. Rather than the dress and manner of the citizens, the streetcar promenader could see chiefly the height, material, and style of the buildings. Boarding a Market Street car at the Ferry Building, Charles Keeler wrote of San Francisco's main business street, "[H]ere and there a fine modern building of stone or terra cotta shows that the city is alive and growing." Particularly good evidence was "[t]he fine Crocker building . . . while across the way . . . a whole block is taken up with the Palace Hotel."[49] This kind of perception assumed that fine buildings were sufficient evidence of the city's good health, something the mid-nineteenth-century urban sketch artists, with their penchant for revealing the evil hidden behind fine facades, would never have done.

Of course, the social distance that the streetcar ride made possible was far from complete, for a cross section of ordinary city residents crowded into the seats and hung onto the straps of every mode of mass transit. Like the Broadway omnibus in Foster's day, streetcars were microcosms of urban social relations. Guidebooks rarely mentioned the social relations of mass transit cars, but turn-of-the-century newspaper sketches and popular songs often did. "On a north side car, one day recently," the Chicago journalist George Ade reported, "a woman calmly handed the conductor a $20 bill and said 'One.'" As the other passengers snickered, the conductor got his revenge by returning the $19.95 change in coins. When the woman promptly discovered that she had a nickel after all, the conductor refused to accept it.[50] Well-to-do women's disdain for streetcar etiquette was a frequent butt of men's jokes.

At night, a streetcar ride revealed the underbelly of urban social relations. "Did you ever ride south on State street in the 4 o'clock car?" Ade asked his readers. "In one corner is a human being, 'drunk.' . . . There are always three or four flashy young colored men who are smoking. . . .

If a Chinaman can squeeze in next to the stove it helps out." The "frowsy girls" who boarded next were so unrefined that the men continued to smoke, and the conductor was often called on to break up fights. Unlike a midcentury urban sketch artist, Ade did not make this anecdote the basis for social or moral criticism. Nor did his night's ride on the cars illuminate the social order and the relations among the different classes. Instead, Ade portrayed nonwhite, lower-class urbanites as occupying a world of their own, available to respectable Chicagoans but hardly a threat to their station. This world need not impinge on the tourist if he or she did not go looking for it.[51]

But Ade's cool distance from the crowd was sometimes hard to achieve. Riding in the cars often exemplified the social and physical discomforts of urban life, as William Jerome's lyrics for "Hold Fast!" (1901) illustrated:

> There wasn't room for breathing and you couldn't turn your head,
> For fear you'd bunk it into someone's face,
> And this is what we call the 'human race,'
> They slammed us in and they jammed us in and piled us up in stacks,
> The Irish, Dutch and Blacks, stuck elbows in our backs.[52]

The cars were renowned for violating sexual proprieties as well as the ethnic ones that Jerome's indignant Anglo-Saxons bemoaned. The 1907 song "I Lost Her in the Subway" chronicled the tragic separation of a young couple just married at city hall:

> When last I saw my dear, just let me shed a tear,
> With both her hands she hung on to a strap,
> The train went 'round a curve, the crowd began to swerve,
> She fell and fourteen men dropped in her lap;
> A youth gave her a seat, then stepped upon her feet. . . .
> I saw him wink his eye, I heard my darling's sigh,
> I hate to think what happened after that.[53]

Here was no deception such as the Young Widow had practiced but simply nature taking its way. Just as cities would grow out of their adolescent flaws, so would city residents become acquainted as the inconvenience of urban life dictated.

But even though visitors and residents often used the same streetcars, each group went to different places at different times and for different reasons. Tourists' goals, and the efforts of guidebook writers to structure them, drew them away from urbanites' everyday routines of work and leisure. Guidebooks accomplished this separation by providing long lists of the "sights" worth seeing and, with increasing frequency, detailed itineraries. As well as listing the various "modes of conveyance," the authors of city guidebooks told visitors where they ought to go.[54]

Once again, the exposition guides provided a precedent. The *Visitors' Guide to the Centennial Exposition* adjured its readers sternly to avoid "an objectless loitering tour" by studying the guide and map carefully to design an itinerary. The anonymous author of the *Official Guide to the World's Columbian Exposition* agreed that such study was "an absolute necessity to one who would not travel aimlessly over the grounds and who has a purpose beyond that of a mere curiosity hunter." Aimlessness and objectlessness caused the tourist to see "nothing in particular but things in general."[55] The educative, uplifting effect that expositions—and refined urban landscapes—were intended to exercise was lost if the sight-seer merely wandered. In spite of the growing acceptance of public, urban leisure, fairgoing and urban tourism still required some didactic purpose if they were to be respectable entertainments. Now that tourists no longer shared residents' aims in moving about the city, they needed some other respectable motive.

Guidebook authors similarly insisted that they provided the itineraries to enable tourists to get the most out of their stays. Frank Morton Todd wrote in his chamber of commerce–sponsored San Francisco guide, "We shall give you your bearings, in time and place. We shall endeavor to show you the way, and smooth it for you too. We shall tell you what to seek and how to find it, and possibly what it may mean when you have found it."[56] The itinerary defined and mapped the city the visitor was to see and guided visitors toward its selection of "sights." It was a means of rationalizing both the urban built environment and tourism.

By the turn of the century, many cities offered a genteel, rational alternative to the streetcars that contributed to this rationalization: the seeing-the-city streetcars and autos. The Seeing Washington Observation Cars were advertised as "Exclusive" as well as "Diverting/Economical/Instructive." A competitor declared: "LADIES Remember our coaches have no awkward ladders to climb. Built for your convenience. Polite, uniformed guides on every trip."[57] Like the railroads and hotels, the sight-seeing cars sought to provide an ideal social space removed from the urban masses. (See figs. 11, 12.) While the trolleys often used the tracks of the local electric rail system, they did not follow the usual routes that moved residents between work, shopping, and home.

When motorized, open-topped buses began to replace trolleys in the early twentieth century, the sight-seeing companies boasted that they of-

Figure 11.   Seeing Washington touring car, "Touring Washington" brochure.
Archives Center, National Museum of American History, Warshaw Collection.

fered tourists a glimpse of what was off the beaten track. Moreover, they
did so in an economical yet comprehensive fashion, as the traveler James
Law found: "A thousand points of interest were passed in review in
about two hours at a total expense of fifty cents." [58] To do the same tour
in a hired carriage would have taken hours longer and cost several dollars. The sight-seeing car was the modern, efficient way to get the job
done right.

The selected sights and the guide's determinedly amusing monologue
directed the attention of the car's riders primarily to the historical and
aesthetic features of the urban landscape: "the public buildings, the
grand boulevards, the residences of great men of the past and of the present, the beautiful parks, the noble monuments. . . , the historic spots
and the 20th century business sections." A focus on the built environment characterized urban handbooks as well, but in those earlier works,
the institutions of government and benevolence had predominated.
Turn-of-the-century sight-seeing cars and guidebook itineraries emphasized instead a city's parks, mansions, and monuments, skyscrapers and
retail palaces. Although government buildings remained an important

Figure 12.   Seeing Chicago auto at Monroe Street near State Street. Detroit
Publishing Company. Library of Congress, Prints and Photographs Division,
LC-D4-39413.

part of the tour, especially in Washington, D.C., hospitals and asylums
no longer made the grade for tourist itineraries.[59]

Moreover, whereas the midcentury urban sketch artists had written
of mansions and magnificent business edifices as evidence of opportunity and opportunism, the later guidebooks presented them as signs of a
general aesthetic awakening. The authors of *King's Handbook of New
York City* declared, "The general art taste of the community is revealed
on every side, especially the local architecture. . . . The Vanderbilt
houses, the Stewart Mansion, the Union-League-Club buildings," and a
series of new, towering hotels all "give architectural distinction to the
city."[60] Replacing biographical sketches as a stategy for personalizing
city landscapes, the descriptions of such mansions allowed tourists to
feel the kind of vicarious domesticity that Isabel March experienced as
she glanced into people's windows along the elevated tracks. The mobile, aesthetic appreciation of the city's architecture encouraged visitors

to perceive private wealth as an expression of the nation's success, just as expositions did.

In addition to turning sight-seers' attention primarily to the built environment, trolley touring furnished a discontinuous, visually oriented experience quite distinct from the promenader's stroll at street level amid the urban crowds. Frank Morton Todd's *How to See San Francisco by Trolley and Cable* (1912) provided a striking example. The first of eight detailed itineraries began at the Ferry Building on the bay and took the tourist "through the edge of Chinatown, over the top of Nob Hill, where the Comstock and railroad millionaires built their mansions." It ended on the western edge of the peninsula at "a point within easy walking distance of the Cliff House and Sutro Garden, Museum, and Baths." Along the way, the rider would glimpse old St. Mary's Church, two Chinese bazaars, Telegraph Hill, Yerba Buena Island, the University Club, the Fairmont Hotel, and more. Some of these "points of interest" stood along the route; others appeared in the medium and far distance.[61]

The visually discontinuous experience that a streetcar ride permitted also may have contributed to a changed sense of locality. A crucial factor enabling the segmentation of cities, mass transit permitted travelers to cross urban social boundaries even as it created them. The ability to travel rapidly through the city might allow a person to be "at home" in several geographically distinct regions. Also, the development of residential suburbs accelerated after the introduction of the electric trolley in 1888. A growing range of well-off but not wealthy Americans could now afford to live outside the city proper while commuting there for work, shopping, and entertainment. Suburbanization created an expanding pool of people familiar with city attractions and yet able to evade urban conflicts, especially when suburbs began resisting annexation at the turn of the century. Although commuting was quite different from pleasure travel, both invited the passenger to experience a city as linked together by patterns of transience rather than residence.[62]

Residents, suburban commuters, and visitors all enjoyed playing in the city's retail and theater districts, but tourists could approach the entire urban landscape as a site of leisure. Guidebooks presented the skyscrapers and banks of the city's business district primarily as aesthetic wonders. Boasting a courtyard with "a tessellated pavement, from which rise lines of rose-colored marble columns with onyx capitals, upholding an entablature of polished red granite," the ensemble topped by a stained-glass dome, the Equitable building in New York was an ornament to lower Broadway.[63] Tourists admired skyscrapers' lavish lobbies, and many took the express elevator to their rooftop observatories for a view of the city. The proliferation of fine retail and office buildings opened the entire business district to refined leisure.

Guidebook writers often noted the cost of construction or number of workers of skyscrapers and banks, but the labors performed there received little attention. Instead, travel writers like Edward Hungerford were more prone to notice what workers—especially the growing numbers of women employed in offices—did during their lunch hours. According to his tale of a day's visit to New York, the female clerks frequented dance halls; men's noontime place of preference seemed to be crowded, hectic cafeterias. Even when travel writers took their readers behind the scenes, to the pressrooms of the great daily newspapers and the back halls and workrooms of department stores, few workers appeared in prose.[64] Fifty years before, urban portraitists had found the sight of such large enterprises, with every man in his place, a powerful symbol of the ability of industrial organization to overcome the centrifugal effects of a market economy.

The lack of attention to work and workers was not unique to urban guidebooks. American tourists had long made a practice of visiting industrial sites and were fascinated to find out how things worked, as many exposition exhibits demonstrated. Factory tours continued to be popular in the twentieth century, although city guidebooks rarely mentioned them. But the interest in workplaces did not amount to an interest in the people laboring there. By the early twentieth century, an "industrial aesthetic" shaped the perceptions of many middling Americans. Tall chimneys pouring smoke into the air, huge, fiery furnaces, and cluttered, sprawling industrial sites demonstrated the nation's industrial prowess and a stark, modern kind of beauty. To perceive factories in terms of chiaroscuro necessarily dulled the viewer's awareness of workers and working conditions. In contributing to the transformation of cities into aesthetic landscapes, guidebooks helped to efface the evidence of the social relations underlying them.[65]

The chief exception to the neglect of industrial sites in urban guidebooks was the near-obligatory visit to Chicago's Union Stockyards and its associated packinghouses. They quickly became one of the city's characteristic attractions after their opening in 1865. With a keen eye for publicity, company officials provided conducted tours for visitors to the complex at least from the 1870s. Most tourists found the operations an awesome example of American organizational genius and industrial might. A few admitted that the mass butchery in the packinghouses made them squeamish. But, as Upton Sinclair found after the publication of his exposé of the industry in 1906, well-to-do Americans were not particularly concerned with the working conditions there. Concerns about health and sanitation probably helped to turn public sentiment against the tour in the early twentieth century. Perhaps equally important, the scale and efficiency of the stockyard and packinghouses were no longer extraordinary.[66]

Mass transportation, guidebook itineraries, and seeing-the-city cars each contributed to distancing tourists from local residents and their uses of the built environment. The corollary of the development of specialized tourist services and spatial practices was that tourists became an increasingly distinct presence in city streets. New York's Fifth Avenue stages, among the last surviving lines of horse-drawn omnibuses, allowed tourists to join and to gawk at the carriage parade and mansions of the wealthy. Turn-of-the-century travel writers frequently noted (and scorned) the groups of "rubberneckers" and the seeing-the-city cars led by the well-rehearsed "man with the megaphone."[67]

Obviously out of place, city visitors could also be annoyingly well informed about the "sights." When Chicago businessman Elden Hartley's brother Jonas came to visit, George Ade wrote, he found that despite several years' residence in the city, Elden had not visited the Art Institute in its new building, did not know where the waterworks were, had never seen the Newberry Library, and did not know how to get to Humboldt Park. Jonas, who did know and planned to visit all these attractions, told his brother, "'I think you had better lay off a week or two and become acquainted with your own town.'" City businessmen, City Beautiful advocates, tour companies, and many Progressives heartily endorsed Jonas Hartley's advice. Elden's admission that he was not well acquainted with some of Chicago's sights because "one has little occasion to be over in this neighborhood" spoke to a physical and social segmentation that many urban reformers hoped to overcome by encouraging the proper use of leisure.[68]

To many city boosters, the creation of beautiful city landscapes and the refined tourists they attracted seemed the key to overcoming this urban parochialism and inspiring a sense of civic belonging that had little to do with the mundane relationships and spatial practices of work, family, and local community. Primers for this new spatial practice, the new guidebooks described the tourist's transient, architectural appreciation of the city as a kind of vicarious, democratic ownership, available to anyone with eyes to see. Aiming to "beautify and adorn San Francisco," the Association for the Improvement and Adornment of San Francisco declared, "We have thought of our parks, our neighbors' houses, our streets and our city as of our own home"—although not, of course, in any literal sense. Tourism, not socialism, was the proper means of realizing this collective possession: "Stay-at-homes know who owns the next house, the adjoining farm, but to the traveler in distant states, there is a sense of ownership in everything."[69]

This sense of corporate ownership through tourism became most clear in two related forms of city visits: historical walking tours and slumming in the neighborhoods of ethnic minorities. Both inscribed on city landscapes the legitimate social authority of well-to-do Americans and encouraged them to repossess large parts of the city given over to commerce and the immigrant working class. Both practices contributed to the erosion of refinement and separate spheres most obviously by easing the social dangers of public places. They also exemplified the uses of a historical narrative and racial ideas to create a broad sense of social ownership that made genteel self-possession less culturally necessary.

SIX

"The Noble Spectacle"

*Historical Walking Tours and Ethnic
Slumming, 1890s–1915*

In 1915 an earnest young San Franciscan brought her Boston beau to
see her hometown. He made the trip only for her sake, as he considered
the city too new to have any attraction for the cultured tourist. "San
Francisco is modern to the core," he sneered. "Boston dates back generations, but you have hardly acquired your three score years and ten."
Determined to prove to him that her city had just as much history as
his and thus was equally worthy of the love of its citizens and visitors,
she took him on a tour. They visited the great cross in Golden Gate Park
that commemorated Francis Drake's presence in 1579, the eighteenth-
century Spanish colonial Mission Dolores with its Mexican and Indian
devotees, and the central plaza, now Portsmouth Square, where a crusty
old forty-niner lounged near a fountain dedicated to Robert Louis Stevenson. They also ate tamales at a "Spanish" restaurant, ambled through
the city's Italian neighborhood, and had tea at a Chinese restaurant. In
the end, our heroine won both her point and his heart.[1]

This didactic little romance titled *The Lure of San Francisco* highlights two important elements that altered the way prosperous Americans perceived their cities by the early twentieth century: the cultivation
of a heroic history and the romanticization of ethnic minorities. Both
were part of the effort to discover (more accurately, invent) a truly national culture, the same enterprise in which domestic travel writing was
involved at the turn of the century.[2] The consolidation of a canonical
narrative of the American past and the fostering of a distinctly Ameri-

can culture in the present required defining which people and events were truly American. Choosing the appropriate ancestors and casting ethnic minorities as picturesque peasants, popular writers participated in the process of reshaping the way that Americans imagined and moved through their cities and, more broadly, their nation.

It is significant that *The Lure of San Francisco* appeared in 1915, that it used the strategy of a city tour to make its claims, and that it was written by two women, Elizabeth Gray Potter and Mabel Thayer Gray. San Francisco hosted the Panama-Pacific International Exposition that year, and the businessmen who organized it conducted both an enormous publicity campaign and an ongoing effort to defeat the powerful labor movement there. The cultivation of history and the romanticization of ethnic differences promised to make a city attractive to tourists by giving them privileged access to its meanings and portraying urban social divisions as evidence of unchanging and unthreatening cultural differences. Commemorative events, statuary, and guidebook descriptions and itineraries constructed on the city's landscape a vision of both past and present community. Many other cities undertook similar campaigns to publicize and preserve certain parts of their past in addressing and masking class and ethnic conflicts in the present.[3]

Finally, this way of envisioning the city presented it as a homelike place for the well-to-do, including women. Riding the trolley through San Francisco, the Bostonian eyed "a Japanese arrayed in a new suit of American clothes and . . . a bright yellow *lei* wound about the hat of a swarthy Hawaiian." He remarked, "Lots of strangers in San Francisco for the Fair." But to the San Franciscan, these men were not foreign: "I smiled as I nodded to the Japanese who had worked in my kitchen for three years, and recognized in the dusky Hawaiian one of the regular singers in a popular café."[4] The domestication of ethnic minorities and the flowering of history in the city meant that refined city dwellers and visitors, especially respectable women, now had a greater degree of freedom in moving through public spaces.

Having acquired both history and peasantry, American cities appeared to the mind's eye more like the cities of Europe. As a result, they became increasingly attractive to tourists. A historically and aesthetically meaningful landscape and a stable social hierarchy generally endorsed by the well-to-do were two of the essential preconditions for genteel tourism. These qualities had long drawn Americans to Europe, where the process of effacing the evidence of work and social conflict from many sites attractive to tourists had been ongoing at least since the eighteenth century. City guidebooks now took up that work in the United States.[5]

Yet the creation of a tourist city did not mean simply the application of nineteenth-century-style tourism from Europe and the countryside to American cities. It drew on and forwarded the growing acceptability of public, commercial leisure among the respectable. Sight-seeing tours, historical pilgrimages, and slumming parties encouraged well-to-do white Americans to enter areas of the city they had abandoned— now, not for moral or immoral ends, but in search of innocent entertainment and in appreciation of their own heritage and that of other peoples. The cultivation of a national history in the urban landscape encouraged well-to-do Americans to feel a kind of vicarious ownership of a city even, or perhaps especially, when they did not live or own property there.[6]

Both the narratives that shaped urban tourism and the itineraries that tourists followed promised to overcome the physical and social segmentation of cities that critics and partisans alike had long feared. But the "community" created through urban tourism hardly lived up to the ideal social order reformers imagined when they praised the social benefits of collective recreation and beautiful buildings. The solidified social distance that made urban tourism possible even for the ladies entailed the reinforcement of class and racial hierarchies. Unlike the urban sketch artists of the 1850s and 1860s, guidebook writers portrayed such divisions as essential to the creation of civic community rather than as dangers to an egalitarian republic. Cities became nice places to visit to the extent that tourists abandoned the moral concerns of their grandparents. Yet the opening of city landscapes to respectable leisure also helped to create a broadly shared public realm in which cultural differences might be celebrated, if only as commodities.[7]

"A SWEET AND STATELY EPIC"

In constructing the tourist city, turn-of-the-century authors of urban description drew on and participated in the cultivation of historical and aesthetic associations, endowing city landscapes with the storied quality Americans had long sought in Europe. At the same time that others sought to cleanse, beautify, and modernize urban areas, a growing number of Americans attempted to preserve selected aging fragments of the cities' built environments and to memorialize a proliferating number of historical sites. Sharing the moral environmentalism of the City Beautiful advocates, they worked to imbue American cities with the physical signs and cultural resonance of a romantic past rather than to construct de novo a meaningful urban landscape.

Widespread interest in cultivating an American past first emerged after the Civil War. Before that time, only a few Americans expressed much concern for preserving historical records, landmarks, or sites. The sheer newness of the United States was one reason. Well into the nineteenth century, the nation's founding was a living memory for some and only a generation away for many. It was relatively continuous with many people's own experiences in building and expanding the boundaries of the country. Moreover, many Americans conceived of history as a reservoir of moral and political lessons rather than as a linear narrative. The ancient Greek and Roman republics were as pertinent to an understanding of contemporary conditions as was the American Revolution. As republicans and children of Europe, most white Americans looked to the ruins of Greece and Rome and the monuments of medieval and Renaissance Europe for traces of their origins.[8]

The notion of a specifically American "heritage" required a new conception of history. Instead of a well-thumbed, eternally timely primer in morality and politics, history had to be understood as the product of the linear, forward movement of time, making the past quite distinct from the present. Rather than a source of universal insight into the human condition, this past had to be reconceived as belonging to one, unique people and illuminating their peculiar genius. Once such a perspective emerged, the collection and preservation of "historical" materials and edifices would become something more than antiquarianism. It would be an essential element of cultural nationalism.[9]

The Civil War helped to stimulate the development of a more "modern" and nationally oriented historical consciousness in the United States. The bloody struggle over slavery gave Americans their first national tragedy. Commemorating it reminded Americans both North and South of their sacrifices and sometimes encouraged sectional reconciliation. After all, both sides had suffered. Although the cult of the Lost Cause kept the Confederacy alive in spirit for many white southerners, the belief that the war must be marked in memory and in the built environment was national in scope. Originating in the South, Decoration or Memorial Day soon became a national occasion to mourn collectively for the dead and celebrate their bravery. Statues to representative or famous soldiers went up in many cities and towns. The reunions of veterans of the Grand Army of the Republic and the Confederate forces, separately and together, reenacted the massive wartime mobilization. These enormous meetings reinforced the links among thousands of men who would otherwise never have traveled so far or met so many strangers.[10]

The slew of national and local centennials at the end of the nineteenth century celebrated national unity less ambiguously than war commemoration. In 1876 the United States celebrated the hundredth anniversary of its founding with an international industrial exposition in Philadelphia. In the years following, other expositions, great and small, would commemorate other historical events. Parades, speeches, and monuments marked the hundredth anniversary of Washington's first inaugural address (1889), the relocation of the national capital to Washington, D.C. (1900), and Chicago's beginning as an American settlement (1903). Chicago's elites staged an enormously successful world's fair in 1893, celebrating a year late the four hundredth anniversary of Columbus's discovery of the Americas. Also fudging the dates a trifle, New Yorkers claimed anniversaries for Henry Hudson and Robert Fulton in 1909, while San Franciscans celebrated the founding of their city by the Spanish governor Gaspar de Portolá.[11]

The role of history in each of these events was not always obvious. By their nature, the industrial expositions tended to emphasize contemporary achievements in manufactures rather than past glories. The organizing categories and exhibits of the 1876 world's fair were notable for their neglect of the nation's past, which functioned chiefly as a foil for its glorious future.[12] Yet the commemorative nature of the event itself encouraged some Americans to consider the previous century. After all, Philadelphia had won the exposition over New York and Washington because of its importance in the American Revolution and the republic's early years. However little interest the fairs demonstrated in the past, the narrative of progress that shaped them indicated the emergence of a linear and specifically national understanding of history. Now Americans could begin to think about a heritage of their own.

The celebration of local events mobilized thousands of city dwellers to participate in events that altered a city's landscape, temporarily and permanently, in the name of commemoration. Requiring months of fund-raising and preparation, they featured massive, multiple parades with historical floats, speeches, and the erection of monuments (see fig. 13). They dominated a city's streets, squares, and newspapers for days, sometimes for more than a week. Teachers and lecturers tutored

Figure 13.   Dewey Arch, New York City, 1899. Library of Congress, Prints and Photographs Division, LC-USZ62-83851.

schoolchildren and adults on the local and national significance of the event. Event organizers encouraged priests, ministers, and rabbis to deliver sermons pertinent to the occasion, and many seem to have done so. Such public anniversary festivals prompted Americans to perceive their cities as historical sites by endowing them with the "associations" so crucial for the practice of refined tourism.[13]

In addition, the industrial fairs forged a link between history and national industrial achievements that worked to legitimize the existing disparities in wealth and the cultural authority of the rich. Both issues had preoccupied the midcentury authors of urban sketches, whatever their politics. The expositions allowed business elites to show their best face by displaying the mechanical marvels and abundant, high-quality goods they produced. Melding commerce and culture, the fairs linked national progress to the development of a market economy and large-scale industry. They portrayed the products of private wealth as evidence of the public wealth. At specifically historical events, the socially prominent

heirs of the founding fathers or "pioneers" might be asked to represent
their honored ancestors at banquets and on floats, demonstrating the
continuity of social status and merit. Many donated their relics from the
hallowed past for public display: private heirlooms became collective
heritage.[14]

The most commonly stated aim of these events was to instruct immigrants in American history and values in order to assimilate them. Many
white, native-born Americans, especially the Anglo-Saxon, Protestant
elites, believed that if the millions of newcomers arriving at the turn of
the century did not adopt distinctively "American" values, the republic
was in danger. As he organized New York City's fête in honor of the hundredth anniversary of George Washington's first inauguration, Charles
Henry Hart noted, "It is well to let the thousands of strangers, that are
pouring into this country every month, know that we have a glorious
past, and that our prosperity as a nation to-day is the result of the foundation laid a hundred years ago." Moreover, the surge in immigration
at the end of the nineteenth century compounded the long-standing anxiety that Americans really had no unique culture. In the face of these
pressures and the political and economic consolidation of the United
States, defining and celebrating a specifically American past became a
pressing national need.[15]

More and more often in the early twentieth century, organized businessmen conceived of and controlled city celebrations, and they sought
to make leisure serve both commercial and civic goals. They hoped that
rationalizing the leisure practices of city dwellers, like teaching American history to immigrants, would overcome the class and ethnic divisions in the city. The Hudson-Fulton Celebration organizer Edward
Hagaman Hall urged Americans to "abandon themselves . . . to a rational festival" in which "the poorest and the richest will share equally in
the enjoyment of the various splendid and artistic spectacles." Like earlier proponents of refinement, Hall did not stop at exhortation. The
New York Herald reported that the subjects of "King Carnival" "will
not be allowed to run riot in the streets. All throwing of confetti has been
prohibited. . . , and any carnival high jinks will be confined solely to the
marching army's maneuvers." [16]

The attractiveness of such safe, brilliant, and business-controlled
events to tourists was not far from the minds of promoters. Seeking to
challenge the growing popularity of New Orleans's Mardi Gras, San
Francisco's Merchants' Association insisted that the "carnival spirit rises

spontaneously in San Francisco at New Year's." Given the spirit, "[a]ll it needs is a little intelligent direction and management to grow into a civic institution of importance and value." After the festival took place on the cusp of 1908–9, the Association approved: "[T]he unmistakable carnival spirit was abroad. . . . The bands, automobiles, electric floats and other features provided by the committee in charge served their purpose and gave the crowds something to talk about." An orderly jubilee in which people enjoyed "such restricted reveling as could keep itself within the bounds of due propriety," the event also reaped a handsome profit for the local businesses who funded the mobile and stationary floats with their bands and maskers. Like festival sponsors elsewhere, the San Francisco Merchants' Association hoped that the New Year's carnival would become "the 'big show' of the year, a recurring custom of the City, attracting visitors from all the Pacific Coast states . . . to enjoy a pleasant vacation and do their yearly shopping at the same time." [17] The cultivation of history, the rehabilitation of public leisure, and the promotion of tourism often went hand in hand.

Historical festivals were not the only occasions for cultivating historical associations in urban landscapes at the turn of the century. More or less assiduously, Americans, including those living in New York, Washington, D.C., Chicago, and San Francisco, sowed the seeds of literary, artistic, and historical significance in their built environments. Like the City Beautiful advocates, they hoped that their efforts to reform the urban landscape, by preserving meaningful artifacts of bygone days, memorializing important sites, and putting up appropriate monuments, would bring citizens together on a higher plane. The City Historical Club of New York declared that its aim was "to awaken a general interest in the history and traditions of New York, believing that such interest is one of the surest guarantees of civic improvement." To that end, the members conducted classes and public lectures, wrote historical sketches, and published a series of historical walking tours that emphasized lower Manhattan but also embraced the outlying boroughs.[18]

Historical societies and preservationists cultivated a very particular past, an *American* heritage in cities once barren of it. This project involved the selection of appropriate founding events and founders—noble Indians, French Jesuit missionaries, and American entrepreneurs in Chicago, for instance, rather than the African-French Jean-Baptiste Point du Sable. As this example suggests, incorporating the traditions of former occupants into a triumphal American narrative was central to the project. The heroine of *The Lure* declared to her Boston beau: "I'm a Californian. I was born here and even if I haven't Spanish blood in my veins, I have the spirit of the old padres." And she was not alone: "The open-hearted hospitality of the Spaniards is a canonical law throughout the West."[19] Combining the best traits of all the earlier European settlers of the area, the true American represented their natural heir. This appropriation of non-Anglo histories erased conflict in the past and naturalized class and ethnic differences in the present.

Commemoration and preservation also addressed peculiarly urban problems that well-to-do Americans faced. Infusing urban landscapes with "heritage" endowed the often bewildering and unrelentingly commercial urban built environment with deeper meanings. The well-to-do Americans who knew and cultivated the invisible significance of the city's built environment could reassert imaginative, if not actual, control over large parts of it that they had abandoned to commerce and working-class slums. Even as it promoted ethnic assimilation, historical commemoration also encouraged well-to-do Americans to reassert their authority in the city by claiming cultural ownership of it. In this way, the activities of historical societies consciously and unconsciously made cities more amenable to tourism.

The activities of the City History Club of New York illustrate the point. In the late 1890s and early 1900s, the society published several pamphlets detailing historical walking tours in various parts of newly established Greater New York. Although they addressed themselves chiefly to residents, their detailed directions and keyed maps resembled those that urban guidebooks were increasingly providing to tourists.[20] The walking tours such clubs designed encouraged both residents and visitors to move through the city in the tourist's manner—engaged in contemplative leisure.

Historical tours were concerned primarily with discovering the signs of a hidden city. Starting at West 14th Street and 10th Avenue, one such tour began with a short walk to the south to "(I.) **Gansevoort Market:** Site of Sappokanican ('carrying place') the Indian village where Hudson is supposed to have anchored in 1609." Only a sign—the "Sign of the Goose"—remained as a visual cue to this history. The historical tour required the participant to acquire an esoteric stock of information about the urban built environment that had nothing to do with present meanings and uses. Drawing on the cultural capital of genteel Americans and giving them a reason to enter otherwise unrefined places, historical tourism helped to expand the public spaces that they could respectably occupy in the city.[21]

An important element in the vogue for local history was an interest in the names of places. Names that expressed a romantic history were far more attractive to American tourists than the local use-names. At the turn of the century, some Chicagoans engaged in a debate over the origins and meaning of their city's name. Although it might, unhappily, derive from an Indian term for "at the place of the skunk," it could also be associated with a more appropriately romantic and ancient incident: "the drowning, at some remote period, of an Indian chief of that name" in the Chicago River.[22] The cultivation of romantic names displaced the ordinary, contemporary uses of a landscape in favor of the tourists'— and city boosters'—preference for evocative associations.

If the city's name did not spark much debate, the origins of street names might be of considerable interest. The New York History Club's published walking tours were sometimes little more than lists of landowners who had at one time or another given their names to a street or village: "Abingdon Square was named for the Countess of Abingdon, Admiral Warren's daughter. . . . Christopher Street was called 'Skinner Road' for one of Sir Peter Warren's sons-in-law. . . . [T]he original 'Fitzroy Road,' [was] named for another son-in-law."[23] Following the sequence of owners offered a genealogy of place that made those who knew the lineage the cultural, if not literal, heirs of the original English proprietors. Moreover, it emphasized an orderly process of change based on marriage, inheritance, and sale, in contrast to the often chaotic and mercilessly competitive real estate market. Renaming or reciting the former names of a street, a site, or a house restored the knower to the cultural ownership of urban spaces.

Evidence of this repossession rests in what the historical forms of city description left out. Often, especially in New York, historical walking tours took the participants into areas of the city long given over to crowded tenements housing working-class Americans and immigrants or to thoroughly modern skyscrapers housing insurance and financial services companies. Yet judging from the historical narratives, the city appeared empty of all but ghosts: "Come with me. . . , and as we walk up Broadway this afternoon, close your eyes to present surroundings, and let me picture the thoroughfare as it looked forty years ago."[24] Few immigrants and fewer bankers appeared in these pages, or did so only in melancholy asides.

Instead, writers invoked the presence of the past and underscored their own sense of belonging. "Every nook and corner in the old quarters of town, rich in its associations with by-gone times, is sacred ground to the man who loves the past," Rufus Rockwell Wilson wrote of lower Manhattan. John Flavel Mines insisted that even in Battery Park, now ringed by warehouses and tenements, "there is no lack of pleasant companionship to those who recall the feet that in old times pressed its gravelled walks." This was no dirty, bewildering metropolis; "To me," Mines wrote, "it is all a sweet and stately epic." Francis Leupp protested, "[My book] is nothing more ambitious than . . . a stroll about Washington with my arm through the reader's, and a bit of friendly chat." Along the way, "we will try to people [the public places] in imagination with the figures which once were so much in evidence there."[25] Promenading among refined ghosts, the genteel individual risked no rude jostling or offense to his or her sensibilities. The evocation of famous past residents, from the perennial favorite, George Washington, to Washington Irving and Robert Louis Stevenson, personalized an otherwise impersonal landscape without reference to the current social order.

In most cities at the turn of the century, the new cultivation of an American past led to few large-scale changes. Not until much later in the twentieth century would local, state, and federal governments involve themselves to any great extent in historic preservation. Here and there a local patriotic or historical society succeeded in purchasing and refurbishing a historic inn or home. Members put up bronze plaques to mark the built-over sites of famous events and noted on maps where an old wall, doorway, or mantelpiece still survived.[26] What mattered more than the physical reshaping of the urban built environment was the visitor's perception and intent in walking through the particular region of the city.

Only on exceptional occasions did the interest in cultivating heritage result in the erection of major public monuments. Richard Watson Gilder, editor of the genteel *Century Monthly Magazine,* led a fundraising campaign to create a permanent replica of the temporary arch raised in New York's Washington Square to celebrate the hundredth anniversary of George Washington's first inauguration. Defending this project against a proposal to preserve one of the other memorial arches, he articulated the intersection between cultivating a heroic past and cementing community in the present. "The whole town has fallen in love, so to speak," with the arch at Washington Square, he declared.

This unifying, apolitical passion arose because the arch "was designed (in the first place) for the square which bears Washington's name;
in the second place this design . . . was appropriate to the surrounding
architecture. The houses near, both inside and out, suggest the Colonial
period." The public had responded just as City Beautiful and commemorative groups hoped to this happy combination of historical and architectural appropriateness: "The movement was started spontaneously
to perpetuate that arch on or near that place." Finally, a wide variety of
New Yorkers had easy access to the square: "Rich and poor [alike use]
its hospitable walks and avenues." As a result, the construction of a permanent arch "will be the beginning of a new era for our city,"[27] one
characterized by love and beauty rather than alienation and ugliness.

The cultivation of historic associations enabled middling Americans
to reassert cultural hegemony over parts of the city they felt they had lost
to the influx of immigrants or the encroachments of business. At the
same time, it cemented a sense of both local and national pride through
a shared past now increasingly visible in the landscape. Like the guidebook itineraries, historical tourism increased the social distance between
the well-to-do tourists and the people they encountered in the streets.
Whereas itineraries and the use of streetcars created a physical and temporal distance, the cultural capital necessary for the appreciation of
"heritage" did so by allowing those in the know to perceive the city as
an orderly, romantic place whose genealogy supported their own social
claims in the present. The members of historical societies certainly hoped
that historical tourists would feel a renewed bond to a city because its
antecedents were their own.

Historic preservation and commemoration also furthered another
kind of distancing. Sacralizing history and its relics widened the imaginative gulf between genteel Americans and the past that they claimed.
Their own activities had the ironic effect not of making history live, of
making it serve as a moral force, but rather of making it seem distant
and quaint. Existing independent of individual or collective daily practices, the past comes to consist of a collection of sacralized relics, frozen
in time, use, and significance. It is designed to be available to just the
kind of vicarious ownership that tourism embodied. This view of American history displaced the question of the ownership of the city onto the
past and into the realm of culture, just as urban tourism offered a vicarious, visual ownership in place of social integration or economic
possession.[28]

The tendency of cultivating heritage in urban landscapes was to put residents and tourists in the same position. Because it privileged knowledge of a canonical past over present uses, the resident's everyday knowledge was no longer useful. He or she needed to learn the specialized knowledge of the tourist. That was the message of Ade's little fable about the Hartley brothers: Chicagoan Elden was woefully ignorant of what was really important about his own city, while his visiting brother, Jonas, had read his guidebook and knew how to find all the best cultural and historical sites.[29] If city dwellers only knew where the historical monuments were and what they meant, if they took pleasure in its architecture, if they could enjoy themselves peacefully in the streets under the aegis and for the profit of local businesses, then they would have a sense of belonging to it along with every other urbanite. Historical tourism promoted this vision of order and stability over against the experience of constant change and antagonism in the built environment and social structure. It encouraged Americans to regard cities as artifacts rather than as social organizations.

But neither the guidebook itinerary, with its focus on landmarks and architecture, nor the historic walking tour, with its eye on fragments of a canonical history, excluded urban residents from their purview entirely. There were people in the tourist city, people whom tourists wanted and expected to see in their perambulations. Chinese, Italian, and eastern European Jewish immigrants and to a lesser degree African Americans were the most often sought out of city dwellers. These ethnic enclaves were the counterparts of the landscapes of progress and heritage.

"A PANOPTICON OF PEEP SHOWS"

At the same time that historical and patriotic societies spearheaded efforts to cultivate a national heritage, guidebook writers and urban sketch artists began to deploy the histories of European and Asian immigrants and African Americans in a new way. The models provided by exposition midways, the growing importance of race and evolutionary thinking, and an emerging unease with the costs of modernity enabled these authors to present ethnic and racial minorities as picturesque urban peasants. Their supposedly traditional, colorful lifestyles became commodities for well-to-do tourists. The result was to encourage respectable Americans to reenter urban, public spaces that had been ceded to the poor at midcentury, but now without the moral dudgeon or evangelical aims of that period. Abandoning the desire to create a single, refined community, tourists also cast aside, at least for the duration of their visit, the assimilationist aims of many reformers. They sought a transient, commercial but vivid experience of what was presented to them as timeless, ineradicable cultural difference.

Even during the heyday of refined and republican anxieties about cities, many Americans had shared a belief that cities were the seat of advanced civilization, and they took pleasure and pride in the fast-paced, bright-hued heterogeneity of city streets and crowds. Urban portraitists had long used the word *cosmopolitan* to express both the architectural grandeur of American cities and their thousands of polyglot residents. New York, Chicago, and San Francisco boosters all claimed for their hometowns the title of the most cosmopolitan city in the United States, although Chicago was more often called the most American of cities, despite its huge foreign-born population.[30]

By the turn of the century, American cities seemed to merit the adjective *cosmopolitan* more than ever, boasting beautiful parks, magnificent business centers, monumental public buildings, lavish, electrically emblazoned retail and theater districts, and well-kept middling and luxurious elite residential neighborhoods. More immigrants from all over the world continued to pour in, adding to the color and variety. The segmentation of the city and the specialization of the literature of urban description now often meant that, in city guidebooks, a fascination with cosmopolitanism accompanied a genial tolerance for the city's flaws rather than a fear for its social fabric. Such an attitude paved the way for the pleasure-seeking but respectable tourist.[31]

The new attitude emerged at a time when the geographic and intellectual organization of racial and ethnic differences was changing rapidly. Between 1880 and 1920, millions of southern and eastern Europeans joined a continuing stream of Germans, Irish, and other western Europeans entering the United States. The "new" immigrants were predominantly Catholic or Jewish, and many white, native-born, Protestant Americans believed them to be less assimilable than western European arrivals. During the same years, the possibility of racial equality raised by the Thirteenth and Fourteenth Amendments withered. The customary segregation and disfranchisement of African Americans were written into law throughout the southern states and often enforced extralegally in the rest of the nation.[32] Both the new immigration and the imposition of a new racial code affected urban description.

They did so most obviously because of the presence of immigrants

and black Americans in urban areas. Most newcomers to the United
States settled in the large industrial cities, finding work in factories and
sweatshops. Of the four cities in my study, New York and Chicago particularly were home to vast and varied foreign-born populations from
both the "old" and "new" waves of immigration. New York's Lower
East Side became well known for its densely crowded neighborhoods of
eastern European Jews and Italians, as well as a small colony of Chinese.
Chicago's sprawling immigrant settlements, curiously, did not much attract travel and guidebook writers, although the claim that Chicago residents spoke as many as forty languages among them was common.[33]

San Francisco also had a "cosmopolitan" population. In addition to
the usual run of European immigrants, by the 1870s the Pacific Coast
city was home to thousands of Chinese men—and a few women—
who comprised its most distinctive ethnic enclave. Laws restricting and
then banning their immigration in 1875 and 1882 set the precedent for
the National Origins Act of 1924. The city's Italian fishermen and their
neighborhoods also attracted considerable attention. Because Washington, D.C., lacked significant industry, it did not attract large numbers of
immigrants, but many African Americans settled there in the late nineteenth century.[34] In urban description, the city's African American residents occupied much the same imaginative space as European and Asian
immigrants in other cities.

Members of the American-born working class, black and white, and
many immigrants often used public, urban spaces in ways that middling
Americans found disreputable. They socialized and worked on stoops
and sidewalks, frequented beer gardens and saloons, danced in concert
halls, and generally were not genteel. In the huge compendiums of the
1860s and 1870s, their drinking and dancing on Sunday often merited
a chapter. Such accounts mingled an attraction to the gaiety, sympathy
for hardworking people enjoying their only day of leisure, and disap-
proval of their religious indifference and unrefined amusements.[35]

These anxieties did not disappear at the turn of the century. The
widespread xenophobia of the period among native-born Americans is
as well known as the ameliorative and assimilative efforts of many reformers. But in the increasingly specialized literature aimed at tourists,
the public presence of "ethnic" city dwellers became a colorful attraction rather than a social danger. "The object of these paragraphs," one
San Francisco writer pointed out in 1897, "is not to descant upon the
Chinaman, his vices and virtues, but to point out the interesting sights"

of Chinatown.[36] Writing about the city's Chinese neighborhood apart from a more or less impassioned discussion of "the Chinese question" had been nearly impossible in the 1870s.

To portray ethnic and racial minorities as sights rather than social problems transformed the thrust of urban description. In the mid-nineteenth-century works, poor immigrants and native-born Americans had posed a serious danger to both the republic and the respectable individual. They had done so because their vices and crimes derived from the fatal mixing of universal human weaknesses with the degraded conditions of urban life. Although immigrants might fall faster and farther than the righteous native-born American, anyone could be fatally deceived or tempted into vice. But the authors of guidebooks and new-style urban sketches assumed no such human similarity. Nor did they anticipate the unwitting social contacts among the virtuous and the vicious believed to be so endemic and so perilous in the city of the 1850s.

Guidebooks and the new style in urban sketches instead portrayed city dwellers as colorful elements in a great spectacle for the enjoyment of the visitor. In doing so, the authors drew on the model provided by the industrial expositions. The main fairgrounds, encompassing the official exhibition, state, and national buildings, represented an ideal city of harmonious architecture and sculpture, broad, well-planned avenues, and good lighting and policing. These areas suggested the refined experience that tourists might experience in a city's downtown business area or retail section; the attractions in both were chiefly architectural and commercial. It was the midway, the amusement section of the expositions, that offered a model for the tourist appreciation and appropriation of other people's cultures.[37]

Often separated from the main grounds, the midway comprised a series of national or ethnic villages, streets, or typical buildings, intermixed with mechanical rides, freak shows, novelties, and food concessions. While national exhibits in the main halls of the exposition displayed fine arts, manufactures, and agricultural products, those on the midway displayed the people themselves. Included in teenager John Lunneen's lists of "[t]he things, etc. that I seen in Chicago and at the Fair," was a list of "[t]he foreigners I seen." He regarded the Japanese, Chinese, "Esquimaux," and Italians with as much enthusiasm as Pope Pius IX's chair, a $15,000 cloak, "[a] very large turtle, [b]lood sucking sharks," and more.[38]

The national exhibits on the midway were designed in a highly conventional way. They relied on prevailing notions of the kinds of architecture, dress, work, and leisure thought "typical" of a people. An advertisement for the concession "Street in Cairo" described it as "a composite structure which combines the most beautiful architectural features of Cairo" peopled by "a throng of natives" who daily performed artisanal crafts, sword, candle, and belly dances, and a full-blown wedding. Just as the advertisement claimed, "Enter the eastern portal. . . , and you realize your dream of the Orient." Not far away from this Egyptian fantasy, the visitor could partake of the European custom of public leisure by sipping coffee at the Viennese café, ride on the Ferris wheel, or visit Hagenbeck's animal show.[39]

The midway exhibits made ethnic difference a salable commodity literally by charging visitors a fee to view dances or skits. They also did so more subtly by packaging them for the tourist's visual appropriation. Claiming to be educational displays and occurring within the genteel boundaries of the exposition, these exhibits allowed visitors to enjoy themselves publicly, watching partly nude men and women perform exotic ceremonies, without risking their respectability. The temporary, stylized quality of the contact between tourists and the peoples on display vacated it of the dangers that such mixing posed in real cities. These were not people with whom the well-to-do Americans who dominated exposition crowds would interact on a daily basis, nor could they be mistaken for the tourist's social equals. Therefore, their lack of refinement could have no moral implication for the spectator. A cartoon lampooning the black Johnson family during its visit to the fair illustrates the point: when Mr. Johnson stopped to shake hands with a grass-skirted Dahomeyan man, Mrs. Johnson exclaimed, "Ezwell Johnson, stop shakin' han's wid dat Heathen! You want de hull Fair ter t'ink you's found a Poo' Relation?"[40]

Guidebook authors and urban sketch artists drew on just this sense of the commercial value of immutable ethnic and racial boundaries in presenting to tourists the minority peoples who lived and worked in American cities. In describing San Francisco's Chinatown as "a panopticon of peep shows," the railroad passenger agent and guidebook writer C. A. Higgins underscored the voyeurism that characterized ethnic slumming. Although the guides "do not include the lowest spectacles except upon request," Higgins continued, "very many visitors, regarding the entire experience as one of the conventional sights of travel, . . . release their conductor from considerations of delicacy."[41] As on the midway, a stable set of aesthetic conventions and commercial transactions established and maintained the social distance between the tourist and the object of the tour.

The slumming tour itself often mimicked the experience of strolling down the midway from concession to concession. In 1891 Rand, McNally's Ernest Ingersoll conducted his reader on a "ramble at night" through the neighborhoods of New York's poor ethnic minorities. Past the missions and police headquarters, one walked into the Italian areas on Mulberry Bend, then strolled to Chinatown on Mott Street to see "an extremely picturesque and foreign scene." The Bowery, the Russian Quarter, and "Judea" appeared in quick succession, and the tour ended in the saloons of Cherry and Water Streets, presumably the haunt of lower-class but native-born white Americans. Although Ingersoll used some of the purple language of his literary ancestors, in his tour the visitor never stopped to banter with the locals or to speculate about the effect of their degradation on respectable society. Rather, visitors sauntered out of Little Italy "with no sense of alarm, since no vendetta has been declared against us," and "have no temptation to heed" the beckoning of the jaunty prostitutes.[42]

As these passages suggest, the turn-of-the-century tourist was not in any danger in venturing to the city's nether parts, according to the guidebooks. "As for danger—pooh!" the anonymous author of *Rand, McNally's Handy Guide to Chicago* (1893) declared. "[A] sober man, of ordinary appearance and tact, can go anywhere on the streets of Chicago. . . , at any hour of the night, without worrying himself a particle as to his safety." The slums had become so safe that sometimes the ladies joined these tours, especially those of Chinatown. Although some works hinted that such behavior was not entirely genteel, the sheltered young Amy Bridges did not hesitate to tour the Chinese neighborhoods of Los Angeles and San Francisco in the 1880s.[43]

The very safety of the city's underbelly dismayed some of the middling men who had previously had sole rights to the practice of *flânerie* there. In 1915 the music and literature critic James Huneker wryly accused the advocates of neighborhood playgrounds for destroying the "East Side with its Arabian Nights entertainment. Twenty years ago you could play the rôle of the disguised Sultan and . . . sally forth at eve from Park Row in pursuit of strange adventures." But that thrilling world was gone; instead, "Oddly enough, human beings like ourselves passed to and fro."[44]

The travel writer Julian Street similarly discovered that the new, improved city attractive to tourists lacked the vice so characteristic of the midcentury city. He went to great lengths to find one of the "pictur-esquely shocking" private apartments for assignations in San Francisco: "Alas for my imaginings, here was no rose-pink boudoir..., but a room like one of those frightful parlor 'sets.' . . . [M]y dream of a setting for sumptuous and esthetic sin was dead."[45] Mocking the earnestness of mid-nineteenth-century urban sketches, Huneker and Street suggested that the real dangers of the modern world were boredom and vulgarity, the consequences of mass production and rationalization.

Slumming lost its luster for its earlier, privileged practitioners just as it became a business soliciting a wide range of patrons. It was no longer a privilege of class and gender but a commercial service that made any personal relationship with the lowly unnecessary. At midcentury, worldly, cynical journalists and police detectives had guided slummers through the haunts of the vicious, but by the turn of the century, guide-books for New York, Chicago, and San Francisco noted firms specializ-ing in slumming tours. The existence of these commercial services deci-sively separated social surveillance from public leisure. This distinction simultaneously made slumming more respectable for a broader clientele and diminished the thrill that had accompanied the transgression of re-fined sociospatial boundaries. Just as organized tours promised to provide the privileges of the rich to the merely well-to-do by industrial means, slumming tours offered stainless social transgression by reducing it to a commercial transaction.[46]

Many city guidebooks included some kind of slumming tour in the itineraries they offered to tourists in the early twentieth century. The in-stitutionalization of slumming contributed to the erosion of refined and republican fears about urban social relations. It stimulated the rise of a worldly cosmopolitanism among a greater range of Americans. Once the residents of city slums became commodities for tourists rather than their companions—however inferior—in an urban, republican experi-ment, they posed no danger. Vice and filth remained titillating, even shocking, but they had lost their ability to threaten the whole of society and became merely exhibits of urban color. Following a summary of the social problems that Chinese immigration posed, Higgins concluded, "Certainly Chinatown, with all its sanitary faults, is the most pictur-esque feature of the city's life."[47]

In addition to providing a model for the commodification of the ur-ban slums, the exposition midway also embodied a concept of racial dif-ference that made it easier for respectable people to do a little slumming while stopping in the city. The midway's human exhibits were meant to

illustrate an evolutionary conception of racial difference. Kept distinct
from the main exhibition halls, they ran from most "civilized"—the
Viennese café, for example—to the most "primitive," such as the Da-
homey or Eskimo villages.[48] While visitors might participate in European pastimes, they only watched performances and bought trinkets
from the "less advanced" peoples.

These carefully designed exhibits demonstrated the increasing importance of race in American society. Race had been central to the way that
white Americans conceived of themselves and organized their society at
least since the late seventeenth century. By the late nineteenth century,
however, the emancipation of American slaves, the rise of European and
American imperialism and of nationalism across the globe, the rising influx of immigrants, and the growing acceptance of evolutionary thought
altered the meaning of the term. Increasingly, race became central to the
definition of American nationality.[49]

In the United States before the Civil War, a political model of citizenship had prevailed. It centered on the belief that contact with American democratic institutions could transform the victims of foreign
tyranny and backwardness into good, progressive citizens. Even then,
many native-born, white Americans doubted the capacity of groups such
as Irish immigrants to become good citizens, and free African American
men were excluded from political participation along with all women.
But by the last half of the nineteenth century, doubts solidified into
certainty about the importance of race. It became common among
many white Americans to locate the roots of the nation's political system not in its republican institutions but in race, usually the "Anglo-
Saxon" race.[50]

"Race" entailed both biological and cultural distinctiveness, encompassing what is now considered national or "ethnic" identity. The inter-
twined Western discourses of civilization and evolution produced a racial hierarchy that placed western European and North American whites
at the top, with southern and eastern European, Asian, Native American, and African peoples below them in that order. Long an important
category, race now expressed an absolute and consummately important
difference that defined a person's place in an evolutionary scheme as well
as in the social order. It defined individual and corporate futures by
defining their origins in the distant past.[51]

In the United States, both the acceleration and changing composition
of immigration and the long retreat from ensuring African American
civil rights contributed to the efforts to define and protect clear racial

boundaries. Xenophobia and racial discrimination intensified at the turn of the century. But the growing importance of nationalism and racial origins also stimulated many Americans, not just native-born whites, to celebrate their heritage and to seek to inscribe it on urban landscapes. Americans with minority ethnic and racial backgrounds participated in the elaboration of the national past, often with the encouragement of Anglo-Americans seeking to overcome the country's heterogeneity.[52]

Ethnic or national origin became increasingly important in the organization of the representation of a city's social order in parades and other public events. Ethnic contingents were beginning to replace trade-based ones in many parades as early as the 1850s, and this trend had accelerated by the turn of the century. After the Civil War, gendered symbols of national origin, such as the Maid of Erin or Columbia, grew more common, symbolizing the idea of the unity of nationality and biology. The businessmen who organized many public festivals deliberately reinforced this sense of cultural affiliation by seeking to include contingents of men from most of the city's immigrant communities. Citing the integrative functions of such events, the organizers of New York's Hudson-Fulton Celebration (1909) arranged for Irish, Italian, Bohemian, Hungarian, and other ethnic delegations to escort the floats in the historical parade. Division Five in Chicago's Centennial parade (1903) marshaled that city's national societies, whose members dressed in their "native" costume. The notable exception was African Americans, who were very rarely asked or permitted to march.[53]

The festive public deployment of race and ethnicity was central to the development of the fledgling urban tourist industry. The floats and marching delegations gave ethnic differences a discrete, conventionalized form, as did the midway exhibit. In celebrating and packaging these differences, both the exposition concessions and the parade floats drew on the notion that culture—literature, arts, and popular folkways—grew out of race or national origins. This belief allowed tourists to regard the living and working conditions of ethnic minorities as cultural expressions of their nature. "About whatever these strange people do, there is an elusive, indefinable touch which is distinctively racial and picturesque," Charles Keeler wrote of San Francisco's Chinese residents. "[I]t serves at once to create atmosphere."[54] Immigrants and African Americans were artifacts of their culture rather than members of a social realm shared with the tourists.

The belief in the racial origin and unchanging character of minority cultures made an externally imposed "authenticity" increasingly impor-

tant. The organizers of the Hudson-Fulton festival, for example, con-
tracted with a broker to provide 125 "real New York State Indians [i.e.,
Iroquois], not halfbreeds," as well as all of the costumes and equipment
they needed to "perform such games, dances, or other motions as may
be necessary for the proper rendition of the scenes in which they take
part." Like most Native Americans who performed at historical festivals, the Iroquois had to present themselves as whites expected to see
them: relics of a lost past, not fellow citizens.[55]

Yet the idea of authenticity also required the incorporation of some
members of ethnic minorities into the new civic order, however marginal
and stereotyped the role. Selected in 1909 to play the part of Gaspar de
Portolá, San Francisco's first Spanish governor, Nicholas A. Covarrubias "will reign over the revels of the Portolá Festival fortified by many
years' experience as a fiesta king." Covarrubias integrated himself into
the urban, industrial order by staging his history and culture for the
entertainment of Anglo-Americans. At the same time, he claimed the
founding of San Francisco for the old Californio elite and asserted a role
for his people in the contemporary civic order, if only symbolically.[56]

A crucial element in transferring the example of the midway to ethnic slumming was the aestheticization of poverty. The journalist Will
Irwin launched a long and successful career with his loving eulogy to
San Francisco's Chinatown after it burned down in the earthquake and
fire of 1906. The old Chinese quarter, he wrote, was "[u]nsanitary to
the last degree. . . . But always beautiful—falling everywhere into pictures." Acknowledging that "the shabby avenues have a picturesqueness
of their own," William Dean Howells nevertheless rejected Irwin's perspective: "[T]here is nothing more infernal than the juggle that trans-
mutes . . . the misery of [our] fellows into something comic or poetic." [57]
But few guidebook writers—and probably few tourists—shared Howells's qualms. Instead they adopted Irwin's pictorial perspective and
treated the neighborhoods of poor ethnic minorities as the picturesque
counterpart to the classical beauty of the business and public buildings.
(See fig. 14.)

Aestheticization was not the only strategy available to the authors of
urban description. Evolutionary thinkers maintained that the different
races represented different stages in the process of evolution. Just as they
occupied the top of the racial pyramid, Caucasians stood at the forefront
of the process of change, nearly always imagined as progress toward the
better. The terms "modern" and "primitive" thus constructed and naturalized a hierarchical social order in the present. White, native-born

Figure 14.   W. A. Rogers, "The Jewish Quarter, Boston," no. 94, Cabinet of American Illustration. Appeared in *Harper's Magazine* 99:845 (November 1899), illustrating an article by Sylvester Baxter, "Boston at Century's End." Library of Congress, Prints and Photographs Division, LC-USZ62-17252.

Americans understood racial and ethnic minorities as living at a different time, meaning both in the past and at a slower pace. Mired in "tradition," nonwhites and non–Anglo-Saxons still lived just as they had centuries (or even millennia) ago. In contrast, white Americans considered themselves the most modern of peoples. In place of tradition, they had reason; in place of superstition, they had science.[58]

Guidebook writers routinely claimed that Little Italy or Chinatown was "just like" a city in Italy or China: "as we jostle through" Mulberry Bend in New York, Ingersoll wrote, "it is hard to believe this is not Naples." Charles Keeler invoked San Francisco's Chinese residents: "Oh, that strange mysterious horde in the center of San Francisco. . . , living in a civilization as old as the pyramids!" Fisherman's Wharf, another San Francisco guidebook writer declared, "is a transplanted 'Little Italy.' The real Mediterranean atmosphere is seen here."[59] Such claims made it irrelevant for the tourists to consider their own relationship to such people, either as well-to-do Americans or as tourists. These peoples were authentic relics of other cultures, not participants in the struggle to get ahead in which native-born, white Americans found themselves enmeshed. (See fig. 15.)

For modern life unfortunately had its costs. Its fast pace, the insistent pressure of "progress," and the erosion of older certainties and social connections made living at the leading edge of civilization stressful, cold, and bland. The elimination of foolish superstitions and useless traditions was the way of civilization, but the rationalized result lacked the warmth, color, and meaningful social ties of "traditional" ways of life. Many well-to-do Americans shared a sense of "weightlessness" as older religious certainties eroded, to be replaced only by the imperative to progress. Although few Americans committed themselves to antimodernism, many sought ways to make their lives more meaningful and vital by drawing on the cultures of more "primitive" peoples.[60]

Because of the way many white Americans understood their racial and national identity, ethnic slumming offered them something more than simply an evening of risqué enjoyment. Time governed their lives. Evolution put them at the forefront of civilization, and their brief history had shorn them of long tradition, making them the newest, most up-to-date of peoples. Clock time regulated their orderly work and living habits. "The pace of urban life" expressed their hardworking hustle and their keenness to get ahead socially. Soothing the strains of such incessant haste, ethnic slumming offered an ersatz, itinerant sense of place

Figure 15.   Arnold Genthe, "The Morning Market, Chinatown [San Francisco]," taken between 1896 and 1906. Library of Congress, Prints and Photographs Division, LC-G403-0051.

to those who could not afford to go abroad to the supposedly more rooted cultures of Europe. Defined as living outside of time, the ethnic peoples who were the objects of tourism embodied, for white American tourists, a strong sense of place both ethnically and socially. The "tradition" said to govern their lives expressed not simply their temporal backwardness but also their acceptance of their low social place.

The urban sketches of Hutchins Hapgood reveal this dynamic clearly. "[T]here is nothing more exhilarating," he wrote, "than to turn yourself loose among the people. I know two or three men of education who, whenever they want to have a good 'temperamental' time, go out at night, alone, and wander for hours about the lowliest streets in the city." Why? Because the "low" were more honest and genuine than the middle classes. "The middle-class person. . . , striving constantly to rise, to get where he is not, is comparatively vulgar, graceless, and unformed." Such people were superficial and inauthentic, leading "a Cook's-tour-like voyage through life." But the Irish tough, the East Side Jew, or the spieling girls in the slums knew and were content in their place; therefore, they were straightforward, honest, and vigorous in their expression. In company with other anxious moderns, interaction with such people was something for which Hapgood's "nerves and his intelligence sometimes longed."[61]

But, significantly, Hapgood himself had no place in his own narrative—except for the crucial fact that he orchestrated it. While celebrating the publicness of the poor, he retained his own privacy by traveling from his world into theirs at his own convenience. To his credit, Hapgood tried to return the favor by publicizing the names and works of some aspiring immigrant Jewish writers and artists. But in his own writing on New York's poor neighborhoods, he remained a tourist.[62] Given organized tours and city sight-seeing cars, even the ladies could indulge in this kind of vacation from the stresses of modernity without risking their privileges.

One of the essential conditions for the romanticization of ethnic minorities was the commercialization of public life in the nation's large cities. Of course, the invasion of urban social relations by commerce was nothing new. It was a central theme of the admonitory writings of the mid-nineteenth-century urban sketch artists. But, by the 1890s, rather than poison relationships among urban dwellers, the cash nexus was becoming the means of maintaining the proper social distance between them. Mid-nineteenth-century city portraitists had either described the fine facades of the new dry goods palaces or warned of the danger of getting cheated. The authors of turn-of-the-century guidebooks, in contrast, blithely sent tourists shopping not just in the fine department stores but all over the city.

Writing in 1912, Helen Throop Purdy urged her readers to spend a leisurely afternoon in San Francisco's Chinatown. She barely mentioned the more usual nighttime slumming tour, for the quarter's lavish bazaars were its chief attraction for her: "Here, in gorgeous and bewildering array, are silks and embroideries to delight the eye and deplete the purse, ivory carvings worthy of the cabinet of an emperor; cloisonné, Satsuma and Canton wares, exquisite lacquer, brass and bronze."[63] Although some "cheap and tawdry" goods might be mingled with the fine, Purdy did not doubt that her readers could tell the difference. That a woman wrote this guide underscored the importance of shopping in opening larger areas of the city to respectable women.

No other ethnic minority's enterprises could rival the draw of San Francisco's Dupont (now Grant) Street Chinese bazaars. But many

cities' public markets provided another stage for their minority populations, especially African Americans and eastern European Jewish immigrants. Neither the markets themselves nor visits to them were new.
Midcentury writers had touted them as evidence of a city's vast hinterland, large population, and generous table. They were important public
institutions, on a par with hospitals, prisons, and even city hall. As they
lost the patronage of well-to-do city dwellers to enclosed retail groceries,
however, the central markets became the objects of political struggles
over the uses of the streets.[64] Avoiding this contest, the authors of guidebooks and urban sketches in the 1890s and 1900s portrayed the markets simply as aspects of the urban picturesque associated with the Old
World and ethnic and racial minorities.

Chicago's "Ghetto market," one guide asserted, "is one of the interesting sights of Chicago and will be enjoyed by the average visitor looking for the unusual." At the public market halls in Washington, D.C.,
"quaint old darkies offer for sale old fashioned flowers and 'yarbs,' live
chickens, and fresh-laid eggs. . . , smoking cob pipes and crooning word-
less melodies just as they used to in 'befo' de wa' days." New York's
street markets and pushcart vendors, who were often from Italy or eastern Europe, elicited similar comments, although there the incursion of
cheap, mass-produced goods led commentators to marvel that people
were willing to buy such items.[65] The entrepreneurial spirit of many Jewish immigrants combined with long-standing anti-Semitism to make it
difficult for white, Protestant Americans to view them as relics of a picturesque past.

Shopping in the slums and identifying various national groups by
what they sold transformed the foreign-born and nonwhite denizens of
the city into "natives" for white tourists. The minority peoples represented racial difference not simply through the color of their skins, their
language, and their customs but also through the sale of their cultures'
baubles and beliefs. This kind of transaction established and solidified a
commercial relationship that also constituted a racial and class hierarchy. The souvenir was the material expression of the changed nature of
social relations among unequals since midcentury. At midcentury commerce had threatened to undermine all social distinctions through its
potential for deceit; now, commerce maintained that social distance and
forged new, cosmopolitan connections.

Ethnic entrepreneurs were quick to take advantage of the growing interest of white Americans in appropriating bits of their cultures. The
outstanding instance occurred in San Francisco's Chinatown. Destroyed

along with most of the downtown in the earthquake and fire of April 1906, the neighborhood survived another of a series of efforts to force the Chinese out of "the heart of the city." Instead, the prominent merchant Look Tin Eli planned to build "an ideal Oriental city." Drawing on Chinese and Chinese American capital, Look helped to finance the construction of two pagoda-topped bazaars in the center of Chinatown and the reconstruction of the pagoda-style telephone exchange. He boasted that "San Francisco's new Chinatown is so much more beautiful, artistic, and so much more emphatically Oriental" than the old. The city's white leaders soon came to agree that making the neighborhood look more "Chinese" was a better idea than eliminating it; a few years later, they cooperated with the Chinese Chamber of Commerce in erecting fanciful "oriental" lampposts. On their own, residents sometimes acted as guides and translators for tourists. Even racism could be turned to some meager benefit.[66]

If you had already found "mementos enough to please all your relations for a year," in San Francisco's Chinatown, "you can walk over to the Telegraph Hill country and find picturesque Italy, Spain and Portugal. You can find epicurean meals at these table d'hôte cafes." Eating at "ethnic" restaurants became increasingly popular around the turn of the century. Before the 1890s Anglo-Americans of all classes seem to have had very limited dietary preferences. They ate "ordinary" American food, meaning plainly cooked roasts, boiled and fried vegetables, and baked and fried breads and cakes. The well-to-do also ate "French" food, meaning more elaborately prepared dishes with sauces and French names, at first-class restaurants and dinner parties. By the 1890s first-class bars and cafés had incorporated German and Celtic themes and foods, although the most exclusive dining establishments remained resolutely "French."[67]

Italian, French, and even Russian and Hungarian tables d'hôte appeared with increasing frequency in guidebooks and city sketches in these years. In San Francisco, one might also find "Spanish" (probably Mexican) restaurants. The restaurants were small and tended to be in less than genteel neighborhoods. They offered simple, set menus for fifty to seventy-five cents, a price lower than one would expect to pay for a meal at a first-class establishment. The portions were generous and often included a bottle or a half bottle of wine. Dining at such a place was strikingly different from dining in a grand hotel restaurant. It required the visitor to go slumming and then to mix with the locals, even partaking of their strange foods. C. A. Higgins wrote that the tourist would find in San Francisco's Italian restaurants "a rare Bohemian sort of entertainment."[68]

The change was most striking with Chinese food. Visiting a restaurant had long been an integral part of the Chinatown tour. Before the 1890s, though, those few daring white Americans who sampled Chinese dishes were uniformly disgusted. Most early slummers did not even order meals, instead requesting only a few plates of sweets and tea. They were always dismayed to find the former odd and the latter unsweetened and milkless. But, by the 1890s, more and more nice white people actually frequented Chinese restaurants because they liked the food—and the "bohemian" atmosphere. Fancy Chinese restaurants opened in Chicago's business district to cater to the lunch crowds. The introduction in the 1890s of chop suey and other dishes combining Chinese and American cuisines contributed to the growing popularity of the restaurants, but clearly white, well-to-do Americans were also beginning to broaden their tastes.[69]

The ethnicity of the servers and the food was an important part of the experience. Maria Sermolino, whose father owned and ran an Italian restaurant in turn-of-the-century New York, recalled, "Whatever 'atmosphere' existed sprang from the fact that papa, and Madama Gonfarone, his partner, and the waiters and bus boys and cooks, and the bartender and the dishwashers and musicians, spoke and thought and acted 'Italian.'" This and other ethnic restaurants benefited from the valorization of immigrant cultures that Hapgood, among others, promoted in an effort to allay the sterility of Anglo-American modernity. Sermolino wrote of the artists who lived nearby, "We did not know why they thought it was so wonderful to be 'Italian' but since they said so we believed it."[70] The commercial, unequal structure of the encounter in restaurants as in bazaars permitted respectable white Americans to partake of the pleasures without sharing the pains of minority status.

The inclusion of quaint ethnics in Washington guidebooks by the early twentieth century marked a transformation in the city's imaginative configuration. Even as other cities developed the impressive public buildings and monumental architecture that had long distinguished the national capital, Washington acquired a picturesque underside to complement its official pomp. Yet, while the "Seeing Washington Cars" showed their passengers a "typical negro shanty" and "quaint negro scenes on market days," the official buildings and canonized historical sites remained the chief sights to be seen. Despite the homogenizing effects of the emerging national tourist industry, significant differences persisted.[71]

Among the four cities in my study, only New York and San Francisco seem to have supported ethnic slumming to a great extent. Although authors commonly noted the great ethnic diversity of Chicago residents, few went on to construct a tour of its huge immigrant neighborhoods or its growing enclave of African Americans. The striking exception to this rule was *Rand, McNally's Handy Guide to Chicago* (1893), which adopted the format and to a large degree the content of the firm's New York guide (1891). Standardization outweighed the conventions for describing Chicago in this unusual work.[72] Rather than eliminate local differences, the national tourist enterprises adapted them to a series of conventions about urban life and tourist desires.

Commercialized ethnic slumming promised to alleviate the boredom, vulgarity, and stress characteristic of modern life for many prosperous white Americans. Yet its very existence indicated the waning of the urgent, often dangerous moral connection that mid-nineteenth-century Americans had felt between the different classes and ethnic groups. A transient practice, slumming, like other forms of tourism, offered a new way of forging social and spatial relationships, one with greater and solidified social distances, but also one allowing for a more cosmopolitan appreciation of cultural differences. The members of ethnic minorities found opportunities in the commodification of their cultures that often gave them ways to make a living and to retain some aspects of their own heritage. Occasionally the racialized notions of culture that supported slumming also offered them a prominent, symbolic place in the local and national communities. Such were the ambiguous consequences of replacing the dream of "the tangible republic" with that of "the noble spectacle."[73]

Conclusion

A Nice Place to Visit

"The regular 3:30 P.M. train on the 'Michigan Central' on July 7th 1894 bore three ladies bent upon a 'pleasure exertion' as it pulled out of the Chicago Depot." The intrepid travelers returned a month later, their journey unhindered by the ongoing economic depression or the great railway strike of that year. In some ways, the tour that the Chicago schoolteacher Helen Boyden, her mother, and a friend undertook was entirely typical of nineteenth-century excursions. Its duration was not unusual and it included conventional elements: the ladies visited Niagara Falls, a perennial attraction, and spent two weeks at an oceanside resort. But, strikingly, they spent the remainder of the month in a rapid tour of cities, visiting Albany, New York, Boston, Philadelphia, Baltimore, Washington, D.C., and Pittsburgh.[1]

Like many travelers before them, Boyden and her companions seem to have toured the smaller cities, Albany and Pittsburgh, mainly because they were there for a day while waiting for another train. But they had clearly planned their visit to the other cities ahead of time. They obtained rooms at good hotels without difficulty and followed rigorous, detailed itineraries almost every day, visiting the major streets, parks, historical sites, and cultural and governmental buildings in each city. The cities they toured were not only open to curious visitors but also prepared for them, so they did not need to stop to secure permission before entering a building. Boyden knew, no doubt from reading a guidebook, which places, sites, and sights were available and appropriate, and she knew how to get there cheaply and quickly. She mentioned few or no city dwellers save the friends or relatives who hosted the party in New York. Later, Boyden joined thousands of other women traveling to National Education Association conventions, becoming another new kind of traveler.[2]

Helen Boyden's ease in travel and city touring marked how much middling Americans had changed since the thrilling, frightening urban sketches of the 1850s and 1860s. She never questioned the propriety of her activities or slackened her determination to see all that was to be seen. Her knowledgeable admiration of paintings, architecture, and historical sites demonstrated her considerable store of cultural capital. She was comfortable enough to poke fun at Horatio Greenough's statue of George Washington in a toga: "Stepping to the door [of the Capitol] we gaze on the fine approach & entrance G.W. sits facing us but which does he say as he holds his hands uplifted: Ein glas bier? or Have a hack?" Pleased to see the "boys in blue" who were suppressing the massive railroad strike of 1893–94, she never raised questions of wealth, morals, and social justice as she toured the cities in her itinerary. "Lafayette, Lincoln, & Washington mutely speak" in New York's Union Square, but no strikers, beggars, or prostitutes did.[3]

The difference between Boyden's commentary and that of mid-nineteenth-century city visitors exemplifies the transformation in the way that well-to-do Americans imagined selfhood and the nature of social bonds. The ideas of refinement and separate spheres located the origins of the independent individual in the private realm. Only self-possession and the ownership of private property enabled full and virtuous participation in public affairs of politics and business. Without the sequestered, affective private family centered on a virtuous mother, the republican realm of male equality and freedom would degenerate into inequality and license—exactly what the sensational urban sketches of the 1850s and 1860s deplored. The refined sociospatial vision sought to redress and yet exacerbated the moral and political dangers in the public spaces of the nation's rapidly expanding commercial cities. True community and true republican equality would result from the acceptance and practice of refinement by all Americans; until then, genteel people had to tread carefully in public spaces.

In the early twentieth century, the separation of spheres and the elaborate etiquette of refinement seemed prudish rather than prudent to many well-to-do Americans. The old sociospatial ideal impeded the cultural economy much as small local or regional businesses impeded the continuing growth of the market. Increasingly, a reformed middle class founded its identity on forms of cultural capital that did not rely as much on the personal networks and local customs so central to refinement. Part of the growing national, corporate economy, the new professionals and managers constituted themselves in part by claiming more "modern" means of making social connections and legitimizing their social power: college degrees, specialized expertise, professional associations. The display of cultural capital and the appropriation of cultural artifacts and experiences marked and justified their social claims to a greater extent than did the ownership of property.[4]

Tourism powerfully embodied the national cultural claims of this re-formed middle class in a particularly modern way, nowhere more than in the dangerous, contested cities. First, as a transient practice, it asserted and enacted the economic and cultural integration of the nation, with tourists—those able to move freely—as the privileged actors. Second, as a leisure activity, it divided the world spatially not so much between private and public (although in an altered form that division remained pertinent) as between work and leisure, between those with meaningful leisure time and those without. Third, it was a thoroughly commercial activity, restructuring existing social relations around the cash nexus as it broadened the access of the well-to-do to places and peoples now cast as nonmodern and noncommercial.

The ability and willingness of well-to-do Americans to tour urban areas required the erosion of an older hope for a moral community among city dwellers. The combination of refinement and republicanism had created that hope as well as the pervasive anxieties of the mid-nineteenth century. No less hierarchical and coercive in practice than the self-indulgent racism of twentieth-century tourists, the sociospatial ideals of refinement and separate spheres had expressed a critique of the ills of urban life and an urgent need to ameliorate them. Both sketches and handbooks offered solutions: refined behavior and an urban wariness of strangers, punitive and rehabilitative institutions, labor discipline, virtuous homes, fine parks, and, of course, the local knowledge of place and people that these works provided.

The cheery banality of the turn-of-the-century guidebooks suggested that cities had no problems and tourists no responsibility but thoroughness. But the guidebooks' jovial assurance that all was well in American cities was not simply capitalist realism at its worst. For one thing, the study and amelioration of urban problems was increasingly becoming something that specialists did. Popular exposés like Jacob Riis's lantern slide lectures and resulting book, *How the Other Half Lives* (1890), urged the well-to-do to support city ordinances reforming tenement housing rather than forge personal, moral relationships with individual poor people. Residents in settlement houses dedicated themselves to the latter task, but in deliberately separating themselves from middle-class society, they contributed to the professionalization of charity and social uplift. The growing importance of statistics, scientific methods, and municipal funding marginalized older forms of middle-class charity and the social assumptions and relationships on which they rested.[5]

Also, despite their specialization, the guidebooks participated in an effort to represent the city to itself that characterized both arts and sciences in this period. In company with scientific studies of working families' budgets, the turn toward "realism" in literature, the growing popularity of the Ashcan school of painters, and the proliferation of romanticized sketches of poor urban neighborhoods and city historical sites were all efforts to find a mode of representation adequate to the strange, new twentieth-century world. Somehow capturing the city's essence, in all its glory or ugliness, on paper in numbers, words, paint, or photography, promised to overcome the yawning gap between haves and have-nots in American society. This new knowledge would then illuminate solutions to all of the problems plaguing a modern, industrial society. The new kinds of urban description promised to show Americans who they really were and thus how to forge a stronger, better society.[6] Urban tourism was one way that prosperous Americans participated in this project and translated imagery into day-to-day patterns of movement and social interaction. Like the earlier era's moralizing, the tourists' thoroughness and efficiency signaled an awareness of the need to cement legitimate social bonds.

The brilliant, exciting, and thoroughly safe city that the guidebooks depicted and that growing numbers of tourists visited was the landscape of an emerging consumer culture. As many critics have persuasively argued and my own account demonstrates, the culture of consumption was far from the social panacea that the promoters of urban tourism, among others, portrayed it to be. Existing inequities persisted, starting with the fact that a majority of Americans had only very slight access to the new abundance. Tourism exemplifies the commodification of cultural differences and social relationships that, for many critics, is the worst feature of a consumer culture. Privileging leisure as the realm of freedom and self-definition concedes workers' alienation from their work and abandons the old equation between the moral self and the production of social value.[7]

Yet, as other scholars have noted, the emergence of a culture of consumption also had positive effects. David Nasaw has argued that turn-of-the-century public amusements created a more expansive, participatory public realm. White men's dominance of both public affairs and public spaces waned along with the rehabilitation of public recreation and the rise of a commercial entertainment industry. The new amusements, like urban tourism, often celebrated and incorporated the cultures of ethnic minorities. The new "need" for leisure could be and was used as a weapon in labor struggles and in defense of ethnic cultures. To be sure, this new public realm was far from egalitarian: it incorporated and ratified the segregation of African Americans; it was controlled by businessmen increasingly distant from the patrons; and it reinforced existing ethnic and sexual stereotypes. Moreover, the cheaper entertainments—amusement parks, for example—offered more opportunities for cross-class and interethnic mingling than did the more expensive tourism. Yet tourism, like many other manifestations of the culture of consumption, did create spaces in which men and women of a range of ethnic and class backgrounds might meet amicably, if not equitably. However impersonal, the cash nexus was a social relationship.[8]

Historians of women have been prominent among those pointing out that the new commercial world had positive effects. Kathy Peiss and Joanne Meyerowitz have analyzed the way that working women used the new commercial amusements to gain some limited autonomy, profoundly altering conventional ideas about female gender roles and sexuality. Middle-class women similarly saw in the world of consumer goods the possibility of freedom from their expected function as self-sacrificing wives and mothers. The new corporate economy opened a growing number of jobs in both factories and offices to single women. While mostly low paying and dead end, these jobs underwrote women's increasing autonomy and legitimized their public presence. Precisely because the rise of a corporate economy severed the links between productive work, the ownership of property, and public participation that characterized refined and artisanal republicanism, women's claim to a public role seemed more reasonable.[9]

Urban tourism had similarly mixed effects. The tourist city was in some ways a more open place than the mid-nineteenth-century city. Respectable white women had access to more places in the city than pre-

viously—and now they did not have to have charitable motives for going there. To the extent that the cash nexus replaced relationships based
on mutual moral involvement, it allowed women greater, although still
limited, latitude in public places. The tourist city also encouraged the
celebration of ethnic differences and supported the enterprises of souvenir sellers and restaurateurs in a select few ethnic minority communities. The range of acceptable difference was limited and accompanied
by dehumanizing stereotypes and the aestheticization of poverty. But
the social distance that tourism drew on and encouraged did open up a
space in which cultural differences became desirable, at least as commodities, for well-to-do white Americans. Urban tourism depended on
the commodification and elaboration of hierarchically ranked differences, yet it also facilitated a kind of cultural pluralism not often found
in the mid-nineteenth century.

Notes

ABBREVIATIONS

AC/NMAH	Archives Center, National Museum of American History
BL	Bancroft Library, University of California, Berkeley
CHS	Chicago Historical Society
HL	Huntington Library
NL	Newberry Library
NYHS	New York Historical Society
NYPL	New York Public Library
PPCC	Pullman Palace Car Company Records, Newberry Library
PPIE	Panama-Pacific International Exposition Records, Bancroft Library
WL	Winterthur Library

INTRODUCTION

1. John Sears, *Sacred Places: American Tourist Attractions in the Nineteenth Century* (Oxford: Oxford University Press, 1989); Neil Harris, "Urban Tourism and the Commercial City," in *Inventing Times Square: Commerce and Culture at the Crossroads of the World*, ed. William R. Taylor (New York: Russell Sage, 1991), 66–82.

2. Henri Lefebvre, *The Production of Space*, trans. Donald Nicholson-Smith (Cambridge, Mass.: Blackwell, 1991), 26, 31, parentheses in the original; see also 33. Neither "the gaze" nor the "public sphere" adequately addresses the issue of space or the importance of historically specific social relations. Further, the "public sphere" by definition excludes nonrational practices from the pro-

cess of constructing and maintaining political community. I argue that urban tourism was a part of American efforts to construct a republican society.

3. Richard Bushman, *The Refinement of America: Persons, Houses, Cities* (New York: Vintage Books, 1993), argues that gentility, or refinement, was a betrayal of American egalitarianism. It certainly had exclusive effects, but it also could serve as a path to upward mobility; see, for example, Daniel Rodgers, *The Work Ethic in Industrial America, 1850–1920* (Chicago: University of Chicago Press, 1978).

4. Karen Halttunen, *Confidence Men and Painted Women: A Study of Middle-Class Culture in America, 1830–1870* (New Haven: Yale University Press, 1982), and Bushman, *The Refinement of America*, address this disjuncture most explicitly; Stuart Blumin, "George G. Foster and the Emerging Metropolis," introduction to *New York by Gas-Light and Other Urban Sketches by George G. Foster,* ed. Stuart Blumin (Berkeley: University of California Press, 1990), 1–61, applies it to city description.

5. Especially good on detailing this struggle are Paul Johnson, *A Shopkeeper's Millennium: Society and Revivals in Rochester, New York, 1815–1837* (New York: Hill and Wang, 1978); Christine Stansell, *City of Women: Sex and Class in New York City, 1780–1860* (Chicago: University of Illinois Press, 1987); and Peter Buckley, "To the Opera House: Culture and Society in New York City, 1820–1860" (Ph.D. dissertation, State University of New York at Stony Brook, 1984).

6. Sears, *Sacred Places,* and Dona Brown, *Inventing New England: Regional Tourism in the Nineteenth Century* (Washington, D.C.: Smithsonian Institution Press, 1995), explore the nature of American tourism in the early to mid-nineteenth century.

7. There is no good way to count tourists in this era. Figures for train ridership exist but do not distinguish by class or among emigrants, business travelers, commuters, and tourists, to name just a few possible categories. Most tourists would have traveled on expensive extra-fare cars, so the number of such cars made and rented provides a good indication of the increase in travel by the turn of the century, but probably the most numerous first-class passengers were traveling salesmen; see John H. White, Jr., *The American Railroad Passenger Car* (Baltimore: Johns Hopkins University Press, 1978), especially the appendixes. The number of extant brochures and advertisements for travel agencies and organized tours in trade journals strongly suggests rapid growth in tourist travel at the turn of the century, but these sources do not yield any figures. See Hal K. Rothman, *Devil's Bargains: Tourism in the Twentieth-Century American West* (Lawrence: University Press of Kansas, 1998), and Cindy S. Aron, *Working at Play: A History of Vacations in the United States* (New York: Oxford University Press, 1999), on the expansion of tourism in the twentieth century and the broadening range of participants.

ONE. STRANGERS AND VISITORS;
OR, THE IMPOSSIBILITY OF TOURISM
IN AMERICAN CITIES, 1830s–1870s

1. Junius Mulvey to his brother Oliver, June 22, 1854, Chicago Description, CHS; Eric Monkkonen, *America Becomes Urban: The Development of U.S. Cities and Towns, 1780–1980* (Berkeley: University of California Press, 1988), 44; Edward K. Spann, *The New Metropolis: New York City, 1840–1870* (New York: Columbia University Press, 1981), 430; James Maitland, *Old and New Chicago: Pen and Pencil Sketches of the Garden City* (Chicago: Hackney & Lane, 1879), 13; William Issel and Robert W. Cherny, *San Francisco, 1865– 1932: Politics, Power, and Urban Development* (Berkeley: University of California Press, 1986), 24; Constance McLauglin Green, *Washington: A History of the Capital, 1800–1950* (Princeton: Princeton University Press, 1962), 1:21. This chapter is unevenly weighted toward New York by necessity. The oldest of the four cities, it also epitomized the American city in the nineteenth century and had more written about it than any other. Still, it was not the only city described in the mid-nineteenth century; see Adrienne Siegel, *The Image of the American City in Popular Literature, 1820–1870* (Port Washington, N.Y.: Kennikat Press/ National University Publications, 1981), chap. 1. Despite the disparate chronologies and quantity of written material, my conclusions draw on sources from all four cities.

2. Siegel, *The Image of the American City,* chap. 1; Stuart Blumin, "George G. Foster and the Emerging Metropolis," introduction to *New York by Gas-Light and Other Urban Sketches by George G. Foster,* ed. Stuart Blumin (Berkeley: University of California Press, 1990), and "Explaining the Metropolis: Perception, Depiction, and Analysis in Mid-Nineteenth-Century New York City," *Journal of Urban History* 11:1 (November 1984): 9–38; also Michael Denning, *Mechanic Accents: Dime Novels and Working-Class Culture in America* (New York: Verso, 1987); Robert Toll, *Blacking Up: The Minstrel Show in Nineteenth-Century America* (London: Oxford University Press, 1974); Warren I. Susman, "The City in American Culture," in his *Culture as History: The Transformation of American Society in the Twentieth Century* (New York: Pantheon, 1984), 231–36. For the use of "strangers and visitors," see Robert Macoy, *History of and How to See New York and Its Environs* (New York: Robert Macoy, 1876), 8, 28–29; *The Stranger's Guide Around New York and Vicinity: What to See and What Is to Be Seen with Hints and Advice to Those Who Visit the Great Metropolis* (New York: W. H. Graham, 1853), preface; *Rand, McNally & Co.'s Historical Description and Guide Map of Chicago, With a Complete Street and Avenue Guide to the Entire City* (Chicago: Rand, McNally, 1879), 45; Charles Prescott, *The Hotel Guests' Guide to the City of New York, 1871–72* (New York: W. P. Cleary & Co., 1871), preface; *Lloyd's Pocket Companion and Guide through New York City, for 1866–67* (New York: Thomas Lloyd, 1866), 7–8; *What to See and How to See It: Phelps' Strangers' and Citizens' Guide to New-York City, with Maps and Engravings* (New York: Phelps and Watson, 1857), "Remarks."

3. Dona Brown, *Inventing New England: Regional Tourism in the Nineteenth Century* (Washington, D.C.: Smithsonian Institution Press, 1995), 16.

4. Brown, *Inventing New England,* chap. 1; Harvey Levenstein, *Seductive Journey: American Tourists in France from Jefferson to the Jazz Age* (Chicago: University of Chicago Press, 1998), chaps. 1, 5; James Buzard, *The Beaten Path: European Tourism, Literature, and the Ways to Culture, 1800–1918* (Oxford: Clarendon Press, 1993), chap. 1.

5. O. B. Bunce, "Chicago and Milwaukee," in Picturesque America: or, the Land We Live In. A Delineation by Pen and Pencil of the Mountains, Rivers, Lakes, Forests, Water-falls, Shores, Cañons, Valleys, Cities, and Other Picturesque Features of Our Country, ed. William Cullen Bryant (New York: D. Appleton & Co., 1872), 2:516. The title gives an accurate sense of the relative importance of urban scenes in the work. See also Sue Rainey, Creating Picturesque America: Monument to the Natural and Cultural Landscape (Nashville: Vanderbilt University Press, 1994).

6. William Dean Howells, *Their Wedding Journey* (Bloomington: Indiana University Press, 1968; orig. 1871), 21.

7. The introduction in Richard Bushman, *The Refinement of America: Persons, Houses, Cities* (New York: Vintage Books, 1992), provides the most explicit discussion of refinement as an ideology.

8. These categories reflect two major tendencies in nineteenth-century urban description, not an absolute distinction. I excluded from consideration works that were primarily city or business directories, almanacs, or histories, although many urban handbooks included that kind of information. Many of the urban handbooks were also classic examples of booster literature, while the urban sketches were often articles published in the penny press of the 1840s and 1850s.

9. James D. McCabe, *New York by Gaslight: A Work Descriptive of the Great American Metropolis* (facsimile rpt., New York: Crown Publishers, 1984; orig. 1882), 29–30.

10. Although I differ with Blumin in some respects, my analysis of the midcentury urban sketches is indebted to his; see his "Emerging Metropolis" and "Explaining the Metropolis." Examples of the urban sketches include Foster, *New York in Slices: By an Experienced Carver; Being the Original Slices Published in the New York Tribune. Revised, Enlarged, and Corrected by the Author. With Splendid Illustrations* (New York: W. F. Burgess, 1849), and his *New York by Gas-Light,* ed. Blumin; Asa Greene, *A Glance at New York: Embracing the City Government, Theatres, Hotels, Churches, Mobs, Monopolies, Learned Professions, Newspapers, Rogues, Dandies, Fires and Firemen, Water and Other Liquids, &c., &c.* (New York: A. Greene, 1837); *The Stranger's Guide Around New York and Vicinity. What to See and What Is to Be Seen with Hints and Advice to Those Who Visit the Great Metropolis* (New York: W. H. Graham, 1853); *Gotham* (New York: Hall and Ruckel, 1870); *Tricks and Traps of Chicago,* pt. 1 (New York: Dinsmore & Co., 1859); Joel Ross, M.D., *What I Saw in New York; or, a Bird's Eye View of City Life* (Auburn, N.Y.: Derby & Miller, 1851); John William Buel, *Metropolitan Life Unveiled; or the Mysteries and Miseries of America's Great Cities, Embracing New York, Washington City, San*

Francisco, Salt Lake City, and New Orleans (St. Louis: Anchor Publishing Co., 1882). Foster embraced Fourierism, a form of communitarian socialism; Ross was an evangelical temperance man.

11. Paul Johnson, *A Shopkeeper's Millennium: Society and Revivals in Rochester, New York, 1815–1837* (New York: Hill and Wang, 1978); Christine Stansell, *City of Women: Sex and Class in New York, 1789–1860* (Chicago: University of Illinois Press, 1987); Peter Buckley, "To the Opera House: Culture and Society in New York City, 1820–1860" (Ph.D. dissertation, State University of New York at Stony Brook, 1984); Clay McShane, *Down the Asphalt Path: The Automobile and the American City* (New York: Columbia University Press, 1994); Robin L. Einhorn, *Property Rules: Political Economy in Chicago, 1833–1872* (Chicago: University of Chicago Press, 1991).

12. In addition to the works listed in the previous note, see Mary Ryan, *Women in Public: Between Banners and Ballots, 1825–1880* (Baltimore: Johns Hopkins University Press, 1990); Paul Boyer, *Urban Masses and Moral Order in America, 1820–1920* (Cambridge, Mass.: Harvard University Press, 1978); Elizabeth Blackmar, *Manhattan for Rent, 1785–1850* (Ithaca: Cornell University Press, 1989); Roy Rosenzweig and Elizabeth Blackmar, *The Park and the People: A History of Central Park* (New York: Henry Holt, 1992); Daniel Bluestone, *Constructing Chicago* (New Haven: Yale University Press, 1991).

13. Karen Halttunen, *Confidence Men and Painted Women: A Study of Middle-Class Culture in America, 1830–1870* (New Haven: Yale University Press, 1982), chap. 2.

14. I disagree with Bushman's contention that refinement was necessarily at odds with Americans' republican leanings, at least in the view of its practitioners; see the introduction to his *Refinement of America*.

15. Bluestone, *Constructing Chicago,* chap. 1; Bushman, *Refinement of America,* chaps. 5, 11; Mary Ryan, *Civic Wars: Democracy and Public Life in the American City during the Nineteenth Century* (Berkeley: University of California Press, 1997); Peter Buckley, "To the Opera House," chaps. 2–4.

16. Blumin, "Emerging Metropolis" and "Explaining the Metropolis," and Denning, *Mechanic Accents,* chap. 6, examine the careers of some journalists and hack novel writers who published urban sketches. Joel Ross, author of *What I Saw,* was a physician; James D. McCabe, a minister, wrote several works on New York.

17. Foster, *New York by Gas-Light,* 69. David Reynolds, *Beneath the American Renaissance: The Subversive Imagination in the Age of Emerson and Melville* (New York: Alfred A. Knopf, 1988), 54–91, labels the subversive, prurient imagery and language "immoral didacticism."

18. Blumin, "Emerging Metropolis" and "Explaining the Metropolis," describes Foster's city map; on Chinatown's place in San Francisco city description, see my unpublished essay, "'Chinatown, Of Course, One Must See': San Francisco's Chinatown as a Tourist Attraction, 1870–1915." Blumin argues that the nonfictional sketches such as Foster's paid more attention to the actual built environment than did the dime novels that Denning describes. In comparison with later tourist guides, however, the absence of explicit directions and locations in the midcentury sketches is striking.

19. Blumin, "Explaining the Metropolis" and "Emerging Metropolis." For examples of the longer works, see James D. McCabe's works; also John B. Ellis, *The Sights and Secrets of the National Capital: A Work Descriptive of Washington City in All Its Various Phases* (New York: United States Publishing Co., 1869); B. E. Lloyd, *Lights and Shades in San Francisco, with Appropriate Illustrations* (San Francisco: A. L. Bancroft, 1876); Junius Henri Browne, *The Great Metropolis: A Mirror of New York. A Complete History of Metropolitan Life and Society* (Hartford: American Publishing Co., 1869); Matthew Hale Smith, *Sunshine and Shadow in New York* (Hartford: J. B. Burr & Co., 1869); Buel, *Metropolitan Life Unveiled.*

20. Greene, *A Glance at New York;* the table of contents of any of the works in the preceding note illustrates the point.

21. For example, Williams, "The City of the Golden Gate," 14–15; *Central Pacific Railroad Guide,* 30–31; John Disturnell, comp., *New York as It Was and as It Is; Giving an Account of the City from Its Settlement to the Present Time; Forming a Complete Guide to the Metropolis of the Nation, Including the City of Brooklyn and the Surrounding Cities and Villages; Together with a Classified Business Directory. With Maps and Illustrations* (New York: D. Van Nostrand, 1876), 66; Greene, *A Glance at New York,* 11–13; also Blumin, "Emerging Metropolis," 53, 55.

22. Browne, *The Great Metropolis,* 329; Ellis, *Sights and Secrets,* 460.

23. Smith, *Sunshine and Shadow,* 26; see also Buel, *Metropolitan Life Unveiled,* 26–28; Halttunen, *Confidence Men and Painted Women,* chap. 2; Blumin, "Explaining the Metropolis," 12–16.

24. Smith, *Sunshine and Shadow,* 405–6; see also Buel, *Metropolitan Life Unveiled,* 28.

25. Ellis, *Washington City,* 406; see also Smith, *Sunshine and Shadow,* 128–29, 203, 407; Browne, *The Great Metropolis,* 186–92; Foster, *New York by Gas-Light,* 178, passim; W. S. L. Jewett, "The Adventures of a Missing Man: Or, Twenty-Four Hours in the Metropolis," *Harper's Weekly* 11:526 (January 26, 1867): 56–57. If authors recognized the presence of newly arrived single women at all, they urged them to go home and stay there. Women more often appeared in urban sketches as prostitutes, their fall from rural innocence already achieved.

26. *Tricks and Traps,* 10, 14–19.

27. Browne, *The Great Metropolis,* 92, 43; see also 243 and chap. 26; Smith, *Sunshine and Shadow,* 48, 249–50, 394–403; McCabe, *New York by Gaslight,* chap. 39.

28. Smith, *Sunshine and Shadow,* 71–72; see also Foster, *New York in Slices,* 16, and his *New York by Gas-Light,* 126–28, 208–13; Browne, *The Great Metropolis,* 92–99, 131, 134; Smith, *Sunshine and Shadow,* 453, 694–704; *Gotham* (New York: Hall & Ruckel, 1870), 22; *The Stranger's Guide,* 33, 55–57; *Tricks and Traps,* 20–21, 51–62; Ross, *What I Saw,* 21–24, 44–61.

29. Foster, *New York by Gas-Light,* 70; see also Browne, *The Great Metropolis,* chap. 20, 36, 49; McCabe, *New York by Gaslight,* chap. 30; Smith, *Sunshine and Shadow,* chap. 43; Deborah Epstein Nord, *Walking the Victorian Streets: Women, Representation and the City* (Ithaca: Cornell University Press, 1995), introd.

30. On separate spheres, see Nancy Cott, *The Bonds of Womanhood: 'Woman's Sphere' in New England, 1780–1835* (New Haven: Yale University Press, 1977); Stansell, *City of Women;* Craig Calhoun, "Introduction: Habermas and the Public Sphere," in *Habermas and the Public Sphere,* ed. Craig Calhoun (Cambridge, Mass.: MIT Press, 1992), 11; Carole Pateman, *The Sexual Contract* (Stanford: Stanford University Press, 1988).

31. Stansell, *City of Women,* 173.

32. *The Stranger's Guide,* 30 (emphasis in the original); Nord, *Walking the Victorian Streets.* Blumin, "Explaining the Metropolis," notes a few female writers about the city, but none seem to have written the kind of gritty, sensationalized work most typical of the urban sketch genre. Some women did write the sober analyses of urban industry, trade, and culture that I discuss in the next section.

33. Browne, *The Great Metropolis,* 30; *Tricks and Traps,* 11–12: "Of course, the *gentleman* is never seen in these gatherings," emphasis in the original; see also Buel, *Metropolitan Life Unveiled,* 83; *Gotham,* 51; Judith Walkowitz, *City of Dreadful Delight: Narratives of Sexual Danger in Late-Victorian London* (Chicago: University of Chicago Press, 1992), chap. 1.

34. McCabe, *Lights and Shadows,* 154; Foster, *New York in Slices,* 4.

35. Browne, *The Great Metropolis,* 124; see also Smith, *Sunshine and Shadow,* 37–38.

36. [Charles Prescott], *The Hotel Guests' Guide for the City of New York, 1871–72* (New York: W. P. Cleary & Co., 1871), 43–44.

37. Foster, *New York in Slices,* 65; see also Ross, *What I Saw,* 169–70; David Scobey, "Anatomy of the Promenade: The Politics of Bourgeois Sociability in Nineteenth-Century New York," *Social History* 17:2 (1992): 203–27; Nord, *Walking the Victorian Streets,* 58–60.

38. Lloyd, *Lights and Shades,* 122; Smith, *Sunshine and Shadow,* 40.

39. Foster, *New York in Slices,* 76; Browne, *The Great Metropolis,* contents; Ellis, *Sights and Secrets,* contents; Samuel Williams, "The City of the Golden Gate, a Description of San Francisco in 1875" (San Francisco: Book Club of California, 1921), BL, 23.

40. Smith, *Sunshine and Shadow,* 58, on Steward; McCabe, *Lights and Shadows,* 657, on Beecher. Earlier writers such as Foster and Greene did not name names except those of public officials and lowlifes.

41. Macoy, *Centennial Illustrated How to See New York* (1875–76), 5; W. M. Steele to Clarinda Steele, March 21, 1857, Chicago Description, CHS; C. N. Brainerd, *My Diary: Or Three Weeks on the Wing. A Peep at the Great West* (New York: Egbert, Bourne & Co., 1868), 11, 13; John Munn diaries, Saturday, June 4, 1853, vol. 21, box 3, CHS; see also Edward Swan Stickney, letter to his sister on Chicago, Milwaukee, and Madison, November 1, 1855, Chicago Description, CHS, 1.

42. See, for example, Caroline Kirkland, "Illinois in Spring-time: With a Look at Chicago," *Atlantic Monthly* 2 (1858): 475–88; A. A. Hayes, "The Metropolis of the Prairies," *Harper's New Monthly Magazine* 61 (1880): 711–31; "City of Chicago," *Inland Monthly Magazine* 10:1 (March 1877): 1184–1224; Charles Dudley Warner, "Studies of the Great West. III—Chicago," no source

(May 1888): 869–79, CHS. Carl Abbott, *Boosters and Businessmen: Popular Economic Thought and Urban Growth in the Antebellum Middle West* (Westport, Conn.: Greenwood Press, 1981); William Cronon, *Nature's Metropolis: Chicago and the Great West* (New York: W. W. Norton, 1991), 31–54.

43. Sears, *Sacred Places,* chap. 5; David Rothman, *The Discovery of the Asylum: Social and Disorder in the New Republic* (Boston: Little, Brown, 1971).

44. Brown, *Inventing New England,* chap. 1; Munn Diaries, vol. 21, passim, CHS; see also Mrs. James A. Finley, journal of a trip from Iowa to Delaware, 1881, Downs Collection, WL.

45. For examples of handbooks, see *The Great Metropolis; or, Guide to New-York for 1849,* 5th ed. (New York: H. Wilson, 1849); *Rand, McNally & Co.'s Historical Description and Guide Map of Chicago, with a Complete Street and Avenue Guide to the Entire City* (Chicago: Rand, McNally, 1879); *Miller's New York as It Is; or Stranger's Guide-Book to the Cities of New York, Brooklyn and Adjacent Places: Comprising Notices of Every Object of Interest to Strangers; Including Public Buildings, Churches, Hotels, Places of Amusement, Literary Institutions, Etc. With Map and Numerous Illustrations* (New York: James Miller, 1861); [Charles E. Prescott], *The Hotel Guests' Guide for the City of New York, 1871–72* (New York: W. P. Cleary & Co., 1871); *Lloyd's Pocket Companion and Guide Through New York City, for 1866–67* (New York: Thomas Lloyd, 1866); Disturnell, *New York as It Was and as It Is . . . ; What to See and How to See It. Phelps' Strangers' and Citizens' Guide to New-York City, with Maps and Engravings* (New York: Phelps & Watson, 1857); J. M. Wing & Co., *Seven Days in Chicago* (Chicago: J. M. Wing & Co., 1878); Henry F. Walling, *The City of New York: A Complete Guide. With Descriptive Sketches of Objects and Places of Interest. With Map* (New York: Taintor Bros., 1867); Macoy, *History of and How to See New York.* Some of these works include small "urban sketch" entries. Unlike the sketches, some handbooks included maps, but unfortunately it is archival practice to remove the maps from the books, so I was unable to make a thorough survey of city maps. The few I did see indicate that midcentury maps included such information as voting wards and school districts, suggesting that handbook writers did not think visitors needed maps different from those residents might use.

46. Brown, *Inventing New England,* notes that Appleton's produced a national guide from the 1840s onward. The earliest edition that I have seen was published in 1853. Appleton's also published railroad and steamer guides, so the company's venture into tourist guides was not surprising. The Baedeker company, founded in 1824, did not produce a guide to the United States until 1893; see Henry Steele Commager, introduction to the facsimile edition of *Baedeker's United States, 1893* (New York: Da Capo Press, 1971). For the term "the stranger's path," see J. B. Jackson, "The Stranger's Path," in *Landscapes: Selected Writings of John Brinckerhoff Jackson,* ed. Ervin Zube (Amherst: University of Massachusetts Press, 1970), 92–106.

47. *Appleton's New and Complete United States Guide Book for Travellers: Embracing the Northern, Eastern, Southern, and Western States, Canada, Nova Scotia, New Brunswick, Etc. Illustrated with Forty-Five Engraved Maps. In-*

cluding Plans of Cities of the Union . . . New and Revised Edition (New York: D. Appleton & Co., 1853), 129; Washington entry, 273–81; Chicago, 93–95. San Francisco seems not to have been included until after the completion of the transcontinental railroad in 1869.

48. *The Great Metropolis,* 69; see also Ross, *What I Saw,* 14; Greene, *A Glance at New York,* 2–3. Blackmar, *Manhattan for Rent,* chap. 3; John Reps, *The Making of Urban America: A History of City Planning in the United States* (Princeton: Princeton University Press, 1965), chap. 11.

49. Greene, *A Glance at New York,* 3; *Miller's New York,* 22; see also *The Great Metropolis,* 2; Ross, *What I Saw,* 14; *Stranger's Guide,* 17–29. The straightness of Chicago's streets attracted less attention at this time than the unevenness of the sidewalks and the depths of the mud. San Francisco's hills made the gridiron especially inappropriate, but it was imposed nevertheless. Washington's combination of radial avenues with the gridiron disoriented many visitors; handbooks explained it carefully.

50. Greene, *A Glance at New York,* 4; see also [Prescott], *Hotel Guests' Guide,* 45; *Stranger's Guide,* 30; Foster, *New York in Slices,* 4; *Lloyd's Pocket Companion,* 16–17; Warner, "Studies of the Great West," 872; McShane, *Down the Asphalt Path,* chaps. 1, 3, 4. Respectable women would have attempted this crossing hobbled by long skirts, corsets, and the requirements of ladylike decorum, not to mention children and packages.

51. Marshall Berman, *All That Is Sold Melts into Air: The Experience of Modernity* (New York: Simon and Schuster, 1982), 150–55, makes this point in reference to Haussman's destruction of Paris's medieval center; see also McShane, *Down the Asphalt Path,* chap. 4.

52. Warner, "Studies of the Great West," 872; see also W. F. Rae, *Westward by Rail: The New Route to the East* (New York: Indian Head Books, 1993; orig. 1870), 48; and Kirkland, "Illinois in Spring-time," 488.

53. *What to See and How to See It,* 20; the description of institutions continues through 46; see also *The Great Metropolis,* 76–82; *Lloyd's Pocket Companion,* 70–75, passim; Prescott, *Hotel Guests' Guide,* 138–68.

54. *McLaughlin's New York Guide and Metropolitan Manual; with New Map of the City and Illustrations of Public Buildings* (New York: Wm. McLaughlin, 1875), 13; David Bailey, *'Eastward Ho!' or, Leaves from the Diary of a Centennial Pilgrim: Being a Truthful Account of a Trip to the Centennial City via Washington, and the Return via Niagara Falls, with a Graphic Description of the Exhibition Itself* (Highland, Ohio: privately printed, 1877), 8; *Miller's New York,* 32–42, Ross, *What I Saw,* 78–79.

55. *The Great Metropolis,* 80.

56. *The Great Metropolis,* 76–77; see also *Miller's New York,* 31–32; *Lloyd's Pocket Companion,* 70–75.

57. Smith, *Sunshine and Shadow,* 149, chap. 15, 172, 182–83, 259; see also 149–51, 162–64. McCabe, *Lights and Shadows* and *New York by Gaslight,* contents, 353; Blumin, "Emerging Metropolis," 60–61.

58. Finley, journal of a trip from Iowa to Delaware, 1881, 18–19, 44–46, 69–71, Downs Collection, WL; David Clapp, journal of a trip from Boston to

New York and Albany, 1831, Downs Collection, WL, 52–55; John W. Kinsey, journal of a trip from Lowell to Chicago, 1850, Downs Collection, WL, 7; Bluestone, *Constructing Chicago,* chap. 3.

59. Bluestone, *Constructing Chicago,* chap. 3–5.

60. The Great Metropolis, 72; Central Pacific Railroad Guide, 31.

61. J. J. Burns and Edwin L. Smart, *In the Heart of New York /Surroundings of the N.Y. Grand Central Station* (New York: n.p., n.d.), 30, with a list of notable churches and preachers through 33. Internal evidence suggests that this guide was published in the 1880s, probably funded by the New York Central Railroad.

62. Kirkland, "Illinois in Spring-Time," 486; Rae, *Westward by Rail,* 36; Carl Smith, *Urban Disorder and the Shape of Belief: The Great Chicago Fire, the Haymarket Bomb, and the Model Town of Pullman* (Chicago: University of Chicago Press), sec. 1.

63. Clarence Chapman Cook, "The Modern Architecture of New York," *New York Quarterly* 4 (April 1855): 109, 107. Cf. George Foster, *New York in Slices,* 3.

64. Halttunen, *Confidence Men and Painted Women,* chap. 6, finds the same lessening of concern about sincerity from midcentury.

65. Bluestone, *Constructing Chicago,* chap. 1; Rosenzweig and Blackmar, *The Park and the People,* sec. 1; Philip Ethington, *The Public City: The Political Construction of Urban Life in San Francisco, 1850–1900* (Cambridge: Cambridge University Press, 1994), 68–76; Holleran, *Boston's 'Changeful Times,'* on changing uses of the Boston Common; Scobey, "Anatomy of the Promenade."

66. Rosenzweig and Blackmar, *The Park and the People,* secs. 1, 2; Bluestone, *Constructing Chicago,* chaps. 1, 2.

67. Rosenzweig and Blackmar, *The Park and the People,* secs. 1, 2; Bluestone, *Constructing Chicago,* chaps. 1, 2; Scobey, "Anatomy of the Promenade."

68. Smith, *Sunshine and Shadow,* 362; see also Browne, *The Great Metropolis,* 123–24.

69. In Prescott's *Hotel Guests' Guide,* 51–90, the Central Park entry took up about half of the volume; *Lloyd's Pocket Companion,* 59–69, devoted an entire chapter/day's walk to the park; see also Clarence Chapman Cook, *A Description of New York Central Park* (New York: Benjamin Blom, 1979; orig. 1869); "More Public Parks! How New York Compares with Other Cities. Lungs for the Metropolis. The Financial and Sanitary Aspects of the Question" (New York: New York Park Association, 1882), 21, pamphlet in the Warshaw Collection of Business Americana, New York, box 6, AC/NMAH; Bluestone, *Constructing Chicago,* chaps. 1, 2.

70. Browne, *The Great Metropolis,* 123; Blackmar and Rosenzweig, *The Park and the People,* chaps. 1, 2, sec. 4.

71. Kenneth T. Jackson, *Crabgrass Frontier: The Suburbanization of the United States* (Oxford: Oxford University Press, 1985), chaps. 2–4.

72. *Morrison's Stranger's Guide for Washington City* (Washington, D.C.: W. H. & O. H. Morrison, 1868) and other editions; *Public Buildings and Architectural Ornaments of the Capitol of the United States at the City of Washington* (Washington: P. Haas, 1840); *Bohn's Hand-Book of Washington. Illustrated*

with Engravings of the Public Buildings and the Government Statuary, 4th ed. (Washington, D.C.: Casimir Bohn, 1856); *Etiquette at Washington: Together with Customs Adopted by Polite Society in Other Cities of the United States. To Which Is Added an Appendix, Containing a Complete Guide Through the Metropolis . . . ,* 7th ed. (Baltimore: Murphy & Co., 1860); Jonathan Elliot, *Historical Sketchs of the Ten Miles Square Forming the District of Columbia . . .* (Washington, D.C.: Elliott, 1830); *Roose's Companion and Guide to Washington and Vicinity* (Washington, D.C.(?): Gibson Bros., 1876–78, and ed. of 1888); John Ellis, *The Sights and Secrets of the National Capital: A Work Descriptive of Washington City in All Its Various Phases* (New York: United States Publishing Co., 1869), esp. 54–55, 451; Viator [Joseph Henry Varnum], *Washington Sketchbook* [title page missing; internal evidence suggests it was published during the Civil War], esp. 17, 116. There were many other handbooks published from 1800 through the 1870s; guidebooks (see chap. 4) began to appear in the 1880s.

73. *Public Buildings* and *Morrison's* cited in the preceding note; Ellis's *Sights and Secrets* was the only full-fledged book of urban sketches I have found for Washington; Buel's *Metropolitan Life Unveiled* has a section on Washington.

74. *Public Buildings . . .* (Washington City: P. Haas, 1840); *Morrison's Stranger's Guide for Washington City, Illustrated with Wood and Steel Engravings. Entirely Rewritten and brought down to the present time* (Washington, D.C.: W. H. & O. H. Morrison, 1868), 9–10, 16; see also *Etiquette at Washington,* 133–34, passim; *Bohn's Hand-Book of Washington,* 6–27; even Ellis, *Sights and Secrets,* 56–399, spent most of his ink on the public buildings and statuary.

75. *Etiquette,* 135; the passage continued with the measurements and furnishings of the hall. Of course, plenty of information on politics and government could be found elsewhere, in newspapers and in memoirs; see, for example, Albert D. Richardson, *Garnered Sheaves from the Writings of Albert D. Richardson, Collected and Arranged by His Wife; To Which Is Added a Biographical Sketch of the Author* (Hartford: Columbian Book Co., 1871); Mary Clemmer Ames, *Ten Years in Washington: Life and Scenes in the National Capital, As a Woman Sees Them* (Hartford: A. D. Worthington; Chicago: Louis Lloyd & Co., 1874).

76. See, for example, *Etiquette; Bohn's* also noted official protocol.

77. *Bohn's,* 84; *Etiquette,* 43, passim.

78. Viator, *Sketches,* 17; Ellis, *Sights and Secrets,* 55.

79. Ellis, *Sights and Secrets,* 87–88, 103–4, 400–7, 445–46, 455, 511–12; Buel, *Metropolitan Life Unveiled,* Washington section.

80. *Appleton's Illustrated Hand-Book of American Cities; Comprising the Principal Cities in the United States and Canada, with Outlines of Through Routes, and Railway Maps* (New York: D. Appleton & Co., 1876), preface.

81. Alan Trachtenberg, *The Incorporation of America: Culture and Society in the Gilded Age* (New York: Hill and Wang, 1982); David Nasaw, *Going Out: The Rise and Fall of Public Amusements* (New York: Basic Books, 1993): chap. 6; Robert Rydell, "The Literature of International Expositions," in *The Books of the Fairs: Materials about World Fairs, 1834–1916, in the Smithso-*

nian Institution Libraries (Chicago: American Library Association, 1992), 1–62. No one has yet examined the connection between the world's fairs and the development of the tourist industry, but exposition records indicate that they played a significant role in encouraging the formation of tour companies, hotel consortia, and railroad organized excursion departments. See, e.g., carton 9, folder 1–35.10, "Tour Companies," carton 15, folder 1–51.50, "Hotel Bureau," and carton 38, folder "Requests for Information re Tours," PPIE papers, BL.

TWO. REFINING TRAVEL:
RAILROADS AND EXTRA-FARE CARS, 1850–1915

1. W. M. Steele to Clarinda Steele, March 21, 1857, Chicago Description, CHS. Spelling and punctuation as in the original. Steele's companions were joining the antislavery community in Kansas; on crossing the border into Canada, he rejoiced to be on free soil.

2. "The Chicago and New York Limited," *Railway Review* (January 30, 1897), PPCC Records 12/00/01, reel 6, vol. 21, NL; John R. Stilgoe, *Metropolitan Corridor: Railroads and the American Scene* (New Haven: Yale University Press, 1987), chap. 3. The "limited" was a train making few stops, consisting of all or chiefly Pullman passenger cars, and costing more to ride than the express or regular trains. The New York Central and the Pennsylvania Railroads sponsored competing high-speed, luxury trains between New York and Chicago, culminating in the Pennsylvania Limited, Broadway Limited, and Twentieth Century Limited, which eventually cut the travel time to eighteen hours.

3. See, for example, *Cook's Excursionist and Home and Foreign Tourist Advertiser, American Edition* (April 1892): 12: "The 'St. Louis Limited,' the new train between Chicago and St. Louis, certainly justifies the most sanguine expectations of the traveling public, and has already taken a prominent place among the representative trains of this country." See also *Hotel Monthly* 5:56 (November 1897): 17, 9:102 (September 1901): 18; *Hotel World* 1:5 (September 16, 1876), 1:16 (December 2, 1875); Raymond & Whitcomb's *Travelers' Guide* (January 4, 1904): title page; and *Tourist* (Southern Pacific Railroad) 1:2 (November 1909): 2–3, 2:1 (January 1910): 1.

4. Stanley Buder, *Pullman: An Experiment in Industrial Order and Community Planning, 1880–1930* (Oxford: Oxford University Press, 1967).

5. John F. Stover, *The Life and Decline of the American Railroad* (New York: Oxford University Press, 1970); John H. White, Jr., *The American Railroad Passenger Car* (Baltimore: Johns Hopkins University Press, 1978); Wolfgang Schivelbusch, *The Railway Journey: The Industrialization of Time and Space in the Nineteenth Century* (Berkeley: University of California Press, 1986, orig. pub. in Germany, 1977); Stilgoe, *Metropolitan Corridor;* Amy G. Richter, "Tracking Public Culture: Modernity and Femininity on the American Railroad, 1865–1920" (Ph.D. dissertation, New York University, 1999). On tourism, see Dona Brown, *Inventing New England: Regional Tourism in the Nineteenth Century* (Washington, D.C.: Smithsonian Institution Press, 1995).

6. Stover, *American Railroad,* chaps. 1–3; Emory Johnson, *American Railway Transportation,* rev. ed. (New York: D. Appleton & Co., 1906), 27.

7. Mrs. James Finley, diary of a journey from Iowa to Delaware in 1881, 2, Downs Collection, WL; punctuation as in the original. [George Amory Bethune], *The Uncertainties of Travel: A Plain Statement by a Certain Traveller. From the Boston Advertiser* (Boston: privately printed, 1880), 5–6, 43.

8. Brad S. Lomazzi, *Railroad Timetables, Travel Brochures & Posters: A History and Guide for Collectors* (Spencertown, N.Y.: Golden Hill Press, 1995): chap. 5; Stover, *American Railroad,* chap. 3.

9. Stover, *American Railroad,* 20–22, chap. 3; Charles B. George, *Forty Years on the Rail: Reminiscences of a Veteran Conductor* (Chicago: R. R. Donnelly & Sons, 1887): 35–36; William Sloane Kennedy, *Wonders and Curiosities of the Railway or Stories of the Locomotive in Every Land* (Chicago: S. C. Griggs, 1884), 233–37.

10. Stover, *American Railroad,* chap. 1; Johnson, *American Railway Transportation,* 24 (chart), chap. 3; James Livingston, *Pragmatism and the Political Economy of Cultural Revolution, 1850–1940* (Chapel Hill: University of North Carolina Press, 1997), 31–40.

11. Stover, *American Railroad,* chap. 3; Johnson, *American Railway Transportation,* 25–26, 29; George Taylor and Irene Neu, *American Railroad Network, 1861–1890* (Cambridge, Mass.: Harvard University Press, 1956), chap. 9; Michael O'Malley, *Keeping Watch: A History of American Time* (New York: Penguin Books, 1990), chaps. 2, 3.

12. White, *American Railroad Passenger Car,* chap. 1; Stover, *American Railroad,* 20–21.

13. John W. Kinsey, journal of a trip from Lowell, Mass., to Chicago, Ill., June to August, 1850, 2 Downs Collection, WL, original spelling; Steele, letter to Clarinda Steele, CHS; White, *American Railroad Passenger Car,* chap. 1; Benjamin F. Taylor, *The World on Wheels and Other Sketches* (Chicago: S. C. Griggs, 1874), 154; PPCC Scrapbooks, 12/00/01, reel 1, vol. 1, March 1865 to September 1867, NL.

14. "Across the Continent/Frank Leslie En Route to the Pacific Coast—Westward from Chicago in a Pullman Hotel Car," *Frank Leslie's Illustrated Newspaper* 44:1143 (August 25, 1877): 421; see also Mrs. Frank (Miriam Florence) Leslie, *California: A Pleasure Trip from Gotham to the Golden Gate* (New York: G. W. Carleton, 1877).

15. Richter, "Tracking Public Culture," analyzes female passengers' efforts to domesticate the cars.

16. Johnson, *American Railway Transportation,* 141–44; White, *American Railroad Passenger Car,* 8; "Nebulae," *Galaxy* (April 1873): 577–78, PPCC Records 12/00/01, reel 1, vol. 3; "A Train for Dudes," *National Car Builder* (September 1883), PPCC Records 12/00/01, reel 2, vol. 8; George, *Forty Years,* 222. By the 1870s, if not earlier, compartment cars with corridors were available; see White, *American Railroad Passenger Car,* 226, 255–56.

17. "Nebulae," PPCC Records 12/00/01, reel 1, vol. 3: 578. American newspapers regularly printed tales of assaults and thefts occurring in the locked European compartment cars en route. The open coach assured the presence of forty to fifty passengers who presumably would prevent such crimes; see White, *American Railroad Passenger Car,* 229, and "Dangers of English Pas-

senger Coaches," *Railway Register* (September 4, 1886): n.p., PPCC Records 12/00/01, reel 3, vol. 10.

18. White, *American Railroad Passenger Car,* chap. 1; Johnson, *American Railway Transportation,* chap. 10; Walter E. Weyl, *The Passenger Traffic of Railways,* Series in Political Economy and Law, no. 16 (Philadelphia: Publications of the University of Pennsylvania, 1901), 15–21, 212, passim.

19. W. H. Cove, "The Charming Young Widow I Met in the Train," n.d. The song appears in a collection titled *Gems of Vocal Melody* (Philadelphia: Lee & Walker, n.d.), in the De Vincent Collection of Sheet Music, 1:7, folder A (1830–89), AC/NMAH. Usually only women got stuck with babies when they lost their virtue. Luckily for the victim of this confidence game, the baby was a doll. See also "Making Up a Shortage," *The Traveler* 1:2 (February 1893): 19.

20. George, *Forty Years,* 223, 211; see also "Side-Scenes on the Central Pacific Railroad," *Leslie's Illustrated Newspaper* 45:167 (February 9, 1878): 389.

21. Taylor, *World on Wheels,* 154–55. The fashionable styles of the period required women to have such large quantities of hair that many purchased hairpieces—thus "back hair." Phrenology, a popular "science" in the mid-nineteenth century, was based on the belief that the shape and location of bumps on the skull revealed a person's character.

22. "The New Era in Railroad Travel," *Chicago Tribune* (June 20, 1865), PPCC Records 12/00/01, reel 1, vol. 1; see also "The Pullman Palace Car Line," *Mechanics Invention* (November 18, 1868), PPCC Records 12/00/01, reel 1, vol. 2.

23. George, *Forty Years,* 211–12; Taylor, *World on Wheels,* 53; the term "railway hog" is Taylor's (51); he also noted with some resentment (54) that women could compel men to give up their seats by crying, "I know a gentleman when I see him!" See also Luke Sharp, "Riding on the Rail," *American Travelers' Journal/Tourists' and Excursionists Companion* 1:1 (March 1881): 4, reprinted from the *Detroit Free Press.*

24. George, *Forty Years,* 222; Taylor, *World on Wheels,* 55. *The Traveler's Guide . . .* (Buffalo: Felton & Bro., 1872), 2, advised travelers to "[a]void those who make your acquaintance on the cars"; the very wording suggests the difficulty of the task.

25. W. M. Steele to Clarinda Steele, March 21, 1857, Chicago Description, CHS; John Munn Diaries, Thursday, June 2, 1853, Saturday, June 4, 1853, in vol. 21, and Wednesday, May 30, 1855, vol. 23, CHS; Finley diary, Downs Collection, WL, passim; see also Jedidiah Bowen to Jane Bowen, June 2, 1850, Chicago Description, CHS.

26. Weyl, *Passenger Traffic,* 19; and Johnson, *American Railway Transportation,* 149, both cite the American railroads' preference for using improved service rather than lower prices to attract more travelers.

27. White, *American Railroad Passenger Car,* chaps. 3–5.

28. See articles clipped from the *Maine Central* [Railroad] journal, PPCC Records 12/00/04, reel 15, vol. 4; White, *American Railroad Passenger Car,* chap. 3; Stilgoe, *Metropolitan Corridor,* chap. 2.

29. Buder, *Pullman,* 43; White, *American Railroad Passenger Car,* chap. 3.

30. "The Pullman Palace Car Line," *Mechanics Invention* (November 18,

1868): n.p., PPCC Records 12/00/01, reel 1, vol. 2; untitled, *Illinois Journal,* Springfield (May 30, 1865), PPCC Records 12/00/01, reel 1, vol. 1. The quotations refer to Pullman cars, but those manufactured by other companies were very similar. On genteel interiors, see Katherine Grier, *Culture and Comfort: People, Parlors and Upholstery, 1850–1930* (Rochester: The Strong Museum, 1988).

31. "Luxuries of Modern Travel," *Louisville Courier Journal* (July 16, 1869), PPCC Records 12/00/01, reel 1, vol. 2; Pullman almost certainly arranged for this journalist to travel on one of its cars; such excursions were one of the company's favorite promotional techniques. White, *American Railroad Passenger Car,* chap. 3, passim; Buder, *Pullman,* chaps. 2, 3. This layout was called a "12 and 1" because it included twelve sections and one compartment.

32. White, *American Railroad Passenger Car,* chaps. 3–5. The $2 fee for use of a berth did not change until the Interstate Commerce Commission mandated that the Pullman Company charge less for the less-desirable upper berth in 1910. Cheaper, less luxurious "tourist" sleeping cars were available on a few lines as early as the 1880s. First-class hotels usually charged about $1 per night for a single-occupancy room without board in the late nineteenth century.

33. "The Great Conventions of the Summer Season," *The Book of the Royal Blue* 4:9 (June 1901): 1; "Legislation on Sleeping Car Fares," *Railway Age* (February 13, 1879), PPCC Records 12/00/01, reel 1, vol. 5; see also untitled, from *Railway Age,* reprinted in *New York Elevated Railroad Journal* (February 17, 1883), PPCC Records 12/00/01, reel 2, vol. 7; "Palace Cars," *The Nation* (December 6, 1877), PPCC Records 12/00/01, reel 1, vol. 4. The poorest men in the 1870s earned less than $2 per day; women wage workers earned on average one-third to one-half of what men did.

34. William Dean Howells, *Their Wedding Journey* (Bloomington: Indiana University Press, 1968; orig. 1871), 52, 60. Probably other racial minorities were also refused entry in first-class and Pullman cars.

35. *Railway Age* (July 3, 1879): n.p., quoted in Buder, *Pullman,* 17; untitled, *Railway Register* (October 6, 1883), PPCC Records 12/00/01, reel 2, vol. 8; "Dining on the Rail," *New York Evening Mail* (January 28, 1870), PPCC Records 12/00/01, reel 1, vol. 2; see also Stilgoe, *Metropolitan Corridor,* chap. 2.

36. Buder, *Pullman,* chaps. 2–3; White, *American Railroad Passenger Car,* chap. 3, passim.

37. "The New Era in Train Travel," *Chicago Tribune* (June 20, 1865), PPCC Records 12/00/01, reel 1, vol. 1; Weyl, *Passenger Traffic,* 212; Johnson, *Railway Transportation,* 143; White, *American Railroad Passenger Car,* chaps. 3–5, appendix B.

38. "Legislation on Sleeping Car Fares," *Railway Age* (February 13, 1879), PPCC Records 12/00/01, reel 1, vol. 5; see also "Ethics of the Sleeping Car," *Chicago Times-Herald* (May 18, 1897), PPCC Records 12/00/01, reel 6, vol. 22.

39. "From Ocean to Ocean," *Philadelphia Evening Bulletin* (June 25, 1870), PPCC Records 12/00/01, reel 1, vol. 2.

40. "Palace Cars," *The Nation* (December 6, 1877), PPCC Records 12/00/01, reel 1, vol. 4; LF, "My Journey from San Francisco to Liverpool, 1872," Huntington Library, original spelling; Anna E. D. Douglas journal, 3, 2,

Downs Collection, WL; see also an excerpt from the *Chicago Tribune* in "The Pullman Palace Dining Car," *Mining Record* (May 31, 1870), PPCC Records 12/00/01, reel 1, vol. 2; "Sleeping Car Charges," *Railway Age* (March 27, 1879), PPCC Records 12/00/01, reel 1, vol. 5.

41. "A Hotel Upon Wheels/The Pullman Dining Car," *San Francisco Bulletin* (June 12, 1869), PPCC Records 12/00/01, reel 1, vol. 2; see also Howells, *Their Wedding Journey,* 51; Elbert Hubbard, untitled editorial on the Harvey dining rooms and dining cars of the Atchison, Topeka, and Santa Fe Railroad (Chicago: Passenger Department of the AT&SF, 1905; reprinted from *The Philistine*), Warshaw Collection, Railroads, box 90, AC/NMAH.

42. "St. Louis, Alton & Chicago R.R.," *St Louis Commercial Bulletin* (August 25, 1868), PPCC Records 12/00/01, reel 1, vol. 2; Bret Harte, "Sleeping-Car Reflections," *Railway Age* (April 12, 1877), reprint from the *New York Sun,* PPCC Records 12/00/01, reel 1, vol. 4; Susan Williams, *Savory Suppers and Fashionable Feasts: Dining in Victorian America* (Knoxville: University of Tennessee Press, 1996); Harvey Levenstein, *Revolution at the Table: The Transformation of the American Diet* (New York: Oxford University Press, 1988), chap. 1.

43. "Board En-Route," no source or date noted, probably 1884, PPCC Records 12/00/04, reel 14, vol. 1; see also "St. Louis, Alton & Chicago R.R.," *St. Louis Commercial Bulletin* (August 25, 1868), PPCC Records 12/00/01, reel 1, vol. 2; "Riding on the Rail," *Chicago Times* (March 29, 1869), PPCC Records 12/00/01, reel 1, vol. 2; Saxon, "The Hotel on Wheels," *Hotel Mail* (March 2, 1878), PPCC Records 09/00/03, Public Relations History Files, box 1, folder 2; LF, "My Journey from San Francisco to Liverpool, 1872," 23; White, *American Railroad Passenger Car,* chaps. 3–5.

44. "The Chicago and New York Limited," *Railway Review* (January 30, 1897), PPCC Records 12/00/01, reel 6, vol. 21; White, *American Railroad Passenger Car,* chaps. 3–5; Peter T. Maiken, *Night Trains: The Pullman System in the Golden Years of American Rail Travel* (Chicago: Lake Press, 1989), 23–27; Stilgoe, *Metropolitan Corridor,* chap. 2.

45. *Car Service Rules of the Operating Department of Pullman's Palace Car Company* (Chicago: C. H. Blakely & Co., 1888), 7; PPCC Records 05/01/06, Employee Instruction Books, box 2, folder 20A. An 1872 version of this manual (box 2, folder 23, p. 6) adjured its readers, "You must labor to *promote the comfort of passengers,* and a *courteous and obliging manner* in your official intercourse with the public is imperatively required" (emphasis in the original).

46. "Politeness Pays/Even a Sleeping Car Porter Can Afford to Treat Travelers Courteously [from the *Philadelphia Times*]," *Chicago Chronicle* (August 10, 1895), PPCC Records 12/00/01, reel 5, vol. 19. This encomium appeared in a eulogy for Henry Carey, a porter on the Pennsylvania Railroad, and included an anecdote about his receiving a $100 tip for his kindness to an ill passenger.

47. "Northwestern Excursion!/Grand Turnout of Railroad Livery/The Pullman Car the Triumph of the Age. . . ," *Council Bluffs* [Iowa] *Daily Nonpareil* (June 19, 1868), PPCC Records 12/00/01, reel 1, vol. 2; Buder reports that black porters joined the white Pullman conductors on the cars in 1867 but does not give a source, *Pullman,* 17; Jack Santino, *Miles of Smiles Years of Struggle:*

Stories of Black Pullman Porters (Chicago: University of Illinois Press, 1989), 7, states that Pullman initially wanted conductors to do the porters' work, then tried hiring women (no doubt white since Santino does not specify race) before turning to black men.

48. Kerry Segrave, *Tipping: An American Social History of Gratuities* (Jefferson, N.C.: McFarland & Co., 1998), 17; Maiken, *Night Trains*, 10; Joseph Husband, *The Story of the Pullman Car* (Chicago: A. C. McClurg & Co., 1917), 155–56. Porters were expected to perform the conductor's duties in addition to their own at times, but they never received the title or the pay. Despite chronic complaints and attempts to organize, the porters' working conditions did not improve much until the formation of the Brotherhood of Sleeping Car Porters in the twentieth century.

49. *Car Service Rules of the Operating Department of Pullman's Palace Car Company, revised Sept. 1st, 1893* (Chicago: W. H. Pottinger, 1893), Pullman Collection, box 3, series 5, AC/NMAH. The manuals in the PPCC Records 05/01/06 provide similar lists of duties. See also William Dean Howells, *The Sleeping Car: A Farce* (Boston: Houghton and Mifflin Co., 1882), 14–15; LF, "My Journey from San Francisco to Liverpool," 8; Amy Bridges diary, December 13, 1886.

50. "Palace Cars," *The Nation* (December 6, 1877), PPCC Records 12/00/01, reel 1, vol. 4; "Robert P. Porter's New York Letter," *Philadelphia Inquirer* (May 22, 1897), PPCC Records 12/00/01, reel 6, vol. 22; "Earful [*sic*] Etchings/Times Mann's [*sic*] Experience on the New York Central's Wagners. . . ," *Kansas City Times* (May 9, 1876), PPCC Records 12/00/01, reel 1, vol. 4; Lawrence Davis, quoted in Santino, *Miles of Smiles*, 71, 116; see also untitled, *St. Louis Railway Register* (October 21, 1882), PPCC Records 12/00/01, reel 2, vol. 7.

51. "Editorial Correspondence/An Outing," *Insurance Agent* (n.d., probably November 1894), PPCC Records 12/00/01, reel 5, vol. 18; "The Slavery of Gratuities," *Chicago Chronicle* (June 3, 1897), PPCC Records 12/00/04, reel 15, vol. 4; "A Sleeping Car Horror," no source, n.d., probably 1890s, PPCC Records, 12/00/04, reel 15, vol. 5; see also "The Insecurity of Pullman Cars," [Madison, Wisc.] *Democrat* (July 19, 1877), PPCC Records 12/00/01, reel 1, vol. 2; "The Sleeping Car Nuisance," *New Orleans Times* (March 22, 1878), PPCC Records 12/00/01, reel 1, vol. 4; "A Sleeping Car Porter Divulges the Secrets of the Craft," *St. Louis Globe-Democrat* (November 1882), PPCC Records 12/00/01, reel 2, vol. 7; and "On a Pullman Sleeper/A Porter's Experiences. . . ," *Philadelphia Press* (March 6, 1883), PPCC Records 12/00/01, reel 2, vol. 7; Santino, *Miles of Smiles*, 71–72, 79, 118.

52. Untitled, *St. Louis Daily Democrat* (February 28, 1873), PPCC Records 12/00/01, reel 1, vol. 3; "A Sleeping Car Porter Divulges the Secrets of the Craft"; no title, no source, n.d., probably 1886, "I asked a sleeping car porter the other day how he managed to live on a salary of $12 a month," PPCC Records 12/00/01, reel 3, vol. 10; no title, no source (May 13, 1897), PPCC Records 12/00/01, reel 6, vol. 22, a petition by porters for higher wages; editorial response noted that tipping constituted a "charity" by the public to the Pullman company, a profitable company; untitled, *Saturday Herald* (Indianapolis) (Feb-

ruary 2, 1878), PPCC Records 12/00/01, reel 1, vol. 4; Santino, *Miles of Smiles*, 70–72; Segrave, *Tipping*, 17.

53. "Sleeping-Car Tyrants/A Discussion of the Ways and Means of the Colored Porter," *New York Times* (n.d., probably 1880), PPCC Records 12/00/01, reel 1, vol. 5; see also untitled, *Missouri Republican* (February 22, 1873), PPCC Records 12/00/01, reel 1, vol. 3; "New Method of Solving Railway Problems," *Railway World* (April 2, 1879), PPCC Records 12/00/01, reel 1, vol. 5; "Advice to Sleeping Car Porters," no attribution, probably 1883, PPCC Records 12/00/01, reel 2, vol. 7.

54. "Dining Cars versus (So-Called) Hotel Cars," *Chicago Times* (June 17, 1877), PPCC Records 12/00/01, reel 1, vol. 4; "About the Niggers," no source, no date, probably 1878, PPCC Records 12/00/01, reel 1, vol. 4. Given the size and efficient use of space in hotel cars, one must conclude that the cook and waiters were required to sleep on the roof. I did not find any evidence that interactions between the porters and white female passengers discomfited whites. One 1940s publicity photo showed three white women in night robes being served breakfast in their compartment by a black porter; the caption advertised the delights of complete privacy on board; see the Pullman Collection, AC/NMAH.

55. See article 101(9), *Car Service Rules* (1893), 12; Santino, *Miles of Smiles*, 84.

56. Article 121(6), *Car Service Rules* (1893): 46; H. H. [Helen Hunt Jackson], *Bits of Travel at Home* (Boston: Roberts Brothers, 1882), 31–33.

57. "Traveling in Comfort," *Detroit Free Press* (n.d., probably 1893–94), PPCC Records 12/00/04, reel 15, vol. 5; "Sleeping Cars for Ladies," *Railway Age* (September 9, 1886), PPCC Records 12/00/01, reel 3, vol. 10; teenager LF, in contrast, worried about "pitching out head first from between the curtains, but refrained, thinking it might astonish the people opposite too much," in "My Journey from San Francisco to Liverpool, 1872," 9; see also Jackson, *Bits of Travel*, 29–34. The sleeping cars did not have much space for the storage of clothing either, at a time when clothing was voluminous and multiparted. Female passengers were noted for usurping the clothing hooks on both ends of the berth; see Howells, *The Sleeping Car*.

58. "Not the Way in England," *Cincinnati Evening Post* (November 18, 1884), PPCC Records 12/00/04, reel 14, vol. 1; "Side-Scenes on the Central Pacific," 389; see also "A Winter Journey Across the Continent," *Boston Advertiser* (February 18, 1870), PPCC Records 12/00/01 reel 1, vol. 2; "Sleeping Car Accommodations," no source, n.d., probably 1884, PPCC Records 12/00/01, reel 2, vol. 9; "Ladies and the Sleeping Car," possibly *New York World* (June 16, 1885), PPCC Records 12/00/01, reel 2, vol. 9; "Sleeping Cars for Ladies," *Railway Age* (September 9, 1886), PPCC Records 12/00/01, reel 3, vol. 10; "Sleeping Cars for Ladies," probably *Daily Graphic* [N.Y.] (October 1886), PPCC Records 12/00/01, reel 3, vol. 10; "Selections from the Mail/Woman on the Sleeping Cars. . . ," *New York Tribune* (October 4, 1896), PPCC Records 12/00/01, reel 6, vol. 21; "Women on Stand in Pullman Car Case/Witnesses Tell How Hard It Is for Feminine Travelers to Get In and Out of Upper Berths of Sleepers. . . ," *Chicago Inter-Ocean* (December 18, 1908), PPCC Records

12/00/01, reel 8, vol. 29; on toilet facilities, see White, *American Railroad Passenger Car*, 429–30.

59. "On Board a Sleeper," *St. Louis Times* (July 30, 1876), PPCC Records 12/00/01, reel 1, vol. 4; "Side-Scenes on the Central Pacific," 389; "Sleeping Cars for Ladies"; "Upper Five," *Chicago Tribune* (August 28, 1886), PPCC Records 12/00/01, reel 3, vol. 10; Howells, *The Sleeping Car*, 11–13; "Palace Sleeping Cars/Kate Field Relates Her Experiences on the New York Central," no attribution, n.d., probably 1886; PPCC Records 12/00/01, reel 3, vol. 10; article 115(3), *Car Service Rules* (1893), 32.

60. Untitled, *Railway Age* (November 2, 1876), PPCC Records 12/00/01, reel 1, vol. 4.

61. "Too Much for the Drummer," *Railroad Gazette* (April 11, 1879), PPCC Records 12/00/01, reel 1, vol. 5; "Sleeping Car Contretemps Caused by a Misplaced Ladder," *Railway Age* (August 7, 1879), PPCC Records 12/00/01, reel 1, vol. 5; "Advice to Sleeping Car Porters," no source, n.d., probably 1883, PPCC Records 12/00/01, reel 3, vol. 8; "Palace Sleeping Cars/Kate Field Relates Her Experiences on the New York Central"; "Scene in a Sleeper. . . ," *Chicago Herald* (February 9, 1890), PPCC Records 12/00/04, reel 14, vol. 1; "A Girl in a Robe de Nuit," no source, n.d., probably mid-1890s, PPCC Records 12/00/04, reel 15, vol. 5; "An Accommodating Crowd," *Cook's Excursionist and Home and Foreign Tourist Advertiser, American Edition* (September 1893): 12. King Vidor's film *The Crowd* (1928) includes a scene invoking all the well-worn jokes about newlyweds traveling to Niagara Falls on the train. The tale about Anthony was meant as a warning about the masculinizing effects of women's rights advocacy, but she might well have endured such practical jokes during her extensive travels.

62. "The Civil Rights Act and the Pullman Sleeping Car," *Mobile* [Ala.] *Register* (March 25, 1875), PPCC Records 12/00/01, reel 1, vol. 3. This story seems to have been widely reprinted; see also "Civil Rights and Railroads/Let White People Stay Out of Pullman's Coaches," *Advertiser and Mail* (Montgomery, Ala.) (March 28, 1875), PPCC Records 12/00/01, reel 1, vol. 3; "A War Against Pullman," *Chicago Times* (April 7, 1875), PPCC Records 12/00/01, reel 1, vol. 3; "Pullman Backs Up Civil Rights," *Post and Mail* [no city] (April 8, 1875), PPCC Records 12/00/01, reel 1, vol. 3; "They 'Go For' Pullman," *Chicago Times* (April 8, 1875), PPCC Records 12/00/01, reel 1, vol. 3; "Pullman—Sleeping Car Companies," *Atlanta Daily Herald* (n.d., probably 1875), PPCC Records 12/00/01, reel 1, vol. 3. The company did not regularly clip from southern newspapers except during this period. The Chicago papers were sympathetic to civil rights in the 1870s. As they pointed out, white southerners did not object to the presence of blacks on the cars when they were servants to white passengers; moreover, white southerners objected to the prominent black politician P. B. S. Pinchback traveling in a sleeper even though he had chartered the entire car. See "The Civil Rights Act and the Pullman Sleeping Cars," *Mobile* [Ala.] *Register*, above; and an excerpt from the *Meridian Mercury* in "A War Against Pullman," *Chicago Times*, above.

63. See the citations in note 61, above; W. F. Storey, "They 'Go For' Pullman," *Chicago Times* (April 8, 1875), PPCC Records 12/00/01, reel 1, vol. 3;

"Pullman Sleeping Car Company," *Atlanta Daily Constitution* (June 16, 1875), PPCC Records 12/00/01, reel 1, vol. 3; *Notice: This Book Contains All the Laws, Notices and Warnings Required by Law to Be Posted in This Car* (n.p., n.d.; dates of laws range from 1897 to 1915), PPCC Records 05/01/06, box 2, folder 27. Scattered references to attempts by prominent blacks to gain access to the extra-fare cars appear throughout the scrapbooks.

64. "Ladies and the Sleeping Car," [*New York World*] (June 16, 1885), PPCC Records 12/00/01, reel 2, vol. 9; "Sleeping Cars for Ladies," *Railway Age* (September 9, 1886), PPCC Records, reel 3, vol. 10; "Sleeping Cars for Ladies," [*Daily Graphic*] (October 1886), PPCC Records 12/00/01, reel 3, vol. 10; "Not that Way in England," *Cincinnati Evening Post* (November 18, 1884), PPCC Records 12/00/04, reel 14, vol. 1; see *Notice: This Book Contains All Laws. . . ,* PPCC Records 05/01/06, box 2, folder 27, for segregation ordinances. As a rule southern railroads did not provide equal facilities for African Americans, who were expected to ride in second-class cars or even the baggage car.

65. "A New Sleeping Car," unattributed (December 14, 1883), PPCC Records 12/00/01, reel 2, vol. 8; "'Inching Along' to Dixie/A Young Lady's Trip to New Orleans/Budoir [*sic*] Cars Utterly Detestable," *Daily Times* (January 12, 1885), PPCC Records 12/00/01, reel 2, vol. 8; "The New Sleeping Car," *Peck's Sun* (Milwaukee) (August 29, 1885), PPCC Records 12/00/01, reel 2, vol. 9; "The Semiramide: A New Patent Palace Car. . . ," *Daily Picayune* (New Orleans) (June 1, 1884), PPCC Records 12/00/04, reel 14, vol. 1.

66. "Proposed Reduction of Sleeping-Car Fare," *Railway Car Journal,* June 1894, PPCC Records 12/00/04, reel 15, vol. 4; "The Woes of the Sleeping-Car," no source, n.d., probably early 1900s, PPCC Records 12/00/04, reel 15, vol. 5; "The Sleeping Car Imposition," *Daily Journal* (Indianapolis), September 5, 1876, PPCC Records 12/00/01, reel 1, vol. 3; "Palace Cars," *The Nation* (December 6, 1877), PPCC Records 12/00/01, reel 1, vol. 3; "Are Sleeping Cars Healthy?" *The Independent* (New York) (January 25, 1883), PPCC Records 12/00/01, reel 2, vol. 7; "America's Sleeping Car Peril—Sanitary Reform Demanded," *New York World* (September 2, 1900), PPCC Records 12/00/01, reel 7, vol. 25.

67. "The Sleeping Car Imposition," *Indianapolis Daily Journal* (September 5, 1876), PPCC Records 12/00/01, reel 1, vol. 4; "Palace Cars," *The Nation* (December 6, 1877), PPCC Records 12/00/01, reel 1, vol. 4; "The Upper Berth," *Railway Review* (October 6, 1883), PPCC Records 12/00/01, reel 2, vol. 8; "America's Sleeping Car Peril—Sanitary Reform Demanded," *New York World* (September 2, 1900), PPCC Records 12/00/01, reel 7, vol. 25; "Sleeping Cars," *Chicago Daily News* (July 8, 1908), PPCC Records 12/00/01, reel 8, vol. 29; "Women in Dread of Upper Berth," *Chicago Tribune* (December 18, 1908), PPCC Records 12/00/01, reel 8, vol. 29; "Women on Stand in Pullman Car Case," *Chicago Inter-Ocean* (December 18, 1908), PPCC Records 12/00/01, reel 8, vol. 29; "Railway Sleeping Car Accommodations," *National Car Builder* (October 1879), PPCC Records 12/00/01, reel 1, vol. 5; "Sleeping Car Accommodations," no source, n.d., probably 1885, PPCC Records 12/00/01, reel 2, vol. 9; "Second Class Travel Made Luxurious," *Railway Age* (May 6, 1887), PPCC Records 12/00/01, reel 3, vol. 10; "Important News for Second-Class

Travelers," *San Francisco Morning Call* (January 31, 1889), PPCC Records 12/00/01, reel 3, vol. 11; "Pullman Car Rates," *Railway Review* (September 29, 1894), PPCC Records 12/00/01, reel 5, vol. 18; "Ethics of the Sleeping Car," *Chicago Times-Herald* (May 18, 1897), PPCC Records 12/00/01, reel 6, vol. 22; "Favor Tourist Cars," *Chicago Record* (November 11, 1897), PPCC Records 12/00/01, reel 6, vol. 23. Criticisms of Pullman's taste in decor had existed at least since the 1870s but now became mainstream, appearing in journals such as the *Ladies' Home Journal*.

THREE. AT HOME IN THE CITY:
FIRST-CLASS URBAN HOTELS, 1850–1915

1. Joel Cook, *An Eastern Tour at Home* (Philadelphia: David McKay, 1889), 14–15; William Smith, "A Word to Travelers," *Hotel World* 1:12 (November 4, 1875): 1. This was the journal's first year of publication. Many of the hotel trade journals began as registers or gazettes that also included editorial matter and often local theater news. In the 1880s they abandoned the newspaper format, dropped the hotel registers, and incorporated more features and more advertisements.

2. Julian Street, *Abroad at Home: American Ramblings, Observations, and Adventures,* illus. by Wallace Morgan (New York: Century Co., 1914), 516; see also "The New Orleans Exposition—Arrivals at the Levee," *Harper's Weekly* 29:1464 (January 10, 1885): cover illus.; *Hotel Monthly* 5:47 (February 1897): 14.

3. See Smith, "A Word to Travelers"; *Forty Days in a Western Hotel, Maga Excursion Papers, Putnam's Railway Classics* (New York: G. P. Putnam & Son, 1867), 281–82; Ernest Ingersoll, *Rand, McNally & Co.'s Handy Guide to New York City,* 11th ed. (New York and Chicago: Rand, McNally, 1901); Junius Mulvey, letter to his brother Oliver, June 22, 1854, Chicago Description, CHS; John Munn diaries, vol. 21, box 3, 167, passim, CHS; Anna E. D. Douglas, diary of a journey from Boston to Daytona, 1892–93, Downs Collection, WL, 8, 26, 52; Henry J. Bohn, "Greater New York Hoteldom," *Hotel World* 59:3 (July 16, 1904): 8. I deal with the difficulties that women traveling alone faced later in the chapter.

4. Samuel Williams, "The City of the Golden Gate, a Description of San Francisco in 1875" (San Francisco: Book Club of California, 1921), BL; Gustav Kobbe, *New York and Its Environs* (New York: Harper Bros., 1891), 39, wrote, "It is presumed that readers of this Guide will not care to patronize any but absolutely unexceptionable hotels. Therefore only such are given." Many of the shorter guides included long lists of hotels; judging from the prices, they were all first-class houses. A single room without board in a first-class hotel by the twentieth century cost $1 to $2 per night and up; rooms in the very best hotels cost much more. Guests paid extra for amenities such as a private bathroom, a corner room, or a sitting room. Until the introduction of the elevator in the 1850s, rooms cost less the higher up they were. Boardinghouse prices differed according to the class of the house but were usually lower than hotel costs.

5. The basic but dated works in American hotel history are Jefferson Wil-

liamson, *The American Hotel: An Anecdotal History* (New York: Knopf, 1930; rpt. New York: Arno Press, 1975); and Doris King, "The First Class Hotel and the Age of the Common Man," *Journal of Southern History* 23:2 (May 1957): 173–88, and "Early Hotel Entrepeneurs and Promoters," *Explorations in Entrepeneurial History* 8 (February 1956): 148–60. Recently, historians and geographers have begun to pay more attention to hotels; see Paul Groth, *Living Downtown: The History of Residential Hotels in the United States* (Berkeley: University of California Press, 1994); Carolyn Brucken, "In the Public Eye: Women and the American Luxury Hotel," *Winterthur Portfolio* 31:4 (Winter 1996): 203–20.

6. Neil Harris, "Urban Tourism and the Commercial City," in *Inventing Times Square: Commerce and Culture at the Crossroads of the World*, ed. William R. Taylor (New York: Russell Sage, 1991), 66–82; Edward Hungerford, *The Story of the Waldorf-Astoria* (New York: G. P. Putnam's Sons, 1925); [Wilbur Dick Nesbit], *Chicago Without a Guidebook* (Chicago: Chicago Association of Commerce, n.d.), 9; *San Francisco* (San Francisco: Chamber of Commerce, 1915), 32–33; *Disturnell's Strangers' Guide to San Francisco and Vicinity* (San Francisco: W. C. Disturnell, 1883), 95. Washington's hotels were less well known, although the Willard was often mentioned in memoirs.

7. Nikolaus Pevsner, *A History of Building Types*, Bollingen Series 35-19 (Princeton: Princeton University Press, 1976), 173–87; King, "The First Class Hotel," 178–81; Williamson, *The American Hotel*, chaps. 1, 2, 4; Katherine Grier, *Culture and Comfort: People, Parlors, and Upholstery, 1850–1930* (Rochester, N.Y.: The Strong Museum, 1988), 19–20, 25–45.

8. Martha M. Taft, letter to the editor of the *Prairie Gem* (September 19, 1863): 2, Chicago Description, CHS; see also accounts by Sir John Leng, Lady Duffus Hardy, and Julian Ralph in Bessie Louise Pierce, ed., *As Others See Chicago: Impressions of Visitors, 1673–1933* (Chicago: University of Chicago Press, 1933), 219–20, 226–29, 287–323.

9. King, "The First-Class Hotel," 176–77; Daniel Boorstin, "Palaces of the Public," in his *The Americans: The National Experience* (New York: Random House, 1965), 146; B. E. Lloyd, *Lights and Shades of San Francisco, with Appropriate Illustrations* (San Francisco: A. L. Bancroft, 1876), 66, 449; Diary of a Boarder at the Astor House, New York, 1857, Downs Collection, WL, 5–7.

10. Boorstin, "Palaces of the Public," 135, 146; King, "The First-Class Hotel," 176–80; cf. Brucken, "In the Public Eye."

11. Boorstin, "Palaces of the Public," 141. The three essential meals were breakfast, dinner (midafternoon), and supper (midevening); some places also offered lunch (noon) and tea (late afternoon or early evening); Williamson, *The American Hotel*, chap. 7; Susan Williams, *Savory Suppers and Fashionable Feasts: Dining in Victorian America* (Knoxville: University of Tennessee Press, 1996; orig. 1984), chap. 2; Brucken, "In the Public Eye," 25.

12. Williamson, *The American Hotel*, Willis quotation, 209; also 194–95; King, "The First-Class Hotel," 176–77; Boorstin, "Palaces of the Public," 144.

13. Alice Morse Earle, *Stage-Coach and Tavern Days* (New York: Macmillan, 1900), 66; Brucken, "In the Public Eye," passim.

14. Williamson, *The American Hotel,* chap. 7; Earle, *Stage-Coach and Tavern Days,* 85–86; *Forty Days in a Western Hotel,* Maga Excursion Papers, Putnam's Railway Classics (New York: G. P. Putnam & Son, 1867), 285, 292–93; M. H. Dunlop, *Sixty Miles from Contentment: Traveling the Nineteenth-Century American Interior* (New York: Basic Books, 1995), chap. 6.

15. Junius Mulvey to his brother Oliver, June 22, 1854, 6, Chicago Description, CHS, original punctuation; see also *Forty Days in a Western Hotel,* 290; *Hotel Monthly* 13:152 (November 1905): 17; Simeon Ford, "Simeon Ford Advocates Condensed Menu," *Hotel Monthly* 15:171 (June 1907): 24: "Ah! Those were the happy days. . . . We used to stow two men in a bed in busy times. Now, even married folks won't sleep together." Ford was in much demand as an after-dinner speaker.

16. Pevsner, *Building Types,* 175–76; Williamson, *The American Hotel,* 55–62; all rooms had washstands, pitchers, and basins.

17. Report of a speech at the Chicago Hotel Association meeting in January 1911, *Hotel Bulletin* 8:3 (February 1911): 151; William Smith, "Hotel Decoration," *Hotel World* 2:4 (September 7, 1876): 5. See also *Hotel Monthly* 5:48 (March 1897): 19; *Hotel Monthly* 11:118 (January 1903): 17; *Hotel World* 2:4 (September 7, 1876): 5; *Hotel World* 63:1 (July 7, 1906): 11.

18. Pevsner, *Building Types,* 174–75, 180–81; Karl Raitz and John Paul Jones III, "The City Hotel as Landscape Artifact and Community Symbol," *Journal of Cultural Geography* 9:1 (Fall–Winter 1988): 23–24; Williamson, *The American Hotel,* 126–29; Henry Mower, *Reminiscences of a Hotel Man of Forty Years' Service* (Boston: Worcester Printing Co., 1912), 20; Grier, *Culture and Comfort,* 35–38, 53–55; John Munn diaries, box 3, vol. 21, CHS, 142, 162–63; given the care of one Mrs. Starr by her relatives, Munn "secured her comfortable rooms . . . & shall care for her in the morning & place her on the cars for her destination."

19. Grier, *Culture and Comfort,* 55, 180; Brucken, "In the Public Eye," 15–19; "A New Feature of the Hotel Plaza," *Town and Country* (November 29, 1913): n.p.; found in Plaza Hotel folder, Hotels box 10, Warshaw Collection of Business Americana, AC/NMAH. Many hotels provided gender-segregated dining rooms in the 1850s and 1860s.

20. *Hotel Monthly* 5:47 (February 1897): 13; see also Brucken, "In the Public Eye"; Williamson, *The American Hotel,* 130; Boorstin, "Palaces of the Public," 139–140; *Hotel World* 55:25 (December 20, 1902): 12.

21. Brucken, "In the Public Eye"; Dunlop, *Sixty Miles,* chap. 7.

22. The parlor appeared in *Chicago Illustrated* (Chicago: Chicago Lithographing Co., 1866–67), 33; the lobby in *From the Lakes to the Gulf* (Chicago: R. R. Donnelly & Sons, 1884), 19. Both rooms were probably in the Palmer House, Chicago's finest hotel in the 1870s and 1880s.

23. *Forty Days in a Western Hotel,* 289, 291; see also John Munn diaries, box 3, vol. 21 (June 4, 1853), CHS, 168: "On entering the public room on alighting from the omnibus, I was struck by the great crowd of young & middle aged men who filled the room, presenting to the eye & ear a scene [ ] & exciting. . . ." Also box 3, vol. 23 (May 30, 1855): 164, 169; James D. McCabe,

Lights and Shadows of New York Life (New York: Farrar, Straus & Giroux, 1970; orig. 1872), 306, 311; Martha Ann Peters, "The St. Charles Hotel: New Orleans Social Center, 1837–1860," *Louisiana History* 1 (1960): 198. Thanks to Steve Deyle for bringing this to my attention.

24. Grier, *Culture and Comfort,* 37; see also 54–55; Brucken, "In the Public Eye"; Dunlop, *Sixty Miles,* chap. 7.

25. Pevsner, *Building Types,* 174–75; Raitz and Jones, "The City Hotel," 23–24; Grier, *Culture and Comfort,* 29; Rome Miller, "The Duties of a Hotel Man. . . ," *Hotel Monthly* 18:210 (September 1910): 51; *Hotel Monthly* 13:150 (September 1905): 17; Charles Martyn and Frank W. Doolittle, *'Fables' of the Hotel Profession and Poems of 'Good Cheer'* (New York: Caterer Publishing Co., 1904), 8–17, on "The Clerk with a Thirst for Glory" and "The Man Who Would Be Manager."

26. "It Affects the Atmosphere," *Hotel World* 66:22 (May 30, 1908): 13: "The dinner brought most of the guests together [but the] . . . European dining plan breeds irregularity." See also *Hotel Monthly* 5:52 (July 1897): 15.

27. "Hotel Keeping as a Science," *Hotel World* 2:4 (September 7, 1876): 8; "Hotel Life in New York," *Hotel World* 3:1 (July 6, 1877): 3; Williamson, *The American Hotel,* chap. 7. Several generations of Leland men managed hotels throughout the United States.

28. *Hotel Monthly* 5:56 (November 1897): 17; *Hotel Monthly* 9:96 (March 1901): 15; *Hotel World* 59:3 (July 16, 1904): 7; Hiram Hitchcock, "The Hotels of America," in *One Hundred Years of American Commerce, 1795–1895,* ed. Chauncey Depew (New York: D. O. Haynes, 1895), 1:150–52. Resort hotels continued to operate on the American plan well into the twentieth century, as did urban "family" hotels, which housed mainly long-term guests. A few major urban hotels maintained both plans, separating residential from transient guests.

29. *Hotel World* 2:2 (August 24, 1876): 10; *Hotel Monthly* 5:52 (July 1897): 15 and 5:56 (November 1897): 17. Hotels had served locals before the institution of the European plan, but these locals had often been living at the hotel or were part of the elite social circle; now the walk-in trade increased.

30. "Resulting Benefits of the Europlan," *Hotel World* 63:17 (October 27, 1906): 9; see also *Hotel Monthly* 3:24 (December 16, 1877): 4, 5:54 (September 1897): 13, and 17:194 (May 1909): 34; Hungerford, *Story of the Waldorf-Astoria,* 7–8.

31. Max Kuhn, *All Happy: A Hint from Mr. Max Kuhn, Chief Controller of the Waldorf-Astoria* (New York: Wynkoop, Hallenbeck, Crawford, 1905), 53–56. The courses included oysters, soups, hot hors d'oeuvres and cold side dishes, fish, first entrée, roasts, punch or sherbet, game, cold dishes or salad, hot and cold sweet dishes, dessert, and coffee. See also George Rector, *The Girl from Rector's* (Garden City, N.Y.: Doubleday, Page, & Co., 1927), 155.

32. "Ins and Outs of Hotel Life," *Hotel World* 55:25 (December 20, 1902): 17; John Goins, "The American Colored Waiter," *Hotel Monthly* 9:101 (August 1901): 30.

33. [Burritt Darrow], *An Account of the Pilgrimage to the Tomb of General Grant, by Cap* (New York: privately printed, 1900), 28–29; Julian Street, *Wel-*

come to Our City (New York: John Lane Co., 1912), 39. Organized tours always promised their patrons first-class meals; see chap. 4.

34. *Hotel World* 71:2 (July 9, 1910): 15.

35. Williamson, *The American Hotel,* chap. 2, 3; Pevsner, *Building Types,* 182–84; *Hotel Monthly* 18:204 (March 1910): 38, and "Three Days in New York," 19:220 (July 1911): 51–56; "A Magnificent Hotel Palace: The New Hotel Sherman," *Hotel Bulletin* 6:1 (December 1910): 25–33; *San Francisco Hotels* (Passenger Department, Southern Pacific Railroad Co., November 1906), 3–4; *Hotel Fairmont, San Francisco* (souvenir pamphlet, n.p., n.d.; post-1906); Van Orman, *A Room for the Night,* chap. 5; David Siefkin, *The City at the End of the Rainbow: San Francisco and Its Grand Hotels* (New York: G. P. Putnam's Sons, 1976), 1–9; Hungerford, *Story of the Waldorf-Astoria,* passim. The hotel journals did frequent surveys of big cities and their hotels but rarely covered Washington, D.C. On rising building heights, see the *Hotel Monthly* 11:126 (September 1903): 19.

36. Hungerford, *Story of the Waldorf-Astoria,* chaps. 2, 4; James R. McCarthy and John Rutherford, *Peacock Alley: The Romance of the Waldorf-Astoria* (New York: Harper and Bros., 1931), 4; Horace Sutton, *Confessions of a Grand Hotel: The Waldorf-Astoria* (New York: Henry Holt and Co., 1951), 9–10, 14; *Souvenir of the Grand Hotel* (San Francisco: Crocker & Co., 1890), 7; Rector, *The Girl from Rector's,* 3–6; [James F. Grady], *Abuses, or, About Hotels* (Chicago: Berg and McCann, 1879), 9; David Scobey, "Anatomy of the Promenade: The Politics of Bourgeois Sociability in Nineteenth-Century New York," *Social History* 17:2 (1992): 225–27; Michael Gillespie, "Democracy and Opulence: Exclusivity for the Masses and the American Grand Hotel" (M.A. thesis, University of California, Berkeley, 1994), 20, cites a *New York Times* article (April 27, 1908), reporting that nearly nineteen thousand people had passed through the Waldorf-Astoria's eight doorways in one day.

37. *Hotel World* 80:11 (March 13, 1915): 13, and 80:17 (April 24, 1915): 13. Brucken, "In the Public Eye," notes that hotels rented out ground-floor areas to shops in the early nineteenth century, but hotel journal editors believed that the practice increased in the 1890s. On conventions, see chap. 4.

38. Diary of a boarder at the Astor House, 1857, Downs Collection, WL, 7; she also noted the lessons learned in "[s]even weeks experience in boarding": "Every word spoken is likely to be overheard and misunderstood. . . . All experience teaches me never to give up, always to keep among people, and embrace means of making acquaintance."

39. Henry J. Bohn, "Greater New York Hoteldom," *Hotel World* 59:3 (July 16, 1904): 8, 10; see also John J. Bohn, "Modern Business Methods," *Hotel World* 71:6 (August 6, 1910): 15.

40. Floyd Miller, *America's Extraordinary Hotelman: Statler* (New York: Statler Foundation, 1968), chap. 14–15; Rufus Jarman, *A Bed for the Night: The Story of the Wheeling Bellboy, E. M. Statler, and His Remarkable Hotels* (New York: Harper & Bros., 1950–52), 126–36.

41. Miller, *America's Extraordinary Hotelman,* 92; Jarman, *A Bed for the Night,* chap. 11; the quotation is from the *Hotel Monthly* 11:128 (November 1903): 17; see also 9:102 (September 1901): 18, and 13:143 (February

1905): 17; May N. Stone, "Hotel Pennsylvania: Strictly First-Class Accommodations at Affordable Rates" (M.S. thesis, Columbia University, 1988), 11–13.

42. "A Modern Hotel Difficulty," *Hotel World* 73:8 (August 1911): 15; *Hotel Monthly* 20:226 (January 1912): 33; Stone, "Hotel Pennsylvania," chap. 1; Neil Harris, "Urban Tourism and the Commercial City," in *Inventing Times Square: Commerce and Culture at the Crossroads of the World,* ed. William R. Taylor (New York: Russell Sage, 1991), 66–82.

43. "The Hotel Building Spasm," *Hotel Bulletin* 12:3 (March 1914): 185; "Wanted: Good Second Class Hotels," *Hotel Monthly* 17:199 (October 1909): 33; see also the *Hotel Monthly* 18:202 (January 1910): 52; "Start of Largest Hotel in the World," *Hotel Bulletin* 10:2 (February 1913): 124.

44. Charles G. Roth, "A Dream of the Future Hotel," *Hotel Monthly* 17:190 (January 1909): 38.

45. "Hotel Service Papers. Number One," *Hotel World* 2:34 (April 5, 1877): 1; *Forty Days in a Western Hotel,* 297; see also a review of the Ebbitt House in Washington, D.C., *Hotel World* 2:2 (August 24, 1876): 6, 72:10 (March 11, 1911): 37; *Hotel Monthly* 5:46 (January 1897): 28, 5:50 (May 1897): 13, 5:55 (October 1897): 38, 5:56 (November 1897): 13, 6:65 (August 1898): 17.

46. "Hotel Service Papers. Number One," 1; William Dean Howells, *Their Wedding Journey* (Bloomington: Indiana University Press, 1968; orig. 1870), 60. See also James McCabe, *Lights and Shadows of New York Life; or, the Sights and Sensations of the Great City* (facsimile ed., New York: Farrar, Straus & Giroux, 1970; orig. 1872): 716; *Forty Days,* 283–85.

47. *Hotel World* 76:15 (April 12, 1913): 12; 2:34 (April 5, 1877): 1; see also 55:24 (December 13, 1902): 11; 60:8 (February 25, 1905): 7; "Training the Colored Waiter," *Hotel World* 66:25 (June 25, 1908): 13; at least one hotel keeper disagreed, finding white men and women to be worse offenders: *Hotel World* 59:7 (August 13, 1904): 7.

48. Street, *Welcome to Our City,* 20–21, passim; see also Kerry Segrave, *Tipping: An American Social History of Gratuities* (Jefferson, N.C.: McFarland and Co., 1998); William Leach, *Land of Desire: Merchants, Power, and the Rise of a New American Culture* (New York: Vintage, 1994): 131–32.

49. "Encourage Travel," *Hotel Monthly* 19:214 (January 1911): 57; Street, *Welcome to Our City,* 44–45; see also "Service—the Modern Idea," *Hotel Bulletin* 12:4 (April 1914): 282; Howells, *Their Wedding Journey,* 18: "It is all but impossible not to wish to stand well with your waiter: I have myself been often treated with conspicuous rudeness by the tribe, yet I have never been able to withhold the *douceur* that marked me for a gentleman in their eyes."

50. "Continue to Collect," *Hotel Bulletin* 6:3 (February 1911): 190; this article referred to the common practice of renting the hat and coat check out to a private service, which then provided equipment and uniformed boys who earned no wages but could keep tips. See also "Encourage Travel," 57; "Service—the Modern Idea," 282; *Hotel World* 72:4 (January 28, 1911): 13.

51. *Hotel World* 60:8 (Feb. 25, 1908): 7; "Training the Colored Waiter," *Hotel World* 66:25 (June 25, 1908): 13; see also *Hotel Monthly* 15:171 (June 1907): 17; in 1893 Anna Douglas stayed at the Florida House in St. Augustine,

which had "[a] very pretty dining room—all col'd waiters—a very elaborate bill of fare," Downs Collection, WL, 29.

52. Rector added that his waiters "were often mistaken for guests. However, an experienced eye could detect that [their] Swiss were too polite to be guests"; *The Girl from Rector's*, 92–93; *Forty Days*, 295–96; Hungerford, *Story of the Waldorf-Astoria*, 87–88. Hotel men now and then called for schools to train waiters, but none was ever noted in the journals; the American Hotel Association made arrangements for Cornell University to open a school of hotel administration in 1922; see Leach, *Land of Desire*, 286; "Schools for Training Hotel Servants," *Hotel Monthly* 11:124 (July 1903): 17–18. Often European immigrants, many waiters probably spoke at least one European language in addition to English and might easily have had a few words of others. Some Chinese men waited tables at western railroad depot restaurants.

53. "Waiters," *Hotel World* 7:1 (July 6, 1878): 1; see also *Hotel World* 54:2 (January 11, 1902): 1 and 63:1 (July 7, 1906): 12; Briton William Ferguson, *America by River and Rail; Or, Notes by the Way on the New World and Its People* (London: James Nisbet & Co., 1856), 49, found to his surprise and dismay that women waited tables at the Clarendon Hotel, New York: "They took time enough before they brought [our dinners] to do a 'smart bit' of flirtation with the cooks." No racial or ethnic designation was ever used in referring to the "girls" who waited tables, so they were most likely white, native-born women. I found almost no material on chambermaids or laundresses in the trade journals except the short-lived column "The Practical Hotel Housekeeper," by Mary Cavanaugh and Mary Bresnan, both hotel housekeepers, in the *Hotel Monthly*; it mostly focused on technical details and the importance of being polite to long-term patrons; see *Hotel Monthly* 5:46 (January 1897): 28–29; 5:47 (February 1897): 24–25; 5:51 (June 1897): 16. Bresnan later published a book of the same title.

54. Lesley Poling-Kempes, *The Harvey Girls: Women Who Opened the West* (New York: Paragon House, 1991); *Hotel World* 60:8 (February 25, 1905): 7, 66:25 (June 25, 1908): 13; Sam J. French, "Rise of Chop Suey Restaurants," *Hotel World* 72:2 (January 14, 1911): 18; the Hotel Raymond in Pasadena used white women to wait table; see Amy Bridges diary, December 21, 1886, HL.

55. Goins, "The American Colored Waiter," *Hotel Monthly* 9:97 (April 1901): 26–27; also 9:99 (June 1901): 25, 9:100 (July 1901): 26, 10:112 (July 1902): 27. Goins published *The American Waiter* at some point before 1908.

56. Hungerford, *Story of the Waldorf-Astoria*, 88–90.

57. "What They Say," *Hotel Monthly* 19:214 (January 1911): 35; Howells, *Their Wedding Journey*, 61–62; see also "A Vindication of the Hotel Clerk," *Hotel World* 7:3 (July 20, 1878): 1; Williamson, *The American Hotel*, chap. 5; Mower, *Reminiscences*, 134–35; "World's Fair Hotel/Clerk" (cartoon), *Harper's Weekly* 37:1907 (July 8, 1893): 654. How to summon bellboys and whether to make them wear uniforms also received some attention in the hotel journals.

58. "A Vindication," 1; Mower, *Reminiscences*, 134–35; Susan Porter Benson, *Counter Cultures: Saleswomen, Managers, and Customers in American*

Department Stores, 1890–1940 (Chicago: University of Illinois Press, 1986); see also "Service—the Modern Idea," 282.

59. "A Vindication of the Hotel Clerk," 1; see also Roth, "A Dream of the Future Hotel," *Hotel Monthly,* 40; Fred C. Ambrose, "Second Thoughts and Other Thoughts from the Hotel Clerk's Point of View," *Hotel Monthly* 17: 190 (January 1909): 40–41. Checking accounts were not common, banks were largely unregulated, and people did not routinely have state-issued forms of identification, so accepting a bank check was a gamble.

60. Bob Parvin, for *Hotel World,* "Tryin'," *Hotel World* 73:13 (September 23, 1911): 23; I have butchered the rhyme for the sake of brevity; *Hotel Monthly* 19:214 (January 1911): 33; see also "Hotel World Would Like to See," *Hotel World* 71:1 (July 2, 1910): editorial page; Martyn and Doolittle, *'Fables' of the Hotel Profession,* 8–11; Mower, *Reminiscences,* 23, 133, 142–43. For an exception, see Jarman's and Miller's biographies of Ellsworth Statler, who went to work in a glass factory at nine, became a bellboy at thirteen, and made himself a millionaire restaurant and hotel owner by the time he was in his forties. As a midwesterner of lower-class origins, Statler was something of an outsider in hotelmen's circles and he may have deliberately set himself up in opposition to the gentlemanly Lucius Boomer, manager of the Waldorf-Astoria and other hotels.

61. Mower, *Reminiscences,* dedication; "That European Trip," *Hotel Bulletin* 7:4 (September 1911): 190.

62. "The Story of a Record Breaking Entertainment," *Hotel Monthly* 18: 206 (May 1910): 47, 50–56. The entertainment included a "wild west" theme smoker at the St. Francis, a Mandarin Chinese banquet, a luncheon at the Fairmont, and tours to Chinatown and other city sights. The hosting hotels invited the membership and apparently donated the costs of lodging and food; related businesses frequently showered the participants with "souvenirs" such as silver spoons and other small items. For another example, see the Washington, D.C., meeting, *Hotel Monthly* 15:171 (June 1907): 18–29. The limited membership of the HMMBA emerged in a controversy over the association's decision to travel to Europe in 1912 or 1913; see "That European Trip," *Hotel Bulletin.*

63. "Need a National Association," *Hotel Bulletin* 9:3 (August 1912): 157–58; *Hotel Monthly* 18:207 (June 1910): 33; Matthew Josephson, *Union House, Union Bar: The History of the Hotel and Restaurant Employees and Bartenders International Union, AFL-CIO* (New York: Random House, 1955).

64. "Need a National Association," 158; *Hotel Bulletin* 10:3 (March 1913): 189; Miller, *America's Extraordinary Hotelman,* 122–26. There were several city, state, and regional hotelmen's associations that worked to increase tourism (the Rocky Mountain Association led the way) and to prevent regulatory legislation. In cities, hotelmen's associations tended to represent the managers and owners only of the first-class hotels.

65. *Hotel Monthly* 5:50 (May 1897): 13; "Palatial Public-Room Publicity," *Hotel World* 72:4 (January 28, 1911): 14–15.

66. "The Horrors of Hotel Life: By a Reformed Landlord" (New York: Connelly and Curtis, 1884), 5–6, passim. The filthy habits of waiters also feature in the 1914 Mack Sennett comedy, *Caught in a Cabaret,* starring Charlie Chaplin.

67. "Apartment-Houses," *Appleton's Journal,* n.s. 5 (1878): 530; see also

Elizabeth Collins Cromley, *Alone Together: A History of New York's Early Apartments* (Ithaca: Cornell University Press, 1990), and Elizabeth Hawes, *New York, New York: How the Apartment House Transformed the Life of the City* (New York: Knopf, 1993).

68. Cromley, *Alone Together*, 21–22; Junius Henri Browne, *The Great Metropolis* (Hartford: American Publishing Co., 1869), 195–204.

69. B. E. Lloyd, *Lights and Shades in San Francisco, with Appropriate Illustrations* (San Francisco: A. L. Bancroft, 1876), 66; see also Cromley, *Alone Together*, 24; "A Good Place to Live," *Hotel World* 72:12 (March 25, 1911): 13.

70. Boorstin, "Palaces of the People," 146, quoting the English traveler Mrs. Bodichon; Browne, *The Great Metropolis*, 205–13; M. H. Smith, *Sunshine and Shadow in New York* (Hartford: J. B. Burr & Co., 1869), 431–32; McCabe, *Lights and Shades*, 313–15, 502–7; Lloyd, *Lights and Shades*, 449.

71. "A Good Place to Live," 13; *Hotel World* 55:3 (July 19, 1902): 11.

72. *Hotel World* 72:13 (September 23, 1911): 15: "It is nearly time for the recirculation of the dreadful story how women traveling alone are not permitted to register and remain at first-class hotels."

73. Browne, *The Great Metropolis*, 195–204; *Hotel Monthly* 9:105 (October 1901): 18; "A Good Place to Live," *Hotel World*, 13; "What Is a Hotel," *Hotel Bulletin* 12:4 (April 1914): 281. The McAlpin and the Plaza and other early-twentieth-century hotels with separate floors for single women had female clerks to aid the guests. Rector, *The Girl from Rector's*, 2; "The Lesson of Rectors [*sic*]," *Hotel Bulletin* 11:1 (July 1913): 17.

74. Ernest Ingersoll, *A Week In New York* (New York: Rand, McNally, 1891), 42. The book has been rebound and broken at the binding, so that words along the inner margins were effaced. Henry Collins Brown, *Valentine's Manual* (New York: Henry Holt Co., 1920), introd., repeated this same warning almost verbatim. The hotel journals occasionally noted lawsuits stemming from denial of service, e.g., *Hotel World* 56:24 (June 13, 1903): 7.

75. *Hotel World* 54:8 (February 22, 1902): 11, 14; "The Modern Hotel," *Hotel World* 63:18 (November 3, 1906): 19; "Greater New York's Greater Hotel," *Hotel World*: 76:1 (January 4, 1913): 29; "The 'Belle' Hop," *Hotel Bulletin* 12:1 (January 1914): 16.

76. Christine Boyer, *Manhattan Manners: Architecture and Style, 1850–1900* (New York: Rizzoli, 1985), 59.

77. Williamson, *The American Hotel*, 129; "Hotel Martha Washington" (n.p., n.d.), circular, Hotel vertical file, NYHS 1–2; "Hotel Martha Washington" (n.p., n.d.), circular in Box 10, Hotels, Warshaw Collection, NMAH. See also Joanne Meyerowitz, *Women Adrift: Independent Wage Earners in Chicago, 1880–1930* (Chicago: University of Chicago Press, 1988).

78. *Hotel Monthly* 6:58 (January 1898): 15, 9:105 (December 1901): 22, 21:238 (January 1913): 92; "Bad Mixup by Night Clerk," *Hotel World* 72:20 (November 11, 1911): 9; and "Correct Hotel Ethics," *Hotel World* 59:20 (November 12, 1904): 9. This last case involved the notorious Henry Thaw and his mistress, Evelyn Nesbit. The manager insisted that Thaw either register Nesbit as his wife or leave the hotel. Thaw refused to do either, and the couple eventually left.

79. "Bad Mixup by Night Clerk," 9; see also *Hotel Monthly* 9:105 (December 1901): 18, 22–23.

80. "Defining the Word Hotel," 14.

81. *Hotel World* 60:2 (January 14, 1905): 7; and 72:4 (January 28, 1911): 13; see also *Hotel World* 71:25 (December 17, 1910): 15. *Hotel World* ridiculed the refusal of a Broadway tearoom to serve two Englishmen who entered without the escort of ladies; see 63:26 (December 29, 1906): 9. As late as 1903, a judge ruled that "the proprietor of a hotel or restaurant has the right to refuse accommodations or service to a lady unattended" as long as all such women were denied entrance; *Hotel World* 56:24 (June 13, 1903): 7.

82. Hardenburgh quoted in Pevsner, *Building Types,* 181; Francis Walker, speech reprinted in *Hotel Bulletin* 8:3 (February 1911): 151; "Hotel Martha Washington" (n.p., n.d.), circular at the Hotel vertical file, NYHS, 1–2; "Hotel Martha Washington" (n.p., n.d.), circular in box 10, Hotels, Warshaw Collection, AC/NMAH; "Hotel Removes Its Ban on Men and Cocktails," *Hotel Record* 6:21 (July 14, 1908): 5. See also the descriptions of the Hotel McAlpin (1912) in *Hotel World* 76:1 (January 4, 1913): 29, and the St. Francis Hotel in *Hotel Monthly* 16:184 (July 1908): 36–37; Hungerford, *Story of the Waldorf-Astoria,* 139, 141. The Waldorf-Astoria claimed to be the first hotel to provide women with a place to get their boots polished, a billiard table, and a Ping-Pong table, but the thoroughly conventional Amy Bridges was delighted to have the chance to play billiards at the Hotel Raymond, Pasadena, in 1886; see Bridges diary, December 21, 1886, HL. The women's bar was a flop, much to the relief of the hotel journal editors.

83. *Hotel World* 80:8 (February 20, 1915): 14; "Fight to Separate Hotels and Saloons," *Hotel Bulletin* 14:2 (February 1915): 107; "The Hotel World Would Like to See," *Hotel World* 71:1 (July 2, 1910): 15; *Hotel Register* 43:16 (February 10, 1904): 3.

84. "What Is a Hotel?" *Hotel World* 72:1 (January 7, 1911): 31; see also *Hotel Bulletin* 10:3 (March 1913): 194; "Defining the Word Hotel," *Hotel World* 76:6 (February 8, 1913): 13; *Hotel Monthly* 8:86 (May 1900): 11, 12:138 (September 1904): 17, 21:238 (January 1913): 42.

85. "Squibs," *Hotel World* 3:1 (July 6, 1877): 2; for a "clarification" of the issue explaining that it was tradesmen, not Jews, who were targeted, see "The Hotel de Snob," *Hotel World* 3:2 (July 12, 1877): 1; see also *Hotel Monthly* 9:102 (September 1901): 18; Gillespie, "Democracy and Opulence," 24 n. 10. The demand for kosher food also contributed to the establishment of many Jewish-owned and run hotels in the early twentieth century, particularly in New York State.

86. *Hotel World* 56:8 (February 21, 1903): 15 and 56:10 (March 7, 1903): 11.

FOUR. "WHY NOT VISIT CHICAGO": TOUR COMPANIES
AND CITY BUSINESS ORGANIZATIONS, 1870–1915

1. Richard Henry Little, "The Charm of Chicago," in a Chicago Association of Commerce (CAC) membership booklet, probably published in 1905–6, the CAC's first year; Chicago Association of Commerce Miscellany, CHS.

2. Richard Wightman Fox, "The Discipline of Amusement," in *Inventing Times Square: Commerce and Culture at the Crossroads of the World*, ed. William R. Taylor (New York: Russell Sage, 1991), 83–98; Daniel T. Rodgers, *The Work Ethic in Industrial America, 1850–1920* (Chicago: University of Chicago Press, 1978), chap. 4; Jane Addams, *The Spirit of Youth and the City Streets* (New York: Macmillan, 1909), 95–97; Simon N. Patten, *The New Basis of Civilization*, ed. Daniel M. Fox (Cambridge, Mass.: Belknap Press of Harvard University Press, 1968; orig. 1907); William H. Wilson, *The City Beautiful Movement* (Baltimore: Johns Hopkins University Press, 1989).

3. Addams, *The Spirit of Youth*, is a good example of the anticommercialism of many Progressives; see also Kathy Peiss, *Cheap Amusements: Working Women and Leisure in Turn-of-the-Century New York* (Philadelphia: Temple University Press, 1986), chap. 7.

4. *Stork's 1700 Mile Summer Tours from Baltimore to New York...* (1879), 1, Warshaw Collection of Business Americana, Tours, box 4, AC/NMAH; see also John R. Stilgoe, *Metropolitan Corridor: Railroads and the American Scene* (New Haven: Yale University Press, 1983), chap. 2, esp. 66.

5. Dona Brown, *Inventing New England: Regional Tourism in the Nineteenth Century* (Washington, D.C.: Smithsonian Institution Press, 1995), chaps. 1–2; Anne Farrar Hyde, *An American Vision: Far Western Landscape and National Culture, 1820–1920* (New York: New York University Press, 1990); the New York Central's *Four-Track Series*, a line of publicity brochures, included No. 31, Charles Barnard's "Seen from the Car: Travel as a Fine Art"; see advertisement in *Four-Track News* 14:1 (January 1903): xviii; "The Road of a Thousand Wonders," Southern Pacific Railroad advertisement in the *Ladies' Home Journal* (July 1906): n.p.; see also "From the Window: A Description of the Scenery, Industries and Points of Historic Interest Along the Queen & Crescent Route," Queen & Crescent Railroad (Cincinnati, 1914), Warshaw Collection, Railroads, box 91, AC/NMAH; the Great Northern Railway's "The Oriental Limited," in the Warshaw Collection, Railroads, box 88, AC/NMAH; and many other examples in boxes 85, 88, and 91. Some people, however, felt that the speed of trains destroyed the possibility of sight-seeing; see Wolfgang Schivelbusch, *The Railway Journey: The Industrialization of Time and Space in the Nineteenth Century* (Berkeley: University of California Press, 1986; orig. 1977).

6. *Proceedings of the Convention of the Northern Lines of Railway, Held at Boston, in December, 1850, and January, 1851* (Boston: J. B. Yerrington & Son, 1851), Warshaw Collection, Railroads, box 86, AC/NMAH, 44.

7. Walter E. Weyl, *The Passenger Traffic of Railways*, Series in Political Economy and Law, no. 16 (Philadelphia: Publications of the University of Pennsylvania, 1901), 63; Emory Johnson, *American Railway Transportation*, rev. ed. (New York: D. Appleton & Co., 1906), 150.

8. Brad S. Lomazzi, *Railroad Timetables, Travel Brochures and Posters: A History and Guide for Collectors* (Spencertown, N.Y.: Golden Hill Press, 1995), chaps. 5–7; Valerie Fifer, *American Progress: The Growth of Transport, Tourist, and Information Industries in the Nineteenth-Century West* (Chester, Conn.: Pequot Press, 1988); the Ask Mr. Foster travel information bureau established branches in department stores, Tours, box 4, Warshaw, AC/NMAH.

9. Piers Brendon, *Thomas Cook: 150 Years of Popular Tourism* (London: Secker & Warburg, 1991); James Buzard, *The Beaten Track: European Tourism, Literature, and the Ways to Culture, 1800–1918* (Oxford: Clarendon Press, 1993), chap. 1; Carole Fabricant, "The Literature of Domestic Tourism and the Public Consumption of Private Property," in *The New Eighteenth Century: Theory, Politics, English Literature*, ed. Felicity Nussbaum and Laura Brown (London: Methuen, 1987), 254–75.

10. Cook quoted in Brendon, *Thomas Cook*, 32; see chaps. 1–3 generally. In the 1840s Cook ran tours mostly as a part of his temperance activities. His son John Mason eventually shifted the company's focus to a wealthier clientele, abandoning his father's philanthropic aims and making the company more profitable.

11. W. Fraser Rae, *The Business of Travel: A Fifty Years' Record of Progress* (New York: Thomas Cook & Son, 1891), 78, quoting the published address "to the People of America," which Cook circulated in the United States in 1865; "Our American Tourist Business," *Cook's Excursionist* 24:2 (June 1874): 3.

12. "Cook's Excursionist and Cook's Tours in America," *Cook's Excursionist* 24:6 (Winter 1874–75): 2.

13. "Our American Tourist Business," *Cook's Excursionist* 24:2 (June 1874): 3; "Cook's Excursionist and Cook's Tours in America," *Cook's Excursionist* 24:6 (Winter 1874–75): 2.

In a joke titled "The Raw and the Cook'd," which appeared in *Cook's Excursionist and Home and Foreign Tourist Advertiser, American Edition* (January 1893): 12, reprinted from the Algiers *Atlas*, a new tourist was advised: "Being new to the business, get Cook'd. Depend upon it, you won't be 'done.'"

14. "The Business of Travel," *Cook's Excursionist* (October 1893): 10. See John Pudney, *The Thomas Cook Story* (London: Michael Joseph, 1953), on the partnership with Jenkins, and Jenkins's publications, including *The Tourist World: A Journal of Travel Devoted to the Interests of Tourists and Travelers* 1:4 (April 1881): 2, and "An Excursion to Colorado, California and the Yosemite Valley, Under the Management of E. M. Jenkins, formerly of Cook, Son & Jenkins" (New York, 1883): 2, Warshaw Collection, Tours, box 5. Hugh De Santis, "The Democraticization of Travel: The Travel Agent in American History," *Journal of American Culture* 1 (Spring 1978): 5; *Raymond's Vacation Excursions . . . Four Spring Tours* (1893). Most of the tour company materials now preserved in archives are Cook & Son and Raymond & Whitcomb publications.

15. Lomazzi, *Railroad Timetables*, chaps. 3–5.

16. *Four-Track News* 1:1 (July 1901): 1; *Central-Hudson Magazine and Monthly Bulletin . . .* 1:7 (January 1891); *Four-Track News: A Monthly Magazine of Travel and Education* 2:4 (April 1902): 121–23, and *Four-Track News* [brochure]: 1–2, in the Warshaw Collection, Railroads, box 85; *Travel Maga-*

zine (A Continuation of the Four-Track News) 12:1 (October 1906): 11. The magazine continued to be published by the New York Central. General passenger agent George Daniels had not been the sole editor at least since 1902, but the 1906 reorganization seems to have established greater distance between the overt advertising of the railroad and its literary arm. Few of the *Four-Track Series* have been preserved, so I do not know when they were first published, but the New York Central seems to have been at the forefront of regional and national advertising among railroads.

17. *Book of the Royal Blue* 1:1 (October 1897); the numbering of this journal is unclear; see also *Tourist/Devoted to the interests of passengers over the Washington-Sunset Route and Southern Pacific Railway* (October 1909); *Sunset* noted its new independence in September 1914 (33:3): 430–31, 504a–d; the quotation is from 504d. *Cook's Excursionist and Home and Foreign Tourist Advertiser, American Edition* (April 1873); the first number apparently appeared in March 1873. Most likely the English edition had been available in the United States since the firm opened its branch in New York in the late 1860s; see Buzard, *The Beaten Track*, 64, on the new version. McCann's Tours published *The Tourist Educator* in the early twentieth century; E. M. Jenkins published a *Cook's Excursionist* lookalike titled *The Tourist World: A Journal of Travel Devoted to the Interests of Tourists and Travelers,* beginning in 1881; Raymond & Whitcomb published a quarterly titled *Travelers' Condensed Guide* that claimed a circulation of thirty thousand by 1904; American Express also published a journal, *Travel, Devoted to the Interests of Travelers in All Lands,* in the 1880s, but it was intended for American travelers to Europe, as were its travelers' checks. Magazines inspired by world's fairs include *The Traveler, an Illustrated Monthly Journal of Travel and Recreation,* published in San Francisco in 1893–94 for the Midwinter Exposition, and *Travel: How, When, Where,* published in St. Louis and much concerned with the 1904 Louisiana Purchase Exposition. See also *American Travelers Journal; Tourists' and Excursionists' Companion,* published out of New York and St. Louis in 1881–82; *The Traveller: Devoted to Travel, Art and Education,* appeared in the early twentieth century.

18. *Reasons Why* (Baltimore: Passenger Department of the Baltimore & Ohio Railroad, 1901); Henry Phelps, comp., "A Literary and Historic Note-Book" (Passenger Department of the Delaware & Hudson Co., n.d.); *The Oriental Limited: The Perfect Train* (Great Northern Railway, 1914); Henry Phelps, *The Golden State Limited* (Chicago: Rock Island System, 190[?]): "It is intended not merely to accommodate passenger traffic but to create it . . . a mighty factor in the promotion, extension and enlargement of first-class travel to the Pacific Coast," n.p.; all of the railroad pamphlets are from the Warshaw Collection, Railroads, box 88. The *Brooklyn Eagle* newspaper had an active information and excursion service, sponsoring trips to the 1893 World's Columbian Exposition and other events; the magazine *Town and Country* also advertised a travel information bureau, as did the *New York Journal*. The Standard Guide Co., a guidebook publisher, supported a service called Ask Mr. Foster. On the trade show, see "Travel and Vacation Exhibition, 2nd Annual," brochure and application form in Warshaw, Tours, box 4; also Neil Harris, "Urban Tourism and the Commercial City," in *Inventing Times Square: Commerce and Culture at the*

Crossroads of the World, ed. William R. Taylor (New York: Russell Sage, 1991), 66–82.

19. "Save Money While Traveling in Comfort" (New York: Lansing's General Ticket Office, n.d.): n.p., in the Warshaw Collection, Tours, box 6; "Ask Mr. Foster," (Buffalo, N.Y.: Wm. Hengerer Co., 1914), 2, Warshaw Collection, Tours, box 4.

20. "Cook's Tours—Some Words of Explanation," *Cook's Excursionist* (April 1873): 5. Letters of credit were written by the tourist's banker requesting that other banks extend privileges to the bearer. Such letters could easily be forged and bankers kept short hours.

21. "Cook's Tours—Some Words of Explanation," *Cook's Excursionist* (April 1873): 5.

22. "Cook's Tours—Some Words of Explanation," *Cook's Excursionist* (April 1873): 5; see also "Holiday Trips," *Cook's Excursionist* (July 1897): 10; and Buzard, *The Beaten Path,* chap. 1. Of course, the conductors did have a class, but because they were approximately of the same class as their passengers, the guide's professional identity shaped the relationship.

23. "Cook's Tours—Some Words of Explanation," *Cook's Excursionist* (April 1873): 5; "California," *Cook's Excursionist* (October 1893): 10; Stephen Merritt, "From Ocean to Ocean! Or, Across and Around the Country. Being an Account of the Raymond and Whitcomb, Pacific, North West [*sic*] and Alaska, Excursion of 1892. Including the Yosemite Valley & Yellowstone Park, By Stephen Merritt, 210 Eighth Ave., New York," HL, 22. Merritt and his wife took the tour to relieve the pressure of a long career and the recent deaths of three family members. Despite Merritt's frequent claim to be doing nothing and enjoying it, he regularly met with fellow Methodist Episcopal ministers and sometimes preached and visited missions.

24. *Cook's Excursionist* (August 1892): 10; see also *American Travelers Journal* 1:1 (March 1881): 6, col. 1: "there is a necessity of the indulgence"; *The Traveler* 3:3 (March 1894): 49; Rodgers, *The Work Ethic in Industrial America,* 94–124; Fox, "The Discipline of Amusement," 83–98.

25. *Raymond's Vacation Excursions, All Traveling Expenses Included, California, The Pacific Northwest, ALASKA, and the World's Columbian Exposition, Four Spring Tours, Leaving Boston April 24 and May 24, 1893* (Boston, 1893), 4–5. The vestibule provided an enclosed passage between the cars, allowing riders to move easily through the entire train. See also *Cook's California Excursions, 1884* (New York, 1884), 4–5, Warshaw Collection, Tours, box 4; Mrs. E. D. Frazar, "World's Fair . . . Philadelphia to Chicago; European Tours for 1893" (Boston, 1893), 3–4, Warshaw Collection, Tours, box 4; *Leve and Alden's American Tours* (January 1882): title page, Warshaw Collection, Tours, box 4; Gillespie and Kinports, "Tours Through Yellowstone Park and California; The Thousand Islands and Canada; The Coast of Maine and Nova Scotia" (1906), 4, Warshaw Collection, Tours, box 5.

26. Raymond & Whitcomb, "Raymond's Vacation Excursions/Ten Grand Summer Trips . . ." (Boston, 1887), 4, Warshaw Collection, Railroads, box 84, AC/NMAH; "Personally Escorted Summer Tours for 1908," Chicago, Union Pacific & Northwestern Line (Chicago, 1908), 6, 24, Warshaw Collection, Rail-

roads, box 85, AC/NMAH; "Who Compose Our Parties," *Tourist World* 1:4 (April 1881): 2; "Special Notices," *Cook's Excursionist* (May 1892): 10; Amy Bridges diary, May 27, 1882, HL: "[T]his train was the first in which we had mingled with other passengers and it did not seem pleasant to me. I'm afraid Pullman cars are making one feel aristocratic." *Raymond & Whitcomb's Tours, Spring Tours through California* (1897), 1, offered three options: California and Alaska, 73 days, $660, just California, 65 days, $560, or a shorter California tour, 53 days, $425; J. F. Muirhead, *Baedeker's Handbook to the United States* (Leipzig and New York, 1893; rept. New York: Da Capo Press, 1971), xxv–xxvi. Shorter tours to northeastern and southeastern resorts costing around $50 were also readily available but not as widely advertised.

27. "Around the World," *Cook's Excursionist* (May 1892): 10; Stephen Merritt, "Ocean to Ocean," 23; his being a minister probably explains his choice of descriptive terms. Amy Bridges also noted making the acquaintance of fellow Raymond & Whitcomb excursionists both on the train and in the Hotel Raymond, Pasadena; see Bridges diary, vol. 1, April 28, 1882; vol. 2, December 9, 1886, passim.

28. Raymond & Whitcomb, *Spring Tours Through California* (1897), 3–4; Augustus Franklin Tripp, "Notes of an Excursion to California in the Winter and Spring of 1893," HL, preface, 2, 7, 11, 17, passim.

29. See Thomas Cook & Son, *Notes for Atlantic Travellers* (n.p., n.d.), 58, Warshaw Collection, Tours, box 4; *Raymond's Vacation Excursions, A Winter in California; Seven Grand Trips . . . 1886–1887* (n.p., 1886): 28; *Cook's California Excursion, 1884*, 5.

30. "A Bostonian Abroad . . . A 'Personally Conducted' Party and Its Adventures. . . ," *Boston Herald* (October 15, 1887), PPCC Records 12/00/04, reel 14, vol. 1; Buzard, *The Beaten Track*, introd. and chap. 1.

31. "The Science of Traveling," *Cook's Excursionist* (January 1892): 14, reprinted from the *Toronto Empire*; "Personally Conducted Parties," *Cook's Excursionist* (November 1893): 10; see also "On the Excursion," *Boston Evening Transcript* (April 21, 1883), PPCC Records 12/00/01, reel 1, vol. 6; Bridges diary, December 13, 1886, HL.

32. "The Science of Traveling," 14; Rae, *The Business of Travel*, 132–33; Brendon, *Thomas Cook*, 62–64 and chap. 2 generally; Pudney, *Cook Story*, chap. 17.

33. "Tours," *Travelers' Condensed Guide, Raymond & Whitcomb Tours and Individual Tickets Everywhere* (January 1904): 58; see also "California" and "Personally Conducted Parties," *Cook's Excursionist* (November 1893): 10; Raymond & Whitcomb, *Grand Summer and Autumn Tours to the Pacific Northwest . . .* (1897): 3; "Raymond's Vacation Excursions/Ten Grand Summer Trips" (July 1887): 3–4; "Cook's California Excursion" (Season 1884): 3–5; "On the Excursion" and "A Bostonian Abroad," cited above.

34. Buzard, *The Beaten Path*, introd. and chap. 1.

35. *Raymond & Whitcomb Tours, Spring Tours Through California* (1897): 3; *Raymond's Vacation Excursions, Thirty Summer Tours!* (July–August, 1890): 6; Pudney, *Cook Story*, 164–65.

36. "On the Excursion" and "A Bostonian Abroad," PPCC Records; Bridges

diary, April 28, 1882, May 18, 1882 (quotation), December 9, 1886, and December 21, 1886; for the numbers, see the *Boston Globe* (April 20, 1890), PPCC
Records 12/00/04, reel 14, vol. 1. There were probably several different departure dates with the tours following each other along the route rather than all
eight hundred traveling at once.

37. "Tours through Yellowstone...," Gillespie and Kinports (1906): 5, Warshaw Collection, Tours, box 5; "Florida/Winter Pleasure Tours" (Philadelphia:
Passenger Department of the Pennsylvania Railroad, 1892), 5; see also *Stork's
1700 Mile Summer Tours,* 5, also in Warshaw, Tours, box 4, all AC/NMAH;
Raymond's Vacation Excursions, Five Grand Summer Trips in August, 1887...,
3; "A Bostonian Abroad," PPCC Records, cited above; and "Find Many Sur-
prises/Eastern Excursionists' Lot," *Chicago Record* (August 14, 1900), PPCC
Records, 12/00/01, reel 7, vol. 25.

38. Harvey Levenstein, *Seductive Journey: American Tourists in France from
Jefferson to the Jazz Age* (Chicago: University of Chicago Press, 1998), 185,
claims that women predominated among nineteenth-century American travelers
to France; see the Tripp, Bridges, and Merritt diaries for evidence that married
couples were more common on American tours. Anna E. D. Douglas, diary of a
journey from Boston to Florida, 1892–93, Downs Collection, WL, seemed quite
comfortable managing the trip and taking care of her two younger sisters. This
kind of criticism appears in well-known twentieth-century essays on tourism; see
Daniel Boorstin, "From Traveler to Tourist: The Lost Art of Travel," in his *The
Image: Or, What Happened to the American Dream* (New York: Atheneum,
1962), 77–117; Paul Fussell, *Abroad: British Literary Traveling between the
Wars* (New York: Oxford University Press, 1980).

39. Rev. Dr. Bridgman, "Vacation Gospel" (Great Northern Railway, 1890),
1, Warshaw Collection, Railroads, Box 88; George G. Eldredge, "On Vacation
Values," *Sunset* 13:3 (July 1904): 254–55; *Stork's 1700 Mile Summer Tours...*
(1879): 1, Warshaw Collection, Tours, Box 4.

40. "When Planning the Summer Outing," Illinois Central Railroad folder,
1917, Warshaw Collection, Tours, box 4, AC/NMAH; *Hints for Strangers,
Shoppers, and Sightsee-ers [sic] in the Metropolis, with a Directory Giving the
Location of the Leading Houses in Many Trades* (New York: New York Infor-
mation Agency, n.d., probably 1900s), 21; *The Guide Magazine for New York*
(November 1902): 3; see also *Rand, McNally & Co.'s Tourist Guide to the
Northwest,* 9–11, 20; *A Guide to the City of Chicago,* 182–87; Mrs. Schuyler
Van Rensselaer, "Midsummer in New York," *Century Magazine* 62:4 (August
1901): 484–85.

41. *Raymond's Vacation Excursions, Thirty Summer Tours!* (1890): 6; see
Cook's Excursionist (April 1892): 30, for the rates; the initial announcement appeared in the January 1892 issue. I was unable to obtain any *Excursionists* for
the 1880s. See also "Tours," *Travelers' Condensed Guide,* Raymond & Whitcomb Tours... (January 1904): 63; "Royal Blue Three-Day Tours from New
York, Philadelphia and Intermediate Points to Washington," *Book of the Royal
Blue* 3:4 (January 1900): inside back cover; "Specimen Tours and Tickets/Pop-
ular Three-Day Tours to Washington, D.C.," *Tourist's Monthly Magazine* 3:1

(January 1908): 30; advertisement for the Pennsylvania Railroad's Washington, D.C., tour, *Harper's Weekly* 44:2254 (March 3, 1900): 204.

42. Harris, "Urban Tourism and the Commercial City," on New York City; "When Planning the Summer Outing," Illinois Central Railroad folder, 1917, Warshaw Collection, Tours, box 4, AC/NMAH.

43. For claims that cities could be excellent summer resorts, see *Wayside Notes Along the Sunset Route (Eastbound)* (San Francisco: Southern Pacific, 1911), 3; *Doxey's Guide to San Francisco and the Pleasure Resorts of California*, 97; Hotel Steward, *San Francisco, Guest's Guide* (San Francisco, n.d., probably 1913–14), 8; *San Francisco Standard Guide . . . Standard Tourists, Sightseers, Shoppers, and Buyers [sic] Guide* (San Francisco: North American Press Association, 1912, proofs), PPIE papers, BL, 7; Sweetser and Ford, *How to Know New York*, 106–10; Van Rensselaer, "Midsummer in New York," *Century Magazine* 62:4 (August 1901): 483–501; J. M. Wing & Co., *Seven Days in Chicago*, 1; Illinois Central Railroad, *Chicago for the Tourist* (1908): 1; *Come to Chicago* (n.p., n.d.; pamphlet in Warshaw, States, Illinois, box 1, 1, AC/NMAH; *A Guide to the City of Chicago* (Chicago: Chicago Association of Commerce, 1909), 182. The earliest claim I have seen is *Rand, McNally & Co.'s Tourist Guide to the Northwest* (Chicago: Rand, McNally, 1880), 9–11, 20; "An Unbiased Examination," *Harper's Weekly* 37:1912 (August 12, 1893): 759. For examples of city filth and the summer exodus, see Edward Spann, *The New Metropolis: New York City, 1840–1857* (New York: Columbia University Press, 1981), chap. 6; middle-class magazines like *Harper's Weekly* regularly chronicled the annual summer flight and the doings at eastern resorts; see, for example, "Out of Town for Summer," *Harper's Weekly* 37:1911 (August 4, 1893): 734.

44. David Nye, *The Electrification of America: Social Meanings of a New Technology* (Cambridge, Mass.: MIT Press, 1990); Daniel Bluestone, *Constructing Chicago* (New Haven: Yale University Press, 1991); William Leach, *Land of Desire: Merchants, Power, and the Rise of a New American Culture* (New York: Vintage, 1994); Clay McShane, *Down the Asphalt Path: The Automobile and the American City* (New York: Columbia University Press, 1994).

45. On sports, see CAC's *Commerce* 7:41 (February 16, 1912): 9; *Official Program for the Portolá Festival* (San Francisco, 1909).

46. Carl Abbott, *Boosters and Businessmen: Popular Economic Thought and Urban Growth in the Antebellum Middle West* (Westport, Conn.: Greenwood Press, 1981); William Cronon, *Nature's Metropolis: Chicago and the Great West* (New York: W. W. Norton, 1991), 41–46; Judd Kahn, *Imperial San Francisco: Politics and Planning in an American City, 1897–1906* (Lincoln: University of Nebraska Press, 1979).

47. Philip Ethington, *The Public City: The Political Construction of Urban Life in San Francisco, 1850–1900* (New York: Cambridge University Press, 1994); Mary Ryan, *Civic Wars: Democracy and Public Life in the American City during the Nineteenth Century* (Berkeley: University of California Press, 1997); Carl Smith, *Urban Disorder and the Shape of Belief: The Great Chicago Fire, the Haymarket Bomb, and the Model Town of Pullman* (Chicago: University of Chicago Press, 1995), 68–69.

48. Ethington, *The Public City,* chaps. 5–8; Ryan, *Civic Wars,* chap. 7; James Livingston, *Pragmatism and the Political Economy of Cultural Revolution, 1850–1940* (Chapel Hill: University of North Carolina Press, 1994).

49. The following analysis is based on the published journals, annual reports, and miscellaneous pamphlets of the Chicago Commerce Association (established in the early twentieth century, exact date unclear from records at the CHS), renamed the Chicago Association of Commerce in 1907; I will use the latter name. I also draw on the publications of the Merchants' Association of New York, founded in 1897; the Board of Trade of Washington, D.C., founded in 1889; and in San Francisco, the Merchants' Association (founded in 1894 to oversee the Midwinter Exposition), the Downtown Association (date of establishment uncertain), the Association for the Improvement and Adornment of San Francisco (1904); several preexisting groups united to form the city's chamber of commerce in 1911. Also pertinent was the San Francisco–based California Promotion Committee (probably established in 1902), whose supposedly statewide propaganda seemed to have focused almost exclusively on the northern part of the state. Unlike earlier chambers of commerce, the early-twentieth-century groups seem not to have been as closely linked with the stock exchanges. These groups addressed broad public issues in addition to promoting business and often abandoned the fiscal conservatism that marked most nineteenth-century elites.

50. Elizabeth Blackmar, *Manhattan for Rent, 1785–1850* (Ithaca: Cornell University Press, 1989); Michael Holleran, *Boston's 'Changeful Times': Origins of Preservation and Planning in America* (Baltimore: Johns Hopkins University Press, 1998); Roy Rosenzweig and Elizabeth Blackmar, *The Park and the People: A History of Central Park* (New York: Henry Holt, 1992); Keith D. Revell, "Regulating the Landscape: Real Estate Values, City Planning, and the 1916 Zoning Ordinance," in *The Landscape of Modernity: Essays on New York City, 1900–1940,* ed. David Ward and Olivier Zunz (New York: Russell Sage, 1992), 19–45.

51. Bluestone, *Constructing Chicago;* Rosenzweig and Blackmar, *The Park and the People,* pt. 1; Revell, "Regulating the Landscape."

52. Alan Trachtenberg, *The Incorporation of America: Culture and Society in the Gilded Age* (New York: Hill and Wang, 1982), chap. 7; Mel Scott, *American City Planning since 1890: A History Commemorating the 50th Anniversary of the American Institute of Planners* (Berkeley: University of California Press, 1969), 32–33, 36–37; James Gilbert, *Perfect Cities: Chicago's Utopias of 1893* (Chicago: University of Chicago Press, 1991), chap. 4.

53. Trachtenberg, *Incorporation,* chap. 7; Gilbert, *Perfect Cities,* chap. 4; Russell Lewis, "Everything Under One Roof: World's Fairs and Department Stores in Paris and Chicago," *Chicago History* 12:3 (Fall 1983): 28–47.

54. Julian Hawthorne, letter to his sister titled "A Description of the Inexpressible" (Chicago Historical Society, 1892), 2.

55. *Going to the Centennial and A Guy to the Great Exhibition, by Bricktop* (New York: Collin and Small, 1876), 21.

56. Gilbert, *Perfect Cities,* chap. 4; Trachtenberg, *Incorporation of America,* chap. 7; Lewis, "Everything Under One Roof."

57. Wilson, *The City Beautiful Movement*, chaps. 1, 2, 4.

58. Review of Charles Mulford Robinson's *Civic Art, Merchants' Association Review* [San Francisco] 7:83 (July 1903): 5. Robinson was a leading spokesman for the movement; see Wilson, *The City Beautiful Movement*, chap. 2.

59. Wilson, *The City Beautiful Movement*, chap. 4; Ethington, *The Public City*, introd.; Livingston, *Pragmatism*, chaps. 3–4.

60. Wilson, *The City Beautiful Movement*, chap. 4; Bluestone, *Constructing Chicago*, chap. 4; Kahn, *Imperial San Francisco*, chap. 3. City Beautiful promoters were not at all anticapitalist; they did want to coordinate profit making with larger aesthetic-cultural goals.

61. Wilson, *The City Beautiful Movement*, chap. 4; Kahn, *Imperial San Francisco*, chap. 3, 4; Bluestone, *Constructing Chicago*, chap. 6; Mario Manieri-Elia, "Toward an 'Imperial City': Daniel H. Burnham and the City Beautiful Movement," in *The American City: From the Civil War to the New Deal*, trans. Barbara Luigia La Penta, ed. Mario Manieri-Elia (Cambridge, Mass.: MIT Press, 1979), 1–123.

62. Henry Rutgers Marshall, "How to Make New York a Beautiful City," address before the Nineteenth Century Club, March 12, 1895 (New York: Nineteenth Century Club, 1895), 9–10.

63. Wilson, *The City Beautiful Movement*, 75–77, passim; Kahn, *Imperial San Francisco*, chap. 8.

64. Joseph D. Redding, "The Practical Benefits of Municipal Adornment," address before the San Francisco Downtown Association, April 19, 1911, pamphlet at BL, 10–11; D. H. Burnham, "The Commercial Value of Beauty," *Park Improvement Papers*, no. 11 (Washington, D.C.: Government Printing Office, 1903), 175–77; the quotation is on 177. Burnham was referring to Chicago in the original essay, but the planners of Washington's improvement saw no difficulty in applying it to their own case. See also the Chicago Association of Commerce's journal, *Commerce* 2:25 (November 2, 1906): 1–2; Henry Rutgers Marshall, (Mrs.) Candace Wheeler, and (Mrs.) E. H. Bashfield, "How to Make New York a Beautiful City," addresses before the Nineteenth Century Club, March 12, 1895 (New York: Nineteenth Century Club, 1895); Montgomery Schuyler, "An Object Lesson in Municipal Decoration," *Harper's Weekly* 44: 2258 (March 31, 1900): 295; *Eleventh Annual Report* of the Washington, D.C., Board of Trade (1911), 42.

65. San Francisco, 1905; New York, 1907, and Chicago, 1909; both the San Francisco and Chicago plans were designed under Burnham's aegis; the Washington Plan, designed by Burnham, architect Charles McKim, and landscape architect Frederick Law Olmsted, Jr., was published in 1902.

66. Report of the Committee on Municipal Art, *Twenty-first Annual Report of the Washington Board of Trade* (Washington, D.C., 1912), 42; see also the *Fifth Annual Report* (Washington, D.C., 1895), 5, and the *Fourteenth Annual Report* (1904), 5; *Merchants' Association Review* [San Francisco] 11:131 (July 1907): 12, 13:150 (February 1909): 6; *Commerce* [Chicago] 2:14 (August 17, 1906): 3, 2:19 (September 21, 1906): 4, 2:25 (November 2, 1906): 1–2, 2:51 (May 3, 1907): 10, 5:9 (July 9, 1909): 20; Report of the Convention Bureau,

Merchants' Association of New York *Yearbook 1914* (New York, 1914), 52. For a dissenting view, see "The Dignity of Cities," in *Commerce* 2:13 (August 10, 1906): 3, quoted from an article in the *Boston Transcript* commenting on the city's plan to establish a partnership with organized business to attract tourists.

67. *Merchants' Association Review* [San Francisco], 8:88 (December 1903): 1; Kahn, *Imperial San Francisco*, chap. 1; John F. Stover, *The Life and Decline of the American Railroad* (New York: Oxford University Press, 1970), 54–56.

68. *Merchants' Association Review* [San Francisco], 9:105 (May 1905): 4; Kahn, *Imperial San Francisco*, chap. 4; William Issel and Robert Cherny, *San Francisco, 1865–1932: Politics, Power, and Urban Development* (Berkeley: University of California Press), chaps. 6, 7.

69. See, for example, *Merchants' Association Review* [San Francisco] 11: 124 (January 1907): 7; 11:125 (February 1907): 12; 11:131 (July 1907): 12; 13:146 (October 1908): 3; 13:147 (November 1908): 12; a City Beautiful–type civic center was built in time for the 1915 Panama-Pacific International Exposition, but no other parts of the plan were constructed; see Issel and Cherny, *San Francisco,* chap. 8.

70. Constance McLaughlin Green, *Washington: Capital City, 1879–1950* (Princeton: Princeton University Press, 1962), chaps. 1–3, 9; John Reps, *Monumental Washington: The Planning and Development of the Capital Center* (Princeton: Princeton University Press, 1967), 53–69.

71. Green, *Washington, 1879–1950,* chap. 2.

72. Green, *Washington, 1879–1950,* chaps. 2, 4; Edmond Jules Le Breton, "The Congressional Mess, 1830–1860" (M.A. thesis, University of Maryland, 1968); "mess" meant boardinghouse.

73. Green, *Washington: A History of the Capital* (Princeton: Princeton University Press, 1962): 1: chaps. 14, 15; and her *Washington, 1879–1950,* chaps. 2, 9.

74. *Eighth Annual Report,* Washington Board of Trade (n.p., 1898), 8; Green, *Washington, 1879–1950,* chaps. 2, 9.

75. Diane Skvarla, "Nineteenth-Century Visitors to Washington: The Beginnings of Tourism," unpublished paper, April 27, 1985, Martin Luther King, Jr., Public Library, Washingtoniana Room; Report of the Committee on Public Buildings, *Second Annual Report of the Washington Board of Trade* (Washington, D.C.: Gibson Bros., 1892), 49; President's Report, *Fourth Annual Report of the Washington Board of Trade* (Washington, D.C.: Judd & Detweiler, 1894), 6; Charles F. Wallraff, "The Capital's Attractions as a Convention Center and Place of Residence," in *Washington, the Capital of the Nation/Descriptive of the Most Important Features of America's Most Beautiful and Interesting City,* comp. George H. Gall (Washington, D.C.: Joint Committee on the Jamestown Exposition, 1907), n.p., second essay; Report of the Committee on Commerce and Manufactures, *Twelfth Annual Report* of the Washington, D.C., Board of Trade (Washington, D.C., 1902), 41–42.

76. Rufus Rockwell Wilson, *Washington, the Capital City, and Its Part in the History of the Nation* (Philadelphia: J. B. Lippincott, 1902), 2:386–87; see also 381–83; *Tourist's Monthly Magazine* 3:3 (March 1908): 4; Henry James, *The American Scene* (New York: Penguin Books, 1994; orig. 1907), 344–45;

Green, *Washington, 1879–1950:* "The capital city from the end of the 1870's to the turn of the century was more nearly a city of leisure than any other in America," 77, and chap. 5 generally. Federal employees were the only workers to have secured an eight-hour workday at this time.

77. "Report of the Publicity Bureau," Merchants' Association of New York *Yearbook* (n.p., 1914), 31; on the Publicity and Convention bureaus of this organization, see 16–18, 49–52; for Chicago, see "Merchants' Meetings," and "National Conventions," *Commerce* [Chicago] 2:5 (June 15, 1906): 1; 2:19 (September 21, 1906): 2, report of the Convention Bureau; also throughout 1906, the CAC tried to promote an annual fall Corn Festival. The Merchants' Association of San Francisco was trying to establish an annual New Year's Eve "Mardi Gras" in 1907–9; see, e.g., "Give Us a Greater and Finer Carnival," *Merchants' Association Review* 11:125 (February 1907): 12.

78. *Commerce* 2:7 (June 29, 1906): 2; President's Report, Merchants' Association of New York *Yearbook* (n.p., 1907), 11; *Commerce* 2:5 (June 15, 1906): 1; 2:7 (June 29, 1906): 1–2; Harris, "Urban Tourism and the Commercial City."

79. Report of the Publicity Bureau, Merchants Association of New York, *Yearbook* (n.p., 1907), 33; *Commerce* 2:7 (June 29, 1906): 2; for notice of the CAC's guidebook, see *Commerce* 4:29 (November 30, 1908): 36.

80. Caroline Kirkland, "Illinois in Spring-time: With a Look at Chicago," *Atlantic Monthly* 2 (1858): 486; *Commerce* 2:51 (May 3, 1907): 10; see also *Life,* Chicago number, 58:1516 (November 16, 1911): centerfold cartoon and passim.

81. *Commerce* 3:5 (June 14, 1907): 3–4; 5:47 (April 1, 1910): 7 (quotation); see also *Commerce* 2:24 (October 26, 1906): 2; 2:46 (March 29, 1907): 10; "Art and the City's Visitors," *Commerce* 2:46 (March 29, 1907): 10. Compare J. M. Wing's insistence, in 1878: "To walk through one of the great packing houses when in full operation is something to be enjoyed, and most visitors to the city avail themselves of the opportunity. . . ," in *Seven Days in Chicago* (Chicago: J. M. Wing Co., 1878), 51. Uneasiness about the propriety of offering the stockyards and packinghouses as a tourist attraction predated Upton Sinclair's sensational exposé but seems to have increased after its publication in 1906.

82. George W. Englehardt, *New York, the Metropolis: The Book of Its Merchants' Association and of Co-operating Public Bodies* (New York: George W. Englehardt Co., 1902), preface.

83. Michael Kammen, *Mystic Chords of Memory: The Transformation of Tradition in American Culture* (New York: Vintage, 1991), chap. 4; "Modern Pilgrimages. How Men and Societies Journey to Far Cities to Attend Reunions . . ." *The* [New York] *Time Table* (October 2, 1886), PPCC Records 12/00/01, reel 3, vol. 10.

84. *Omaha Daily Republican* (September 20, 1886) and the *Louisville Courier Journal* (September 30, 1886), PPCC Records 12/00/01, reel 3, vol. 10, on the Grand Army of the Republic reunion in San Francisco; the veterans used 150 specially chartered Pullman cars in addition to the regular service. The articles also note that the Chicago Odd Fellows required 50 to 55 sleeping cars to

travel to a convention in Boston, and the Knights Templars used about 200 extra cars to get to their conclave in St. Louis. See also the Report of the Convention Bureau, Merchants' Association of New York *Yearbook* (New York, 1914), 51; *Commerce* 2:19 (September 21, 1906): 2, 2:21 (October 5, 1906): 5, 2: 34 (January 4, 1907): 5, 3:5 (June 14, 1907): 6–8; *First Annual Report,* Washington Board of Trade (Washington, D.C., 1890), 17–18; *Second Annual Report* (Washington, D.C.: Gibson Bros., 1892), 3–4; *Twelfth Annual Report* (1902): 8–9; *Merchants' Association Review* [San Francisco] 9:98 (October 1904): 3.

85. *Merchants' Association Review* [San Francisco] 7:73 (September 1902): 1; 9:98 (October 1904): 3; *Commerce* 5:36 (January 14, 1910): 38; and the PPCC Records clippings cited above. The National Education Association held frequent large conventions that drew many women.

86. On Boston, see the CAC's *Commerce* 2:13 (August 10, 1906): 2–3; I do not know what became of this proposal. See also the Report of the Convention Bureau, Merchants' Association of New York *Yearbook 1914* (New York, 1914), 52.

87. See Issel and Cherny, *San Francisco,* chap. 8, on that city's efforts to build a civic auditorium.

88. *The Town Hall of the Nation: Why Chicago Must Have a Municipal Auditorium. Chicago, though by Geographical Location the Convention Center of the United States, Loses Half Its Advantage Through Lack of a Suitable Convention Hall. An Appeal to the Mayor, the City Council and the Voters of Chicago. With Maps and Drawings* (Chicago: Chicago Association of Commerce, 1914), 4; "Chicago Convention City," *Commerce* 3:41 (February 21, 1908): 4–5; "San Francisco as a Convention City," *Merchants' Association Review* 11:133 (September 1907): 12; 14:157 (September 1909): 12; Report of the Committee on Public Buildings, *Second Annual Report* of the Washington Board of Trade (1892), 25–26; President's Report, Washington Board of Trade *Fifteenth Annual Report* (Washington, D.C., 1905), 10, 34. New York's Merchants' Association seems not to have taken much interest in building a convention center, but I found few records.

89. *Merchants' Association Review* 14:157 (September 1909): 12.

90. *The Town Hall of the Nation,* "public home," 12; for estimates of the hall's profitability, see 4, 10.

91. *The Town Hall of the Nation,* 6.

92. *A Guide to the City of Chicago* (Chicago: Chicago Association of Commerce, 1909), preface; "Special Report of the San Francisco Convention League" (May 15, 1914), carton 10, folder: San Francisco Convention League, Panama-Pacific International Exposition Records, BL, 3, 4; see also Keeler, *San Francisco and Thereabout,* preface; Helen Throop Purdy, *San Francisco as It Was; as It Is; and How to See It* (San Francisco: Paul Elder, 1912), introd.; the CAC's journal, *Commerce* 2:14 (August 17, 1906): 3, and 2:25 (November 2, 1906): 1–2; Merchants' Association of New York *Yearbook* (New York, 1914), 52; *Merchants' Association Review* [San Francisco] 5:50 (October 1900): 3 and 6:71 (July 1902): 12. The Washington Board of Trade was more concerned with raising the interest of non-Washingtonians, since residents of the city had no political leverage.

FIVE. "AN INDIVIDUALITY ALL ITS OWN":
TOURIST CITY AND TOURIST CITIZENS, 1876–1915

1. *The Tourist's Hand-Book of New York: Old Landmarks, Memorial Tablets, Origin of Street Names, Old Sites of Playhouses, Historical Features, Special Trips for Visitors, Chronology of Manhattan, from 1524 to 1905, for the Resident and Visitor Alike* (New York: Historical Press, 1905), cover and introd.; emphasis in the original.

2. Southern Pacific Railroad, *New York/New Orleans Sunset Route* (Southern Pacific Railroad, 1914–15), 45.

3. Edward Hungerford, *The Personality of American Cities: San Francisco* (San Francisco: Chamber of Commerce, 1915), 3; Frank Morton Todd, *The Chamber of Commerce Handbook for San Francisco, Historical and Descriptive; a Guide for Visitors* (San Francisco: Chamber of Commerce, 1914), 29. See also James W. Shepp and Daniel B. Shepp, *Shepp's New York Illustrated* (New York: Shepp & Shepp, 1893), 4; Julian Street, *Abroad at Home: American Ramblings, Observations, and Adventures* (New York: Century Co., 1914), 18: "places, no less than persons, have characters and traits and habits of their own." Warren Susman, "'Personality' and the Making of Twentieth-Century Culture," in his *Culture as History: The Transformation of American Society in the Twentieth Century* (New York: Pantheon, 1984), 271–86.

4. Hungerford, *Personality of American Cities*, 23–24; Susan Strasser, *Satisfaction Guaranteed: The Making of the American Mass Market* (New York: Pantheon, 1989).

5. On Washington, see Rufus Rockwell Wilson, *Washington, the Capital City, and Its Part in the History of the Nation* (Philadelphia: J. B. Lippincott, 1902), 2:386–87; Stilson Hutchins and Joseph West Moore, *The National Capital, Past and Present: The Story of Its Settlement, Progress, and Development, with Profuse Illustrations of Its Historical Objects, Public Buildings, Memorial Statuary, and Beautiful Homes* (Washington, D.C.: Post Publishing Co., 1885), 303–4; and Henry James, *The American Scene* (New York: Penguin Books, 1994; orig. 1907), 345. On Chicago, see Frederick Francis Cook, speech before the Chicago Historical Society, 1910, 8–10 and passim, Chicago Description, CHS; Hungerford, *Personality of American Cities*, 200–204; *Commerce* 5:30 (December 3, 1909): 30. On New York, see Hungerford, *Personality of American Cities*, 17, 19; M. F. Sweetser and Simeon Ford, *How to Know New York City; a Serviceable and Trustworthy Guide*, . . . revised to October 1, 1890, with map, 8th ed. (New York: J. J. Little & Co., 1891), 4–6. On San Francisco, see William Doxey, *Doxey's Guide to San Francisco and the Pleasure Resorts of California* (San Francisco: William Doxey, 1897), 97; Southern Pacific Railroad, *Wayside Notes Along the Sunset Route (Eastbound)* (San Francisco: Southern Pacific Passenger Department, 1911), 3–4; Benjamin Ide Wheeler, "The New San Francisco," *American Monthly Illustrated Review of Reviews* 33:197 (June 1906): 683; Charles Sedgwick Aiken, *San Francisco, California's Metropolis; the City that Fronts the Orient* (San Francisco: San Francisco Commissioners for the Louisiana Purchase Exposition, 1904), n.p.

6. See, for example, Robert Harlan, *At the Sign of the Lark: William Dox-*

ey's San Francisco Publishing Venture (San Francisco: Book Club of California, 1983); Doxey published his city guidebook, *Doxey's Guide to San Francisco and the Pleasure Resorts of California,* as he launched his business as a bookseller and publisher.

7. For example, George Englehardt, *New York, the Metropolis: The Book of Its Merchants' Association and of Co-operating Public Bodies* (New York: George W. Englehardt Co., 1902); Ernest Ingersoll, *A Week in New York* (New York: Rand, McNally, 1891); and idem, *Rand, McNally & Co.'s Handy Guide to New York City,* 11th ed. (New York: Rand, McNally, 1901); note the title change.

8. "Ask Mr. Foster" (Buffalo, N.Y.: W. Hengerer Co., 1914), Warshaw Collection, Tours, box 4; Cynthia H. Peters, "Rand, McNally and Company in the Nineteenth Century: Reaching for a National Market," *Chicago History* 13:1 (Spring 1984): 64–72; Andrew McNally III, *The World of Rand McNally* (New York: Newcomen Society in North America, 1956).

9. Ingersoll, *A Week in New York* (1891); idem, *Rand, McNally & Co.'s Handy Guide to New York City* (1901); a very similar guide was published for Chicago in 1893 with no author listed. C. A. Higgins, *To California and Back* (Chicago: Passenger Department, Santa Fe Route [Southern Pacific], 1893); and a similar work with the same title and notes by Charles Keeler (New York: Doubleday, Page & Co., 1904); Keeler himself wrote *San Francisco and Thereabouts* (San Francisco: A. M. Robertson, 1902–6) for the California Promotion Committee. Higgins was assistant passenger agent for the Atchison, Topeka, and Santa Fe Railroad and played a role in developing tourism in the Southwest as well as in California.

10. Ingersoll, *A Week in New York,* introd.; Michael Schudson, *Discovering the News: A Social History of American Newspapers* (New York: Basic Books, 1978).

11. Dona Brown, *Inventing New England: Regional Tourism in the Nineteenth Century* (Washington, D.C.: Smithsonian Institution Press, 1995); William Stowe, *Going Abroad: European Travel in Nineteenth-Century American Culture* (Princeton: Princeton University Press, 1994); Stuart Blumin, introduction to *New York by Gas-Light and Other Urban Sketches by George F. Foster* (Berkeley: University of California Press, 1990), 225–27.

12. William Taylor, "The Launching of a Commercial Culture: New York City, 1860–1930," in *Power, Culture, and Place: Essays on New York City,* ed. John Hull Mollenkopf (New York: Russell Sage, 1988), 107–27; and James Gilbert, *Perfect Cities: Chicago's Utopias of 1893* (Chicago: University of Chicago Press, 1991), chap. 4, both analyze turn-of-the-century guidebooks.

13. Christopher Wilson, "The Rhetoric of Consumption: Mass-Market Magazines and the Demise of the Gentle Reader, 1880–1920," in *The Culture of Consumption: Critical Essays in American History, 1880–1980,* ed. Richard Wightman Fox and T. J. Jackson Lears (New York: Pantheon, 1983), 39–64. Julian Street's *Abroad at Home* was sponsored by the Century Co.; Julian Ralph's *Harper's Chicago and the World's Fair* (New York: Harper & Bros., 1893) stated its backing in the title; and his *Our Great West: A Study of the Pres-*

ent Conditions and Future Possibilities of the New Commonwealths and Capitals of the United States (New York: Harper & Bros., 1893) was based on the same journey; cf. Caroline Kirkland, "Illinois in Spring-time: With a Look at Chicago," *Atlantic Monthly* 2 (1858): 475–88.

14. Hungerford, *The Personality of American Cities*, i.

15. Street, *Abroad at Home*, 6–7, italics and punctuation in the original; Warren Susman, "The City in American Culture," in his *Culture as History*, 237–51.

16. Street, *Abroad at Home*, 3–4, 19. He also refused to use statistics, a staple of guidebooks and guided tours.

17. Street's reference to whimsical leisure was deceptive, as the journey gave him material for several articles and a book. On tourism and its critics, see James Buzard, *The Beaten Track: European Tourism, Literature, and the Ways to Culture, 1800–1918* (Oxford: Clarendon Press, 1993), introd., chap. 1.

18. *Merchants' Association Review* [San Francisco], 6:71 (July 1902): 12; see also William H. Wilson, *The City Beautiful Movement* (Baltimore: Johns Hopkins University Press, 1989), 47–48.

19. Newton Dent, "The Romance of Chicago: The Record of a Dominant Spirit of Hustle; the Growth of the Western Metropolis—Its Tremendous Impetus and Its Contribution to the Making of America," *Munsey's Magazine* 37:1 (April 1907): 20; Todd, *The Chamber of Commerce Handbook for San Francisco*, 29.

20. See, for example, Carl Smith, *Urban Disorder and The Shape of Belief: The Great Chicago Fire, the Haymarket Bomb, and the Model Town of Pullman* (Chicago: University of Chicago Press, 1995).

21. Amy Kaplan, *The Social Construction of American Realism* (Chicago: University of Chicago Press, 1988), especially her analysis of William Dean Howells's *A Hazard of New Fortunes;* Rebecca Zurier, Robert W. Snyder, and Virginia M. Mecklenburg, *Metropolitan Lives: The Ashcan Artists and Their New York* (New York: National Museum of American Art and W. W. Norton, 1995).

22. J. B. Jackson, "The Stranger's Path," in *Landscapes: Selected Writings of John Brinckerhoff Jackson*, ed. Ervin H. Zube (Amherst: University of Massachusetts Press, 1970), 92–106.

23. Frank Morton Todd, *How to See San Francisco by Trolley and Cable* (San Francisco: San Francisco Chamber of Commerce Publicity Committee, 1912), 4; see also *New York City Illustrated/Visitor's Guide and Tourist's Directory of Leading Hotels. . .*, 3d ed. (New York: New York Journal System of Information Bureaus, 1902), 3; Merchants' Association of New York, *Pocket Guide to New York* (New York: Merchants' Association, 1906), 166; *A Visitor's Guide to the City of New York, Prepared by the Brooklyn Daily Eagle on the occasion of the Return of Admiral Dewey . . .* (New York: Brooklyn Daily Eagle, 1899), 5; Ethel Shackelford, "The New Method of Seeing New York," *Boston Evening Transcript*, December 23, 1903, n.p.; *Chicago's Checkerboard Guide, World's Fair Edition . . . Compiled Especially for the Visitor of a Few Days or Weeks*, compliments of Phelps, Dodge & Palmer Co., Manufacturers (Chicago: A. H. Pokorny & Co., 1893), preface; Chicago Association of Com-

merce, *A Guide to the City of Chicago* (Chicago: Chicago Association of Commerce, 1909), 68, 86; *The Rand, McNally Souvenir Guide to Chicago: A Compendium of Reliable Information for Shoppers and Sightseers Desiring to Visit the Stores and Manufacturing Districts, and the Points of Special Interest . . .* (Chicago: Rand, McNally, 1912; published under the auspices of the Publicity Committee of the Chicago Association of Commerce), 59; C. A. Higgins, with Charles Keeler, *To California and Back: A Book of Practical Information for Travelers to the Pacific* (New York: Doubleday, Page & Co., 1904), 204.

24. Joseph West Moore, *Picturesque Washington, Pen and Pencil Sketches of Its Scenery, History, Traditions, Public and Social Life . . .* (Providence: J. A. and R. A. Reid, 1884), 296; see also J. M. Wing & Co., *Seven Days in Chicago* (Chicago: J. M. Wing & Co., 1878), 17.

25. *The Tourist's Hand-Book of New York. . . ,* title page and introd.; Hutchins Hapgood, *Types from the City Streets* (New York: Funk & Wagnalls, 1910), 114, 117; see also *The Heart of Chicago/At a Glance. Free Guide . . . A Handy Companion for Visitors,* 16th ed. (n.p., n.d., probably 1893): 1; Chicago Association of Commerce, *A Guide to the City of Chicago,* 3; *Rand, McNally & Co.'s Bird's-Eye Views and Guide to Chicago . . .* (Chicago: Rand, McNally, 1898), introd.; Gustav Kobbé, *New York and Its Environs; with maps and illustrations* (New York: Harper & Bros., 1891), preface.

26. *New York City Illustrated/Visitor's Guide and Tourist's Directory,* 5; "Information/What to See in Washington," *Ask Mr. Foster* brochure (1906), box 1, Washington, D.C., Warshaw Collection, AC/NMAH; see also *Rand, McNally & Co.'s Handy Guide to Chicago and World's Columbian Exposition. Illustrated. What to See and How to See It* (Chicago: Rand, McNally, 1893), 83; Sweetser and Ford, *How to Know New York,* 4. Other guides noted that their itineraries required the tourist to spend no more than a few minutes at each "sight."

27. Hapgood, *Types,* 120; Amy Dru Stanley, "Beggars Can't Be Choosers: Compulsion and Contract in Postbellum America," *Journal of American History* 78:2 (March 1992): 1267. When capitalized, "Bohemian" also named the people now called Czech; the broader meaning seems to have developed from the association of the southern German habit of gemütlichkeit with anyone who combined beer drinking with more or less serious conversation about art and music.

28. The term "cultural capital" is from Pierre Bourdieu, *Distinction: A Social Critique of the Judgement of Taste,* trans. Richard Nice (Cambridge, Mass.: Harvard University Press, 1984), 12, 53–54; Richard Ohmann, *Selling Culture: Magazines, Markets, and Class at the Turn of the Century* (New York: Verso, 1996), examines the cultural formation of an American "professional-managerial" class at the turn of the century.

29. Helen Boyden diary, vol. 2, July 10 and July 30, 1894, CHS; Hapgood, *Types,* 120.

30. Anne Farrar Hyde, *An American Vision: Far Western Landscape and National Culture, 1820–1920* (New York: New York University Press, 1990); Marguerite Shaffer, *See America First: Tourism and National Identity, 1905–1930* (Washington, D.C.: Smithsonian Institution Press, 2001).

31. William Leach, "Transformations in a Culture of Consumption: Women and Department Stores, 1890–1925," *Journal of American History* 71:2 (September 1984): 319–42; Daniel Bluestone, *Constructing Chicago* (New Haven: Yale University Press, 1991), chap. 4; Kenneth Jackson, *Crabgrass Frontier: The Suburbanization of the United States* (New York: Oxford University Press, 1985).

32. John Disturnell, comp., *New York as It Was and as It Is; Giving an Account of the City from Its Settlement to the Present Time; Forming a Complete Guide to the Metropolis of the Nation, Including the City of Brooklyn and the Surrounding Cities and Villages; Together with a Classified Business Directory. With Maps and Illustrations* (New York: D. Van Nostrand, 1876), 53. By Disturnell's own account in the preface, he had been publishing both New York City and state directories, almanacs, and guides to scenic tours since 1833; another Disturnell continued in the business: *Disturnell's Strangers' Guide to San Francisco and Vicinity* (San Francisco: W. C. Disturnell, 1883). David Clapp recorded on his first visit to New York: "There was nothing very striking in the appearance of New York, as it first presented itself [from the water]," diary, 1831, Downs Collection, WL, 39.

33. Ingersoll, *A Week in New York* (1891), 189–90; on imagery of New York City, see Angela Blake, "Beyond Darkness and Daylight: Constructing New York's Public Image, 1890–1930" (Ph.D. dissertation, American University, 1999).

34. William Taylor, "New York and the Origin of the Skyline: The Commercial City and the Visual Text," in his *In Pursuit of Gotham: Culture and Commerce in New York* (New York: Oxford University Press, 1992), 23–33; Peter Bacon Hales, *Silver Cities: The Photography of American Urbanization, 1839–1915* (Philadelphia: Temple University Press, 1984); the Underwood & Underwood stereograph collection and the postcard collection at the AC/NMAH offer a representative sample of popular urban imagery.

35. "New York Illustrated," 1914, brochure in the Warshaw Collection, AC/NMAH, New York, box 4, cover and centerfold illustration.

36. Keith D. Revell, "Regulating the Landscape: Real Estate Values, City Planning, and the 1916 Zoning Ordinance," and Gail Fenske and Deryck Holdsworth, "Corporate Identity and the New York Office Building, 1895–1915," in *The Landscape of Modernity: Essays on New York City, 1900–1940*, ed. David Ward and Olivier Zunz (New York: Russell Sage, 1992), 19–45, 129–59; Mona Domosh, "The Symbolism of the Skyscraper: Case Studies of New York's First Tall Buildings," *Journal of Urban History* 14:3 (May 1988): 321–45; Bluestone, *Constructing Chicago*, chap. 4.

37. Taylor, "The Launching of a Commercial Culture," in Mollenkopf, ed., *Power, Culture, and Place*, 107–33; Gilbert, *Perfect Cities*, 55–73.

38. *Visitors' Guide to the Centennial Exposition and Philadelphia* (Philadelphia: J. B. Lippincott & Co., 1876), inside front cover. Keyed maps began to appear in the early twentieth century; handbooks and national-circulation guides such as Appleton's included city plans from the 1850s, but these were not specially designed for tourists. *The Guide to the Centennial Exposition, Presented by J. A. Ephraim & Son, Importers of Diamonds and Watches* (Philadelphia:

J. Henry Smythe, 1876), flanked its description of the fairgrounds with historical sketches and a tour of Philadelphia's historical sights.

39. C. B. Norton, *World's Fairs from London 1851 to Chicago 1893* (Chicago: Milton Weston Co. for the World's Columbian Exposition, 1890), 42; Robert Rydell, "The Literature of Expositions," in *The Books of the Fairs: Materials about World Fairs, 1834–1916, in the Smithsonian Institution Libraries* (Chicago: American Library Association, 1992), 4.

40. *Visitors' Guide,* 10; Emory R. Johnson, *American Railway Transportation,* rev. ed. (New York: D. Appleton & Co., 1906), 24.

41. Charles C. Moore, "San Francisco Knows How! An Answer to the World's Question: Can This Exposition Be Different?" *Sunset: The Pacific Monthly* 28:1 (January 1912): 5.

42. Peter Bacon Hales, "Photography and the World's Columbian Exposition: A Case Study," *Journal of Urban History* 15:3 (May 1989): 247–73; Russell Lewis, "Everything Under One Roof: World's Fairs and Department Stores in Paris and Chicago," *Chicago History* 12:3 (Fall 1983): 28–47.

43. Michele Bogart, *Public Sculpture and the Civic Ideal in New York City, 1890–1930* (Chicago: University of Chicago Press, 1989); Kirk Savage, *Standing Soldiers, Kneeling Slaves: Race, War, and Monument in Nineteenth-Century America* (Princeton: Princeton University Press, 1997); Michael Kammen, *Mystic Chords of Memory: The Transformation of Tradition in American Culture* (New York: Vintage, 1991).

44. J. M. Wing wrote in 1878 that in order to see Chicago "we shall be obliged to patronize the public hacks more or less in our daily excursions," *Seven Days in Chicago* (Chicago: J. M. Wing & Co., 1878), 17. Walking was the chief mode of transit in most mid-nineteenth-century works, just as it was for city residents.

45. Clay McShane, *Down the Asphalt Path: The Automobile and the American City* (New York: Columbia University Press, 1994), chaps. 1–5; Charles W. Cheape, *Moving the Masses: Urban Public Transit in New York, Boston, and Philadelphia, 1880–1912* (Cambridge, Mass.: Harvard University Press, 1980), 1–17.

46. [Wilbur Dick Nesbit], *Chicago without a Guide Book* (Chicago: Chicago Commercial Association, n.d., probably 1910s), 3; Anna E. D. Douglas, journal of a trip from Boston to Daytona in 1892–93, Downs Collection, WL, 11–12, 15–16. See also Ingersoll, *Rand, McNally & Co.'s Handy Guide to New York City,* chap. 2; *Washington Sight-Seeing and Shopping Guide* (Washington, D.C.: Whitman Osgood, 1904), 6; W. J. Elliott, ed., *Washington: C. T. Hunter's Official Guide Book* (Washington, D.C., 1909), 13; *A Hand-Book to the Nation's Capital. Published Gratuitously by the Brooklyn Daily Eagle, Washington Bureau,* 3d ed. (1897), 7, 39–41; Doxey, *Doxey's Guide to San Francisco,* 23–24; *San Francisco and Its Environs* (San Francisco: California Promotion Committee, 1903), 11, 45–50; Sweetser and Ford, *How to Know New York City,* 19; *New York City Illustrated/Visitor's Guide and Tourist's Directory of Leading Hotels,* 61–62; Keeler, *San Francisco and Thereabout,* 36–41; *The Guide Magazine for New York* (November 1902): 81–83.

47. Perry Duis, "Whose City? Public and Private Places in Nineteenth-

Century Chicago," pt. 1, *Chicago History* 12:1 (Spring 1983): 21; on the development of the panorama, see Shelley Rice, *Parisian Views* (Cambridge, Mass.: MIT Press, 1997), 127–29.

48. William Dean Howells, *A Hazard of New Fortunes* (New York: Oxford University Press, 1990), 63. The novel was completed in 1889.

49. Keeler, *San Francisco and Thereabout*, 36, 37–38, 40. Keeler only noted the people in the streets after he got off the cars.

50. [George Ade], "The Conductor Has His Woes," in *Stories of the Streets and of the Town* (Chicago: Chicago Record, 1894), 1:19; see also the "Things Talked Of" column, *Harper's Weekly* 37: 1909 (July 22, 1893): 687.

51. Ade, "The Conductor Has His Woes," 19–20; Gilbert, *Perfect Cities*, chap. 3, analyzes Ade's works; Taylor, "The Launching of a Commercial Culture," discusses O. Henry's short stories.

52. "Hold Fast!" lyrics by William Jerome, music by Jean Schwartz (New York: Shapiro, Bernstein & Von Tilzer, 1901), folder A, box 29, Series 1.8, de Vincent Sheet Music Collection, AC/NMAH.

53. "I Lost Her in the Subway," lyrics by Al. Bryan, music by S. R. Henry (New York: Jos. A. Stern, 1907), folder A, box 29, Series 1.8, de Vincent Sheet Music Collection, AC/NMAH.

54. See, for example, *A Guide to the City of Chicago* (Chicago: Chicago Association of Commerce, 1909), 68–84; Todd, *How to See San Francisco by Trolley and Cable; Rand, McNally's Handy Guide to New York* (1891) and *Handy Guide to Chicago* (1893).

55. *Visitors' Guide*, 10; *Official Guide to the World's Columbian Exposition* (Chicago: Columbian Guide Co., 1893), 5; letter from Robert D'Erlach to H. D. H. Connick, Director of Works, April 12, 1915, on behalf of the exposition guides, folder "Guide Service," carton 93, Panama-Pacific International Exposition papers, BL.

56. Frank Morton Todd, *San Francisco* (San Francisco: Chamber of Commerce, 1915), 3.

57. "Seeing Washington Observation Cars," brochure in box 1, Street Cars and Subways, Warshaw Collection, AC/NMAH; "The Sight-Seeing Automobile Coach of Washington," n.d., brochure, Washington, D.C., box 2, Warshaw Collection, AC/NMAH; see also "Royal Blue Line Motor Tours" (1916), broadside in box 1, Transportation, Warshaw Collection, AC/NMAH; the Royal Blue Line (or Baltimore & Ohio Railroad) ran these tours in Washington, New York, and Boston; *A Guide to the City of Chicago* (Chicago: Chicago Association of Commerce, 1909), 86–87; *San Francisco and Its Environs* (San Francisco: California Promotion Committee, 1903): 50; Helen Throop Purdy, *San Francisco as It Was; as It Is; and How to See It* (San Francisco: Paul Elder, 1912), 59–60; "Road of a Thousand Wonders" (San Francisco: Southern Pacific Railroad, n.d., probably 1909–10), 7: "Suppose you begin with the obvious—take a sightseeing car."

58. James D. Law, *Here and There in Two Hemispheres* (Lancaster, Penn.: Home Publishing Co., 1903), 449; see also Ethel Shackelford, "The New Method of Seeing New York," *Boston Evening Transcript* (December 23, 1903), n.p.

59. "Seeing Washington Observation Cars," 2. Public institutions had not

disappeared entirely; many guidebooks had long sections following their list
or schedule of sights that included the public schools and universities, hospitals,
banks, churches, and other institutions. However, these buildings were no longer
the focus of the work and most were no longer "sights."

60. *King's Handbook of New York City: An Outline History and Description of the American Metropolis* . . . (Boston: Moses King, 1893), 66; see also
Joel Cook, *An Eastern Tour at Home* (Philadelphia: David McKay, 1889).

61. Todd, *How to See San Francisco by Trolley and Cable*, 6–7. Todd wrote
several publicity pieces for the Chamber and was also the official historian of the
Panama-Pacific International Exposition. This kind of line-of-sight touring produced a more discontinuous experience in hilly San Francisco than it might in
flatter cities. The development of the skyline in Chicago and New York in this
era also encouraged the identification of sometimes widely dispersed landmarks,
rather than specific neighborhoods, as characteristic of a city.

62. Jackson, *Crabgrass Frontier*, chaps. 6, 7, 8 and tables A-7, A-8, A-9;
Leach, "Transformations in a Culture of Consumption"; Susan Porter Benson,
*Counter Cultures: Saleswomen, Managers, and Customers in American Depart-
ment Stores, 1890–1940* (Chicago: University of Illinois Press, 1986).

63. Sweetser and Ford, *How to Know New York*, 89; see also *Official Guide
to the World's Columbian Exposition*, 177. Bluestone, *Constructing Chicago*,
chap. 4; Fenske and Holdsworth, "Corporate Identity."

64. Hungerford, *Personality of American Cities*, 30–34; Street, *Abroad at
Home*, chap. 12; see also Angel Kwollek-Folland, *Engendering Business: Men
and Women in the Corporate Office, 1870–1930* (Baltimore: Johns Hopkins
University Press, 1994).

65. John Sears, *Sacred Places: American Tourist Attractions in the Nineteenth Century* (New York: Oxford University Press, 1989), chap. 8; Strasser,
Satisfaction Guaranteed, 113–15; John R. Stilgoe, *Metropolitan Corridor: Railroads and the American Scene* (New Haven: Yale University Press, 1987); Raymond Williams, *The Country and the City* (London: Chatto and Windus, 1973),
120–25. For an example of the industrial aesthetic, see *A Guide to the City of
Chicago* (1909), 125–26.

66. Ralph, *Harper's Chicago*, chap. 7; Street, *Abroad at Home*, chap. 12;
A Guide to the City of Chicago (1909), 88–91; Upton Sinclair, *The Jungle* (New
York: Signet, 1960; orig. 1906). The protagonist's initial admiration of the pack-
inghouses, 36–46, was typical.

67. Irving Lewis Allen, *The City in Slang: New York Life and Popular Speech*
(New York: Oxford University Press, 1993), 83, dates the word from the 1890s;
Street, *Abroad at Home*, 4; Nesbit, *Chicago without a Guide Book*, 1–2; Fran-
cis Leupp, *Walks about Washington* (Boston: Little, Brown, 1915), 284; James
Barnes, "Fifth Avenue," *Metropolitan Magazine* 33:5 (August 1910): 644;
Shackelford, "The New Method of Seeing New York," n.p.; W. L. Jacobs, "See-
ing New York," *Harper's Weekly* 55:2866 (November 25, 1911): 14–15;
C. Clyde Squiers, "And They Wrote Home That the Scenery Was Unforget-
table," *Harper's Weekly* 56:2898 (July 6, 1912): 22.

68. George Ade, *Stories of the Streets and of the Town*, 3d ser. (1895), 176–

78, 177; see also Shackelford, "The New Method of Seeing New York," n.p.; "Your City," *Chamber of Commerce Journal* (San Francisco) 1:9 (July 1912): 2.

69. F. W. Dohrman, president of the Merchants' Association, in "Testimonial to Claus Spreckels," *Merchants' Association Review* (San Francisco), 5:50 (October 1900): 1; *Tourist's Educator* 2:12 (December 1907): 4.

SIX. "THE NOBLE SPECTACLE": HISTORICAL WALKING TOURS AND ETHNIC SLUMMING, 1890s–1915

1. Elizabeth Gray Potter and Mabel Thayer Gray, *The Lure of San Francisco: A Romance Amid Old Landmarks* (San Francisco: Paul Elder & Co., 1915), 4, passim.

2. Eric Hobsbawm, "Introduction: Inventing Traditions," in *The Invention of Tradition*, ed. Eric Hobsbawm and Terence Ranger (Cambridge: Cambridge University Press, 1983), 1–14; David Glassberg, *American Historical Pageantry: The Uses of Tradition in the Early Twentieth Century* (Chapel Hill: University of North Carolina Press, 1990).

3. William Issel and Robert Cherny, *San Francisco, 1865–1932: Politics, Power, and Urban Development* (Berkeley: University of California Press, 1988); Marjorie Dobkin, "A Twenty-Five-Million-Dollar Mirage," in *The Anthropology of World's Fairs: San Francisco's Panama-Pacific International Exposition of 1915*, ed. Burton Benedict et al. (Berkeley: Lowie Museum of Anthropology, 1983), 66–93; Glassberg, *American Historical Pageantry*.

4. Potter and Gray, *The Lure of San Francisco*, 7.

5. Raymond Williams, *The Country and the City* (London: Chatto and Windus, 1973); Carole Fabricant, "The Literature of Domestic Tourism and the Public Consumption of Private Property," in *The New Eighteenth Century: Theory, Politics, English Literature*, ed. Felicity Nussbaum and Laura Brown (London: Methuen, 1987), 254–313; Henry James, *The American Scene* (New York: Penguin Books, 1994; orig. 1907), is famous for his catalog of American lacks; he also noted the dislocation of class and ethnic hierarchy in the United States and how it made social relations difficult, e.g., 91.

6. David Handler, "On Having a Culture: Nationalism and the Preservation of Québec's *Patrimonie*," in *Objects and Others: Essays on Museums and Material Culture*, ed. George W. Stocking (Madison: University of Wisconsin Press, 1988), 192–215.

7. David Nasaw, *Going Out: The Rise and Fall of Public Amusements* (New York: Basic Books, 1993); and Michele Bogart, *Public Sculpture and the Civic Ideal in New York City* (Chicago: University of Chicago Press, 1989), chap. 11, both address the question of public amusements and citizenship.

8. Michael Kammen, *The Mystic Chords of Memory: The Transformation of Tradition in American Culture* (New York: Vintage Books, 1991), pt. 1.

9. Kammen, *Mystic Chords*; Glassberg, *American Historical Pageantry*; David Handler, *Nationalism and the Politics of Culture in Québec* (Madison: University of Wisconsin Press, 1988), chaps. 2, 6.

10. Kammen, *Mystic Chords*, chap. 4; see also Nina Silber, *The Romance of*

Reunion: Northerners and the South, 1865–1900 (Chapel Hill: University of North Carolina Press, 1993); Kirk Savage, *Standing Soldiers, Kneeling Slaves: Race, War, and Monument in Nineteenth-Century America* (Princeton: Princeton University Press, 1997).

11. The first U.S. president, George Washington, delivered his inaugural address in New York City in 1789; in the nineteenth century, the site was marked by a statue. Fort Dearborn, the first official American outpost at the site of Chicago, dated from 1803; the site had long hosted Native Americans, and there had been an intermittent French presence since the seventeenth century. Few guidebook accounts mentioned the trading post established there in the eighteenth century by the African-French Jean-Baptiste Point du Sable. An English navigator employed by the Dutch, Hudson explored the bay and river named after him in 1609; New York resident Fulton floated a successful steamboat, the *Clermont,* in 1807. Portolá headed the garrison town of Yerba Buena intended to protect the mission established on the peninsula. The town's American residents changed its name to the more august San Francisco in the 1840s as part of their bid for urban prominence.

12. Kammen, *Mystic Chords,* chap. 5.

13. See, for example, *Hudson-Fulton Celebration Souvenir* (New York: Hudson-Fulton Celebration Committee, n.d.), 8–9; this event included three major parades—military, civic, and carnival—which were staged in Manhattan and the other boroughs of Greater New York as well as in the towns along the Hudson River over a period of weeks; a naval parade sailed through the bay and up the Hudson River. Edward Hagaman Hall, *Hudson and Fulton: A Brief History . . . with Suggestions Designed to Aid the Holding of General Commemorative Exercises and Children's Festivals . . . ,* 2d ed. (New York: Hudson-Fulton Celebration Committee, 1909); *Official Program/Chicago Centennial Jubilee, Containing a Complete Daily Program of Events . . .* (Chicago: Chicago Centennial Committee, 1903); *Portolá Festival, Official Souvenir Program* (San Francisco, October 19–23, 1909). Newspaper coverage of such events was extensive.

14. Matthew Hale Smith, *Sunshine and Shadow in New York* (Hartford, Conn.: J. B. Burr, 1896), 52–59; Glassberg, *American Historical Pageantry,* notes that the "pioneers" lost their privileged place around the turn of the century and less elitist forms of community representation prevailed.

15. "The Centennial of Washington's Inauguration, Grand Celebration in New York, on April 30th, Next," New York, December 1988, ms. of proposed promotional article, box 3, Charles Henry Hart Papers, Rare Books and Manuscripts Division, NYPL.

16. Edward Hagaman Hall, *The Hudson-Fulton Celebration: 1909* (New York: Hudson-Fulton Celebration Commission, 1909), 12; and Hall, *Hudson and Fulton,* 316; "Great Pageant of Light to Form Climax of Fetes," *New York Herald* (September 23, 1909): 6.

17. The first, fourth, and fifth quotations are from "A Carnival of the Pacific," *Merchants' Association Review* 13:147 (November 1908): 12; the second, "Give Us a Greater and Finer Carnival," *Merchants' Association Review* 11:125 (February 1907): 12; and the third, "San Francisco Carnival to Become an Annual Event," *Merchants' Association Review* 13:150 (February 1909): 6.

For the New Year's celebration before the Merchants' Association took an interest, see "Noisy New Year's Eve on Downtown Streets," *San Francisco Chronicle* (January 1, 1898): 3. On city festivals, see my essay, "The Chamber of Commerce's Carnival: City Festivals and Urban Tourism in the United States, 1890–1915," in *Being Elsewhere: Tourism, Consumer Culture, and Identity in Modern Europe and America*, ed. Shelley Baranowski and Ellen Furlough (Ann Arbor: University of Michigan Press, 2001).

18. Maud Wilder Goodwin, Alice Carrington Royce, and Ruth Putnam, eds., *Half-Moon Series: Papers on Historic New York* (New York, 1897), n.p. Glassberg, *American Historical Pageantry*, 13, notes that the number of state and local historical societies rose from 140 to 300 between 1870 and 1890; Kammen, *Mystic Chords*, 260–61, points to the establishment of the first historic preservation societies, the Association for the Preservation of Virginia Antiquities (1890) and the Society for the Preservation of New England Antiquities (1910).

19. Potter and Gray, *The Lure of San Francisco*, 14; see also the *Official Program/Chicago Centennial Jubilee*, n.p., entry for Thursday, October 1 [1903].

20. Frank Bergen Kelley, *Excursion Planned for the City History Club of New York, No. II—Greenwich Village and Lispenard's Meadows*, 2d rev. ed. (New York, 1906); on p. 16 was a list of of the seven other excursion leaflets available, five cents apiece, as well as several other publications, including a "club game." See also Esther M. Thurber, *Historic Landmarks of Philadelphia* (Philadelphia: Press of the Leeds & Biddle Co., 1899).

21. Kelley, *Excursion . . . Greenwich Village*, 5; Pierre Bourdieu, *Distinction: A Social Critique of the Judgement of Taste*, trans. Richard Nice (Cambridge, Mass.: Harvard University Press, 1984), 228.

22. Ernest Ingersoll, *Rand, McNally & Co.'s Handy Guide to Chicago* (Chicago: Rand, McNally, 1901), 12; see also Hobart Chatfield Chatfield-Taylor, *Chicago* (Boston: Houghton Mifflin, 1917), 6.

23. Kelley, *Excursion . . . Greenwich Village*, 5–6.

24. John Flavel Mines, *A Tour Around New York and My Summer Acre, Being the Recreations of Mr. Felix Oldboy* (New York: Harper and Bros., 1893), 58.

25. Rufus Rockwell Wilson, *New York: Old & New; Its Story, Streets, and Landmarks*, 3d ed. (Philadelphia: J. B. Lippincott, 1909), 2:12; Mines, *A Tour Around New York*, 161, 75; Francis Leupp, *Walks about Washington* (Boston: Little, Brown, 1915), vii–viii. The walks were for the most part conventional, encompassing the official buildings of the city. More historically oriented was his "Lincoln pilgrimage," 282–83, which followed the steps of both the president and his assassin on the day of Lincoln's murder.

26. Kelley, *Excursions Planned for the City History Club of New York, to Greenwich Village, Fraunces Tavern* (site of Washington's Farewell Address, preserved by the Sons of the American Revolution) (New York, 1906); and *The Nineteenth Century City* (New York, 1908, 1905).

27. Letter to Minot S. Morgan, Letterbook 3, box 19, Richard Watson Gilder Papers, Rare Books and Manuscripts Division, NYPL, 254–56.

28. Handler, "On Having a Culture," 192–215; Bourdieu, *Distinction,* 227–28.

29. George Ade, *Stories of the Streets and of the Town,* 3d ser. (Chicago: Chicago Record, 1895), 176–78.

30. See, for example, *A Trip Across the North American Continent from Ogden to San Francisco* (New York: Central Pacific Railroad, n.d., probably 1870), 30; Samuel Williams, *The City of the Golden Gate, a Description of San Francisco in 1875* (San Francisco: Book Club of California, 1921), 14–15; B. E. Lloyd, *Lights and Shades in San Francisco, with Appropriate Illustrations* (San Francisco: A. L. Bancroft, 1876), 58; *Rand, McNally & Co.'s Handy Guide to Chicago and World's Columbian Exposition* (Chicago: Rand, McNally, 1893), 21; J. J. Burns and Edwin L. Smart, *In the Heart of New York/Surroundings of the New York Grand Central Station* (New York: n.p., n.d., probably 1880s), 30.

31. See, for example, *San Francisco* (San Francisco: Chamber of Commerce, 1915), 3; Charles Keeler, *San Francisco and Thereabout* (San Francisco: A. M. Robertson, 1906; orig. 1902, by the California Promotion Committee), 45; *A Guide to the City of Chicago* (Chicago: Chicago Association of Commerce, 1909), 26; Charles Henry White, "Chicago," *Harper's Monthly Magazine* 118 (1909): 730; James Huneker, *New Cosmopolis: A Book of Images . . .* (New York: Charles Scribners' Sons, 1915); *The Guide Magazine for New York* (November 1902): 66; *King's Handbook of New York City: An Outline History and Description of the American Metropolis . . .* (Boston: Moses King, 1893), 140; James W. Shepp and Daniel B. Shepp, *Shepp's New York City Illustrated . . .* (Philadelphia: Globe Bible Publishing Co., 1894), 20; Frederick Francis Cook, speech for the Chicago Historical Society, May 24, 1910, CHS, 8–11, 15, 20.

32. John Higham, *Strangers in the Land: Patterns of American Nativism, 1860–1925,* 2d ed. (New Brunswick, N.J.: Rutgers University Press, 1988; orig. 1955); C. Vann Woodward, *The Strange Career of Jim Crow* (New York: Oxford University Press, 1955); Gail Bederman, *Manliness and Civilization: A Cultural History of Gender and Race in the United States, 1880–1917* (Chicago: University of Chicago Press, 1995).

33. See, for example, *Official Guide to the World's Columbian Exposition* (Chicago: Columbian Guide Co., 1893), 172; *A Guide to the City of Chicago* (Chicago: Chicago Association of Commerce, 1909), 26–27. James Gilbert, *Perfect Cities: Chicago's Utopias of 1893* (Chicago: University of Chicago Press, 1991), 58 n. 32, notes that the authors of 1893 guidebooks seem to have all used the same table showing the population of the city by national origin. Those who did comment on the predominance of foreign-born people in Chicago usually went on to demonstrate that the city was nevertheless typically American; e.g., "City of Chicago," *Inland Monthly Magazine* 10:1 (March 1877): 1184–1224; Frederick Francis Cook, speech for the Chicago Historical Society, May 24, 1910, Chicago Description, CHS.

34. Sucheng Chan, "Public Policy, U.S.-China Relations, and the Chinese American Experience: An Interpretive Essay," in *Pluralism, Racism, and Public Policy: The Search for Equality,* ed. Edwin G. Clausen and Jack Birmingham (Boston: G. K. Hall, 1981), 5–38; Constance McLaughlin Green, *Washington,*

Capital City, 1879–1950 (Princeton: Princeton University Press, 1962), ix, chap. 6, 11.

35. James McCabe, *Lights and Shadows of New York Life; or, the Sights and Sensations of the Great City* . . . (New York: Farrar, Straus & Giroux, 1970; facsimile of original 1872 ed.), chap. 32, "The Sabbath in New York"; Lloyd, *Lights and Shades in San Francisco,* "Sunday in San Francisco," 121–24.

36. William Doxey, *Doxey's Guide to San Francisco and the Pleasure Resorts of California* (San Francisco: William Doxey, 1897), 116; see also my unpublished essay, "'Chinatown, Of Course, One Must See': San Francisco's Chinatown as a Tourist Attraction, 1870–1915" (1993).

37. Gilbert, *Perfect Cities,* 52–55, argued that this kind of writing was a "literary cosmetic" (55) responding to the anxieties of white, native-born Americans about immigration, urbanization, and municipal government. More than simply a response, the new style in urban description derived from and helped to create an alternative vision of the city, one linked to the developing culture of consumption and a Progressive social vision rather than that of refinement.

38. John Lunneen, "My Visit to Chicago and the World's Fair," diary, October 1893, World's Columbian Exposition Personal Narratives, Box 1, CHS, 7–8. Fifteen years old in 1893, Lunneen also visited dime museums during his stay and his mother dragged him to the opera. He died of tuberculosis in his twenties. On the midways, see Robert Rydell, *All the World's a Fair: Visions of Empire at American International Expositions, 1876–1916* (Chicago: University of Chicago Press, 1984).

39. "Street in Cairo, World's Columbian Exposition," box 8, World's Expositions, Warshaw Collection, AC/NMAH. Edward Said, *Orientalism* (New York: Vintage, 1979); see also Adelaide N. Evenden diary, World's Columbian Exposition Personal Narratives, box 1, folder Evenden, CHS, 66; Frances W. Sever letters, World's Columbian Exposition Personal Narratives, box 2, folder Sever, CHS, second letter, Sunday evening, 3 C; Beatty diary, World's Columbian Exposition Personal Narratives, box 1, folder Beatty, Wednesday and Thursday, September 20–21, 1893, CHS.

40. *Harper's Weekly* 37:1913 (August 19, 1893): 797, original spelling and punctuation; Curtis M. Hinsley, "The World as Marketplace: Commodification of the Exotic at the World's Columbian Exposition, Chicago, 1893," in *Exhibiting Cultures: The Poetics and Politics of Museum Display,* ed. Ivan Karp and Steven D. Levine (Washington, D.C.: Smithsonian Institution Press, 1991), 344–65.

41. C. A. Higgins, *To California and Back: A Book of Practical Information for Travelers to the Pacific* (New York: Doubleday, Page & Co., 1904), 235–36.

42. Ernest Ingersoll, *Rand, McNally & Co.'s Handy Guide to New York City,* 11th ed. (Chicago: Rand, McNally, 1901), chap. 7; quotations on 152 and 157.

43. *Rand, McNally & Co.'s Handy Guide to Chicago and the World's Columbian Exposition* (1893), 105; whole passages from this work are borrowed from the company's *Handy Guide to New York* (1891), which in turn was scarcely revised for its reprinting in 1901; see also *New York City Illustrated/*

Visitor's Guide and Tourist's Directory . . . (New York: New York Journal System of Information Bureaus, 1902), 64. Tours of San Francisco's Chinatown had included both men and women since the 1870s; see Mrs. Frank Leslie, *California: A Pleasure Trip from Gotham to the Golden Gate in April, May, and June 1876* (New York: G. W. Carleton, 1877), chaps. 15, 16; Amy Bridges diaries, June 13, 1882, in vol. 1, March 31, 1887, in vol. 2, HL.

44. Huneker, *New Cosmopolis*, 4.

45. Julian Street, *Abroad at Home: American Ramblings, Observations, and Adventures* (New York: Century Co., 1914), 495–96.

46. See Mrs. Frank Leslie, *California*, chaps. 15, 16, on hiring a detective; on guides, Higgins, *To California and Back*, 237; *Rand, McNally's Handy Guide to Chicago*, 104–5, and *Handy Guide to New York*, 157, referred to the "professional slummer." The guide services were also mentioned and advertised in guidebooks and hotel brochures; see, e.g., *San Francisco Guide and Souvenir*, October 1902 (Palace Hotel News Stand, 1901), 3, 18; *San Francisco* (Chicago: Passenger Department, Santa Fe Route [Atchison, Topeka, and Santa Fe Railroad], 1901), 94.

47. Higgins, *To California and Back*, 242. The commodification coexisted with continuing fears about the social and physical ills thought to originate in the slums, especially those of minorities like the Chinese.

48. Rydell, *All the World's a Fair*.

49. Philip Ethington, *The Public City: The Political Construction of Urban Life in San Francisco, 1850–1900* (Cambridge: Cambridge University Press, 1994), chap. 4, 5; Bederman, *Manliness and Civilization;* Eric Hobsbawm, "Mass Producing Traditions: Europe, 1870–1914," in *The Invention of Tradition*, ed. Eric Hobsbawm and Terence Ranger (Cambridge: Cambridge University Press, 1983), 263–307.

50. Ethington, *The Public City*, introd., chap. 1; T. J. Jackson Lears, *No Place of Grace: Antimodernism and the Transformation of American Culture, 1880–1920* (New York: Pantheon, 1981), chap. 3; Bederman, *Manliness and Civilization*, chap. 1.

51. Bederman, *Manliness and Civilization*, chap. 1.

52. Kammen, *Mystic Chords*, chap. 8; Bogart, *Public Sculpture*, details the efforts of ethnic minorities in New York to erect statues and memorials to their national heroes, sometimes in opposition to Anglo-Saxon elites.

53. Herman Ridder and Henry Sackett, introduction to Edward Hagaman Hall's *Hudson and Fulton*, 10; *Hudson-Fulton Celebration Souvenir Program* (New York: Board of Aldermen, 1909). *Official Program/Chicago Centennial Jubilee, Containing a Complete Daily Program* . . . (Chicago: Chicago Centennial Committee, 1903), Tuesday, September 29. Mary Ryan, *Women in Public: Between Banners and Ballots, 1825–1880* (Baltimore: Johns Hopkins University Press, 1990), 32–34, 44–45; Glassberg, *American Historical Pageantry*, chap. 5. An "African" contingent did march in the Hudson-Fulton parade.

54. Keeler, *San Francisco and Thereabout*, 60.

55. Contract between the Hudson-Fulton Celebration Commission and F. E. Moore, August 15, 1909, in the HFCC Papers, New York Historical Society, 1. See also "Golden Days Come Again," *San Francisco Chronicle* (Janu-

ary 21, 1898): 5; "Indians Invade City at Dawn," *Chicago Tribune* (September 27, 1903): 2; "The Lighter Side of Big Celebration," *New York Herald* (September 28, 1909): 5; L. G. Moses, *Wild West Shows and the Images of American Indians, 1883–1933* (Albuquerque: University of New Mexico Press, 1996).

56. *Portolá Festival, Official Souvenir Program* (San Francisco, October 19–23, 1909), BL, 55. The festival queen, on the other hand, was the young Anglo-American winner of a beauty contest. The press did not remark on this interracial, May-December pairing.

57. *Old Chinatown: A Book of Pictures,* by Arnold Genthe, with text by Will Irwin (New York: Mitchell Kennerley, 1912), 45; William Dean Howells, *Impressions and Experiences* (New York: Harper & Bros., 1896), 278–79; see also Ingersoll, *New York,* 156; Theodore Dreiser, *The Color of a Great City* (New York: Boni and Liveright, 1923), viii, passim.

58. Bederman, *Manliness and Civilization,* chaps. 1, 2; Johannes Fabian, *Time and the Work of Anthropology: Critical Essays, 1971–1991* (Philadelphia: Harwood Academic Publishers, 1991).

59. Ingersoll, *New York,* 151; Keeler, *San Francisco and Thereabout,* 59; *San Francisco* (San Francisco: Chamber of Commerce, 1915), 31; see also Dreiser, *The Color of a Great City,* 267–70; *A Guide to the City of Chicago,* 26–27; *Glimpses of New York: An Illustrated Handbook of the City* (New York: Compiled and Edited by the New York Edison Co., 1911), 35.

60. See, for example, Lears, *No Place of Grace;* Bederman, *Manliness and Civilization,* chaps. 2, 3; Leah Dilworth, *Imagining Indians in the Southwest: Persistent Visions of a Primitive Past* (Washington, D.C.: Smithsonian Institution Press, 1996); David Whisnant, *All That Is Native and Fine: The Politics of Culture in an American Region* (Chapel Hill: University of North Carolina Press, 1983).

61. Hutchins Hapgood, *Types from the City Streets* (New York: Funk and Wagnalls, 1910), 23, 18, 158.

62. Hutchins Hapgood, *Spirit of the Ghetto,* ed. Moses Rischin (Cambridge, Mass.: Belknap Press of Harvard University Press, 1967; orig. 1902); David Minter, "Hapgood, Hutchins," in *American National Biography,* ed. John A. Garraty and Mark C. Carnes (New York: Oxford University Press, 1999), 10: 34–35; see also Howells, *Impressions and Experiences,* 135–36, on poor New Yorkers' assumption that tourists were social workers, detectives, or journalists. While they might expect to be paid, they did not protest the intrusion.

63. Helen Throop Purdy, *San Francisco as It Was; as It Is; and How to See It* (San Francisco: Paul Elder & Co., 1912), 139; see also Lillie Hampton French, "Shopping in New York," *Century Magazine* 61 (December 1901); and my "'Chinatown, Of Course, One Must See'"; Edward Hungerford, *The Personality of American Cities: San Francisco* (San Francisco: Chamber of Commerce, 1915), 296, labeled Chinatown as it was rebuilt after 1906 "frankly commercial."

64. Daniel Bluestone, "'The Pushcart Evil,'" in *The Landscape of Modernity: Essays on New York City, 1900–1940,* ed. David Ward and Olivier Zunz (New York: Russell Sage, 1992), 287–312.

65. *A Guide to the City of Chicago,* 125; W. J. Elliott, ed., *Washington: C. T.*

Hunter's Official Guide Book (Washington, D.C., 1909), 10; see also Joseph West Moore, *Picturesque Washington, Pen and Pencil Sketches . . .* (Providence, R.I.: J. A. and R. A. Reid, 1884), 248–50. Moore noted that black women no longer took kindly to being called "aunty" as they had before emancipation. See also French, "Shopping in New York," 647; Dreiser, *The Color of a Great City,* 112–18, 275–83.

66. Look Tin Eli, "Our New Oriental City—Veritable Fairy Palaces Filled with the Choicest Treasures of the Orient," in *San Francisco, The Metropolis of the West* (San Francisco: Western Press Association, 1910?), n.p.; Robert Howe Fletcher and Ernest C. Peixotto, *Ten Drawings in Chinatown with Certain Observations* (San Francisco: A. M. Robertson, 1898), hired a Chinese American guide; Thomas W. Chinn, *Bridging the Pacific: San Francisco Chinatown and Its People* (San Francisco: Chinese Historical Association of America, 1989), 16, 37–41; Thomas W. Chinn, H. Mark Lai, and Philip P. Choy, eds., *A History of the Chinese in California: A Syllabus* (San Francisco: Chinese Historical Association of America, 1969), 80, speculate that "Look" was probably Lu Jun-Ch'ing.

67. "Road of a Thousand Wonders: San Francisco, The Metropolis of the Pacific" (Southern Pacific Railroad, probably San Francisco 1909–10), 24–25; on food, see "The Hotel Sherman of Chicago," *Hotel Monthly* 19:216 (March 1911): 38–39, for the Celtic Bar and Celtic Cafe; the hotel also had private dining rooms decorated in French, English, Italian, Dutch, Japanese, and Venetian styles, but the food served would most likely have been "French." Harvey Levenstein, *Revolution at the Table: The Transformation of the American Diet* (New York: Oxford University Press, 1988); Donna Gabaccia, *We Are What We Eat: Ethnic Food and the Making of Americans* (Cambridge, Mass.: Harvard University Press, 1998), chap. 2.

68. Higgins, *To California and Back,* 213; see also *New York City Illustrated,* 63; Potter and Gray, *The Lure of San Francisco,* 25; *Glimpses of New York,* 47; Huneker, *New Cosmopolis,* chap. 5. Once again Chicago writers neglected the "ethnic" in describing their city, but see *Chicago for the Tourist* (Chicago: Illinois Central Railroad, 1908), 15–18.

69. See, for example, Leslie, *California: A Pleasure Trip,* 170–71; contrast an approving review in Purdy, *San Francisco,* 138; and *A Guide to the City of Chicago,* 103. Chicago did not have a significant Chinese population at this time, so the appearance of these restaurants is good evidence for white Americans' new fondness for an altered Chinese cuisine.

70. Maria Sermolino, *Papa's Table d'Hôte* (Philadelphia: J. B. Lippincott, 1952), 15, 14. Sermolino's parents arrived in New York in 1892; see also Gabaccia, *We Are What We Eat,* chaps. 3, 4.

71. James D. Law, *Here and There in Two Hemispheres* (Lancaster, Penn.: Home Publishing Co., 1903), 449; "Seeing Washington Observation Cars," 2, brochure in box 1, Street Cars and Subways, Warshaw Collection, AC/NMAH.

72. *Rand, McNally's Handy Guide to Chicago* (1893) and *Rand, McNally's Handy Guide to New York* (1891, 1901); Gilbert, *Perfect Cities,* chap. 3, argued that Chicago represented the future for Americans and so urban description focused on its industries and skyscrapers to a greater extent than elsewhere. The

city's vast sprawl and ethnic and class segregation may also have diminished the awareness of well-to-do, native-born whites of its heterogeneity in a way not possible in narrow Manhattan. Claiming to be the most American of cities, in contrast to "European" New York, was also an important part of Chicago's rivalry with the eastern city.

73. Isaac F. Marcosson, "The New Washington," *Munsey's Magazine* 46:3 (December 1911): 312.

CONCLUSION: A NICE PLACE TO VISIT

1. Helen Boyden diary, vol. 2 (1890s–1910), CHS, 1; the diary is unpaginated, so page numbers represent my count. Boyden's handwriting is so clear and her descriptions of sights so detailed that one suspects she wrote her accounts afterward in consultation with a guidebook. The third woman seems to have accompanied Boyden and her mother only as far as the ocean resort.

2. Boyden diary, vol. 2, passim. That Boyden was traveling with her mother probably made it easier for them to find hotel rooms. Although she traveled fairly often, she always did so accompanied by her family, as in an early trip to Denver, described in vol. 1, or by her mother or female friends, as in National Education Association meetings and a voyage to South America, described in vol. 2. Unfortunately, from my point of view, she never recorded doing any slumming.

3. Boyden diary, vol. 2, CHS, 71, 23, passim.

4. Burton J. Bledstein, *The Culture of Professionalism: The Middle Class and the Development of Higher Education* (New York: W. W. Norton, 1978); Richard Ohmann, *Selling Culture: Magazines, Markets and Class at the Turn of the Century* (New York: Verso, 1996).

5. Michael Schudson coined the term "capitalist realism" in his *Advertising: the Uneasy Persuasion: Its Dubious Impact on American Society* (New York: Basic Books, 1984), 5–6, 209–33; Jacob Riis, *How the Other Half Lives,* ed. Sam Bass Warner, Jr. (Cambridge, Mass.: Belknap Press of Harvard University Press, 1970; orig. 1890).

6. Amy Kaplan, *The Social Construction of American Realism* (Chicago: University of Chicago Press, 1988); Peter Bacon Hales, *Silver Cities: The Photography of American Urbanization, 1839–1915* (Philadelphia: Temple University Press, 1984); Rebecca Zurier, Robert W. Snyder, and Virginia M. Mecklenburg, *Metropolitan Lives: The Ashcan Artists and Their New York* (New York: National Museum of American Art and W. W. Norton, 1995).

7. James Livingston, *Pragmatism and the Political Economy of Cultural Revolution, 1850–1940* (Chapel Hill: University of North Carolina Press, 1997); Richard Wightman Fox and T. J. Jackson Lears, *The Culture of Consumption: Critical Essays in American History, 1880–1980* (New York: Pantheon, 1983); Dona Brown, *Inventing New England: Regional Tourism in the Nineteenth Century* (Washington, D.C.: Smithsonian Institution Press, 1995); and Hal Rothman, *Devil's Bargains: Tourism in the Twentieth-Century American West* (Lawrence: University Press of Kansas, 1998), argue that tourism is worse than other exploitive, extractive industries because it sells the community itself.

8. David Nasaw, *Going Out: The Rise and Fall of Public Amusements* (New

York: Basic Books, 1993); Robert W. Snyder, *The Voice of the City: Vaudeville and Popular Culture in New York* (New York: Oxford University Press, 1989); John Kasson, *Amusing the Million: Coney Island at the Turn of the Century* (New York: Hill and Wang, 1978); Lizabeth Cohen, *Making a New Deal: Industrial Workers in Chicago, 1919–1939* (Cambridge: Cambridge University Press, 1991); Roy Rosenzweig, *Eight Hours for What We Will: Workers and Leisure in an Industrial City, 1870–1920* (Cambridge: Cambridge University Press, 1983); Michael Denning, *The Cultural Front: The Laboring of American Culture in the Twentieth Century* (New York: Verso, 1998).

9. William Leach, "Transformations in a Culture of Consumption: Women and Department Stores, 1890–1925," *Journal of American History* 71:2 (September 1984): 319–42; Kathy Peiss, *Cheap Amusements: Working Women and Leisure in Turn-of-the-Century New York* (Philadelphia: Temple University Press, 1986); Joanne Meyerowitz, *Women Adrift: Independent Wage Earners in Chicago, 1880–1930* (Chicago: University of Chicago Press, 1988); Susan Porter Benson, *Counter Cultures: Saleswomen, Managers, and Customers in American Department Stores, 1890–1940* (Chicago: University of Illinois Press, 1986); Angel Kwolek-Folland, *Engendering Business: Men and Women in the Corporate Office, 1870–1930* (Baltimore: Johns Hopkins University Press, 1994).

Bibliographic Essay

When Earl Pomeroy published *In Search of the Golden West: The Tourist in Western America* (Lincoln: University of Nebraska Press, 1957), tourism was not a topic historians paid much attention to. When they and other scholars did notice it, they usually invoked tourism in order to condemn mass culture. Daniel Boorstin's *The Image: A Guide to Pseudo Events in America* (New York: Atheneum, 1973; orig. 1963) and Paul Fussell's *Abroad: British Literary Traveling between the Wars* (New York: Oxford University Press, 1982) are exemplary. In *The Beaten Track: European Tourism, Literature, and the Ways to Culture, 1800–1918* (Oxford: Clarendon Press, 1993), James Buzard challenges the assumptions underlying this critique of tourism and offers an alternative analytic approach, as does Mary Louise Pratt, *Imperial Eyes: Travel Writing and Transculturation* (London: Routledge, 1992).

American historians began to follow Pomeroy's lead in the 1970s and 1980s. Hugh DeSantis's article, "The Democratization of Travel: The Travel Agent in American History," *Journal of American Culture* 1 (Spring 1978): 1–17, sketches the development of a tourist industry in the United States and suggested its meaning: the opening of previously elite pastimes to ordinary people. This theme persists, though challenged and complicated, in the growing body of scholarship on tourism.

John Sears launched the recent surge in interest with *Sacred Places: American Tourist Attractions in the Nineteenth Century* (Oxford: Oxford University Press, 1989). Examining several of the more popular nineteenth-century tourist attractions, he argues that Americans made such natural wonders as Niagara Falls and the Natural Bridge tourist attractions in part because they could rival the splendid historical and cultural monuments of Europe in a way that the new commercial cities of the United States could not.

Scholars following in Sears's footsteps have tended to study particular regions, especially the Far West. Dona Brown, *Inventing New England: Regional Tourism in the Nineteenth Century* (Washington, D.C.: Smithsonian Institution Press, 1995), like Sears links pleasure travel to class and ethnic identities. Agreeing with Sears and DeSantis that access to pleasure travel broadened over time, she places this change in the context of the development of a modern consumer culture with contradictory implications for the host communities. Marguerite Shaffer's study of early-twentieth-century western tourism, *See America First: Tourism and National Identity, 1905–1930* (Washington, D.C.: Smithsonian Institution Press, 2001), investigates the close connections between the expanding western tourist industry and nationalism. Leah Dilworth, *Imagining Indians in the Southwest: Persistent Visions of a Primitive Past* (Washington, D.C.: Smithsonian Institution Press, 1996), examines the link between tourism and the romantic appropriation of the native peoples of the Southwest.

M. H. Dunlop, *Sixty Miles from Contentment: Traveling the Nineteenth-Century American Interior* (New York: Basic Books, 1995), pays particular attention to gender differences and the perception of the landscape. Valerie Fifer's *American Progress: The Growth of Transport, Tourist, and Information Industries in the Nineteenth Century West* (Chester, Conn.: Pequot Press, 1988), provides a vast amount of detail about the career of the pioneer western guide writer George Crofutt but little interpretation. Anne Farrar Hyde, *An American Vision: Far Western Landscape and National Culture, 1820–1920* (New York: New York University Press, 1990), explores one of the important changes supporting the industry's growth without directly addressing tourism.

In *Devil's Bargains: Tourism in the Twentieth-Century American West* (Lawrence: University Press of Kansas, 1998), Hal K. Rothman begins in the 1890s, where Brown and Sears ended their studies, and offers a more theoretically informed analysis than most other historians have done. The relationship between class and the character of tourism and tourist attractions and the social and economic consequences of growth of the tourist industry are his chief concerns. Returning to the national scale is Cindy S. Aron's *Working at Play: A History of Vacations in the United States* (New York: Oxford University Press, 1999). Rather than focus on attractions as Sears did, Aron examines vacationers of many stripes and the changing social contexts in which they took their leisure.

The ultimate destination for American travelers, of course, was Europe—the Old World. On American tourists in Europe, see William Stowe, *Going Abroad: European Travel in Nineteenth-Century American Culture* (Princeton: Princeton University Press, 1994), and Harvey Levenstein, *Seductive Journey: American Tourists in France from Jefferson to the Jazz Age* (Chicago: University of Chicago Press, 1998).

American cities, never as popular with tourists as domestic rural or European destinations, have also been less popular among historians. Neil Harris, "Urban Tourism and the Commercial City," in William R. Taylor, ed., *Inventing Times Square: Commerce and Culture at the Crossroads of the World* (New York: Russell Sage, 1991), 66–82, places the development of urban tourism in the context of the rise of a commercial culture centered in New York City. James Gilbert, *Perfect Cities: Chicago's Utopias of 1893* (Chicago: University of Chicago Press,

1991), and William R. Taylor, "The Launching of a Commercial Culture: New York City, 1860–1930," in John Mollenkopf, ed., *Power, Culture, and Place: Essays on New York City* (New York: Russell Sage, 1988), 107–33, use guidebooks to illuminate the cultural character of these cities.

Scholars have unveiled lurking touristic impulses in apparently virtuous social reformers more often than they have studied actual urban tourists. Deborah Epstein Nord's "The Social Explorer as Anthropologist: Victorian Travelers among the Urban Poor," in William Sharpe and Leonard Wallock, eds., *Visions of the Modern City: Essays in History, Art, and Literature* (Baltimore: Johns Hopkins University Press, 1987), 122–34, is illustrative. In her book, *Walking the Victorian Streets: Women, Representation, and the City* (Ithaca: Cornell University Press, 1995), Nord analyzes the difficulties that women travel writers faced in moving around and writing about the city. Judith Walkowitz, *City of Dreadful Delight: Narratives of Sexual Danger in Late-Victorian London* (Chicago: University of Chicago Press, 1992), also demonstrates the extent to which walking the city was a middle-class male pastime that others challenged at their own risk.

Sociologists and anthropologists preceded historians and literary scholars to the study of tourism. The classic work is Dean MacCannell, *The Tourist: A New Theory of the Leisure Class* (New York: Schocken Books, 1976). Arguing that tourism provides a metaphor for modern life, MacCannell detailed the structure of tourist attractions and its social-psychological effects. A valuable stimulus to serious research on tourism, the work is largely ahistorical and posits a singular, universal experience of tourism that ignores the way that pleasure travel embodies and constructs social differences. Judith Adler, "Origins of Sightseeing," *Annals of Tourism Research* 16:1 (1989): 7–29, describes the transformations in pleasure travel across the globe and throughout recorded time. The pioneering anthropological work was Valene L. Smith, ed., *Hosts and Guests: The Anthropology of Tourism*, 2d ed. (Philadelphia: University of Pennsylvania Press, 1989; lst ed., 1977). Among other issues, the essays in this volume address the racial and local meanings of tourism. John Urry, *Consuming Places* (London: Routledge, 1995), studies a more recent concern, the commodification of places and histories.

It is more difficult to recover the business history of tourism than its literary expression. Archives have obtained few records from tour companies, and the plethora of brochures, tickets, souvenirs, and schedules these businesses produced has largely gone the way of most interesting ephemera. The giant of the nineteenth-century tourist industry, Thomas Cook & Son, has received most attention because of its importance, its continuing existence, and its institutional records. The most up-to-date and scholarly study is Piers Brendon, *Thomas Cook: 150 Years of Popular Tourism* (London: Secker & Warburg, 1991), written with the company's cooperation. See also Lynne Withey, *Grand Tours and Cook's Tours: A History of Leisure Travel, 1750–1915* (New York: William Morrow, 1997), and John Pudney, *The Thomas Cook Story* (London: Michael Joseph, 1953). DeSantis's "The Democratization of Travel" provides information on American tourist agencies, especially the leading firm, Boston-based Raymond & Whitcomb.

The historical literature on cities is much larger than that on tourism. Especially valuable for this study were those that combined attention to the city's political and material environment with interest in class, gender, and the uses of space. Thomas Bender's *Toward an Urban Vision: Ideas and Institutions in Nineteenth-Century America* (Baltimore: Johns Hopkins University Press, 1975), and Drew McCoy, *The Elusive Republic: Political Economy in Jeffersonian America* (New York: W. W. Norton, 1980), illuminated the intellectual context shaping early-nineteenth-century Americans' view of cities and urban life.

Stuart Blumin, "Explaining the New Metropolis: Perception, Depiction, and Analysis in Mid-Nineteenth-Century New York City," *Journal of Urban History* 11:1 (November 1984): 9–38, and his introduction to *New York by Gas-Light, and Other Sketches by George G. Foster* (Berkeley: University of California Press, 1990), 1–61, are an essential foundation for understanding mid-nineteenth-century urban description. Other important analyses of urban representation include Michael Denning, *Mechanic Accents: Dime Novels and Working-Class Culture in America* (New York: Verso, 1987); Peter Bacon Hales, *Silver Cities: The Photography of American Urbanization, 1839–1915* (Philadelphia: Temple University Press, 1984); Amy Kaplan, *The Social Construction of American Realism* (Chicago: University of Chicago Press, 1988); David Reynolds, *Beneath the American Renaissance: The Subversive Imagination in the Age of Emerson and Melville* (New York: Alfred A. Knopf, 1988); and Rebecca Zurier, Robert W. Snyder, and Virginia M. Mecklenburg, *Metropolitan Lives: The Ashcan Artists and Their New York* (New York: National Museum of American Art and W. W. Norton, 1995).

On politics, the urban landscape, and the uses of space, see Elizabeth Blackmar, *Manhattan for Rent, 1785–1850* (Ithaca: Cornell University Press, 1989); Daniel Bluestone, *Constructing Chicago* (New Haven: Yale University Press, 1991); Peter Buckley, "To the Opera House: Culture and Society in New York City, 1820–1860" (Ph.D. dissertation, State University of New York at Stony Brook, 1984); Robin Einhorn, *Property Rules: Political Economy in Chicago, 1833–1872* (Chicago: University of Chicago Press, 1991); Philip J. Ethington, *The Public City: The Political Construction of Urban Life in San Francisco, 1850–1900* (Cambridge: Cambridge University Press, 1994); and Mary P. Ryan, *Civic Wars: Democracy and Public Life in the American City during the Nineteenth Century* (Berkeley: University of California Press, 1997).

Works examining the consolidation of the middle class and the relationship among class, gender, and the urban landscape and social relations include Stuart Blumin, *The Emergence of the Middle Class: Social Experience in the American City, 1760–1900* (Cambridge: Cambridge University Press, 1989); Richard Bushman, *The Refinement of America: Persons, Houses, Cities* (New York: Vintage Books, 1993); Nancy Cott, *Bonds of Womanhood: 'Woman's Sphere' in New England, 1780–1835* (New Haven: Yale University Press, 1977); Karen Halttunen, *Confidence Men and Painted Women: A Study of Middle-Class Culture in America, 1830–1870* (New Haven: Yale University Press, 1982); Paul Johnson, *The Shopkeeper's Millennium: Society and Revivals in Rochester, New York, 1815–1837* (New York: Hill and Wang, 1978); John Kasson, *Rudeness and Civility: Manners in Nineteenth-Century Urban America* (New York: Hill and Wang, 1990); Daniel T. Rodgers, *The Work Ethic in Industrial America, 1850–1920* (Chicago: University of Chicago Press, 1978); Roy Rosenzweig, *Eight Hours for What We Will: Workers and Leisure in an Industrial City, 1870–1920* (Cambridge: Cambridge University Press, 1983); Roy Rosenzweig and Elizabeth Blackmar, *The Park and the People: A History of Central Park* (New York: Henry Holt & Co., 1992); Mary Ryan, *Women in Public: Between Banners and Ballots, 1825–1880* (Baltimore: Johns Hopkins University Press, 1990); David Scobey, "Anatomy of the Promenade: The Politics of Bourgeois Sociability in Nineteenth-Century New York," *Social History* 17:2 (1992): 203–27; and Christine Stansell, *City of Women: Sex and Class in New York, 1789–1860* (Chicago: University of Illinois Press, 1987).

Helpful works outside United States history include Marshall Berman, *All That Is Solid Melts into Air: The Experience of Modernity* (New York: Simon and Schuster, 1982); Lenore Davidoff and Catherine Hall, *Family Fortunes: Men and Women of the English Middle Class, 1780–1850* (Chicago: University of Chicago, 1987); H. J. Dyos and Michael Wolff, eds., *The Victorian City: Images and Reality* (London: Routledge and Kegan Paul, 1973); Donald Olsen, *The City as a Work of Art: London, Paris, Vienna* (New Haven: Yale University Press, 1986); Shelley Rice, *Parisian Views* (Cambridge, Mass.: MIT Press, 1997); and Carl Schorske, *Fin-de-Siècle Vienna: Politics and Culture* (New York: Knopf, 1980).

Equally important for understanding urban tourism are works on the development of a culture of consumption at the turn of the century. Most useful were Susan Porter Benson, *Counter Cultures: Saleswomen, Managers, and Customers in American Department Stores, 1890–1940* (Chicago: University of Illinois Press, 1986); Richard Butsch, ed., *For Fun and Profit: The Transformation of Leisure into Consumption* (Philadelphia: Temple University Press, 1990); Richard Wightman Fox and T. J. Jackson Lears, eds., *The Culture of Consumption: Critical Essays in American History, 1880–1980* (New York: Pantheon, 1983); William Leach, *Land of Desire: Merchants, Power, and the Rise of a New American Culture* (New York: Vintage, 1994); Joanne Meyerowitz, *Women Adrift: Independent Wage Earners in Chicago, 1880–1930* (Chicago: University of Chicago Press, 1988); David Nasaw, *Going Out: The Rise and Fall of Public Amusements* (New York: Basic Books, 1993); Richard Ohmann, *Selling Culture: Magazines, Markets, and Class at the Turn of the Century* (New York: Verso, 1996); Kathy Peiss, *Cheap Amusements: Working Women and Leisure in Turn-of-the-Century New York* (Philadelphia: Temple University Press, 1986); Susan Strasser, *Satisfaction Guaranteed: The Making of the American Mass Market* (New York: Pantheon, 1989); and William R. Taylor, ed., *Inventing Times Square: Commerce and Culture at the Crossroads of the World* (New York: Russell Sage, 1991). James Livingston, *Pragmatism and the Political Economy of Cultural Revolution, 1850–1940* (Chapel Hill: University of North Carolina Press, 1997), challenges the orthodox condemnation of consumer culture and outlines some of its implications for American conceptions of self and society.

No one could write about public spaces and spheres in the 1990s without addressing Jürgen Habermas's *The Structural Transformation of the Public Sphere:*

An Inquiry into a Category of Bourgeois Society, trans. Thomas Berger and Frederick Lawrence (Cambridge, Mass.: MIT Press, 1991). Nancy Fraser's and Geoff Eley's critiques of Habermas in Craig Calhoun, ed., *Habermas and the Public Sphere* (Cambridge, Mass.: MIT Press, 1992); Henri Lefebvre's *The Production of Space,* trans. Donald Nicholson-Smith (Cambridge, Mass.: Blackwell, 1991); and Pierre Bourdieu's *Distinction: A Social Critique of the Judgement of Taste* (Cambridge, Mass.: Harvard University Press, 1984), offer approaches that encompass the political meanings of nonrational social practices, including spatial relations.

The literature on American railroads is enormous and addresses both scholarly and popular audiences. Among the most useful works were John F. Stover, *The Life and Decline of the American Railroad* (New York: Oxford University Press, 1970), and George R. Taylor and Irene D. Neu, *The American Railroad Network, 1861–1890* (Cambridge, Mass.: Harvard University Press, 1956). John H. White, Jr.'s *The American Railroad Passenger Car* (Baltimore: Johns Hopkins University Press, 1978), is the definition of definitive. Works addressing the physical, aesthetic, and social experience of nineteenth-century railroad travel include Amy G. Richter, "Tracking Public Culture: Modernity and Femininity on the American Railroad, 1865–1920" (Ph.D dissertation, New York University, 1999); Wolfgang Schivelbusch, *The Railway Journey: The Industrialization of Time and Space in the Nineteenth Century* (Berkeley: University of California Press, 1986; orig. pub. in Germany, 1977); John R. Stilgoe, *Metropolitan Corridor: Railroads and the American Scene* (New Haven: Yale University Press, 1983); and many popular works on luxury travel.

On George Pullman and the Pullman Palace Car Company, see Stanley Buder, *Pullman: An Experiment in Industrial Order and Community Planning, 1880–1930* (London: Oxford University Press, 1967), and Carl Smith, *Urban Disorder and the Shape of Belief: The Great Chicago Fire, the Haymarket Bomb, and the Model Town of Pullman* (Chicago: University of Chicago Press, 1995), chap. 10. White's *Passenger Car* offers information on Pullman's competitors and the open-section plan that prevailed in the industry. On porters, see Jack Santino, *Miles of Smiles, Years of Struggle: Stories of Black Pullman Porters* (Chicago: University of Illinois Press, 1989).

Like tourism, hotels have not received much attention from historians until recently. Jefferson Williamson's dated *The American Hotel: An Anecdotal History* (rpt. New York: Arno Press, 1975; orig. Knopf, 1930) remains the standard; see also Doris King, "The First Class Hotel and the Age of the Common Man," *Journal of Southern History* 23:2 (May 1957): 173–88; her "Early Hotel Entrepreneurs and Promoters," *Explorations in Entrepreneurial History* 8 (February 1956): 148–60; and Daniel Boorstin, "Palaces of the Public," in his *The Americans: The National Experience* (New York: Random House, 1965), 134–47. Focusing exclusively on the finest hotels, these authors accepted the assertion of nineteenth-century Americans that the hotels were democratically open "palaces of the people."

More recent works have been less credulous but continue to focus on first-class hotels. Carolyn Brucken examines hotels' place in the staging of middle-class wealth and gender ideals in "In the Public Eye: Women and the American

Luxury Hotel," *Winterthur Portfolio* 31:4 (Winter 1996): 203–20, based on her "Palaces for the People: Luxury Hotels and the Building of a New Public in Antebellum America" (Ph.D. dissertation, George Washington University, 1997). See also Richard Guy Wilson, ed., *Victorian Resorts and Hotels: Essays from a Victorian Society Autumn Symposium* (Philadelphia: Victorian Society in America, 1982); Katherine Grier, *Culture and Comfort: People, Parlors and Upholstery, 1850–1930* (Rochester, N.Y.: The Strong Museum, 1988); and M. H. Dunlop, *Sixty Miles from Contentment*, chap. 6. Karl Raitz and John Paul Jones III, "The City Hotel as Landscape Artifact and Community Symbol," *Journal of Cultural Geography* 9:1 (Fall–Winter 1988): 17–36, place architecture and the use of space in its historical context. Tracing the emergence of new, "businessmen's" hotels is May N. Stone, "Hotel Pennsylvania: Strictly First-Class Accommodations at Affordable Rates" (M.S. thesis, Columbia University, 1988). Molly Berger, "The Modern Hotel in America, 1829–1929" (Ph.D. dissertation, Case Western Reserve University, 1997), details the technological developments in hotel keeping. In *Living Downtown: The History of Residential Hotels in the United States* (Berkeley: University of California Press, 1994), Paul Groth examines a wide range of hotels and analyzes Americans' declining tendency to live in them.

Doris King's articles shed some light on hotel owners and managers. Only Matthew Josephson's union-sponsored *The History of the Hotel and Restaurant Employees and Bartenders International Union, AFL-CIO* (New York: Random House, 1955), addresses hotel workers, chiefly male waiters and bartenders. It focuses on organizing efforts and factional struggles within the union rather than on work experiences.

On city boosters and businessmen, see Elizabeth Blackmar's *Manhattan for Rent* (cited above); Carl Abbott, *Boosters and Businessmen: Popular Economic Thought and Urban Growth in the Antebellum Middle West* (Westport, Conn.: Greenwood Press, 1981); William Cronon, *Nature's Metropolis: Chicago and the Great West* (New York: W. W. Norton, 1991); Judd Kahn, *Imperial San Francisco: Politics and Planning in an American City, 1897–1906* (Lincoln: University of Nebraska Press, 1979); and Carl Smith, *Urban Disorder and the Shape of Belief.*

On the City Beautiful and urban planning, see William H. Wilson's revisionist *The City Beautiful Movement* (Baltimore: Johns Hopkins University Press, 1989), which debunks the long-standing view that this movement was the offspring of the 1893 World's Columbian Exposition. See also Mel Scott, *American City Planning since 1890: A History Commemorating the 50th Anniversary of the American Institute of Planners* (Berkeley: University of California Press, 1969); Mario Manieri-Elia et al., eds., trans. Barbara Luigia La Penta, *The American City: From the Civil War to the New Deal* (Cambridge, Mass.: MIT Press, 1979); Judd Kahn, *Imperial San Francisco;* and Daniel Bluestone, *Constructing Chicago.*

For an overview of the considerable but lopsided work on expositions, see Robert Rydell, "The Literature of International Expositions," in *The Books of the Fairs: Materials about World's Fairs, 1834–1916, in the Smithsonian Institution Libraries* (Chicago: American Library Association, 1992), 1–62. Other valuable works include Burton Benedict et al., *The Anthropology of World's Fairs: San Francisco's Panama-Pacific International Exposition of 1915* (Berkeley, Calif.: Lowie Museum of Archaeology in association with Scolar Press, 1983); James Gilbert, *Perfect Cities,* chap. 4; Curtis M. Hinsley, "The World as Marketplace: Commodification of the Exotic at the World's Columbian Exposition, Chicago, 1893," in Ivan Karp and Steven D. Levine, eds., *Exhibiting Cultures: The Poetics and Politics of Museum Display* (Washington, D.C.: Smithsonian Institution Press, 1991), 344–65; Rydell's *All the World's a Fair: Visions of Empire at American International Exposition, 1876–1916* (Chicago: University of Chicago Press, 1984); and Alan Trachtenberg, *The Incorporation of America: Culture and Society in the Gilded Age* (New York: Hill and Wang, 1982).

On city streets and the development of urban mass transit, see Charles W. Cheape, *Moving the Masses: Urban Public Transit in New York, Boston, and Philadelphia, 1880–1912* (Cambridge, Mass.: Harvard University Press, 1980); Stanley I. Fischer, *Moving Millions: An Inside Look at Mass Transit* (New York: Harper & Row, 1979), chaps. 1–6; Clay McShane, *Down the Asphalt Path: The Automobile and the American City* (New York: Columbia University Press, 1994); David Nye, *Electrifying America: Social Meanings of a New Technology, 1880–1940* (Cambridge, Mass.: MIT Press, 1990), chap. 3; and John R. Stilgoe, *Metropolitan Corridor,* chap. 11.

On the uses and cultivation of history, see Eric Hobsbawm, "Introduction: Inventing Traditions," in Eric Hobsbawm and Terence Ranger, eds., *The Invention of Tradition* (Cambridge: Cambridge University Press, 1983), 1–14, and David Handler, *Nationalism and the Politics of Culture in Québec* (Madison: University of Wisconsin Press, 1988). David Glassberg, *American Historical Pageantry: The Uses of Tradition in the Early Twentieth Century* (Chapel Hill: University of North Carolina Press, 1990), chronicles the boom in community historical performances in the United States. Michael Kammen, *Mystic Chords of Memory: The Transformation of Tradition in American Culture* (New York: Vintage Books, 1991), addresses the growing importance of history in multiple aspects of American life. Michele H. Bogart, *Public Sculpture and the Civic Ideal in New York City, 1890–1930* (Chicago: University of Chicago Press, 1989), examines the politics of New York's aesthetic adornment. Michael Holleran, *Boston's 'Changeful Times': Origins of Preservation and Planning in America* (Baltimore: Johns Hopkins University Press, 1998), examines the emergence of preservation in Boston.

On city festivals at the turn of the century, see Glassberg, *American Historical Pageantry;* James Gill, *The Lords of Misrule: Mardi Gras and the Politics of Race in New Orleans* (Jackson: University of Mississippi Press, 1997); and Catherine Cocks, "The Chamber of Commerce's Carnival: City Festivals and Urban Tourism in the United States, 1890–1915," in Shelley Baranowski and Ellen Furlough, eds., *Being Elsewhere: Tourism, Consumer Culture, and Identity in Modern Europe and America* (Ann Arbor: University of Michigan Press, 2001).

My understanding of ethnic slumming was shaped by the following analyses of the discourses of time, primitiveness, and modernity: Gail Bederman, *Man-*

liness and Civilization: A Cultural History of Race and Gender in the United States, 1880–1917 (Chicago: University of Chicago Press, 1995); Dipesh Chakrabarty, "Postcoloniality and the Artifice of History: Who Speaks for 'Indian' Pasts?" *Representations* 37 (Winter 1992): 1–26; Leah Dilworth, *Imagining Indians in the Southwest;* Johannes Fabian, *Time and the Work of Anthropology: Critical Essays, 1971–1991* (Philadelphia: Harwood Academic Publishers, 1991); Lata Mani, "Contentious Traditions: The Debate on Sati in Colonial India," in Kumkum Sangari and Sudesh Vaid, eds., *Recasting Women: Essays in Indian Colonial History* (New Brunswick, N.J.: Rutgers University Press, 1990), 88–126; Mary Louise Pratt, *Imperial Eyes;* and Marianna Torgovnick, *Gone Primitive: Savage Intellects, Modern Lives* (Chicago: University of Chicago Press, 1990).

On Americans' changing eating habits and the growing centrality of previously "ethnic minority" foods, see Donna Gabaccia, *We Are What We Eat: Ethnic Food and the Making of Americans* (Cambridge, Mass.: Harvard University Press, 1998); Harvey Levenstein, *Revolution at the Table: The Transformation of the American Diet* (New York: Oxford University Press, 1988); and Susan Williams, *Savory Suppers and Fashionable Feasts: Dining in Victorian America* (Knoxville: University of Tennessee Press, 1996).

On Chicago, see Daniel Bluestone, *Constructing Chicago* (cited above); William Cronon, *Nature's Metropolis;* Robin Einhorn, *Property Rules;* Carl Smith, *Chicago and the Literary Imagination, 1880–1920* (Chicago: University of Chicago Press, 1984); and Carl Smith, *Urban Disorder and the Shape of Belief.* The Chicago Historical Society's journal, *Chicago History,* is also very useful.

On New York, see Elizabeth Blackmar, *Manhattan for Rent;* Angela Blake, "Beyond Darkness and Daylight: Constructing New York's Public Image, 1890–1930" (Ph.D. dissertation, American University, 1999); John Hull Mollenkopf, ed., *Power, Culture, and Place: Essays on New York City* (New York: Russell Sage, 1988); Roy Rosenzweig and Elizabeth Blackmar, *The Park and the People;* Edward Spann, *The New Metropolis: New York City, 1840–1857* (New York: Columbia University Press, 1981); William R. Taylor, ed., *Inventing Times Square;* David Ward and Olivier Zunz, eds., *The Landscape of Modernity: Essays on New York City, 1900–1940* (New York: Russell Sage, 1992).

On San Francisco, see Philip Ethington, *The Public City* (cited above); William Issel and Robert W. Cherny, *San Francisco, 1865–1932: Politics, Power, and Urban Development* (Berkeley: University of California Press, 1988); Judd Kahn, *Imperial San Francisco.* On Chinatown, see Thomas W. Chinn, *Bridging the Pacific: San Francisco Chinatown and Its People* (San Francisco: Chinese Historical Association of America, 1989), and John Kuo Wei Tchen, *Genthe's Photographs of San Francisco's Old Chinatown* (New York: Dover Publications, 1984). On the neighborhood's emergence as a tourist attraction, see my unpublished essay, "'Chinatown, Of Course, One Must See'" (University of California, Davis, 1993).

On Washington, see Constance McLaughlin Green, *Washington: A History of the Capital, 1800–1950* (Princeton: Princeton University Press, 1962), for a traditional chronicle. John Reps, *Monumental Washington: The Planning and*

Development of the Capital Center (Princeton: Princeton University Press, 1967), celebrates the creation of the Mall and provides splendid illustrations. More recent and more critical works include Alan Lessoff, *The Nation and Its City: Politics, Corruption, and Progress in Washington, D.C., 1861–1902* (Baltimore: Johns Hopkins University Press, 1994); and Howard Gillette, *Between Justice and Beauty: Race, Planning, and the Failure of Urban Policy in Washington, D.C.* (Baltimore: Johns Hopkins University Press, 1995).

Index

98; bathing and bathrooms in, 76, 86; Bohn, Henry, 81; Boldt, George, 92, 93; businessmen's hotels, 86–87; Chicago, 26, 72, 76, 78–80, 85, 100; clerks, front desk, 81, 93–95, 96; commercialization and, 76–77, 81–85, 88, 97–102, 104–5; conventions and, 85, 95–96; cultural transformation and, 7, 70–105; definition of, 103; dining in, 72–75, 80–84, 90–91, 98; European plan, 81–84; familial ideal of, 73–82, 94, 98; first-class, 71–72 and passim; government regulation of, 103; Harvey, Fred, 92; Jews and, 103–4; lobby (rotunda), 77–80; managers of, 74–75, 81, 95–96; mid-nineteenth century, 72–73; morality and, 98–102; Mower, Henry, 93–94, 95; New York, 72, 76, 79, 80, 81, 83, 84, 85, 86, 91–93, 100–102; parlors, 77–80; privacy in, 76, 81, 86; professional organizations for, 94–96; prohibition movement and, 103; Rector, George, 83, 91, 100; refinement and, 70–74, 78–79, 85, 88, 96, 102, 104–5; Republicanism and, 71, 72–93, 96, 104–5; residents, long-term, 26, 71, 73, 86, 98, 101; San Francisco, 72, 95; separate spheres and, 71–72, 76–79, 83, 85, 88, 97–103; servants in, 88–97; Smith, William, 89; Statler, Ellsworth, 86; tourism and, 72, 85, 87, 95–96, 104–5; turn of the twentieth century, 84–88, 96, 101–2; urban space and, 70–72, 76–78, 82, 84; waiters in, 83, 89–93, 96; Willy, John, 87, 92, 95; women and, 77–78, 80, 92, 98–101; women's hotels, 98–102
Howells, William Dean: aestheticization of poverty and, 195; African Americans, 89–90; clerks, hotel, 93; *A Hazard of New Fortunes,* 164; *Impressions and Experiences,* 195; mass transit, 164; New York, 11; railroad travel, 54–55; *Their Wedding Journey,* 11, 54–55, 89–90, 93; waiters, 89–90
Huneker, James, 191
Hungerford, Edward, 145, 150, 171

immigrants and immigration: Americanization of, 180; attitudes toward, 89, 187–99; Chicago, 188; Chinese, 15–16, 89, 166, 188, 194, 200–201; entrepreneurs, 200–202; historical preservation and commemoration and, 180–85; Irish, 91, 193; Italian, 186, 197, 202; New York, 188, 191, 200,

202; San Francisco, 175, 188; tourism, objects of, 174–76, 186–203; turn of the twentieth century, 187; urban description and, 189; waiters, 91–93
Ingersoll, Ernest, 100, 148, 191, 197
Irwin, Will, 195

Jackson, Helen Hunt, 64
Jenkins, E. M., 112, 113
Jews, 32, 103–4, 186, 196, 199, 200

Keeler, Charles, 165, 194
Kinsey, John, 31, 46
Kirkland, Caroline, 33, 137

Lefebvre, Henri, 2
leisure: cultural transformation and, 2, 5–6, 108, 118, 121–22, 125, 145, 151, 206; dangers of, 12, 17–19, 21, 24, 154–55; expositions and, 127–30, 163, 167; festivals and, 178–81; market economy and, 13–14, 17, 18–19; mid-nineteenth century, 12; parks and, 36; rationalization of, 180–81; rehabilitation of, 5, 107, 108, 109, 112–13, 116–17, 121–22, 124–25, 145, 180–81; separate spheres and, 13–14, 19–22; sports, 124; tourism and, 5–6, 108, 112–14, 116–18, 121–22, 123–25, 144–45, 151, 154–55, 167, 176, 206; urban description and, 12, 17, 19, 149; urban space and, 170–71; Washington, D.C., 136, 146; women and, 20–21, 39, 121; working class and, 188
Leupp, Francis, 184
Little, Richard Henry, 106
Lloyd, Benjamin, 23, 98
Look Tin Eli (prob. Lu Jun-Ch'ing), 201
Los Angeles, 7–8, 133, 191
Lunneen, John, 189

market economy: consumer culture and, 207–8; growth of, 3–4, 13; leisure and, 13–14, 17, 19; middle class and, 3–5, 11, 13–14, 19–20; prostitution and, 17, 20; republicanism and, 3, 11, 13, 22; separate spheres and, 13–14; social relations and, 13–14, 18–19; urban space and, 11, 13–14; women and, 20–21
mass transit: African Americans and, 165–66; cable cars, 164; Chicago, 164, 165–66; elevated railroad, 164, 204; expositions and, 162–63; horsecars, 164; guidebooks and, 163–65; New York, 164, 172; omnibuses

Text:	10/13 Sabon
Display:	Sabon
Composition:	G&S Typesetters, Inc.
Printing and binding:	Data Reproductions Corporation